Tourism and Degrowth

T0371914

Tourism and Degrowth develops a conceptual framework and research agenda for exploring the relationship between tourism and degrowth.

Rapid and uneven expansion of tourism as a response to the 2008 economic crisis has proceeded in parallel with the rise of social discontent concerning so-called "overtourism." Meanwhile, despite decades of concerted global effort to achieve sustainable development, socioecological conflicts and inequality have rarely reversed, but in fact increased in many places. Degrowth, understood as both social theory and social movement, has emerged within the context of this global crisis. However, thus far the vibrant degrowth discussion has yet to engage systematically with the tourism industry in particular, while, by the same token, tourism research has largely neglected explicit discussion of degrowth.

This volume brings the two discussions together to interrogate their complementarity. Identifying a growth imperative in the basic structure of the capitalist economy, the contributors contend that mounting critique of overtourism can be understood as a structural response to the ravages of capitalist development more broadly. Debate concerning overtourism thus offers a valuable opportunity to re-politicise discussion of tourism development generally.

Exploring the potential for degrowth to facilitate a truly sustainable tourism, *Tourism and Degrowth* will be of great interest to scholars of tourism, environmental sustainability and development. The chapters were originally published as a special issue of the *Journal of Sustainable Tourism*.

Robert Fletcher is Associate Professor in the Sociology of Development and Change Group at Wageningen University in the Netherlands. He is the author of *Romancing the Wild: Cultural Dimensions of Ecotourism* (2014) and co-editor of *Nature™ Inc.: Environmental Conservation in the Neoliberal Age* (2014).

Ivan Murray Mas holds a PhD in Geography from the University of the Balearic Islands and an MsC in Environmental Sustainability from the University of Edinburgh. He is Associate Professor of Geography at the University of the Balearic Islands, where he is also a member of the research group on sustainability and space. His research merges political ecology, political economy and ecological economics of tourism. Recently, he co-edited *Turistificación global: Perspectivas críticas en turismo* with Ernest Cañada. He is also involved in social movements.

Asunción Blanco-Romero is Associate Professor of Geography at the Universitat Autònoma de Barcelona and also participates with the National University of Distance Education, the Universitat Oberta de Catalunya and the OSTELEA School of Tourism and Hospitality in Spain. She is a member of the TUDISTAR research group (tourism and new social and territorial dynamics), with which she has participated in several research projects. Her research focuses on cultural and heritage tourism, new tourisms and local development, tourism and degrowth and geography and gender issues in regional development.

Macià Blázquez-Salom is Associate Professor in the Department of Geography at the University of the Balearic Islands. His research interests include tourism, territorial planning and nature conservation from a sustainability perspective. He has been a visiting scholar in several European and Central American universities. His most recent publications deal with urban and regional planning regulation and the expansion of the Balearic Islands' hotel chains in Central America and the Caribbean.

Tourism and Degrowth

Towards a Truly Sustainable Tourism

Edited by
**Robert Fletcher, Ivan Murray Mas,
Asunción Blanco-Romero and
Macià Blázquez-Salom**

Routledge
Taylor & Francis Group

LONDON AND NEW YORK

First published 2020
by Routledge
2 Park Square, Milton Park, Abingdon, Oxon, OX14 4RN

and by Routledge
605 Third Avenue, New York, NY 10017

First issued in paperback 2021

Routledge is an imprint of the Taylor & Francis Group, an informa business

British Library Cataloguing in Publication Data
A catalogue record for this book is available from the British Library

Typeset in Myriad Pro
by Newgen Publishing UK

ISBN 13: 978-0-367-49098-0 (pbk)
ISBN 13: 978-0-367-86152-0 (hbk)

Publisher's Note
The publisher has gone to great lengths to ensure the quality of this reprint but points out that
some imperfections in the original copies may be apparent.

Disclaimer
Every effort has been made to contact copyright holders for their permission to reprint
material in this book. The publishers would be grateful to hear from any copyright holder
who is not here acknowledged and will undertake to rectify any errors or omissions in future
editions of this book.

Contents

Citation Information

The chapters in this book were originally published in the *Journal of Sustainable Tourism*, volume 27, issue 12 (November 2019). When citing this material, please use the original page numbering for each article, as follows:

For any permission-related enquiries please visit:
www.tandfonline.com/page/help/permissions

Notes on Contributors

Made Adityanandana, Agrarian, Food and Environmental Studies, International Institute of Social Studies, Erasmus University, The Hague, the Netherlands

Asunción Blanco-Romero, Department of Geography, Universitat Autònoma de Barcelona, Spain

Macià Blázquez-Salom, Department of Geography, University of the Balearic Islands, Palma de Mallorca, Spain

Karla Boluk, Department of Recreation and Leisure Studies, Faculty of Applied Health Sciences, University of Waterloo, Canada

Sandro Carnicelli, School of Business and Enterprise, University of the West of Scotland, Paisley, UK

Natasha Chassagne, Centre for Social Impact, Swinburne University of Technology, Melbourne, Australia

Joseph M. Cheer, Centre for Tourism Research, Wakayama University, Japan

Phoebe Everingham, Department of Human Geography, University of Newcastle, Australia

Robert Fletcher, Sociology of Development and Change Group, Wageningen University, the Netherlands

Jordi Gascón, Department of History of Art and Social History, University of Lleida, Catalonia, Spain

Julien-François Gerber, Agrarian, Food and Environmental Studies, International Institute of Social Studies, Erasmus University, The Hague, the Netherlands

Stefan Gössling, Western Norway Research Institute, Sogndal, Norway

Ivar Petter Grøtte, Western Norway Research Institute, Sogndal, Norway

Sabina Habegger, Spain CIMAS Network (Observatory of Citizenship and Sustainable Environment), Rizoma Foundation, Málaga, Spain

C. Michael Hall, School of Business and Economics, Linnaeus University, Kalmar, Sweden, and Department of Management, Marketing and Entrepreneurship, University of Canterbury, Christchurch, New Zealand

Freya Higgins-Desbiolles, School of Management, University of South Australia, Adelaide, Australia

Josep Ivars-Baidal, Department of Regional Geographic Analysis and Physical Geography, University of Alicante, Spain

Jens Kristian Steen Jacobsen, Institute of Transport Economics, Oslo, Norway

Chris Krolikowski, School of Management, University of South Australia, Adelaide, Australia

Scott McCabe, Nottingham University Business School, Jubilee Campus, UK

Claudio Milano, the OSTELEA School of Tourism and Hospitality, University of Lleida, Barcelona, Spain

Rubén Mora-Esteban, Urban Planning and Land Planning Research Group, Complutense University of Madrid, Spain

Joan Moranta, Oceanographic Centre of the Balearic Islands, Palma de Mallorca, Spain

Ivan Murray Mas, Earth Sciences Department, University of the Balearic Islands, Palma de Mallorca, Spain

Enrique Navarro-Jurado, Institute of Tourist Investigation, Intelligence and Innovation, Faculty of Tourism, Department of Geography, University of Málaga, Spain

Marina Novelli, School of Sport and Service Management, University of Brighton, Eastbourne, UK

Ove Oklevik, Department of Business Administration, Western Norway University of Applied Sciences, Bergen, Norway

Sarah Rachelle Renkert, School of Anthropology, University of Arizona, Tucson, USA

José María Romero-Martínez, Department of Graphic Expression in Architecture and Engineering, ETS Architecture, University of Granada, Spain

Yolanda Romero-Padilla, Faculty of Commerce and Tourism, Complutense University of Madrid, Spain

Eduardo Serrano-Muñoz, "Territorial Generation" Research Group, Rizoma Foundation, Málaga, Spain

Joaquín Valdivielso, Department of Philosophy and Social Work, University of the Balearic Islands, Palma de Mallorca, Spain

Fernando Vera-Rebollo, Department of Regional Geographic Analysis and Physical Geography, University of Alicante, Spain

Gayathri Wijesinghe, School of Management, University of South Australia, Adelaide, Australia

Foreword

Filka Sekulova

"I am not against tourism, and actually the citizens of Barcelona are not against tourism as such."
A member of the city hall and co-author of the plan for touristic regulation in Barcelona at a
public meeting in Spring 2017

There is something steadfast that blocks any major criticism of tourism per se. As if tourism is the sacred grail which cannot fail; as if tourism is the benchmark of a good life which our social imaginary increasingly lures us into – just like economic growth. From this perspective, it is awkward and ridiculous to denounce tourism per se; just like it is to denounce economic growth per se.

It is difficult to understand the roots, logic and impacts of tourism without situating it within the mechanics of economic growth, whether in capitalist or socialist-capitalist configurations. The degrowth literature points to a key friction, or a chronic disease, of modern industrial societies that has to do with the very *addiction to* growth. Material accumulation through economic growth is the new all-pervasive global common sense acting both as an end in itself and as a fix for any trouble at any point in time and space (Latouche, 2009). Degrowth as a topic of discursive debate and a concept breaks with the illusion of and fixation around the pursuit of infinite growth. Degrowth writers try to thin out the "inflated" modern Western subject to liberate ontological and epistemological space for other human and non-human worlds (D'Alisa, 2019). The basic and simple hypothesis brought forward here is that a good life could exist, and actually could be *easier* to achieve and sustain with four to five (or more) times lower material and energy throughput in that of *rich* nations, i.e. the *Global North* (Capellan-Perez et al., 2015; Kallis, 2019). This would, however, imply letting go of our capitalist mindset; letting go of and transforming gender relations and roles, including the distribution of paid and unpaid work. It would also mean confronting our fears and vulnerabilities in their material and immaterial manifestations, while acknowledging and savoring inter-dependency in both human and beyond-human senses.

From this perspective, tourism is one of the world's largest industries, precisely because of its steady and merciless growth track. Given that the multiple downsides of tourism have been surfacing over the past two decades, some argue for a shift towards truly sustainable tourism (Hall, 2009). The increasing number of complaints relating to economic growth have so far mostly resulted in adding a "sustainability" prefix to the pursuit. Sustainable growth has been particularly useful in maintaining and strengthening the fortress of the "growth religion" (Latouche, 2009). This is also the case with empty signifiers such as "development" and "progress" (Escobar, 2014). The sustainability add-on to tourism could do the same. Perhaps we need to start thinking of *unmaking tourism* as a concept, imaginary and industry, just like unmaking development (Escobar, 1995).

Tourism means consumption, and stimulating further consumption, unnecessary consumption, vain consumption, consumption aiming at distracting our attention from what really matters (Kasser, 2002). Tourism, as shown in this book, often means destruction: destruction of mountain slopes for skiing, of wild beaches for resorts, of relational and convivial practices and values at the level of local neighborhoods. Tourism creates an illusionary paradise, thus hiding dirty and sad realities, secluding those who are there to serve, in a semi-slavery mode of operation, from those who indulge with the idea of buying an experience of "disconnect" or "relaxation" (Büscher & Fletcher, 2016). Tourism is further grounded in the illusion that the best experience can and should be bought with money. It is like a drug that helps one escape and recharge in order to carry on business as usual in an accelerated and warming planet.

Tourism is an engine of development and growth, based on high socio-metabolic flows. From a degrowth perspective, touristic industry, behavior and desires cannot be simply repaired and tagged as sustainable in a "less-of-the-same" type of fashion (D'Alisa, Demaria, & Kallis, 2014). Reducing and transforming, or dissipating, tourist activities around hot spots would not change, transform and deconstruct its extractivist logic. To get rid of the faults of tourism, we need to look at their source: which is not only in the number of visitors, but in the lifestyles it brings about; or in the system it supports, and the system that supports it. And even more importantly, to deconstruct tourism from the outside, we also need to look at the projection of the tourism industry inside of us.

"We need to acknowledge reality, Barcelona is a touristic city", the same official cited in the epigraph also said. But reality is also created by what we believe and say. Saying is also believing and making it so, by fortifying it. If development is a discourse invented by the West for the cultural domination of non-Western societies (Escobar, 2014), tourism might be one of its Trojan horses. This book offers a concerted and diverse approach to rethinking tourism and the lifestyles, economies and societies that go along with it, like a breath of fresh air amidst the dim fogs of the cultural and ideological bases of development.

The impossibility of decoupling economic growth from environmental harms (Hickel & Kallis, 2019) is proportional to the impossibility of decoupling the troubles of (over)tourism from the need to undertake political inquiry and (re)action that decompose structural lock-ins. This publication demonstrates that the troubles around tourism are not to be taken at face value only. They are more than what they seem. They are symptoms of a regime, logic and structure(s) set on a race for survival through further growth/accumulation with pervasive power dynamics yet thinner and thinner intellectual and moral grounding.

References

Büscher, B., & Fletcher, R. (2016). "Destructive creation : Capital accumulation and the structural violence of tourism". *Journal of Sustainable Tourism, 25*(5), 651–667.
Capellan-Perez, I., Mediavilla, M., de Castro, G., Carpintero, O., & Javier Miguel, L. (2015). "More growth? An unfeasible option to overcome critical energy constraints and climate change". *Sustainability Science, 10*(3), 397–411.
D'Alisa, G., Demaria, F., & Kallis, G. (Eds.). (2014). *Degrowth: A Vocabulary for A New Era*. New York: Routledge.
D'Alisa, G. (2019). "Degrowth". *Dicionário Alice*. Retrieved from https://alice.ces.uc.pt/dictionary/?id=23838&pag=23918&id_lingua=2&entry=24248. ISBN: 978-989-8847-08-9.
Escobar, A. (1995). *Encountering Development*. Princeton, NJ: Princeton University Press.
Escobar, A. (2014). "Development, critiques of". In G. D'Alisa, F. Demaria, & G. Kallis (Eds.), *Degrowth: A Vocabulary for a New Era* (pp. 29–32). New York: Routledge.
Hall, C. M. (2009). "Degrowing tourism: Decroissance, sustainable consumption and steady-state tourism". *Journal of Sustainable Tourism, 20*(1), 46–61.
Hickel, J., & Kallis, G. (2019). "Is green growth possible?". *New Political Economy*. doi:10.1080/13563467.2019.1598964
Kallis, G. (2019). "Socialism without growth". *Capitalism Nature Socialism, 30*(2), 189–206.
Kasser, T. (2002). *The High Price of Materialism*. Cambridge, MA: MIT Press
Latouche, S. (2009). *Farewell to Growth*. Malden, MA: Polity Press.

Tourism and degrowth: an emerging agenda for research and praxis

Robert Fletcher, Ivan Murray Mas, Asunción Blanco-Romero ⓘD and Macià Blázquez-Salom

ABSTRACT
This article outlines a conceptual framework and research agenda for exploring the relationship between tourism and degrowth. Rapid and uneven expansion of tourism as a response to the 2008 economic crisis has proceeded in parallel with the rise of social discontent concerning so-called "overtourism." Despite decades of concerted global effort to achieve sustainable development, meanwhile, socioecological conflicts and inequality have rarely reversed, but in fact increased in many places. Degrowth, understood as both social theory and social movement, has emerged within the context of this global crisis. Yet thus far the vibrant degrowth discussion has yet to engage systematically with the tourism industry in particular, while by the same token tourism research has largely neglected explicit discussion of degrowth. We bring the two discussions together here to interrogate their complementarity. Identifying a growth imperative in the basic structure of the capitalist economy, we contend that mounting critique of overtourism can be understood as a structural response to the ravages of capitalist development more broadly. Debate concerning overtourism thus offers a valuable opportunity to re-politicize discussion of tourism development generally. We contribute to this discussion by exploring of the potential for degrowth to facilitate a truly sustainable tourism.

Introduction

On 22 May 2019, Nirmal Purja, a mountaineer and former British soldier, published a photograph of his view from the rear of a long queue of climbers snaking towards the summit of Mt. Everest. This image quickly went viral (see Hill, 2019), prompting – combined with the fact that this congestion led to the death of at least five other climbers in the days surrounding the photo's publication – widespread complaints that the peak had become dangerously overcrowded (e.g., Beaumont, 2019). This event crystallized several years of increasingly vocal critique in popular destinations worldwide concerning a phenomenon now commonly labelled "overtourism", which the United Nations World Tourism Organization (UNWTO) defines as "the impact of tourism on a destination, or parts thereof, that excessively influences perceived quality of life of citizens and/or quality of visitors experiences in a negative way" (2018, p. 4). How had it reached the point, critics now complained, that such overcrowding had come to affect even the highest point on Earth?

At the heart of this discussion stands the sustained yearly increase in growth the global tourism industry has experienced since at least 1950, which the United Nations World Tourism Organization (UNWTO) (2019) claims averages 4% per annum. Critique of overtourism thus calls into question this growth itself and the extent to which it can remain sustainable in the face of a mounting range of negative impacts. In this way, the critique touches the heart of discussion concerning the potential for sustainable tourism more generally. As we demonstrate further below, the bulk of this discussion takes as its starting point the necessity of sustaining tourism *growth*. Yet if this growth is itself an essential obstacle in the face of sustainability then this perspective may need to be questioned in its entirety.

In this way, the overtourism discussion dovetails with longstanding critique of a similar growth imperative at the heart of sustainable development policy more generally (e.g., Escobar, 1995; Wanner, 2015). An increasingly popular response to this imperative has been a call to move away from a growth-based economy altogether and instead pursue "degrowth." Emerging from a conjunction of activist social movements and critical scholarship, degrowth is a proposal for a radical socio-political transformation, for a "planned economic contraction" (Alexander, 2012) intended to shift the societal metabolic regime towards a decabornized one based on lower material throughput. In contrast to proposals for "decoupling," "dematerialization" or "green growth" (see e.g., Fletcher & Rammelt, 2017; Parrique et al., 2019; Smil, 2013), degrowth advocates a re-politization of sustainability discourse and radical transformation of the political economy within which sustainability is pursued (Asara, Otero, Demaria, & Corbera, 2015). It includes calls to (re)build societies and economies around principles of commons creation and governance, care and conviviality (see esp. D'Alisa, Demaria, & Kallis, 2014).

Research and advocacy concerning degrowth has developed rapidly over the last decade in particular (see Kallis et al., 2018). Yet to date this discussion has, with few exceptions (outlined below), largely neglected sustained attention to tourism specifically. Tourism is, however, one of the world's largest industries and hence a main form of global economic expansion (Fletcher, 2011; United Nations World Tourism Organization (UNWTO), 2019). Moreover, the industry is forecasted to continue to grow dramatically into the foreseeable future as the basis of the development aspirations of many low- and high-income societies alike (United Nations World Tourism Organization (UNWTO), 2019). To seriously pursue degrowth at both global and most national levels would, therefore, likely require drastic transformation of the tourism industry and its metabolism.

By the same token, notwithstanding important initial explorations (also detailed below), widespread discussion of the potential for sustainable tourism has thus far neglected to seriously engage with the discourse of degrowth. This collection thus seeks to bring discussions of sustainable tourism and degrowth together as a foundation for future research and praxis. In this introduction to the collection, we describe the building blocks upon which this discussion is erected then explore how it is operationalized in the ten articles that follow. Our overarching aim is to contribute to exploration of the potential for degrowth to facilitate a truly sustainable tourism, promoting academic discussion particularly within the fields of political economy and political ecology of tourism.

We begin by outlining the mounting discussion of overtourism, explaining how it builds on yet also departs from a venerable tradition of critique concerning the myriad negative impacts of conventional tourism development. We then describe how "sustainable tourism" has been promoted as an antidote to these problems. Here we elaborate our previous assertion that this discussion has, like sustainable development writ large, generally taken sustained growth as its starting point (as Michael Redclift pointed out already in the late 1980s; see Redclift, 1987, 2018). We identify this growth imperative in the basic structure of the capitalist economy, which demands continual growth in order to stave off internal contradictions that would otherwise threaten its survival. From this perspective, tourism growth can be seen to provide essential support to the global capitalist system as a whole (Fletcher, 2011). We show how this imperative has intensified since the 2008 economic crisis, after which stimulation of tourism growth has been increasingly relied upon as a mechanism for economic recovery more generally. This has been compounded by the rise of so-called platform capitalism in the same period, whereby "cyberspace" has been harnessed as a new arena for time-space displacement of excess accumulated capital (Harvey, 1982, 1989), in terms of which tourism development can be seen to function as an associated capitalist fix (Fletcher, 2011; Fletcher & Neves, 2012). In our analysis, consequently, critique of overtourism can be understood as a structural response to the ravages of capitalist development more broadly – a far cry from its frequent dismissal as a form of "anti-tourism" or even "tourism-phobia" (for discussion see esp. Milano, 2017a, 2017b). Overtourism, we contend, must therefore provoke reconsideration of the political economy of tourism as a whole and not merely debate concerning the appropriate number of tourists ("carrying capacity") within a given location. From this perspective, the question of overtourism and its proliferation offers a valuable opportunity to re-politicize tourism development within critical inquiry on the part of both academia and social movements.

From there we turn to degrowth, outlining a vibrant groundswell of research and practice concerning this theme that has proliferated over the past decade. Returning to discussion of capitalism's growth imperative, we build on Foster's (2011) early contention that degrowth within capitalism constitutes an "impossibility theorem" to argue that serious degrowth likely demands pursuit of post-capitalism. Moving back to tourism once more, we outline the small spate of previous research pointing to the potential for degrowth to facilitate a truly sustainable tourism. Here again we emphasize that this must go beyond capitalist development to pursue post-capitalist forms of production, consumption and exchange. We finish by outlining how other researchers can build on all of this to elaborate various aspects of the analysis further in the future and how the different articles in the special collection initiate this important project.

(Over)tourism and its discontents

Discussion of overtourism grew exponentially over the last decade to become one of "the buzzwords of 2017" (Milano, Cheer, & Novelli, 2019, p. 354) and focus of a burgeoning literature in both popular and scholarly media (see esp. Koens, Postma, & Papp, 2018; Milano, 2017a, 2017b; Milano, Cheer et al., 2019; Milano, Novelli, & Cheer, 2019; United Nations World Tourism Organization (UNWTO), 2018). This literature has documented an increasingly critical response to tourism expansion in a wide range of the world's most popular destinations, including Amsterdam, Athens, Barcelona, Berlin, Dubrovnik, Lisbon, London, Malaga, Palma (Mallorca), Paris, Reykjavík, Venice and many more.

As most contributors to the overtourism discussion acknowledge, concern with the negative impacts of tourism development is anything but new. On the contrary, growing discontent with these impacts, on the part of both residents and visitors, has frequently accompanied such development in destinations throughout the world. Globally, discontent with the impacts of unfettered tourism development promoted scathing critique from the Ecumenical Coalition on Third World Tourism as early as 1992, which succinctly summarized many of the most common concerns in asserting:

> [T]ourism, especially Third World Tourism, as it is practiced today, does not benefit the majority of people. Instead it exploits them, pollutes the environment, destroys the ecosystem, bastardizes the culture, robs people of their traditional values and ways of life and subjugates the women and children in the abject slavery of prostitution. In other words, tourism epitomises the present unjust world economic order where the few who control wealth and power dictate the terms. As such, tourism is little different from colonialism. (Srisang, 1992, p. 3, cited in Mowforth & Munt, 2016, p. 58).

Consequently, a substantial portion of tourism research has long been devoted to documenting and explaining discontent of this sort. In his controversial *Tourism: Blessing or Blight?*, Young (1973) had in the 1970s already raised many of the issues that are still at the forefront of critical tourism studies, including impacts related to tourism growth. Building on this, Butler's (1980) famous Tourism Area Life Cycle (TALC) model depicts a series of regular phases of destination development leading to stagnation and decline if not proactively addressed. Doxey (1975), meanwhile, offers an "Irritation Index" depicting am evolution towards increasing hostility in hosts' attitudes vis-à-vis visitors as tourism expands.

Despite this long pedigree of discontent concerning tourism development, however, there does seem to be something particular and unprecedented about the present moment, wherein a common set of complaints have been voiced by different sets of actors in so many disparate places simultaneously. This pattern suggests that we are dealing with something systemic and structural that has yet to be highlighted by the existing overtourism literature. In what follows, we offer an original structural analysis of the causes and consequences of the current wave of overtourism as a foundation for our subsequent discussion of the potential for degrowth to offer a constructive response to it. We begin by delving deeper into the nature of the "sustainable tourism" that is frequently advocated as a corrective to the negative impacts of conventional tourism development outlined above.

A "sustainable" tourism development?

The dominant response to adverse impacts of conventional tourism development has always been to call for transition to a "sustainable" form of tourism, as exemplified by this journal among many other media. Such calls have paralleled the rise of sustainable development policy more generally and have similarly defined sustainability in terms of the conventional three pillars highlighting interrelated environmental, social, and economic dimensions (Mowforth & Munt, 2016). Like sustainable development (see Hopwood, Mellor, & O'Brien, 2005), what precisely sustainable tourism means has always been understood differently by different people (Butler, 1999). Yet foundational to both discussions has long been a common concern to sustain economic growth as the basis for both projects (Naess & Høyer, 2009). As the UN's foundational Bruntland Report famously asserted,

> Far from requiring the cessation of economic growth, [sustainable development] recognizes that the problems of poverty and underdevelopment cannot be solved unless we have a new era of growth in which developing countries play a large role and reap large benefits (World Commission on Environment and Development (WCED), 1987, p. 40).

This perspective has been reiterated in the newly implemented Sustainable Development Goals (SDGs), which include tourism development as one explicit foci and readily admit their central concern to promote "sustained, inclusive and sustainable economic growth" (United Nations (UN), 2016). Nonetheless, and despite sustainable tourism's popularity as a widespread buzzword, business-as-usual scenarios forecast a dramatic expansion of tourism and its impacts in coming years (Gössling & Peeters, 2015).

Yet it is this very growth that has prompted mounting concern within discussions of overtourism. Again, as with sustainable development broadly, such concern is commonly met with assertions that a shift to "green growth" based in "decoupling" can reconcile sustainability with continued economic expansion (see e.g., United Nations Environment Programme (UNEP), 2011a, 2011b). Yet abundant evidence questions whether such green growth is actually attainable (Fletcher & Rammelt, 2017; Hickel & Kallis, 2019; Parrique et al., 2019). And even if it were this would not address the social implications of tourism expansion at the heart of the overtourism discussion.

Consequently, questioning growth itself as the basis of sustainable tourism has now become part of sustainable tourism discourse (Büscher & Fletcher, 2017; Fletcher, 2019; Hall, 2009, 2010; Higgins-Desbiolles, 2010, 2018). Higgins-Desbiolles, for instance, asserts that the global tourism industry "is addicted to growth, which is incompatible with sustainability goals" (2018, p. 157). Consequently, she argues that achieving a truly "sustainable tourism necessitates a clear-eyed engagement with notions of limits that the current culture of consumerism and pro-growth ideology precludes" (Higgins-Desbiolles, 2010, p. 125). Fletcher, similarly, calls for a "new model [of] tourism management, as well as economic governance more generally, that does not depend on continual growth" (2019, p. 532). Yet achieving this entails addressing the nature of the political-economic system within which most tourism is embedded. We turn to this in the next section.

Tourism growth as capitalist "fix"

Frequently underappreciated within tourism studies is the extent to which the industry can be understood not merely as an instrument of capitalist development (Britton, 1991; Bianchi, 2009; Mosedale, 2011, 2016) but as a primary means by which the capitalist system as a whole sustains itself in the face of fundamental contradictions that threaten its long-term survival (Fletcher, 2011). This analysis begins with understanding the ways that various spatial and/or temporal "fixes" help to resolve problems of capital overaccumulation more broadly via displacing excess capital through time and space and thereby helping to resolve crisis in the short term (Harvey, 1982, 1989; Smith, 1984). As a principle capitalist industry, tourism development can be seen to offer a whole series of such fixes for the capitalist system more generally (Fletcher, 2011; Fletcher & Neves, 2012).

It should be little surprise, consequently, that one of the most common responses to the 2008 global economic crisis was to endeavor to re-stimulate tourism growth as a stimulus to economic recovery generally (Murray, 2015). This was, Harvey (2010) explains, a textbook overaccumulation crisis in which global production outstripped demand – even with the copious quantity of cheap credit available to many consumers – and hence precipitated a deep and persistent recession. As a sink for reinvestment of this accumulated capital, tourism development could thus help to resolve this recession. Hence the UNWTO, in a self-styled "Roadmap to Recovery" published shortly after the initial collapse (in March 2009), asserted the need to resume tourism growth, in the interest of which "it is now crucial to remove all obstacles to tourism, especially taxation and over regulation" (United Nations World Tourism Organization (UNWTO), 2009a, 2009b). For this to occur it was deemed imperative for "governments to remove unnecessary regulatory and bureaucratic restrictions on travel which hamper its flow and reduce its economic impacts" (ibid.). Specifically, the organization recommended state intervention to "boost trade, simplify regulation, build infrastructure and rationalize taxes" (ibid.).

Heeding such advice, nations around the world undertook an unprecedented push to attract increased tourism flows as a means not only to re-stimulate the industry but to promote economic recovery more broadly (Nicolae & Sabina, 2013; Murray, 2015; Murray, Yrigoy, & Blázquez-Salom, 2017). In this spirit, then UNWTO Secretary-General Taleb Rifai asserted in 2013 that "international tourism continues to grow above expectations, supporting economic growth in both advanced and emerging economies and bringing much needed support to job creation, GDP and the balance of payments of many destinations" (United Nations World Tourism Organization (UNWTO), 2013). This was compounded by the rise of what has come to be called "platform capitalism" also in the wake of the 2008 crisis (see Langley & Leyshon, 2017; Rushkoff, 2016; Slee, 2017; Srnicek, 2017). Platform capitalism comprises "digital infrastructures that enable two or more groups to interact" (Srnicek, 2017, p. 43). These platforms seek to centralize and capture activity within a particular domain and thereby appropriate the monopoly rents generated by this privileged market position. The most prominent platforms globally include Amazon,

Google, and Facebook (in the realms of online commerce, web searching and social media, respectively). Srnicek (2017, p. 49–50) distinguishes five main types of platforms:

1. *"advertising platforms* (e.g. Google, Facebook), which extract information on users, undertake a labour of analysis, and then use the products of that process to sell ad space."
2. *"cloud platforms* (e.g. AWS, Salesforce), which own the hardware and software of digital-dependent businesses and are renting them out as needed."
3. *"industrial platforms* (e.g. GE, Siemens), which build the hardware and software necessary to transform traditional manufacturing into internet-connected processes that lower the costs of production and transform goods into services."
4. *"product platforms* (e.g. Rolls Royce, Spotify), which generate revenue by using other platforms to transform a traditional good into a service and by collecting rent or subscription fees on them."
5. *"lean platforms* (e.g. Uber, Airbnb), which attempt to reduce their ownership of assets to a minimum and to profit by reducing costs as much as possible."

The "lean" platform Airbnb is the main arena of contention within the tourism industry (Blanco-Romero, Blázquez-Salom, & Cànoves, 2018; Crommelin, Troy, Martin, & Pettit, 2018; Roelofsen & Minca, 2018). In providing the opportunity for ordinary residents (and increasingly, large firms as well) to offer their private spaces for rental to inbound tourists, Airbnb, along with a number of similar if smaller platforms, has enabled a dramatic expansion of tourism into areas previously outside of the major tourism circuits. Common consequences of this expansion include sharp increases in real estate and rental prices and subsequent displacement of residents in favor of transient visitors, thereby transforming the character of entire neighborhoods and cityscapes (see esp. Blanco-Romero, Blázquez-Salom, & Cànoves, 2018; Cocola-Gant & Gago, 2019).

Srnicek contends that the rise of platforms can be understood as a direct response to the 2008 crisis, in the aftermath of which "capitalism has turned to data as one way to maintain economic growth and vitality in the face of a sluggish production sector" (2017, p. 6). Digital platforms are a particularly seductive arena for pursuit of capital accumulation in an era of general stagnation, in that "the ability to rapidly scale many platform businesses by relying on pre-existing infrastructure and cheap marginal costs means that there are few natural limits to growth" (Srnicek, 2017, p. 45). In this way, platforms offer an entirely new arena – cyberspace – in which to pursue time-space fixes for the overaccumulation crisis.

From this political economic perspective, current discussion of overtourism must be understood as a product of structural dynamics within the global capitalist system as a whole. This provides a very different vantage point than the common focus on the ostensibly "anti-tourist" or even "tourism-phobic" attitudes commonly ascribed to disgruntled residents (see Milano, 2017a; Blanco-Romero, Blázquez-Salom, & Morell, 2018; Blanco-Romero, Blázquez-Salom, Morrell, & Fletcher, 2020). Rather, it places the focus squarely on a systemic push towards tourism growth more broadly pursued by powerful actors at local, national and global levels simultaneously. Widespread pushback against overtourism is thus a reflection of this campaign. This response may therefore be understood as something of a Polanyian double movement, in terms of which capitalist development commonly provokes popular resistance contesting the negative impacts of this development (Polanyi, 1944). More than this, it can be seen as what Nancy Fraser labels a "triple movement" that goes beyond the state-centered "social protection" central to Polanyi's analysis to advocate an autonomous, emancipatory politics pursued beyond state institutions (Fraser, 2013; Fraser & Jaeggi, 2018). And if the problem to which these movements respond is promotion of tourism growth itself, then a potential resolution to this conflict would be to instead demand containment of such growth, either through social protection (a double movement) or, as we are increasingly witnessing, calls for tourism degrowth (a triple movement) altogether.

Enter degrowth

The theoretical and political fundaments that nourish degrowth can be traced back at least to the 1960s and 1970s in the early voices in political and social ecology (e.g., André Gorz, Jacques Ellull, Ivan Illitch, Cornelius Castoriadis, Murray Bookchin, and Manuel Sacristán) as well as ecological economics (e.g., Nicolai Georgescu-Roegen, Joan Martínez-Alier, Herman Daly and José Manuel Naredo). Although many of those thinkers did not explicitly mentioned the term degrowth they are crucial for introducing some of the key ideas and questions that would subsequently be elaborated in the degrowth literature. Explicit discussion of degrowth has grown quickly since the turn of the twenty-first century in particular to comprise a number of interconnected threads (for a useful recent overview see Kallis et al., 2018). However, it is important to acknowledge that other political and scholarly projects very similar to degrowth have developed in parallel utilizing different concepts, such as *Sumak Kawsay* or *Buen Vivir* (Kothari, Salleh, Escobar, Demaria, & Acosta, 2019; see also below).

In an influential stream of initial discussion in the early 2000s, Latouche (2003, p. 3–4) contributed to degrowth discourse by defining it as "a necessity, not a principle, an ideal, but the objective of a post-development society." His thesis was rooted in the idea of achieving social prosperity without the need for the infinite growth demanded by mainstream development pundits. Latouche (2006, 2007) claimed to unravel the contradictions entailed in pursuit of unlimited growth by defining this as precisely what degrowth is *not*. In this way, he responded to common criticisms in arguing that degrowth does not intend to condemn impoverished countries to poverty, nor does it mean zero growth, nor a return to the past, nor to a patriarchal or authoritarian social order incompatible with democracy.

Building on this foundational work by Latouche and others, the degrowth conversation has developed through social activism within the new century, been elaborated through a series of international conferences held yearly since 2008 (D'Alisa, Demaria, & Cattaneo, 2013), and been propagated through a great profusion of recent academic writing (see inter alia Akbulut, Demaria, Gerber, & Martinez-Alier, 2019; Cattaneo, D'Alisa, Kallis, & Zografos, 2012; D'Alisa et al., 2014; Demaria, Kallis, & Bakker, 2019; Kallis, Schneider, & Martinez-Alier, 2010; Kallis, Kerschner, & Martinez-Alier, 2012a; Kallis, Kerschner, & Martinez-Alier, 2012b; Paulson, 2017; Saed, 2012; Sekulova, Kallis, Rodríguez-Labajos, & Schneider, 2013). Links among such initiatives have facilitated their scaling up into national and transnational networks (D'Alisa et al., 2013).

Within this diverse discussion, degrowth is understood in different ways, from a narrow economic transformation to a far broader cultural paradigmatic shift. Central to most strands of degrowth discourse, however, is "to understand critically and undo the phenomenon of growth – a material, ecological, historical, discursive and institutional phenomenon that is at the heart of the Western imaginary and its colonial dominance – and to propose alternatives to it" (Kallis, 2018, p. 9). This project comprises both macro- and micro-level initiatives. At the macroeconomic level, "degrowth refers to a trajectory where the 'throughput' (energy, materials and waste flows) of an economy decreases while welfare, or well-being, improves" (Kallis, 2018, p. 9). Specific proposals for implementing such a shift include:

> resource and CO_2 caps; extraction limits; new social security guarantees and work-sharing (reduced work hours); basic income and income caps; consumption and resource taxes with affordability safeguards; support of innovative models of "local living"; commercial and commerce free zones; new forms of money; high reserve requirements for banks; ethical banking; green investments; cooperative property and cooperative firms. (Kallis et al., 2012b, p. 175)

At the micro-level, meanwhile, degrowth proponents advocate activities such as "cycling, car-sharing, reuse, vegetarianism or veganism, co-housing, agro-ecology, eco-villages, solidarity economy, consumer cooperatives, alternative (so-called ethical) banks or credit cooperatives as well as decentralized renewable energy cooperatives" (D'Alisa et al., 2013, p. 218).

As a discussion emerging primarily from the high-income Global North, degrowth's applicability to low income and Southern societies has been questioned (Escobar, 2015; Rodríguez-Labajos et al., 2019). Thus Escobar depicts a widespread perception "that degrowth is 'ok for the North' but that the South needs rapid growth, whether to catch up with rich countries, satisfy the needs of the poor, or reduce inequalities" (2015, p. 6). Yet degrowth advocates commonly call not merely for economic contraction but rather "contraction and convergence" – that is, economic degrowth in societies experiencing excessive resource use and (limited) growth in others. Yet growth alone cannot redress inequality within a capitalist system based on uneven geographical development (Smith, 1984). Hence, as Daly (2008, p. 12) reminds us, "Without aggregate growth poverty reduction requires redistribution." For degrowth to be "socially sustainable" (Martinez Alier, 2009) in any society therefore demands dramatic redistribution in control of existing land, wealth and resources.

A common misunderstanding equates degrowth with simple economic decline or recession. Yet as Kallis and colleagues explain, "involuntary declines are not degrowth in themselves, and countries in recession or depression are not degrowth experiments" (2018, p. 294). In this sense, moments and places of crisis, economic busts, burst financial bubbles, natural disasters, and similar events have nothing to do with degrowth. Rather, degrowth can be conceptualized as a "radical political and economic reorganization leading to drastically reduced resource and energy throughput" (Kallis et al., 2018, p. 291).

An important question concerns the extent to which degrowth is compatible with a capitalist economy and society (Foster, 2011; Liodakis, 2018). Raising this question some time ago, Foster indeed pronounced degrowth within capitalism an "impossibility theorem," arguing, "The ecological struggle ... must aim not merely for degrowth in the abstract but more concretely for *deaccumulation*—a transition away from a system geared to the accumulation of capital without end" (2011, p. 33, emphasis in original). Responding to this challenge, Kallis and co-authors indeed acknowledge that "[c]apitalist economies can ... either grow or collapse: they can never degrow voluntarily" (2012b, p. 177), and hence that degrowth advocacy often "fails to explain how a capitalist economy would work without a positive profit rate, a positive interest rate or discounting." Summarizing this discussion more recently, Kallis concludes, "Growth is part and parcel of capitalism: abandoning the pursuit of growth requires a transition beyond capitalism" (2018, p. 163). Yet in contrast to some post-capitalist literature that envisions a future of abundance enabled by information technology (i.e., the internet of things, which will, ostensibly, lead to abolition of the law of value, echoing Rifkin's (2014) argument for a 'zero marginal cost' society) (e.g., Bastani, 2019; Mason, 2015; Srnicek & Williams, 2015), degrowth advocates tend to eschew techno-promethean utopias and instead take seriously the need for a metabolic shift towards a future entailing living with less and with a lower footprint (Kerschner, Wächter, Nierling, & Ehlers, 2018) – what Latouche (2009) calls "frugal abundance" and Salleh (2009) "ecofeminist sufficiency."

Tourism and degrowth

Potential for degrowth has been explored in relation to a variety of economic sectors and other social spaces. Yet application of the perspective to the realm of tourism has been relatively limited thus far. Bourdeau and Berthelot (2008) offer an initial exploration of this potential in a contribution to the first international degrowth conference in Paris in 2008. This was then elaborated by Hall, who asserted that "the contribution of tourism to sustainable development should be understood in the context of degrowth processes that offer an alternative discourse to the economism paradigm that reifies economic growth in terms of GDP" (2009, p. 46). To operationalize this alternative, Hall advocated a "steady-state tourism ... that encourages qualitative development but not aggregate quantitative growth to the detriment of natural capital (2010, p. 131). Building on all of this, Büscher and Fletcher subsequently assert, "Tourism, clearly, must not just come to terms with the fact that its exponential growth has to halt, but that it needs to radically 'degrow' in line with broader, more sustainable patterns of consumption and production" (2017, p. 664). In a rare empirical intervention in this discussion, meanwhile, Panzer-Krause (2019) identifies a nascent degrowth-oriented faction within a network of ecotourism operators in rural Ireland.

The most sustained exploration of the potential for degrowth within tourism thus far is provided by Andriotis (2018). While he spends some time outlining core degrowth principles and their potential to facilitate sustainable tourism promotion more generally, his focus is primarily on the potential for individuals to travel in a manner that reduces resource use and other negative impacts – for instance, backpackers who move slowly between destinations and spend substantial time in one place trying to minimize consumption. In this way, Andriotis and others (e.g., Hall, 2009) point to the potential for tourism degrowth to converge with a variety of other campaigns seeking to reduce or reverse the negative impacts of tourism growth in various ways, including advocacy of "slow" (Fullagar, Markwell, & Wilson, 2012), "responsible" (Spenceley, 2012), "pro-poor" (Scheyvens, 2009) and "justice" (Higgins-Desbiolles, 2008) tourism.

Industry insiders defending growth

Notwithstanding this small yet growing stream of commentary, a focus on tourism growth itself as a core obstacle to sustainable tourism remains far from popular within the overarching public sphere. On the contrary, it has been inspired heated reactions from industry insiders, who commonly portray tourism as a relatively "clean" sector whose growth is associated with increased economic welfare and job creation (Stroebel, 2015). From the consumer side, questioning tourism development implies questioning the very mechanisms that allow modern subjects to channel discontent produced by the increasing speed, competition and stress experienced in their work lives (Fletcher & Neves, 2012). On the producer side, challenging mass tourism implies questioning hegemonic economic structures, provision of precarious/seasonal jobs, and increases in the prices of land/housing. In short, questioning tourism development is tantamount to challenging the current capitalist productive model and its growth imperative.

Consequently, the 11th edition of the UNWTO/WTM Ministers' Summit (convened in November 2017 just as the overtourism discussion was peaking) carried the explicit title "Overtourism: growth is not the enemy; it is how we manage it" (World Trade Market (WTM) 2017). In announcing this meeting Rifai (2017) was quoted as asserting:

> Growth is not the enemy. Growing numbers are not the enemy. Growth is the eternal story of mankind. Tourism growth can and should lead to economic prosperity, jobs and resources to fund environmental protection and cultural preservation, as well as community development and progress needs, which would otherwise not be available.

Following from this perspective, the dominant response to complaints of overtourism has thus far been to propose ways to better "manage" rather than question tourism growth. Hence, in its most elaborate contribution to the discussion, a report entitled 'Overtourism'? Understanding and Managing Urban Tourism Growth beyond Perceptions, the UNWTO asserts that "[t]ourism congestion is not only about the number of visitors but about the capacity to manage them" (United Nations World Tourism Organization (UNWTO), 2018, p. 5). At the same time, however, the report moves further towards actually addressing critics' concerns in also acknowledging, "Measures cannot focus only on altering tourist visitor numbers and tourist behaviour – they should also focus on local stakeholders. To ensure the positive aspects of tourism remain visible to and understood by residents, it is necessary to understand residents' concerns and grievances and include them in the tourism agenda" (United Nations World Tourism Organization (UNWTO), 2018, p. 7). Yet the laundry list of actions proposed to resolve the issue – from "Promot[ing] the dispersal of visitors within the city and beyond" to "Improv[ing] city infrastructure and facilities"

– do little to tackle its root causes in the capitalist political economy and its imperative for continual growth to stave off overaccumulation crises.

At the municipal level, meanwhile, containment of tourism growth has in some places been partially assumed by public institutions seeking to regulate tourist accommodation capacity. (This can be understood as a double movement rather than the genuine degrowth envisioned as a civil society-based triple movement.) Measures introduced to operationalize this aim include: growth moratoria; management plans; eco-taxes and other special taxes on accommodation or traveling for tourism purposes; and limiting the capacity of transport infrastructure (airports, ports, highways, tunnels, bridges, etc.) or facilities (e.g., golf courses, ski slopes, marinas) (see Blázquez-Salom, 2006). Yet a common consequence of such measures is that their implementation generally causes a destination to become more expensive and elitist. In this way, regulations to merely contain tourism growth risk employing such measures in favour of the richest classes (Blázquez-Salom, 2016). The question of how to reconcile tourism degrowth with social equity thus remains fundamental.

Towards a post-capitalist tourism?

Initial exploration of the potential to pursue degrowth within tourism has largely neglected explicit discussion of the capitalist political economy underpinning most tourism development today. However, both social movements and critical scholarship contesting tourism commodification and promoting non-capitalist forms of tourism have highlighted issues and themes that could be embedded within a broad discussion of tourism degrowth (see e.g., Britton, 1978; Britton & Clarke, 1989; Cañada & Murray, 2019; Christine, 2014; Cordero, 2006; Gascón & Cañada, 2005; Mowforth & Munt, 2016; Wall, 1997). Building on this, Büscher and Fletcher (2017) explicitly link their advocacy of degrowth with critique of capitalist tourism and hence ask how "might tourism look if conceptualized from the point of view of a more general anti- or post-capitalist politics?" (2017, p. 664). They answer by asserting that "tourism should move radically from a private and privatizing activity to one founded in and contributing to the common" (2017, p. 664). Elsewhere, Fletcher expands on this to suggest that a properly post-capitalist tourism would pursue "(1) forms of production not based on private appropriation of surplus value; and (2) forms of exchange not aimed at capital accumulation; that (3) fully internalize the environmental and social costs of production in a manner that does not promote commodification and (4) are grounded in common property regimes" (2019, p. 532).

Advocacy of post-capitalism is certainly not to assume that merely moving away from capitalism is sufficient to reverse tourism growth. Actually existing socialist societies in the twentieth century, after all, were as deeply committed to pursuit of continual economic growth as the capitalist ones they contested. (Of course, it could also be argued with Wolff (2012) that such societies were not really socialist at all but rather forms of "state capitalism.") Consequently, "a transition beyond capitalism does not necessarily bring the abandonment of growth" (Kallis, 2018, p. 163). Rather, deliberate pursuit of degrowth, in tourism as elsewhere, "requires a systemic overhaul of established institutions, imaginaries and modes of living" (ibid.) with post-capitalism as its starting point. As with degrowth generally, it is important to distinguish between the type of simple decline in tourist numbers caused by such factors as economic crisis, loss of destination popularity or natural disaster, on the one hand, and on the other genuine tourism degrowth, which would require a concerted process of political-economic reorganization.

As with degrowth more generally, such a transition towards tourism degrowth could comprise both top-down and bottom-up elements, with pushes for systemic structural change at global and societal levels combined with more localized and individual practices contributing to downsizing on the ground. How the abstract principles of post-capitalist tourism outlined above might manifest within policy and practice at each of these scales remains largely unexplored thus far, however. Following Latouche, advocacy of touristic degrowth need not be viewed as wholesale denunciation of tourism per se – in other words, as an "anti-tourism" position, as popular media accounts often frame it. Rather, it is about searching for strategies for "de-touristification" in terms of which leisure activities are reconfigured, reorganized and practiced in different ways that aim to privilege local communities and ecosystems (Blanco-Romero, 2019).

Outline of an agenda for research and praxis

Building on the preceding discussion, we can begin to conceptualize a number of interrelated lines of inquiry for a future program of research and political engagement focused on the potential for tourism degrowth:

1. *Tourism and sustainability as a political question* (cf. Swyngedouw, 2010). This strand of analysis would use the banner of tourism degrowth as a strategy to re-politicize tourism development generally and sustainable tourism in particular.
2. *Distribution of costs and benefits within tourism development and management.* This line of research would undertake critical analysis of the political economy and political ecology of tourism's function as a form of capital accumulation, particularly in terms of who gains and who loses in the process of tourism development.
3. *The biophysical limits to tourism growth.* This research would investigate the social and biophysical costs of tourism development under capitalism, providing an assessment of the ecological costs and forms of metabolism entailed in this process.
4. *Post-capitalist tourism in practice.* This agenda would study practices of tourism degrowth (explicit or implicit) and their contradictions currently in operation or gestation throughout the world.
5. *Commoning tourism and redistributing value.* Following from the preceding, this line of investigation would explore the potential for tourism degrowth to transform the political and economic organization of the industry, particularly in pursuit of collectivization or redistribution of surplus value.
6. *Tourism degrowth as de-touristification.* This research would contribute to exploring the potential of tourism degrowth to function as de-touristification or "detourism" – that is, in reducing the intensity and impacts of tourism particularly in saturated destinations, and in this way facilitating a truly sustainable tourism.
7. *The right to metabolism.* This agenda would seek to more clearly define and conceptualize tourism degrowth as a reduction of the material and energy flows required by tourism capital, on the one hand, as well as a transformation of the political organization of material and energy flows within a triple movement scenario, on the other, in this way promoting the "right to metabolism" as a radical political project.

Overview of the collection

The articles that follow engage diverse aspects of the degrowth discussion via concrete case studies as well as more abstract theoretical exploration. While they do not all take post-capitalism as either their starting or ending point, they offer a productive basis for beginning to explore this potential. They also illustrate several of the lines of inquiry outlined above, providing a fertile foundation for further exploration of these themes.

Concerning the function of degrowth to serve as a provocation to re-politicize the question of sustainability within tourism development, Gascón (2019) leads off the collection by taking issue with growing assertions that travel should constitute a human right, advanced by the UNWTO and other industry insiders. He views this as preemptive attempt to squelch critique of the tourism growth imperative that degrowth among other perspectives mobilizes. Following Alston (1984), Gascón contends that such advocacy constitutes a "frivolous claim" that threatens both to distract from the need to consider touristic degrowth seriously and to trivialize the human rights discourse that it seeks to piggyback.

Turning to the theme of the political economy of tourism and its consequences, Navarro-Jurado et al. (2019) argue that tourism development in Malaga – the principle destination on Spain's fabled Costa del Sol – should be understood as a component of an "urban growth machine" (Logan & Molotch, 1987) more generally that seeks to harness grand infrastructural projects as the engine of capital accumulation and expansion. They document a growing push-back against this development model by local social movements that have banded together to advance an alternative economic model emphasizing smaller-scale, bottom-up initiatives aimed to minimize environmental impact. The authors view this resistance as a symptom of a need to develop a more systematic planning process integrating tourism with other forms of development grounded explicitly in degrowth principles.

The next three contributions continue the focus on Spain's Mediterranean coast, where the promotion of tourism growth as an outlet for persistent economic crisis has been particularly intense, as has the social fallout from this promotion. The epicentre of this conflict is likely Barcelona, the focus of the intervention by Milano, Novelli, et al. (2019). They chart the rise of social movements critical of the impacts of ever-increasing tourist numbers that organized themselves under the label ABTS (*Assemblea de Barris per un Turisme Sostenible* [Assembly of Neighbourhoods for Sustainable Tourism]) and called explicitly for touristic degrowth ("decreixement turístic"). This movement then expanded outward to network with similar movements in other cities to constitute the *Red de Ciudades del Sur de Europa ante la Turistización* (Network of Southern European Cities against Touristification), or SET. The authors document how, despite initial resistance, the Barcelona government increasingly responded to these movements' demands by instituting a variety of measures aimed to mitigate tourism development and, in some spaces, actually degrow tourism facilities. They end on an ambivalent note by observing, on the one hand, that despite initial optimism some of these measures remain more in the realm of rhetoric than realization while, on the other hand, whatever its practical impact in situ the Barcelona discussion has nonetheless helped to stimulate a global debate concern the implications and future of tourism development generally.

Next, Valdivielso and Moranta (2019) take us off the coast to another popular destination – the Balearic Islands – to explore mounting discussion of degrowth as a response to the dramatic recent surge in tourism arrivals to the islands. Through the lens of critical discourse analysis (CDA), they frame degrowth as a contested signifier that is adopted both to advocate for radical transformation of the tourism industry and to greenwash more reformist policy measures aimed merely to manage the industry's development. Based on this analysis, the authors conclude that the Balearic debate is not merely about different ways to address and manage tourism development but is in fact a "social struggle" that has stimulated the formation of "new democratic political subjects" and their organization within a revitalized civil society.

Building on the preceding contributions, Blázquez-Salom, Blanco-Romero, Vera-Rebollo, & Ivars-Baidal (2019) offer a more synthetic overview of tourism development within the region. Comparing Barcelona, the Balearics and Valencia, they identify a growing prevalence of territorial planning measures intended to reduce or at least contain tourism expansion. Yet the authors assert that these ostensibly progressive processes suffer from crippling contradictions due to their inability to directly confront the capitalist accumulation model underlying the tourism growth they address. Consequently, they call for much stronger measures capable of transcending this accumulation model in pursuit of "genuine and fair degrowth."

Subsequently, Adityanandana and Gerber (2019) turn our focus to an entirely different region – Southeast Asia – to explore a potential example of tourism degrowth in practice. Their focus is a tourism megaproject in the Benoa Bay of Bali, Indonesia, whose development has been subject to fierce contestation by local interest groups that alternately support and denounce the project. Despite these differences, the authors find that local actors on different sides of the debate all espouse a similar philosophy of *Tri Hita Karana* (THK), translated as the "three causes of well-being." This perspective, however, is understood quite differently by different disputants within the debate. One prominent position the authors describe as a "radical-integral" perspective bearing "similarities with post-growth views" that, they contend, might be drawn upon to promote a degrowth-oriented approach to tourism development more broadly.

The next two articles continue this exploration of potential degrowth in practice by examining two similar cases of community-based ecotourism in the same country in South America: Ecuador. First, Renkert (2019) draws on Gibson-Graham's (2006) diverse economies framework to describe how involvement in a Kichwa-owned ecolodge "is locally embraced as a vehicle for livelihood wellbeing, cultural reclamation and environmental stewardship" grounded in a philosophy of *Sumak Kawsay* (commonly translated as *Buen Vivir* or the "good life"). While fully cognisant that small-scale projects of this sort cannot redress all of the ills associated with tourism overdevelopment, Renkert asserts that it still offers valuable lessons for how tourism can potentially be harnessed to cultivate a "localized degrowth society."

Taking the growing prominence of a *Buen Vivir* (BV) perspective generally with the country and region as their starting point, Chassagne and Everingham (2019) then examine how this philosophy is embodied within another community-based project in Ecuador's Cotacachi County. They explore how the BV principles embodied in this initiative resonate with the pillars of degrowth as conceptualized by Latouche (see above). Based upon this resonance, the authors assert that BV can provide the impetus for degrowing damaging extractive industries while simultaneously growing community-based tourism as a more socially and environmentally sustainable alternative. Importantly, however, they explain that within this process degrowth is a "consequence of BV, rather than the objective."

Taking us back to Europe once more, Oklevik et al. (2019) turn the focus from community-based initiatives to how Destination Marketing Organisations (DMOs) such as government tourism bureaus might encourage tourism "optimization" as opposed to the dominant emphasis on "maximizing" visitor numbers. Based on a survey of international tourists in southwestern Norway, they ask whether an emphasis on promotion of varied "'activities', i.e., the development of local, small-scale and ideally more sustainable experiences, can contribute to economic growth without necessarily increasing numbers of arrivals". To facilitate further exploration for this potential they propose an innovative methodology that might be applied in other contexts as well.

Finally, Higgins-Desbiolles, Carnicelli, Krolikowski, Wijesinghe, and Boluk (2019) round out the collection by offering a provocative conceptual reflection on the rocky road that has led us to this moment of unprecedented public discussion concerning the potential for degrowth in tourism planning. Drawing on diverse examples from around the world, they demonstrate how continual expansion of the global tourism industry has increasingly been confronted by the spectre of "limits to growth" first conjured by the famous Club of Rome report in the early 1970s (Meadows, Meadows, Randers, & Behrens, 1972). At the present juncture, the authors assert, the only way for the industry to truly achieve the sustainability it purportedly pursues is to rethink its aims fundamentally in order to refocus on degrowth. Central to this effort, they argue, must be an emphasis on supporting the rights of local community members over those of inbound tourists or firms comprising the tourism industry.

Conclusion: another tourism is possible

Tourism development, as we have shown, has become a principle fix for the 2008 financial crisis. The rapid and uneven expansion of tourism has proceeded in parallel with the rise of social discontent concerning so-called overtourism, which has affected particularly cities in the Global North. After decades of concerted global effort to achieve sustainable development, socioecological conflicts and inequality have rarely reversed, but in fact increased in many places. Degrowth, understood as both social theory and social movement, has emerged within the context of this global crisis. Since many authors and institutions have acknowledged that we have entered an age of economic stagnation combined with high levels of social inequality and expanding ecological degradation, the search for post-growth, post-capitalist, post-development and/or degrowth alternatives has become a social and intellectual imperative. In this regard, the agenda of tourism degrowth research that we have outlined herein aims to re-politicize the debate on sustainable tourism, where the point of this research should be not only to document and understand tourism development, but to contribute to its transformation (Castree, 2010).

In order to do so, we must first acknowledge the previous work by radical scholars who have long critically analyzed the socio-ecological costs of tourism – work that provides the foundation upon which a conceptual framework for analyzing tourism degrowth is erected. But most importantly, we must recognize the essential inspiration for this analysis in the organization of grassroots movements and their struggles against tourism dispossession, as well as the alternative and post-capitalist tourism projects such movements have nurtured. While many projects of this sort have not self-identified as degrowth initiatives per se, their vision and goals often match closely with principles of tourism degrowth. Since tourism degrowth is a proposal that aims to bring social movements and research/praxis together, scholars will have to pay particular attention to and cooperate with social movements to make another tourism possible within planetary boundaries.

Disclosure statement

No potential conflict of interest was reported by the authors.

Funding

This article was supported by the research project "Overtourism in Spanish coastal destinations: Tourism degrowth strategies" (RTI2018-094844-B-C31) funded by the Spanish Ministry of Science, Innovation and Universities.

ORCID

Asunción Blanco-Romero ⓘ http://orcid.org/0000-0002-5869-8603

References

Adityanandana, M., & Gerber, J.-F. (2019). Post-growth in the tropics? Contestations over *Tri Hita Karana* and a tourism megaproject in Bali. *Journal of Sustainable Tourism, 27*(12), 1–18. doi:10.1080/09669582.2019.1666857

Akbulut, B., Demaria, F., Gerber, J.-F., & Martinez-Alier, J. (2019). *Ecological Economics* 157, special issue on "Theoretical and political journeys between environmental justice and degrowth." doi:10.1016/j.ecolecon.2019.106418

Alston, P. (1984). Conjuring up new human rights: A proposal for quality control. *The American Journal of International Law, 78*(3), 607–621. doi:10.2307/2202599

Alexander, S. (2012). Planned economic contraction: The emerging case for degrowth. *Environmental Politics, 21*(3), 349–368. doi:10.1080/09644016.2012.671569

Andriotis, K. (2018). *Degrowth in tourism: Conceptual, theoretical and philosophical issues.* New York, NY: CABI.

Asara, V., Otero, I., Demaria, F., & Corbera, E. (2015). Socially sustainable degrowth as a social–ecological transformation: Repoliticizing sustainability. *Sustainability Science, 10*(3), 375–384. doi:10.1007/s11625-015-0321-9

Bastani, A. (2019). *Fully automated luxury communism: A manifesto.* London: Verso.

Beaumont, P. (2019, May 25). British climber latest to die on Everest amid overcrowding. *Guardian.* Retrieved from https://www.theguardian.com/world/2019/may/25/british-climber-latest-to-die-on-everest-amid-overcrowding-robin-fisher

Bianchi, R. (2009). The 'critical turn' in tourism studies: A radical critique. *Tourism Geographies, 11*(4), 484–504. doi:10.1080/14616680903262653

Blanco-Romero, A. (2019). Decrecimiento turístico. In E. Cañada (Ed.). *El turismo en la geopolítica del Mediterráneo* (pp. 66–71). Barcelona: Alba Sud Editorial.

Blanco-Romero, A., Blázquez-Salom, M., & Cànoves, G. (2018). Barcelona, housing rent bubble in a tourist city: Social responses and local policies. *Sustainability, 10*(6), 2043. doi:10.3390/su10062043

Blanco-Romero, A., Blázquez-Salom, M., & Morell, M. (2018). La turismofobia como arma arrojadiza. *Abaco: Revista de Cultura y Ciencias Sociales, 98*, 55–64.

Blanco-Romero, A., Blázquez-Salom, M., Morrell, M., & Fletcher, R. (2019). Understanding stakeholders' perceptions of urban touristification. *BAGE.* Forthcoming. doi:0.21138/bage.2834

Blázquez-Salom, M. (2006). Calmar, contenir i decréixer: Polítiques provades (1983-2003) i possibles de planificació urbanística. *Territoris, 6*, 159–172.

Blázquez-Salom, M. (2016, May 26). Per on decréixer turísticament? Una alternativa ecosocialista. Alba Sud. Retrieved from http://www.albasud.org/blog/ca/883/c-mo-decrecer-tur-sticamente-una-alternativa-ecosocialista

Blázquez-Salom, M., Blanco-Romero, A., Vera-Rebollo, J. F., & Ivars-Baidal, J. (2019). Territorial tourism planning in Spain: From boosterism to tourism degrowth? *Journal of Sustainable Tourism. 27*(12).

Bourdeau, P., & Berthelot, L. (2008). *Tourisme et decroissance: De la critique it l'utopie?* In F. Flipo & F. Schneider (Eds.), Proceedings of the First International Conference on Economic De-Growth for Ecological Sustainability and Social Equity, Paris, 18–19 April, pp. 78–85. Paris: Research & Degrowth.

Britton, R. A. (1978). *International tourism and indigenous development objectives. A study with special reference to the West Indies* (PhD thesis). University of Minnesota, Minneapolis, MN.

Britton, S. (1991). Tourism, capital, and place: Towards a critical geography of tourism. *Environment and Planning D: Society and Space, 9*(4), 451–478. doi:10.1068/d090451

Britton, S., & Clarke, W. C. (Eds.) (1989). *Ambiguous alternative: Tourism in small developing countries.* Suva: University of the South Pacific Press.

Butler, R. W. (1980). The concept of a tourist area cycle of evolution: Implications for management of resources. *The Canadian Geographer/Le Géographe Canadien, 24*(1), 5–12. doi:10.1111/j.1541-0064.1980.tb00970.x

Butler, R. W. (1999). Sustainable tourism: A state-of-the-art review. *Tourism Geographies, 1*(1), 7–25. doi:10.1080/14616689908721291

Büscher, B., & Fletcher, R. (2017). Destructive creation: Capital accumulation and the structural violence of tourism. *Journal of Sustainable Tourism, 25*(5), 651–667. doi:10.1080/09669582.2016.1159214

Cañada, E., & Murray, I. (Eds.) (2019). *Turistificación global: Perspectivas críticas en turismo.* Barcelona: Icaria.

Castree, N. (Ed.) (2010). *The point is to change it: Geographies of hope and survival in an age of crisis*. New York, NY: John Wiley & Sons.

Cattaneo, C., D'Alisa, G., Kallis, G., & Zografos, C. (2012). *Futures, 44*(6), special issue on "Degrowth futures and democracy." doi:10.1016/j.futures.2012.03.012

Chassagne, N., & Everingham, P. (2019). Buen Vivir: Degrowing extractivism and growing wellbeing through tourism. *Journal of Sustainable Tourism, 27*(12), 1–17. doi:10.1080/09669582.2019.1660668

Christine, R. (2014). *L'Usure du monde: Critique de la déraison touristique*. Paris: L'échappée.

Cocola-Gant, A., & Gago, A. (2019). Airbnb, buy-to-let investment and tourism-driven displacement. A case study in Lisbon. *Environment and Planning A*. Forthcoming.

Cordero, A. (2006). *Nuevos ejes de acumulación y naturalez: El caso del turismo*. Buenos Aires: CLACSO.

Crommelin, K., Troy, L., Martin, C., & Pettit, C. (2018). Is Airbnb a sharing economy superstar? Evidence from five global cities. *Urban Policy and Research, 36*(4), 429–444. doi:10.1080/08111146.2018.1460722

D'Alisa, G., Demaria, F., & Cattaneo, C. (2013). Civil and uncivil actors for a degrowth society. *Journal of Civil Society, 9*(2), 212–224. doi:10.1080/17448689.2013.788935

D'Alisa, G., Demaria, F., & Kallis, G. (Eds.). (2014). *Degrowth: A vocabulary for a new era*. London: Routledge.

Daly, H. (2008). A steady-state economy. Presentation for the UK Sustainable Development Commission, London, UK.

Demaria, F., Kallis, G., & Bakker, K. (2019). *Environment and Planning E, 2*(3). special section on "Geographies of degrowth."

Doxey, G. V. (1975). *A causation theory of visitor-resident irritants, methodology and research inferences*. Conference Proceedings: Sixth Annual Conference of Travel Research Association, pp. 195–198. CTRA, San Diego, CA.

Escobar, A. (1995). *Encountering development: The making and unmaking of the Third World*. Princeton: Princeton University Press. doi:10.1086/ahr/101.5.1523

Escobar, A. (2015). Degrowth, postdevelopment, and transitions: A preliminary conversation. *Sustainability Science, 10*(3), 451–462. doi:10.1007/s11625-015-0297-5

Fletcher, R. (2011). Sustaining tourism, sustaining capitalism? The tourism industry's role in global capitalist expansion. *Tourism Geographies, 13*(3), 443–461. doi:10.1080/14616688.2011.570372

Fletcher, R. (2019). Ecotourism after nature: Anthropocene tourism as a new capitalist 'fix'. *Journal of Sustainable Tourism, 27*(4), 522–535. doi:10.1080/09669582.2018.1471084

Fletcher, R., & Neves, K. (2012). Contradictions in tourism: The promise and pitfalls of ecotourism as a manifold capitalist fix. *Environment and Society, 3*(1), 60–77. doi:10.3167/ares.2012.030105

Fletcher, R., & Rammelt, C. (2017). Decoupling: A key fantasy of the post-2015 sustainable development agenda. *Globalizations, 14*(3), 450–467. doi:10.1080/14747731.2016.1263077

Foster, J. B. (2011). Capitalism and degrowth: An impossibility theorem. *Monthly Review, 62*(8), 26–33. doi:10.14452/MR-062-08-2011-01_2

Fraser, N. (2013). A triple movement? Parsing the politics of crisis after Polanyi. *New Left Review, 81*, 119–132.

Fraser, N., & Jaeggi, R. (2018). *Capitalism. A conversation in critical theory*. Cambridge: Polity.

Fullagar, S., Markwell, K., & Wilson, E. (Eds.). (2012). *Slow tourism: Experiences and mobilities* (Vol. 54). New York, NY: Channel View Publications.

Gascón, J. (2019). Tourism as a right: A "frivolous claim" against degrowth? *Journal of Sustainable Tourism, 27*(12), 1–14. doi:10.1080/09669582.2019.1666858

Gascón, J., & Cañada, E. (2005). *Viajar a todo tren: Turismo, desarrollo y sostenibilidad*. Barcelona: Icaria.

Gibson-Graham, J. K. (2006). *A postcapitalist politics*. Minneapolis, MN: University of Minnesota Press.

Gössling, S., & Peeters, P. (2015). Assessing tourism's global environmental impact 1900–2050. *Journal of Sustainable Tourism, 23*(5), 639–659. doi:10.1080/09669582.2015.1008500

Hall, C. M. (2009). Degrowing tourism: Décroissance, sustainable consumption and steady-state tourism. *Anatolia, 20*(1), 46–61. doi:10.1080/13032917.2009.10518894

Hall, C. M. (2010). Changing paradigms and global change: From sustainable to steady-state tourism. *Tourism Recreation Research, 35*(2), 131–143. doi:10.1080/02508281.2010.11081629

Harvey, D. (1982). *The limits to capital*. Chicago, IL: University of Chicago Press. doi:10.1086/ahr/88.5.1243

Harvey, D. (1989). *The condition of postmodernity: An inquiry into the origins of cultural change*. Oxford: Basil Blackwell.

Harvey, D. (2010). *The Enigma of Capital: And the crises of capitalism*. London: Profile Books.

Hickel, J., & Kallis, G. (2019). Is green growth possible? *New Political Economy*, 1–18. doi:10.1080/13563467.2019.1598964

Higgins-Desbiolles, F. (2008). Justice tourism and alternative globalization. *Journal of Sustainable Tourism, 16*(3), 345–364. doi:10.1080/09669580802154132

Higgins-Desbiolles, F. (2010). The elusiveness of sustainability in tourism: The culture ideology of consumerism and its implications. *Tourism and Hospitality Research, 10*(2), 116–129. doi:10.1057/thr.2009.31

Higgins-Desbiolles, F. (2018). Sustainable tourism: Sustaining tourism or something more? *Tourism Management Perspectives, 25*, 157–160. doi:10.1016/j.tmp.2017.11.017

Higgins-Desbiolles, F., Carnicelli, S., Krolikowski, C., Wijesinghe, G., & Boluk, K. (2019). Degrowing tourism: Rethinking tourism. *Journal of Sustainable Tourism*, *27*(12), 1–19. doi:10.1080/09669582.2019.1601732

Hill, K. (2019, May 26). 'I became a traffic controller': Viral Everest photo's weird back story. *Daily News*. Retrieved from https://10daily.com.au/news/a190527cgbsr/i-became-a-traffic-controller-viral-everest-photos-weird-back-story-20190528

Hopwood, B., Mellor, M., & O'Brien, G. (2005). Sustainable development: Mapping different approaches. *Sustainable Development*, *13*(1), 38–52. doi:10.1002/sd.244

Kallis, G. (2018). *Degrowth (The economy: Key ideas)*. New York, NY: Agenda Publishing.

Kallis, G., Kerschner, C., & Martinez-Alier, J. (2012a). The economics of degrowth. *Ecological Economics*, *84*, 172–180. doi:10.1016/j.ecolecon.2012.08.017

Kallis, G., Kerschner, C., & Martinez-Alier, J. (2012b). *Ecological Economics*, *84*, special section on "The economics of degrowth." doi:10.1016/j.ecolecon.2012.08.017

Kallis, G., Kostakis, V., Lange, S., Muraca, S., Paulson, S., & Schmelzer, M. (2018). Research on degrowth. *Annual Review of Environment and Resources*, *43*(1), 291–316. doi:10.1146/annurev-environ-102017-025941

Kallis, G., Schneider, F., & Martinez-Alier, J. (2010). *Journal of Cleaner Production*, *18*(6), special issue on "Growth, recession or degrowth for social equity and sustainability.

Kerschner, C., Wächter, P., Nierling, L., & Ehlers, M. H. (2018). Degrowth and technology: Towards feasible, viable, appropriate and convivial imaginaries. *Journal of Cleaner Production*, *197*(2), 1619–1636. doi:10.1016/j.jclepro.2018.07.147

Koens, K., Postma, A., & Papp, B. (2018). Is overtourism overused? Understanding the impact of tourism in a city context. *Sustainability*, *10*(12), 4384. doi:10.3390/su10124384

Kothari, A., Salleh, A., Escobar, A., Demaria, F., & Acosta, A. (Eds.) (2019). *Pluriverse: A post-development dictionary*. New Delhi: Tulika Books.

Langley, P., & Leyshon, A. (2017). Platform capitalism: The intermediation and capitalisation of digital economic circulation. *Finance and Society*, *3*(1), 11–31. doi:10.2218/finsoc.v3i1.1936

Latouche, S. (2003). Por una sociedad del decrecimiento. *Le Monde Diplomatique*, 97. Edición Española.

Latouche, S. (2006). *Le Pari de la décroissance*. Paris: Fayard.

Latouche, S. (2007). *Petit traité de la décroissance sereine*. Paris: Mille et Une Nuits.

Latouche, S. (2009). *Farewell to growth*. Cambridge: Polity.

Liodakis, G. (2018). Capital, economic growth, and socio-ecological crisis: A critique of de-Growth. *International Critical Thought*, *8*(1), 46–65. doi:10.1080/21598282.2017.1357487

Logan, J., & Molotch, H. (1987). *Urban fortunes: The political economy of place*. Berkeley, CA: University of California Press.

Martinez Alier, J. (2009). Socially sustainable economic de-growth. *Development and Change*, *40*(6), 1099–1119. doi:10.1111/j.1467-7660.2009.01618.x

Mason, P. (2015). *Postcapitalism: A guide to our future*. London: Penguin.

Meadows, D. H., Meadows, D. L., Randers, J., & Behrens, W. W. III. (1972). *The limits to growth: A report for the Club of Rome's project on the predicament of mankind*. New York, NY: Universe Books.

Milano, C. (2017a). Turismofobia: Cuando el turismo entra en la agenda de los movimientos sociales. *Marea Urbana*, 1. Retrieved from https://mareaurbanabcn.wordpress.com/2017/04/25/turismofobia-cuando-el-turismo-entra-en-la-agenda-de-los-movimientos-sociales/

Milano, C. (2017b). *Overtourism y turismofobia: Tendencias globales y contextos locales*. Barcelona: Ostelea School of Tourism & Hospitality. Retrieved from https://www.researchgate.net/publication/323174699_Overtourism_y_Turismofobia_Tendencias_Globales_y_Contextos_Locales

Milano, C., Cheer, J. M., & Novelli, M. (Eds.) (2019). *Overtourism: Excesses, discontents and measures in travel and tourism*. New York, NY: CABI.

Milano, C., Novelli, M., & Cheer, J. M. (2019). Overtourism and tourismphobia: A journey through four decades of tourism development, planning and local concerns. *Tourism Planning and Development*, *16*(4), 353–357.

Mosedale, J. (Ed.). (2011). *Political economy of tourism: A critical perspective*. London: Routledge.

Mosedale, J. (Ed.). (2016). *Neoliberalism and the political economy of tourism*. London: Routledge.

Mowforth, M., & Munt, I. (2016). *Tourism and sustainability: Development, globalisation and new tourism in the Third World* (4th ed.). London: Routledge.

Murray, I. (2015). *Capitalismo y turismo en España: Del "milagro económico" a la "gran crisis"*. Barcelona: Alba Sud Editorial.

Murray, I., Yrigoy, I., & Blázquez-Salom, M. (2017). The role of crises in the production, destruction and restructuring of tourist spaces: The case of the Balearic Islands. *Investigaciones Turísticas*, *13*, 1–29.

Naess, P., & Høyer, K. G. (2009). The emperor's green clothes: Growth, decoupling, and capitalism. *Capitalism Nature Socialism*, *20*(3), 74–95. doi:10.1080/10455750903215753

Navarro-Jurado, E., Romero-Padilla, Y., Romero-Martínez, J. M., Serrano-Muños, E., Habegger, S., & Mora-Esteban, R. (2019). Growth machines and social movements in mature tourist destinations: Costa del Sol—Malaga. *Journal of Sustainable Tourism*. *27*(12).

Nicolae, C., & Sabina, M. (2013). Travel and tourism as a driver of economic recovery. *Procedia Economics and Finance, 6*, 81–88.

Oklevik, O., Gössling, S., Hall, C. M., Steen Jacobsen, J. K., Grøtte, I. P., & McCabe, S. (2019). Overtourism, optimisation, and destination performance indicators: A case study of activities in Fjord Norway. *Journal of Sustainable Tourism, 27*(12), 1–19. doi:10.1080/09669582.2018.1533020

Panzer-Krause, S. (2019). Networking towards sustainable tourism: Innovations between green growth and degrowth strategies. *Regional Studies, 53*(7), 927–938. doi:10.1080/00343404.2018.1508873

Parrique, T., Barth, J., Briens, F., Kerschner, C., Kraus-Polk, A., Kuokkanen, A., & Spangenberg, J. H. (2019). *Decoupling debunked: Evidence and arguments against green growth as a sole strategy for sustainability.* Bruxelles: European Environmental Bureau.

Paulson, S. (2017). *Journal of Political Ecology, 24*(1), special section on "Degrowth: Culture, power, and change." doi:10.2458/v24i1.20882

Polanyi, K. (1944). *The great transformation: The political and economic origins of our time.* Boston, MA: Beacon.

Redclift, M. C. (1987). *Sustainable development: Exploring the contradictions.* London: Methuen.

Redclift, M. C. (2018). Sustainable development in the age of contradictions. *Development and Change, 49*(3), 695–707. doi:10.1111/dech.12394

Renkert, S. R. (2019). Community-owned tourism and degrowth: A case study in the Kichwa Añangu community. *Journal of Sustainable Tourism, 27*(12), 1–16. doi:10.1080/09669582.2019.1660669

Rifai, T. (2017). Tourism: Growth is not the enemy; it's how we manage it that counts. Retrieved from http://media.unwto.org/press-release/2017-08-15/tourism-growth-not-enemy-it-s-how-we-manage-it-counts

Rifkin, J. (2014). *The zero marginal cost society: The internet of things, the collaborative commons, and the eclipse of capitalism.* New York, NY: Palgrave Macmillan.

Rodríguez-Labajos, B., Yánez, I., Bond, P., Greyl, L., Munguti, S., Ojo, G. U., & Overbeek, W. (2019). Not so natural an alliance? Degrowth and environmental justice movements in the Global South. *Ecological Economics, 157*, 175–184. doi:10.1016/j.ecolecon.2018.11.007

Roelofsen, M., & Minca, C. (2018). The Superhost: Biopolitics, home and community in the Airbnb dream-world of global hospitality. *Geoforum, 91*, 170–181. doi:10.1016/j.geoforum.2018.02.021

Rushkoff, D. (2016). *Throwing rocks at the Google bus: How growth became the enemy of prosperity.* New York, NY: Penguin.

Saed. (2012). *Capitalism Nature Socialism, 23*(1), symposium on "Degrowth."

Salleh, A. (2009). *Eco-sufficiency and global justice: Women write political ecology.* London: Pluto Press.

Scheyvens, R. (2009). Pro-poor tourism: Is there value beyond the rhetoric? *Tourism Recreation Research, 34*(2), 191–196. doi:10.1080/02508281.2009.11081590

Sekulova, F., Kallis, G., Rodríguez-Labajos, B., & Schneider, F. (2013). *Journal of Cleaner Production, 38*, special issue on "Degrowth: From theory to practice." doi:10.1016/j.jclepro.2012.06.022

Srisang, K. (1992). Third world tourism: The new colonialism. *In Focus, 4*, 2–3.

Slee, T. (2017). *What's yours is mine: Against the sharing economy.* London: Scribe.

Smil, V. (2013). *Making the modern world: Materials and dematerialization.* New York, NY: Wiley.

Smith, N. (1984). *Uneven development: Nature, capital, and the production of space.* Oxford: Basil Blackwell.

Spenceley, A. (2012). *Responsible tourism: Critical issues for conservation and development.* London: Routledge.

Srnicek, N. (2017). *Platform capitalism.* New York, NY: John Wiley & Sons.

Srnicek, N., & Williams, A. (2015). *Inventing the future: Postcapitalism and a world without work.* London: Verso Books.

Stroebel, M. (2015). Tourism and the green economy: Inspiring or averting change? *Third World Quarterly, 36*(12), 2225–2243. doi:10.1080/01436597.2015.1071658

Swyngedouw, E. (2010). Apocalypse forever? Post-political populism and the spectre of climate change. *Theory, Culture & Society, 27*(2–3), 213–232. doi:10.1177/0263276409358728

United Nations (UN). (2016). Sustainable development goals. Retrieved from https://sustainabledevelopment.un.org/sdgsproposal

United Nations Environment Programme (UNEP). (2011a). *Towards a green economy: Pathways to sustainable development and poverty reduction.* Nairobi: UNEP.

United Nations Environment Programme (UNEP). (2011b). *Decoupling natural resource use and environmental impacts from economic growth.* Nairobi: UNEP.

United Nations World Tourism Organization (UNWTO). (2009a). Roadmap to recovery. Retrieved from http://www.unwto.org/media/news/en/press_det.php?id=4181&idioma=E

United Nations World Tourism Organization (UNWTO). (2009b). Tourism status update. Retrieved from http://www.unwto.org/media/news/en/press_det.php?id=5061

United Nations World Tourism Organization (UNWTO). (2013). International tourism: An engine for the economic recovery. Press Release # 13081. Retrieved from http://media.unwto.org/press-release/2013-12-12/international-tourism-engine-economic-recovery

United Nations World Tourism Organization (UNWTO). (2018). *'Overtourism'? Understanding and managing urban tourism growth beyond perceptions*. Madrid: UNWTO.

United Nations World Tourism Organization (UNWTO). (2019). *World tourism highlights 2018*. Madrid: UNWTO.

Valdivielso, J., & Moranta, J. (2019). The social construction of the tourism degrowth discourse in the Balearic Islands. *Journal of Sustainable Tourism, 27*(12), 1–17. doi:10.1080/09669582.2019.1660670

Wall, G. (1997). Sustainable tourism—Unsustainable development. In S. Wahab & J. Pilgrim (Eds.). *Tourism development and growth: The challenge of sustainability* (pp. 29–43). London: Routledge.

Wanner, T. (2015). The new 'passive revolution' of the green economy and growth discourse: Maintaining the 'sustainable development' of neoliberal capitalism. *New Political Economy, 20*(1), 21–41. doi:10.1080/13563467.2013.866081

Wolff, R. D. (2012). *Democracy at work: A cure for capitalism*. New York, NY: Haymarket Books.

World Commission on Environment and Development (WCED). (1987). *Our common future*. Oxford: Oxford University Press.

World Trade Market (WTM). (2017). 11th Ministers summit. Retrieved from http://london.wtm.com/en/events/wtm-ministerial-programme/Ministers-Summit/

Young, G. (1973). *Tourism: Blessing or blight?* London: Penguin.

Territorial tourism planning in Spain: from boosterism to tourism degrowth?

Macià Blázquez-Salom (iD), Asunción Blanco-Romero (iD), Fernando Vera-Rebollo (iD) and Josep Ivars-Baidal (iD)

ABSTRACT

Tourism saturation and unsustainability have been studied in urban political ecology. Both of these problems are inseparable from tourism planning and they have resulted in proposed solutions based on growth containment and even degrowth. These types of measures have been applied to varying degrees in mature coastal destinations in Spain since the 1990s, and they are currently being used for the country's main urban destinations due to problems generated by tourism saturation. This study examines the progressive incorporation of these measures in territorial tourism planning in Spain and it points out that the traditional emphasis on urban-tourism growth is declining and that more restrictive policies are now being implemented. This shift is illustrated through the analysis of three innovative territorial tourism planning instruments in Barcelona, the Balearic Islands and the Autonomous Region of Valencia. These ostensibly progressive processes suffer from crippling contradictions due to their inability to directly confront the capitalist accumulation model underlying the tourism growth they address. Consequently, much stronger measures capable of transcending this accumulation model in pursuit of genuine, and fair degrowth without systemic constraints are needed.

Introduction

Mounting interest in tourism growth containment and tourism degrowth is due to increasing concern about socio-ecological problems and support for initiatives that favour local empowerment through municipal and regional policies. Problems such as the exhaustion of non-renewable natural resources or environmental pollution have given cause for alarm and they have generated a demand for the control of the more detrimental production activities, such as tourism, due to their contribution to global change (Lezen et al., 2018; Scott, & Gössling, 2015).

Furthermore, the deterioration of democracy, political and business corruption and the systemic economic crisis (Streeck, 2014), which is particularly acute in the context of the bursting Spanish housing bubble (López & Rodríguez, 2011), have given rise to the emergence of counter-hegemonic movements of *"indignados"* (Asara, 2016), driven by the dispossessions in the city centres and the difficulty to access housing (Wachsmuth & Weisler, 2018; Blanco-Romero, Blázquez-Salom, & Cànoves, 2018).

In Spain, action aimed at resolving the aforementioned socio-environmental challenges has traditionally been based on a territorial planning process implemented through regional policies. The institutional structure of the state has assumed the planning function of the economic and territorial activities using these planning policies in order to optimise the use of natural resources, in favour of general interest and to resolve or mitigate the socio-ecological conflicts. Its principal instruments have been sectoral planning and other urban and tourism planning tools. Within a global context of unequal geographic development, the territorial rebalance has been addressed, on the whole, through the economic promotion of disadvantaged regions. There are fewer cases of action that aim at containing growth or promoting degrowth of those areas where wealth is more highly concentrated. Some of these experiences in containing growth have involved: the protection of natural spaces, the limitation of urban development (Rullan, 2011) or of the capacity of infrastructures, such as airports (Hilbrandt, 2017). The objectives established in these actions are the assumption of environmental limits, sufficiency (Hayden, 2014), degrowth (Kallis et al., 2018) or the redistribution of opportunities to access well-being.

Although the design of the territorial and tourism planning instruments is based on discourse that defends a conventional model of sustainability, occasionally it is claimed that they are also being used to solve the crisis of capital accumulation, creating a lock-in to a conventional growth model (Hof & Blázquez-Salom, 2015), based on elitist 'quality tourism', which favours individual interests and those of the hegemonic project of the dominant classes (Bianchi, 2004), thus contradicting their purported objectives. The very existence of the state apparatus was considered by Henry Lefebvre (1968) to be a rationalising and commercialising instrument that enabled relationships of domination to be maintained. Its control through planning gives rise to spaces filled with ideological baggage, materializing the interests defended by urban planners, and economic lobbies (Soja, 1989). Government policy instruments have been studied as a further expression of the neoliberal hegemonic project, consisting in rolling-back the Keynesian welfare state in terms of territorial development regulation (Peck & Tickell, 2002).

This study explores these issues through the analysis of three innovative territorial tourism planning instruments in Barcelona, the Balearic Islands and the Autonomous Region of Valencia. Our hypotheses are: first, that territorial tourism planning has evolved in Spain from boosterism to attempted containment and even degrowth; and second, these regulatory measures applied have underlying contradictions and inconsistencies in relation to the objectives of socio-environmental justice.

In accordance with this critical approach, the objectives of this study are:

- To periodise the regulatory framework of urban-tourism planning in Spain between 1960 and the present day.
- To discover and analyse three innovative territorial planning instruments for Spanish coastal areas that are subjected to the greatest urban and tourism pressure –the Territorial Action Plan for the Green Coastal Infrastructure (PATIVEL) in the Autonomous Community of the Region of Valencia, the Special Urban Plan for Tourist Accommodation (PEUAT) in Barcelona (Catalonia) and the Plan for Intervention in Tourism Areas (PIAT) in Mallorca (Balearic Islands)– which are intended to contain tourism growth in order to mitigate its harmful effects.
- To identify the possible environmental and social contradictions associated with applying these measures to regulate growth in comparison to their own discourse of degrowth, which in this way, seems to be used rhetorically.
- By way of conclusion, to assess the extent to which tourism planning in Spain is evolving towards the principles of fair or genuine degrowth.

The article is structured in the following sections: firstly, an explanation about our methodology; secondly, the literature review; thirdly, analysing the periodisation of the urban-tourism regulatory framework in Spain (1960-2018); and, fourthly, analysing the three instruments to contain growth and new intervention mechanisms to address overtourism. In accordance with the objectives proposed, our three case studies have been chosen in view of their different dimensions. They are not going to be compared, instead an analysis will be carried out in the discussion section, on their regulations aimed at containing urban-tourism growth or promoting degrowth, their socio-ecological contradictions and the discourse that they are based on. Finally, the conclusions sum up our contribution.

Methodology

A qualitative methodology based on different tools has been used to develop the objectives described. First, secondary sources of previous studies have been consulted to establish the periodisation of the Spanish regulatory framework, based on five approaches or traditions of public tourism planning (Getz, 1986; Hall, 2008), updated with recent contributions (Hall, 2014; Saarinen, Rogerson, & Hall, 2017). Second, each of the planning instruments has been studied based on the public and private documentation available, particularly sources related to public participation during its administrative processing. Lastly, a critical study of participatory action research has been carried out (Kemmis, Mc Taggart, & Nixon, 2013). The participant observation of the authors has been developed in discussion groups and activist meetings of resident associations, in order to critically analyse, as accurately as possible, public discourse and the governance processes. The interviewed stakeholder groups were: Assembly of Neighbourhoods for Sustainable Tourism (ABTS), Grup Balear d'Ornitologia i Defensa de la Naturalesa (GOB), Terraferida, Ciutat per qui l'habita, Palma XXI, and the residents of the neighbourhoods that are the most affected by the phenomenon.[1] In order to organize the information obtained, Grounded Theory methods have been taken into account in the research (Charmaz & Belgrave, 2015), which is considered to be the most suitable method for the theoretical construction in social science research (Denzin & Lincoln, 2005), and it is one of the most frequently used tools in human and social sciences (Corbin & Strauss, 1990). To determine qualified opinions, semi-structured in-depth interviews were conducted with different qualified spokespeople of the stakeholders (social movements', hoteliers' and local administration representatives). These include individuals who are in charge of the administrative policies implemented in the three study areas (PEUAT, PIAT and PATIVEL).

In accordance with the objectives proposed, our study has been conducted taking into account case studies of three different spatial scales (the Autonomous Community of the Region of Valencia, the island of Majorca and the city of Barcelona), which have similar historical tourism backgrounds and are characterised by saturation and more complex experiences of territorial planning for tourist growth containment. Each territorial and tourism planning measure has been studied in terms of its different dimensions, in order to attain the defined objectives: to analyse their regulations aimed at containing urban-tourism growth or stimulating degrowth, their socio-ecological contradictions and the discourses on which they are based.

According to the theoretical sampling in Grounded Theory, our sample of sources and informants is intended to maximise the differences among them, by choosing the divergent discourses that are available (Charmaz & Belgrave, 2015).

Literature review

Authors in the field of political ecology explain the interest in degrowth in relation to the criticism of hegemonic neoliberal ideology that naturalizes the need for economic growth, individualism, consumerism or competitiveness (Asara, 2016). From this same perspective, it can be interpreted that economic growth has been used as a mechanism to favour the pacification of class conflicts (Kallis et al., 2018), through its promises of employment and social mobility, bolstering profit rates through public investment and labour and territorial flexibility. Growth is also fuelled by the extension of the tourism business frontiers through the rhetoric use of the so-called "sharing economy", motivated by job insecurity and the chance to boost income (Slee, 2017), for example, through the possibility of renting properties to tourists for short stays (Wachsmuth & Weisler, 2018).

Alternative proposals, such as sufficiency (Princen, 2005) and degrowth (Kallis et al., 2018) suggest that the opulent classes are historically those who are the most responsible for global change and they also have a greater margin to reduce their production and consumption patterns (Sachs, 2001; Hall, 2009). However, degrowth can also be proposed in demographic or Malthusian terms, by prioritising economic profitability and treating the population differently according to their income levels. Certain authors claim that the enclosure and containment of growth are related to dispossession, which benefits class hegemonic projects (Bianchi, 2004; Büsher & Fletcher, 2014; Sevilla-Buitrago, 2015; Artigues & Blázquez-Salom, 2016). The resulting social segregation fosters the exclusive and elitist use of space (Kondo, Rivera, & Rullman, 2012), creating a consensus that favours the interests of the ruling classes (Eisenschitz, 2016), which monopolise incomes (Harvey, 2002) or expand and commodify new spaces and aspects of life to address the inherent contradictions in capitalism (Fletcher, 2011; Fletcher & Neves, 2012).

Similarly, a rhetorical use of sustainability discourse is already thought to contribute to the consolidation of the hegemony of the historically dominant classes, facilitated by growth at the heart of capitalism (Igoe, Neves, & Brockington, 2010; Sklair, 2000). The dominance of the ruling class is achieved through a combination of force and the creation of a discourse that neutralises the counter-hegemonic challenges aimed at the dominating order, co-opting and neutralising them through changes and concessions that re-establish the consensus (Wanner, 2015). Antonio Gramsci called this process the "absorption of the antithesis" (Gramsci 1971, p. 110).

For example, the World Travel & Tourism Council analyses the way that complaints about tourism oversaturation are assimilated without altering the *status quo* (McKinsey & Company, 2017). The WTTC proposes to mitigate overtourism through deseasonalisation, spatial deconcentration, price increases, limiting accommodation places and regulating the access to overcrowded sites.

A partial concept of the socio-ecological variables at stake lies at the root of these contradictions. Certain territorial and tourism planning instruments are aimed at improving environmental conditions, such as the landscape quality of the environments in terms of weak sustainability, although they neglect socio-economic aspects that are taken into consideration in political ecology and environmental justice studies.

However, a genuine degrowth project involves a socio-ecological transition (Escobar, 2015) using new forms of radical democracy, guided by environmental justice, solidarity and autonomy (Cattaneo, D'Alisa, Kallis, & Zografos, 2012). Social movements are thought to promote a new "epistemic community", moving the struggle further beyond the boundary of greenwash rhetoric, thus corroborating tourism growth in a transformative "triple movement of emancipation" (Fraser, 2013), against the expansion of the tourist frontier, i.e. touristification (Moranta & Valdivielso, 2020). Otherwise, regulatory measures to contain growth, such as territorial and tourism planning instruments used by the state can be considered to be double movements of social protection rather than a genuine degrowth (Fletcher, Murray, Blanco-Romero, & Blázquez-Salom, 2019). The resulting proposals for ecological transition are directed by the principles of environmental justice and they prioritise the schemes that improve the living conditions of the most disadvantaged (Moreno, 2010; Perles-Ribes, Ramón-Rodríguez, Vera-Rebollo, & Ivars-Baidal, 2017). Genuine degrowth also aims at recognising the ecological dependence of the human species on the ecological systems. It is therefore linked to the strong approach to sustainability in terms of the weak commensurability of natural capital and man-made capital, and accepting that there are limits on the global systemic resilience.

Given this current state of knowledge, we critically analyse the limitations of territorial tourism planning instruments, by studying three innovative experiences, in the light of the different interpretations of degrowth. Thus, we intend to expand on the knowledge of its practical application by this means.

Analysis and periodisation of the urban-tourism regulatory framework in Spain (1960-2018)

Recent Spanish history, particularly with regard to the Mediterranean coastline, highlights the effects of the functional specialisation in tourism and real estate. In this period of almost 60 years, different tourist and territorial planning approaches have been applied to the tourism spaces, which depend on the changes in the socio-economic and tourism context, the associated economic cycles and the transformations experienced by the country (Murray, Yrigoy, & Blázquez-Salom, 2017). It is possible to observe how five main approaches have worked in practice and how they have addressed specific problems related to tourism planning, which have resulted in responses to overtourism and setting limits on growth and degrowth measures. Below, the phases contained in Table 1 are described.

The "spanish tourism miracle" as a prime example of boosterism (until 1975)

The configuration of mass tourism coastal destinations in Spain from the 1960s took place within a dictatorial political regime that used tourism as a way to obtain foreign exchange earnings in order to palliate the balance of payment deficit and improve the country's image to the outside world (Murray, 2015). Within this context, tourism planning displayed the characteristics of *boosterism,* in which the growth in the tourism supply was considered to be a priority, concentrated in coastal towns.

The three Economic and Social Development Plans of the period 1964-1975 show how profitability was the primary objective of the economic approach. The effects of the territorial implementation of tourism in the *boosterism* years were still visible in the coastal destinations and they have resulted in structural problems that are difficult to overcome. The meteoric growth of supply with deficient urban planning led to deficits in infrastructure and quality standards of the supply, the deterioration of natural and cultural heritage, and even, the first saturation problems of tourist sites (Cals, 1974; Murray, 2015).

The decentralisation of policies and the first boost to protectionist measures (1975-1989)

After the economic crisis of 1973 and with the new Land Act (1975), a new stage of growth began that was linked more to the construction of housing than the supply of hotels. In general, the new municipal plans legalised previous urban-tourism action and favoured urban expansion. With the return of democracy in Spain (1978), a new stage of decentralising tourism and urban policy began. In the mid-1980s, the Ley de Bases de Régimen Local (1986) (Law regulating the Basis of the Local Government) was passed. It conferred a wide range of competencies in terms of urban planning to the municipalities and urban-tourism growth became a source of municipal finance.

In parallel, the Autonomous Regions passed spatial planning laws on a regional level, which enabled this public policy to be consolidated during the 1990s (Benabent, 2006). These initiatives established the base for a more territorial approach to urban planning, while the macroeconomic perspective continued to be fundamental in policies related to the tourism sector. On a local scale, the *laissez faire* approach of *boosterism* was limited through exercising greater administrative control and a greater reflection of the effects of planning in the territorial model. Pioneering

Table 1. Synthesis of the evolution of the tourist and territorial planning approaches in Spain and measures to contain growth. Source: Compiled by the author.

	Boosterism (Until 1975)	Decentralisation and first protectionism (1975-1989)	Restructuring of destinations (1992-1997)	"Urbanisation tsunami" (1998-2007)	Crisis and neoliberal reaction (2008-2014)	Response to overtourism (From 2014)
Economic/ tourism cycle	Expansive cycle until the crisis of 1973. 1964-1974: 1st property bubble in Spain*	Delayed effects of the 1973 crisis. 1986-1992: 2nd property bubble*	Crisis that ended the property bubble	Expansive economic cycle 1996-2007: 3rd property bubble*	Fast recovery of the tourism crisis but not of the socio-economic crisis. Favourable international scenario	Gradual recovery of real estate activity. Rent bubble?
Processes of territorial implementation	Hotel establishments on the seafront	Housing development for tourism use in coastal areas	Predominance of housing development; scarce renovation of traditional nuclei and pressure on rustic land	Conventional expansion together with large urban operations, also in the pre-coastal area	Enterprise-based reassessment projects. "Zombie urbanisations"	Touristification and gentrification of urban spaces
Predominant approach	Boosterism and economic approach	Greater relevance of physical (urban plans) and community (regulatory participation) approach	Strategic and sustainable tourism planning as a rhetorical principle: local plans and Agenda 21	Contradictory physical planning on a regional level. Resurgence of boosterism	Delegitimisation of public planning in favour of private interests	Broader social participation in urban planning, particularly in large cities
Principal containment measures	Non-existent Growth as an objective	Ley de Costas (Coastal Law) (1988). Declaration of Protected Natural Spaces. Tourism density ratios (Balearic Islands)	POOT of Mallorca (1995). Limitations to growth on designated land. Consolidation of regional spatial planning policies	New Spanish Land Act (1998), catalyst of growth. Urban construction moratoriums (Balearic and Canary Island). Sub-regional planning of growth containment (Menorca, Catalonia …)	Austerity policies (slowing down of the renovation of destinations). Regulatory flexibility: Declaration of Regional Interest	Limitations to creating new urban tourism rental places (sectoral and urban planning regulations): PEUAT, PIAT … Reinforcement of sub-regional planning as a limit to growth (PATIVEL)

*Periodisation of the property bubbles in Lois, González, and Escudero (2012).

measures to protect natural spaces were applied in the Balearic Islands from 1984 (Blázquez-Salom, 1999). An attempt was made to modify the development inertia of *boosterism* with pro-tectionist legislation through effects that were more palliative than preventative: Environmental Impact Assessment Act (1986), Coastal Law (1988) or the Law for the Conservation of Natural Spaces and Wild Flora and Fauna (1989).

The restructuring of destinations: planning initiatives without the capacity/will for structural transformation (1990-1997)

At the end of the 1980s and the beginning of the 1990s, there was a recession in the inter-national tourist demand for Spain, within a context of global turbulence that gave rise to a neo-liberal economic modernisation (Murray et al., 2017). The weaknesses of the "Spanish economic miracle" included a disordered urban growth of the main tourist destinations, which are addressed in the White Paper on Spanish Tourism (1990).

In the 1990s, the corporate desire to monopolise hotel revenue and over-supply fuelled the formation of an increased social consensus in favour of nature conservation, rhetorically based on mitigating the risk of losing tourism competitiveness. In the Balearic Islands, tourism restruc-turing focused on adopting measures to contain urban-tourism growth through "hotel moratoriums" but, at the same time, promoting residential development (Aguiló, 1990), with the announcement that the regional government wanted to convert the islands into Europe's second residence (Amer, 2006). The restructuring of tourism urbanisation was promoted through reduc-tions in density with the establishment of "spongy" urban ratios to create free spaces, foster con-tainment and the redirection of growth. The Tourism Supply-side Regulation Plans (POOT) for the Balearic Islands was the first decisive action on a regional scale to contain the growth of coastal tourist areas (Blázquez-Salom and Yrigoy, 2016).

The restructuring of the tourist destinations was considered in terms of the maturity and obsolescence of their supply (Vera and Rodríguez, 2012), basing the tourism policies on the discourse of renovation, excellence and sustainability (Future Plans I and II, 1992-1999) and overall quality (Integral Plan of Spanish Tourism Quality, PICTE, 2006). Strategic tourism plan-ning continued to be dependent on urban planning instruments which were binding in nature. The discourse of sustainability promoted social participation in tourism planning proc-esses, for example, through Local Agenda 21 programmes, environmental audits and, less fre-quently, action and monitoring plans with tracking indicators. Moreover, in the Balearic Islands, the municipality of Calvià applied an Agenda 21 to the review of a developmentalist urban plan (approved in 1991), limiting urban expansion through the declassification of developable land, although there was still a considerable growth margin for the land classi-fied as urban (Blázquez-Salom, 2001).

The "urban development tsunami" and the debate on tourism models (1998-2007)

The expansion of tourism and urbanisation characterised the so-called "urban development tsunami" that affected the coastal strip of the Spanish Mediterranean (Gaja i Díaz, 2008). In the period 1997-2006, a total of 4.7 million properties were finished, which was a completely dispro-portionate figure in the European context (Burriel de Orueta, 2008), attracting international cap-ital within a climate of strong credit expansion (López & Rodríguez, 2011). The new reform of the Land Law (1988) introduced liberalising measures that favoured real estate expansion. The insistence of pro-growth lobbies (Romero and Vidal, 2018) and the use of urban expansion for municipal financing explain the low incidence of urban planning to contain real estate and tour-ism growth (Peñín, 2006). Territorial tourism planning was based on the rhetoric of sustainability but urban growth was given priority (Mantecón, 2008). The palliative measures are associated with a weak sustainability approach, for example, improving water management or protecting spaces of environmental interest, with no real transformation of the urban and tourism model (Vera & Ivars, 2003).

The urban development tsunami threatened hotel profitability and aggravated the environmental conflicts. The denouncement of the excessive tourism-residential urbanisation was supported by the large hotel owners who criticised the diffused urban development and low profitability of disperse building models (Deloitte & Exceltur, 2005). Their support for the environmental cause called for a new territorial tourism planning that would determine the mature tourism spaces, coordinate the municipal planning and incorporate measures to contain urban growth. There was a myriad of territorial planning measures and instruments on different regional and local levels which clashed, overlapped and, sometimes contradicted each other (Górgolas Martín, 2016).

In short, for our field of study we can identify three distinct models of regional territorial tourism policy: 1) the Balearic region, which is similar to the Canary Islands, in that they both impose moratoriums and apply integrated regional tourism planning (Blázquez-Salom & Yrigoy, 2016; Rullan, 2005, 2011; Simancas, 2015); 2) regions such as Catalonia that introduce urban planning measures to protect the coastline, which are binding for the municipalities (Nel lo, 2012); 3) and the autonomous regions, such as Valencia, which, without renouncing the rhetoric of sustainability, are committed to urban expansion through large real estate operations (Burriel de Orueta, 2009) and, belatedly, have applied instruments that limit growth, such as the PATIVEL.

The crisis as a catalyst of neoliberal approaches (2008-2014)

The slowdown of urban expansion came about as a result of the international economic crisis of 2008, with the bankruptcy of construction companies, real estate agencies and banks (Méndez, Abad, & Echaves, 2015). The management of the crisis made regulation more flexible, creating conditions that fostered investment and public funds were used to bail out financial entities (Murray, 2015); meanwhile, austerity policies were applied, slowing down public investment in a whole range of areas including the reconstruction of mature tourism destinations (Yrigoy, 2015).

The conditions for tourism growth were restored using new neoliberal territorial and tourism policies. The Comprehensive National Tourism Plan (2012-2015) emphasised the need for private investment implemented through, for example, the financing of hotel corporations (Yrigoy, 2016). New regulations stimulated capital investment through the streamlining of the administrative procedures that were necessary to process urban planning projects, for example, through declarations of autonomic interest (Blázquez-Salom, Artigues, & Yrigoy, 2015), among other measures.

The excess supply of housing, the result of the urban development tsunami, the high level of private borrowing and job insecurity are arguments in favour of the expansion of the tourism business frontiers and the legalisation of renting properties to tourists (Blanco-Romero et al. 2018).

Instruments to contain growth and new intervention mechanisms to address overtourism

In accordance with the objectives proposed, our study has been conducted taking into account case studies (Map 1) of three different spatial scales (the Autonomous Community of the Region of Valencia, the island of Majorca and the city of Barcelona), which have similar historical tourism backgrounds and are characterised by saturation and more complex experiences of territorial planning for tourist growth containment. The instruments analysed below are: the PATIVEL (2018), the PIAT (2018) and PEUAT (2017).

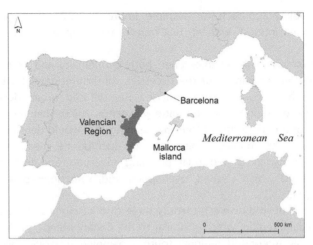

Map 1. Location of the study cases: The Autonomous Community of the Region of Valencia, the island of Majorca and the city of Barcelona. Source: Compiled by the author.

PATIVEL: the territorial action plan of the green coastal infrastructure

The tourism specialisation of the Region of Valencia is suffering from environmental deterioration, particularly on the coast and a social demand is emerging, which is calling for its protection through urban planning. Within this context, the regional government of the Region of Valencia has approved a new planning framework instrument called Estrategia Territorial de la Comunidad Valenciana (Territorial Strategy of the Region of Valencia) (ETCV) (2011). This document explicitly highlights the commitment to sustainable planning in accordance with the principles established by the European Territorial Strategy (1999) and it denotes landscape management as a tool of spatial planning.

One of the key elements of the territorial model proposed by the ETCV is the so-called "Green Territorial Infrastructure". The origins of this concept lie in the architecture of the North American landscape (*Law Olmstead*), which has been incorporated into territorial planning. The Green Infrastructure is defined as being an interconnected network made up of landscapes of great environmental, cultural and visual value. It includes the natural spaces protected in the regional, state or international legislation, the spaces of the Natura 2000 network (Directive 92/43/EEC), the landscapes of cultural and visual value and those fragile spaces with restrictions for urbanisation: the areas with natural risks, the risk of erosion and aquifer recharge. In spatial planning processes, these spaces should be connected by ecological corridors and functional connections. In this way, the future uses of the land that may be applied in the space must comply with the requirements of protection and conservation of the Green Infrastructure, which forms the basic structure of the environmental sustainability of a geographic space (Vera-Rebollo, Olcina, Sáinz-Pardo Trujillo 2019).

The ETCV is specified in the PATIVEL (Decree 58/2018) and its essential objective is to protect the coastal areas of the Region of Valencia that are unaffected by urban development. The PATIVEL delimits and orders a total of 52 areas that should be kept free from construction (Conselleria de Vivienda, Obras Públicas y Vertebración del Territorio, 2018). Its scope of protection includes areas that were already declared as non-buildable land and the urban declassification of 1,426 ha of land on the coastal strip. Overall, the PATIVEL seeks to protect a total of 7,500 ha of the region's coastline, which is equivalent to 12% of the land that has not been urbanised yet in the 2,000 m-wide strip of the coastline (Map 2).

The principal objectives of the PATIVEL are: 1) to define and organise the supramunicipal Green Infrastructure of the coastline, thus protecting its environmental, territorial, landscape, cultural, educational and protection values against natural and induced risks; 2) to guarantee

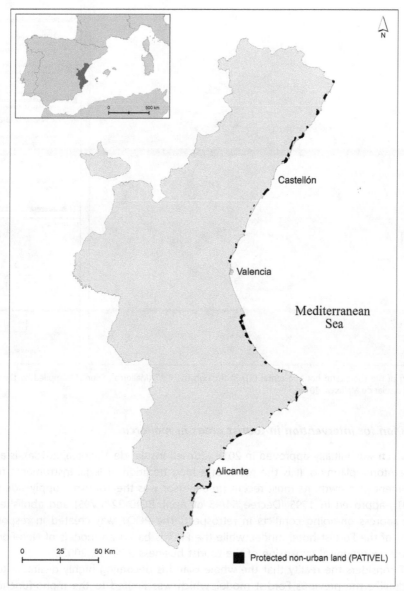

Castellón

Valencia

Mediterranean
Sea

Alicante

0   25   50 Km

■ Protected non-urban land (PATIVEL)

Map 2. Areas protected by the PATIVEL (Autonomous Community of the Region of Valencia). Source: Compiled by the author based on the Conselleria de Vivienda, Obras Públicas y Vertebración del Territorio (2018).

the ecological and functional connectivity between the coastal and inland spaces and to prevent the fragmentation of the pieces that make up the Green Infrastructure; 3) to improve the maintenance of the free spaces on the coastal strip, thus preventing the consolidation of continuous buildings and urban barriers; 4) to guarantee the effectiveness of the protection of the easements of the coastal public domain; 5) to improve the quality and functionality of the coastal spaces that are already built up, particularly a quality tourism supply; 6) to favour pedestrian and cyclist accessibility and mobility on the coast and along its connections with the inland territory.

The PATIVEL is a relevant initiative for protecting the little coastal land that is still undeveloped or for which there is no urban plan that has been approved or is in the process of being developed. This new direction already represents a significant change in policy with regard to the land liberalising measures of previous decades. However, its application is not exempt from contradictions, which are discussed in the following section.

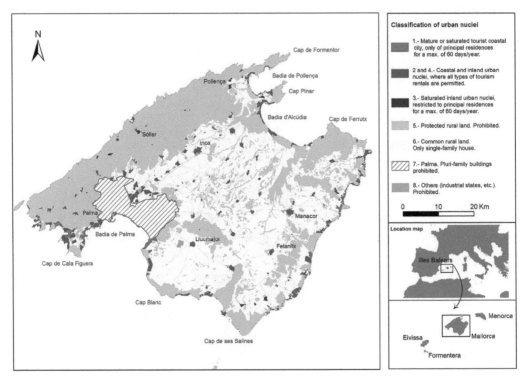

Classification of urban nuclei

1.- Mature or saturated tourist coastal city, only of principal residences for a max. of 60 days/year.

2 and 4.- Coastal and inland urban nuclei, where all types of tourism rentals are permitted.

3.- Saturated inland urban nuclei, restricted to principal residences for a max. of 60 days/year.

5.- Protected rural land. Prohibited.

6.- Common rural land. Only single-family house.

7.- Palma. Pluri-family buildings prohibited.

8.- Others (industrial states, etc.). Prohibited.

Map 3. Zoning of the short term housing rental (STHR) through the PIAT (Mallorca). Source: Compiled by the author based on the Consell Insular de Mallorca, 2018a.

The PIAT: Plan for intervention in tourist areas in mallorca

The PIAT, which was initially approved in 2018 (Consell Insular de Mallorca, 2018a), is an example of tourist territorial planning. It is the result of a long tradition of legal instruments to promote the containment of growth. Its most recent predecessor was the Tourism Supply-side Regulation Plans (POOT), approved in 1995 (Decree 54/95 of April, BOIB 22/06/95) and abolished in 2012. Both plans address on-going conflicts in retrospect. The POOT was created in response to the dysfunctions of the Fordist hotel model, while the PIAT is based on models of Neo-Fordism flexibilisation and geographical expansion of the tourist business (Bianchi, 2002).

The PIAT considers the reality that the whole island is becoming highly desirable to the tourism sector, unlike the previous Fordist model, which was limited to the mono-functional urban development of the coast. During the 1990s, the tourism business frontiers widened; the supply became more diversified with the introduction of new geographic areas, aspects of daily life and residential properties were excluded from the tourism sector in the Fordist hotel model. This extension of the geographical area was linked to the introduction of new tangible and intangible elements in the tourism sector. Among them, housing is the asset added to the tourism market, which generates the greatest social conflict due to its essential function for residential use that competes with the tourism and speculative uses.

The PIAT acknowledges the diagnosis of overtourism and seeks to address four objectives: 1) to regenerate tourist cities; 2) to limit the tourism use depending on the territorial capacities; 3) to determine the capacity of the tourism supply, differentiating hotel supply and housing: 4) and to improve the sustainability of the facilities through the promotion of efficiency measures (Consell Insular de Mallorca, 2018a).

The PIAT deploys territorial tourism planning measures, particularly aimed at limiting the accommodation supply, especially apartments and houses. The approval of the PIAT was

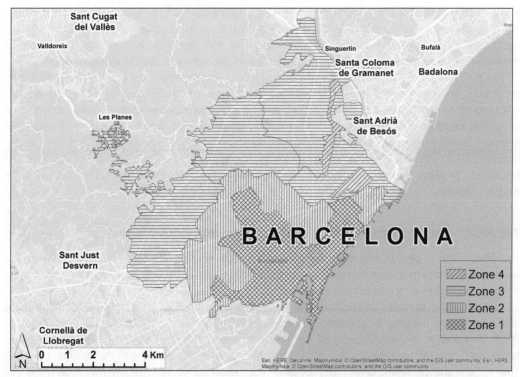

Map 4. Zoning of the PEUAT (Barcelona). Source: Compiled by the author based on Barcelona City Council data. 2017.

accompanied by the approval of a zoning plan that is intended to organise its expansion (Consell Insular de Mallorca, 2018 b). This zoning determines in which urban nuclei different types of short term housing rental (STHR) are permitted, which depends on four variables: 1) the density of inhabitants and tourism beds per hectare of urban and developable land; 2) the percentage of tourist beds with regard to the resident population; 3) the proportion of empty properties with regard to total properties; 4) and the proportion of legalised STHR with regard to the total properties in the urban nucleus.

Therefore, the rental of housing to tourists is zoned according to a classification of all of the urban nuclei (Map 3): 1) the mature or saturated tourist coastal cities where the rental of the main residences of property owners to tourists is only allowed for 60 days per year; 2) the rest of the coastal tourist nuclei, in which all types of tourism rentals are allowed; 3) the inland urban nuclei, where the rental of main residences to tourists is allowed for 60 days per year; 4) the rest of the inland urban nuclei, where all types of rental of properties to tourist are permitted; 5) the protected rural land (natural spaces) where this type of use is prohibited; 6) the rest of common rural land, which has agricultural, forestry or natural uses, and where only holiday rentals of single-family houses are permitted; 7) and finally, the municipality of Palma, with the island's capital, which is governed by its own regulations and where, currently, the rental of housing in pluri-family buildings is prohibited, but not that of single family properties.

The PIAT establishes a maximum capacity of tourist accommodation in Mallorca at being 430,000 beds, although this increased from 292,435 tourist places in 2016 to 395,798 in 2018, which is mainly due to the avalanche of legalisations on tourist accommodation properties (Consell Insular de Mallorca, 2018a). This figure does not include the illegal supply of properties rented to tourists, which the PIAT acknowledges as being the same as the number of legalised properties. The difference between the maximum capacity permitted and the real amount of tourism rental beds in 2018 is the "margin of places" available for growth. The arguments given in the PIAT in favour of this containment are: 1) the space limits of the island; 2) the overburdening of resources and infrastructures; 3) the threat to the social structure of an excessive specialisation in tourism; 4) the feeling of congestion in the peak season; 5) the saturation of infrastructures and facilities, including housing; 6) and the fight against climate change.

The PIAT diagnoses an over-saturation of the main tourism resources: cycling tour paths, hiking routes, golf courses, dry marina or beaches. In the case of the beaches, an available theoretical ratio of 1.68 m2/places is calculated, considering the distribution of the useful surface area of all the beaches at the maximum frequentation of the island, which, in 2017 was 1,477,157 people (Consell Insular de Mallorca, 2018a). Its diagnosis identifies the beaches that have a low occupation, it estimates an optimum ratio of 15m2/person and proposes the building of regulated car parks (with one parking space for every 4 users) in order to facilitate access to 16 isolated beaches.

The PEUAT: Special urban plan for tourist accommodation in barcelona

The PEAUT forms part of the intervention and containment measures adopted to address the overtourism problem arising from the success of Barcelona, which was forced to reformulate its policy and tourism intervention measures (López Palomeque, 2015).

Following the bursting of the financial and housing bubble in 2008, the built environment has once again become a guarantor of the credit system as 'spatio-temporal fixes' (Harvey, 2006), and also in the restructuring of the tourism space (Murray et al., 2017). The citizen-based social and cultural identity (Capel, 2005) becomes a new attraction for the tourist business. This is how the de-industrialised city became the target of tourism regeneration through the commercialisation of its civic culture, or city marketing (Eisenschitz, 2016); and how the "touristification of everyday life" (Bourdeau, François, & Bensahel, 2013) has given rise to conflicts regarding social segregation, inflation, congestion, privatisation and the trivialisation of the space (Russo and Scarnatto, 2017). Within this context, the multifunctional city provides opportunities to earn monopoly rents for its capital with policies that impose limitations and contribute uniqueness. Paradoxically, the social tension that aims at limiting this homogenising mass tourism contributes to creating a differentiated and unique city brand, which makes it more attractive and more profitable (Harvey, 2002).

The conflicts generated by tourism massification have transformed tourism into one of the greatest concerns of citizens. This is why the City Council of Barcelona has been developing different measures to manage tourist accommodation since 2014, such as the moratorium initiated by Convergència i Unió (conservative nationalist party). After 2015, the city council, governed by a coalition of left-wing parties, approved new intervention instruments: the fight against illegal tourist accommodation (mainly available on the online platforms), the reorganisation of the port in order to move certain cruise terminals away from the centre, or the first plan of its kind in Europe, the PEUAT, designed around new dynamics based on increased citizen participation through dialogue with neighbourhood associations (Blanco-Romero et al., 2018; Russo & Scarnatto, 2017).

In January 2017, the City Council of Barcelona passed the PEUAT (Diputación de Barcelona, 2017) and put an end to the previous moratorium. This initiative, which is a pioneer in its field, stands for the regulatory framework of the city's urban planning and tourist accommodation management criteria through the application of the urban planning law of Catalonia (Legislative Decree 1/2010). This decree regulates the creation of new tourist accommodation establishments (hotels, apartments, youth hostels, collective residences, etc.) and STHR (HUTs, Housing Used for Tourism). The former HUTs are one of the most controversial aspects of the current situation, for which zero growth has been imposed throughout the whole city.

The objective of PEUAT, drawn up by the City Council of Barcelona, is to improve the quality of life of the city's citizens, aiming to: 1) alleviate tourist pressure; 2) contain the increase in tourist accommodation; 3) preserve the quality of the public space and diversify it with other activities: 4) promote the diversity of the urban fabric; 5) guarantee the right to housing, rest, privacy, well-being, sustainable mobility and a healthy environment.

The PEUAT has been designed as an urban planning instrument, distinguishing between four specifically regulated zones (Map 4). Each of these zones is characterised by the distribution of the accommodation throughout the territory, the ratio between the number of tourist beds offered and the resident population, the ratio and conditions of certain uses, the incidence of the activities in the public space and the presence of tourist attractions (Ayuntamiento de Barcelona, 2017). The innovative aspect resides principally in the regulation of the HUTs, establishing zero growth throughout the city so as to prevent excessive concentration and to guarantee a balanced territorial distribution. In this way, when a HUT ceases its activity in a congested area, a new licence will be granted in uncongested areas or accommodation regrouping will be allowed in the maintenance or growth areas.

Therefore, Zone 1, which is considered to be the zone of negative growth, does not allow any type of tourist establishment to be introduced or the increase in the number of places in the existing establishments. It includes whole districts, such as Ciutat Vella or the Poble Sec, where the majority of establishments are concentrated (more than 60% of the city's supply) and they receive an average visiting population of 69% of the total population, in cases such as the Gothic quarter. This measure is intended to attain degrowth and, in some zones, such as Ciutat Vella, maintain the specific regime with regard to the HUTs that contemplate the regrouping in a whole building and the possibility of relocating the potential fewer places.

In Zone 2, the current number of places and establishments is to be maintained and the existing establishments are not allowed to expand. It includes areas such as Sants or Sagrada Familia, among others, where the visiting population stands for, on average, 11% of the total population.

Zone 3 is the largest in size and the opening of new establishments and the expansion of existing ones is allowed, provided that the growth is contained. Growth is permitted provided that the maximum density of places in terms of the morphological capacity of the area and the current availability of supply of tourist accommodation are not exceeded.

Zone 4 includes all other areas of the city with specific regulations as they are considered to be three large redevelopment areas: la Marina del Prat Vermell, la Sagrera and the northern part of 22@ quarter, with very different characteristics in terms of territory, building density, use and development. In these areas, the introduction of new HUTs is forbidden.

Discussion. Inconsistencies in the growth containment and degrowth measures

The analysis of the regulatory framework and the three study tools reveal inconsistencies and undesirable collateral effects in the transition towards the containment of growth and degrowth of tourism. These contradictions are found in the actual concept of the tools and their rhetorical discourse in relation to their practical application.

In the case of the Region of Valencia, in 2018, the PATIVEL took on the tradition of protecting the coast, which had been applied in the Balearic Islands in 1999 and in Catalonia in 2005 during the phase called the "urban development tsunami" (Górgolas Martín, 2019). It is a physical/spatial planning tool that applies sub-regional planning measures in order to limit growth. This first characteristic, its late development, particularly when it is compared to the growth containment policies that have been implemented in other Spanish regions for more than two decades, is one weakness.

Furthermore, it specifies the applicability of different interpretations of degrowth, linked to ideological stances. One meaning of degrowth, related just to the quantitative demographic variable, is based on neo-Malthusian proposals that blame unsustainability on the most disadvantaged social classes, in quantitative terms. A more genuine interpretation of degrowth maintains that it should favour the social vulnerable classes (Perles-Ribes et al., 2017). The first is achieved through the creation, in certain cases, of a pro-degrowth consensus in the oversaturated tourist destinations, in which a reduction of the amount of customers is desired, getting rid of those with the lowest purchasing power. These coalitions between the upper class and hegemonic power take advantage of the containment measures through their control of the revenue of the urban-tourism business. Consequently, territorial protection, with the elimination of the expectation of further property development, increases the value of the real estate in the area, thanks to the generation of unpaid externalities. The decrease in the supply, due to growth containment, deals with the increase of its economic profitability.

The same applies to the operating licences of the tourist establishments, after using moratoriums that paralysed the granting of new licences, generally with a significant "pull effect" and high growth ceilings. In the case of the PIAT in Mallorca and the PEUAT in Barcelona, the hotel sector, property owners and real estate investors benefit from the increased value of their assets due to the higher value in the market of a product that is becoming more scarce and selective. The image attached to a commitment to contain growth favours competitiveness through restructuring and social-spatial segregation in order to replace the mass tourism supply for a more exclusive and expensive offer.

Another contradiction of the curbing of the expansion of urbanisation is its elitisation, with the adoption of mobility habits that involve a more intense energy consumption (Scott, & Gössling, 2015), together with urban planning patterns of single family homes with gardens and swimming pools that consume greater amounts of water. This territorial model of quality tourism uses the discourse of sustainability as a "fix" to favour capital accumulation (Hof & Blázquez-Salom, 2015), monopolised by powerful regional cliques that control the mechanisms to exercise power (Bianchi, 2004).

The tourism pressure on urban spaces and the changes in the rental legislation favours the eviction of tenants with low rents, they foster, among other factors, gentrification processes (Blanco-Romero et al., 2018; Vives-Miró, Rullan, & González, 2018), which can be aggravated by degrowth measures that do not contemplate social policies to facilitate residents' access to housing. In this sense, in 2017, the Balearic Parliament added a new objective of "investing in the acquisition and rehabilitation of dwellings intended for social housing" in order to raise funds with the tourism tax.

Moreover, a geographical expansion of the tourism business frontiers can be observed, which is paradoxically related to the application of the restrictions. In this way, the traditional and multifunctional city or the rural and natural spaces close to the city tourist destinations become attractive for tourism development as well. The promise of a greater monopolistic profitability, fuelled by the restrictions on growth, attracts capital in search of profitability and proximity (Hof & Blázquez-Salom, 2013). New actors appear with conflicting interests, such as associations in favour of tourist rental properties and social movements condemning tourism gentrification, demanding the right to the city and access to housing.

The strategic diagnosis of the plan calls for degrowth, but the regulations have not put this into practice. Therefore, the discourse has become rhetoric. According to stakeholders' statements (ABTS' evaluation dated 17/05/2017[2]), the PEAUT does not consider Barcelona as a unit in terms of the degrowth of its tourist accommodation capacity, generally allowing growth in the neighbourhoods of the outer ring, which are not yet tourist oriented. Also, in Mallorca, the discourse regarding the containment of growth has been a feature of the whole territorial tourism planning process, from the POOT with its hotel moratorium to the PIAT with its promise to impose a ceiling on the increase in the supply of places. The rhetoric of the hegemonic discourse goes to the extent of portraying the PIAT as a degrowth measure. This rhetorical discourse seeks to pacify the resident population that has campaigned for the defence of the territory, in a context of social conflict due to overtourism. Overtourism is battled, but to benefit capital accumulation, commodification of a wider spectrum of everyday life and dispossessing disadvantaged social classes (Moranta & Valdivielso, 2019).

The changes brought about by the legalisation on the use of dwellings to accommodate tourists have been studied in the rural context (Hof & Blázquez-Salom, 2013) and in the central district of the city (Vives-Miró et al., 2018; Blanco-Romero et al., 2018). Changes from a residential to tourism function are altering the area's internal zoning. When tourists are accommodated in neighbourhoods, which the plan considers as being residential, certain mandatory facilities do not make sense. Tourists do not need educational centres, social or religious services, which the plan establishes as being obligatory in residential areas. The tourists' demand for free public spaces (from children's play areas to beaches), healthcare facilities, water and energy supply and waste treatment is different from the residential demand. The same applies to the retail structure, given that the type of stores intended for the residential population are different to those that attract tourists (Blázquez-Salom et al., 2019).

In terms of the practical application of the regulatory measures regarding the use of dwellings for tourism, the planning shows inconsistencies in terms of its fulfilment. One major weakness of these regulations is the failure to apply inspection or sanctioning measures in order to curb inequality. In Mallorca, the increase in the number of tourist rental properties does not respect the margins established by the legislation, with a supply of non-registered or illegal properties representing 54% of the total tourist stays in dwellings in 2016 (Consell Insular de Mallorca, 2018a). Similarly, in Barcelona, the neighbourhood platforms have focused their criticism on denouncing the illegal activities related to tourism accommodation in dwellings and the need for a Citizens Monitoring Committee that controls the compliance with the PEUAT and the inspection and sanctioning mechanisms that are established.

The protection of unique coastal areas through the PATIVEL does not include environmental management measures, a key factor for the subsequent land management (Farinós Dasí, 2012). Many areas affected by the urbanisation pressure run the risk of becoming dumping grounds and "socially fallow" (Vera-Rebollo, Olcina-Cantos & Sáinz-Pardo Trujillo2019). Classifying land as non-developable under special protection should go hand-in-hand with an environmental and landscape management that requires the collaboration of the regional and local governments and the development of agreements with the land owners that determine the land stewardship (Capdepón & Durá, 2019).

Although decisions are made through consultation and citizen participation processes, another inconsistency of the plans is related to the social conflicts. Even though the PEUAT, the PATIVEL or the PIAT were intended to be created through participative governance processes, their application highlights lines of debate and tension between the different groups involved, mainly due to the fact that governance has been understood as being the relativisation of the State, whereby the government of the city is shared with private agents and the most powerful continue to exercise control, by establishing a consensus to maintain their class hegemony (Garnier, 2011). Their instrumental political use legitimises growth as social glue, due to its virtuous cycle of wealth creation, capital gains, job positions, etc. (Logan and Molotch, 1987). Therefore, both the hotel sector and the citizens' associations (ABTS among others) have already expressed their disagreement, each in their respective field of action. According to its representatives, the *Gremi d'Hotelers,* has presented a contentious-administrative appeal against the PEUAT, so as to stop and request the elimination of the restrictions imposed on the growth of tourist accommodation in the city, in the same way as town councils and land owners reject and appeal against the PATIVEL with respect to the protection of land along the coastline. Meanwhile, while acknowledging the need for the PEUAT as a containment tool, the ABTS considers it to be insufficient, given that it does not address the underlying problem of tourist saturation as it allows an increase in the number of tourist accommodation places despite the degrowth and desaturation proposals put forward by the citizens.

Furthermore, the PATIVEL lacks a programme to monitor and assess the effectiveness of the approved model, over an appropriate time span, using a system of basic indicators (Wang &

Banzhaf, 2018). There is another inconsistency in the PEUAT in terms of its duration, which is established at four years. This means that it is impossible to implement long-term action and it is necessary to contemplate the licences previously granted in addition to those granted by the PEUAT (approximately 23,000 places in four and a half years).

Conclusions

There are clear trends in the historical territorial tourism planning sequence in Spain. The boom of mass tourism in the 1960s and the first half of the 1970s is a clear example of *boosterism*. The first measures to contain growth date back to the mid-1990s. They were applied to mature coastal areas and were, on the whole, implemented by regional governments. These measures were particularly prominent in the Balearic and Canary Islands.

On a local scale, from the mid-1980s, urban planning incorporated a greater reflection of the city model compared to previous stages. However, the plans were too rigid and based on bloated developable land classifications, which generated enormous growth potential. The community-based approach was tentatively developed in the design of local urban plans, and from the 1990s, through selective social participation in the creation of tourism and local Agenda 21 strategic plans.

Sustainable tourism development as a focus of planning in Spain requires a highly critical balance. From the mid-1990s, sustainability was incorporated into planning as a rhetorical principle, but very little real progress was made, with the exception of certain processes related to Local Agenda 21 programmes, such as the case of Calvià (Mallorca) or Menorca, which established limits on urban and tourism development. From a physical-spatial point of view, measures for protecting natural spaces, regulating construction on non-developable land or establishing moratoriums and measures to limit urban growth have been implemented by regional governments.

During the urban development tsunami, the hegemonic discourse regarding the virtue of tourism development and the legal and administrative tangle into which tourist urban development had evolved are reminiscent of *boosterism*, with solutions that generally favoured business interests. This social aspect should be taken into account in view of the potential reactivation of the real estate activity. In fact, the effects of the 2008 crisis do not appear to have caused a reconsideration of the tourism urban development processes. According to the analysis of our case studies, the stagnation of construction in coastal destinations is a consequence of the economic crisis and it does not respond to a new sustainable development strategy. On the other hand, the crisis has served to justify neoliberal approaches in favour of the strategic nature of the new urban-tourism operations.

However, some evidence points to a change of scenario that is more favourable for growth containment policies and, to a lesser extent, for degrowth. The accumulated effect of the real estate growth cycles has generated structural deficits and a growing awareness of the saturation of tourist areas, particularly in mature coastal destinations and large cities, aggravated by the dizzying increase in tourist accommodation available on online platforms. In this way, real qualitative progress will be made in terms of the intervention instruments in the destinations that are most affected by overtourism, which are also those with progressive governments (Barcelona, Madrid or Palma), where citizen participation is promoted in planning processes in order to correct and avoid the effects of mass tourism.

The three instruments analysed (PATIVEL, PIAT and PEUAT) all follow this trend. The impact of tourism on the transformation of the territorial and socio-economic organisation and that of the spaces affected by this activity is more visible than ever. The comparison of their discourses clashes with the evaluation of their real effectiveness. According to the analysis carried out preliminary conclusions can be drawn, which should be included in the emerging debate about tourism degrowth and compared in future case studies. First, these instruments are being promoted as paradigmatic tools for content urban growth, although they have come late, once the successive waves of urban-tourist development have already artificialized the Spanish coast (such in the case of the Region of Valencia). Second, although they help reduce the demographic pressure in quantitative terms in these saturated tourist destinations, they favour property rental (in the tourist but also in the real estate sectors). Third, the curbing of the urbanisation expansion becomes elitist, where the less favoured inhabitants are being evicted and moved, while more affluent customers invest and gentrify the built environment and behave with more intensive energy and water consumption habits. Fourth, the application of tourist territorial planning tools to curb growth, without any other measure of social redistribution of the benefits, favours capital accumulation, which is monopolised by cliques that control the mechanism to exercise power. Fifth, the adoption of innovative tourist territorial plans stimulates the geographical expansion of the tourist business frontier (towards the designated natural areas, the rural areas, the central district of the historical city or the outskirts). Sixth, the enactment of the plans does not mean that they are actually implemented, due to lack of inspection and sanctioning measures. Seventh, setting aside land from urban development turns it into "socially-fallow" areas, which become dumping grounds without environmental management measures. And finally, private agents and the most powerful continue to exercise control, establishing a consensus to maintain their class hegemony, taking advantage of the generation of unpaid externalities.

Consequently, more restrictive measures are justified in those destinations that are the most affected by tourism, if degrowth is to be applied in an effective way. However, like all types of public action, these measures are not neutral and they can produce inconsistencies with the risk of the discourse of degrowth being orchestrated in such a way that it favours individual interests. The future research agenda should consider new ways of defining planning instruments to make up for these contradictions and also explore paths to fulfil genuine and fair degrowth without systemic constraints.

Notes

1. The in-depth interviews were carried out in 2018 in Barcelona and Palma, and they are stored on file at the TUDISTAR research group headquarters, at the Universitat Autònoma de Barcelona. They can be consulted by contacting us (tudistar@uab.cat). With regard to PATIVEL, an in-depth analysis was carried out on the public participation process, and as an expert an author took part in the claims stage presented in the Plan, which is available in http://www.habitatge.gva.es/auto/planes-accion-territorial/PATIVEL/08%20Plan%20de%20participaci%c3%b3n%20p%c3%bablica/Plan%20de%20participaci%c3%b3n%20p%c3%bablica.pdf
2. https://assembleabarris.wordpress.com/2017/05/17/comunicat-de-premsa-abts-valoracio-del-peuat/ (consulted on the 24/07/2018).

Funding

This article was funded by Ministerio de Economía y Competitividad (MINECO) and the European Regional Development Fund (ERDF). Projects codes: CSO2015-64468-P, RTI2018-094844-B-C31, CSO2016-74861-R and CSO2017-82592-R.

ORCID

Macià Blázquez-Salom (iD) http://orcid.org/0000-0002-5522-6539
Asunción Blanco-Romero (iD) http://orcid.org/0000-0002-5869-8603
Fernando Vera-Rebollo (iD) http://orcid.org/0000-0002-0576-0151
Josep Ivars-Baidal (iD) http://orcid.org/0000-0002-9238-2792

References

Aguiló, E. (1990). Baleares. *Papeles de Economía Española, 45*, 135–150.

Amer, J. (2006). *Turisme i política. L'empresariat hoteler de Mallorca*. Palma: Documenta Balear.

Artigues, A., & Blázquez-Salom, M. (2016). Huidas al paraíso y la realización mercantil del sueño [Escape to paradise and the commercial realization of the dream]. XIV Coloquio Internacional de Geocrítica. Las utopías y la construcción de la sociedad del futuro, *Barcelona*.

Asara, V. (2016). The Indignados as a Socio-Environmental Movement: Framing the Crisis and Democracy. *Environmental Policy and Governance, 26*(6), 527–542. doi:10.1002/eet.1721

Ayuntamiento de Barcelona (2017). *Plan Especial Urbanístico de Alojamiento Turístico*. Retrieved from: http://ajunta-ment.barcelona.cat/pla-allotjaments-turistics/es/(2/3/2017).

Benabent, M. (2006). *La ordenación del territorio en España*. Sevilla, Junta de Andalucía and Universidad de Sevilla.

Bianchi, R. (2002). Towards a New Political Economy of Global Tourism. In Sharpley, R. and D. Telfer (eds.). *Tourism & Development: Concepts and Issues*. Clevedon: Channel View Publications, 265–299

Blanco-Romero, A., Blázquez-Salom, M., & Cànoves, G. (2018). Barcelona, Housing Rent Bubble in a Tourist City. Social Responses and Local Policies. *Sustainability, 10*(6), 2043. doi:10.3390/su10062043

Blázquez-Salom, M. (1999). La protección de espacios naturales en Baleares: Patrimonio común y recurso turístico. Proceso histórico, situación actual y proyección futura. In B. Valle-Buenestado (Ed.), *Geografía y Espacios Naturales* (pp. 47–59). Murcia: Asociación de Geógrafos Españoles and Federación de Espacios Protegidos de Andalucía.

Blázquez-Salom, M. (2001). Auditorías ambientales de destinos turísticos: Diagnosis territorial para el desarrollo de Agendas 21 locales. *Cuadernos de turismo, 8*, 39–60.

Blázquez-Salom, M., Artigues, A. A., & Yrigoy, I. (2015). Crisis y planificación territorial turística neoliberal en las Islas Baleares. *Investigaciones Turísticas, 9*, 24–49. doi:10.14198/INTURI2015.9.02

Blázquez-Salom, M., & Yrigoy, I. (2016). Caso 1. La planificación del turismo en áreas litorales en España. In M. Simancas-Cruz (Coord.). *La planificación y gestión territorial del turismo* (pp. 175–204). Barcelona: Síntesis.

Blázquez-Salom, M., Blanco-Romero, A., Gual Carbonell, J., & Murray, I. (2019). Tourist gentrification of retail shops in Palma (Majorca.). In C. Milano, J. M. Cheer & M. Novelli (Eds.), *Overtourism: Excesses, Discontents and Measures in Travel and Tourism* (pp. 39–69). Abingdon: .Cabi

Bianchi, R. (2004). Tourism Restructuring and the Politics of Sustainability: A Critical View From the European Periphery (The Canary Islands). *Journal of Sustainable Tourism, 12*(6), 495–529. doi:10.1080/09669580408667251

Bourdeau, P., François, H., & Bensahel, L. (2013). *Fin (?) et confins du tourisme: Interroger le statut et les practiques de la récréation contemporaine*. Paris: L'Harmattan.

Burriel de Orueta, E. L. (2008). La década prodigiosa del urbanismo español (1997-2006), *Scripta Nova. Revista Electrónica de Geografía y Ciencias Sociales, XII*(270), 64.

Burriel de Orueta, E. L. (2009). La planificación territorial en la Comunidad Valenciana (1986-2009), *Scripta Nova. Revista Electrónica de Geografía y Ciencias Sociales, XIII*, 306.

Büsher, B., & Fletcher, R. (2014). Accumulation by Conservation. *New Political Economy, 20*(2), 1–26. doi:10.1080/13563467.2014.923824

Cals, J. (1974). *Turismo y política turística en España: una aproximación*. Barcelona: Ariel.

Capdepón Frías, M., & Durá Alemañ, C. J. (2019). Introducción al concepto de la conservación privada. Nuevas herramientas para la protección de la biodiversidad, Ciudad y territorio. *Estudios Territoriales, 199*, 27–42.

Capel, H. (2005). *El Modelo Barcelona: un examen crítico*. Barcelona: Ediciones del Serbal.

Cattaneo, C., D'Alisa, G., Kallis, G., & Zografos, C. (2012). Degrowth futures and democracy. *Futures, 44*(6), 515–523. doi:10.1016/j.futures.2012.03.012

Charmaz, K., & Belgrave, L. L. (2015). Grounded theory. In G. Ritzer (Ed.). *The Blackwell encyclopedia of sociology*. New York, NY: John Wiley & Sons.

Consell Insular de Mallorca. (2018a). Aprovació inicial del Pla d'Intervenció en Àmbits Turístics de Mallorca (PIAT). *Butlletí Oficial de les Illes Balears*. 93, 28/07/2018. Retrieved from: http://www.conselldemallorca.net/?&id_parent=444&id_class=532&id_section=15489&id_son=19134.

Consell Insular de Mallorca. (2018b). Acord del Ple del Consell Insular de Mallorca d'aprovació inicial de la delimitació provisional de les zones aptes per a la comercialització de les estades turístiques a habitatges d'ús residencial a Mallorca, prevista en l'article 75 de la Llei 8/20. *Butlletí Oficial de les Illes Balears*, núm. 13, 27/01/2018.

Conselleria de Vivienda, C, Obras Públicas y Vertebración del Territorio (2018). *PATIVEL: The Territorial Action Plan of the Green Coastal Infrastructure*. - Retrieved from: http://www.habitatge.gva.es/es/web/planificacion-territorial-e-infraestructura-verde/plan-de-accion-territorial-de-la-infraestructura-verde-del-litoral.

Corbin, J., & Strauss, A. (1990). *Basics of qualitative research: techniques and procedures for developing grounded theory*. Thousand Oaks, CA: SAGE Publications.

Deloitte & Exceltur (2005). *Impactos sobre el entorno, la economía y el empleo de los distintos modelos de desarrollo turístico del litoral mediterráneo español, Baleares y Canarias*. Madrid: Exceltur, Alianza Para la Excelencia Turística.

Denzin, N. K., & Lincoln, Y. S. (Eds.). (2005). *Handbook of qualitative research*. (3rd ed.). Thousand Oaks, CA: Sage Publications.

Diputación de Barcelona (2017). Normativa Pla especial urbanístic per a la regulació dels establiments d'allotjament turístic, albergs de joventut, residències col·lectives d'allotjament temporal i habitatges d'ús turístic a la ciutat de Barcelona. *Butlletí Oficial de la Província de Barcelona*. 2017. Retrieved from: https://bop.diba.cat/scripts/ftpisa.aspx?fnew?bop2017&03/022017003806.pdf&1.

Eisenschitz, A. (2016). Tourism, class and crisis. *Human Geography, 9*(3), 110–124.

Escobar, A. (2015). Degrowth, post development, and transitions: A preliminary conversation. *Sustainability Science, 10*(3), 451–462. doi:10.1007/7s11625-015-0297-5

Farinós Dasí, J. (ed.). (2012). *De la Evaluación Ambiental Estratégica a la Evaluación de Impacto Territorial: Reflexiones acerca de la tarea de evaluación*. Valencia: Publicaciones de la Universitat de València.

Fletcher, R. (2011). Sustaining Tourism, Sustaining Capitalism? The Tourism Industry's Role in Global Capitalist Expansion. *Tourism Geographies, 13*(3), 443–461. doi:10.1080/14616688.2011.570372

Fletcher, R., & Neves, K. (2012). Contradictions in tourism: The promise and pitfalls of ecotourism as a manifold capitalist fix. *Environment and Society, 3*(1), 60–77. doi:10.3167/ares.2012.030105

Fletcher, R., Murray, I., Blanco-Romero, A., & Blázquez-Salom, M. (2019). Tourism and degrowth: an emerging agenda for research and praxis. *Journal of Sustainable Tourism*,

Fraser, N. (2013). A Triple Movement? Parsing the Politics of Crisis after Polanyi. *New Left Review, 81*, 119–132.

Gaja i Díaz, F. (2008). El tsunami urbanizador el litoral mediterráneo. El ciclo de hiperproducción inmobiliaria 1996-2006. *Scripta Nova. Revista electrónica de Geografía y Ciencias Sociales, XII*(270). 66. doi:10.1344/sn2016.20.16793

Garnier, J. P. (2011). Del derecho a la vivienda al derecho a la ciudad: ¿De qué derechos hablamos... y con qué derecho? *Biblio3W. Revista Bibliográfica de Geografía y Ciencias Sociales, XVI*, 909.

Getz, D. (1986). Models in tourism planning: Towards integration of theory and practice. *Tourism Management, 7*(1), 21–32. doi:10.1016/0261-5177(86)90054-3

Górgolas Martín, P. (2019). Del «urbanismo expansivo» al «urbanismo regenerativo» directrices y recomendaciones para reconducir la herencia territorial de la década prodigiosa del urbanismo español (1997-2007). Aplicación al caso de estudio del litoral andaluz. *Ciudad y territorio. Estudios territoriales, 199*, 81–100.

Górgolas Martín, P. (2016). *La planificación de la ciudad en el cambio de milenio (1997-2017). Propuestas para reconducir la herencia recibida. Los casos de Casares (Málaga) y Chiclana de la Frontera (Cádiz)*, Doctoral Thesis, Seville University.

Gramsci, A. (1971). *Selections from the Prison Notebooks*. New York: International Publishers.

Hall, C. M. (2008). *Tourism planning: Policies, processes and relationships* (2nd ed.). Harlow, England; New York: Pearson/Prentice Hall.

Hall, C. M. (2009). Degrowing Tourism: Décroissance, Sustainable Consumption and Steady-State Tourism. *Anatolia: An International Journal of Tourism and Hospitality Research, 20*(1), 46–61. doi:10.1080/13032917.2009.10518894

Hall, C. M. (2014). Economic greenwash: On the absurdity of tourism and green growth. In V. Reddy, & K. Wilkes (Eds.), *Tourism in the Green Economy*. London: Earthscan.

Harvey, D. (2002). The art of rent: Globalization, monopoly and the commodification of culture. *Socialist Register, 38*, 93–110.

Harvey, D. (2006). *Limits to Capital*. London: Verso, 1982.

Hayden, A. (2014). Stopping Heathrow Airport Expansion (For Now): Lessons from a Victory for the Politics of Sufficiency. *Journal of Environmental Policy & Planning*, *16*(4), 539–558. doi:10.1080/1523908X.2013.873713

Hilbrandt, H. (2017). Insurgent participation: Consensus and contestation in planning the redevelopment of Berlin-Tempelhof airport. *Urban Geography*, *38*(4), 537–556. doi:10.1080/02723638.2016.1168569

Hof, A., & Blázquez-Salom, M. (2013). The Links between Real Estate Tourism and Urban Sprawl in Majorca (Balearic Islands, Spain). *Land*, *2*(2), 252–277. doi:10.3390/land2020252

Hof, A., & Blázquez-Salom, M. (2015). Changing tourism patterns, capital accumulation, and urban water consumption in Mallorca, Spain: A sustainability fix? *Journal of Sustainable Tourism*, *23*(5), 770–796. doi:10.1080/09669582.2014.991397

Igoe, J., Neves, K., & Brockington, D. (2010). A spectacular eco-tour around the historic bloc: Theorising the convergence of biodiversity conservation and capitalist expansion. *Antipode*, *42*(3), 486–512. doi:10.1118/330.2010.00761.x.

Kallis, G., Kostakis, V., Lange, S., Muraca, B., Paulson, S., & Schmelzer, M. (2018). Research on Degrowth. *Annual Review of Environment and Resources*, *43*(1), 291–316. doi:10.1146/annurev-envoiron-10207-025941

Kemmis, S., Mc Taggart, R., & Nixon, R. (2013). *The Action Research Planner: Doing Critical Participatory Action Research*. Berlin: Springer Science & Business Media

Kondo, M. C., Rivera, R., & Rullman, S. (2012). Protecting the idyll but not the environment: Second homes, amenity migration and rural exclusion in Washington State. *Landscape and Urban Planning*, *106*(2), 174–182. doi:10.1016/j.landurbplan.2012.03.003

Lefebvre, H. (1968). The right to the city. In E. Kofman & E. Lebas (eds.) *Writings on cities*. Cambridge: Blackwell.

Lezen, M., Sun, Y.-Y., Faturay, F., Ting, Y.-P., Geschke, A., & Malik, A. (2018). The carbon footprint of global tourism. *Nature Climate Change*, *8*(6), 522–531. doi:10.1038/s41558-018-0141-x

Logan, J., & Molotch, H. (1987). *Urban fortunes: The political economy of place*. Berkeley: University of California Press.

Lois, R. C., González, J. M., & Escudero, L. A. (2012). *Los espacios urbanos: El estudio geográfico de la ciudad y la urbanización*. Madrid: Biblioteca Nueva.

López, I., & Rodríguez, E. (2011). The Spanish model. *New Left Review*, *69*(3), 5–29.

López Palomeque, F. (2015). Barcelona, de ciudad con turismo a ciudad turística. Notas sobre un proceso complejo e inacabado. *Documents D'Anàlisi Geogràfica*, *61*(3), 483–506. doi:10.5565/rev/dag.296

Mantecón, A. (2008). *La experiencia del turismo: Un estudio sociológico sobre el proceso turístico-residencial*. Barcelona: Icaria. doi:10.6018/turismo.40.310041

McKinsey & Company (2017). *Coping with success. Managing overcrowding in tourism destinations*. McKinsey & Company and World Travel & Tourism Council, London. Retrieved from: https://www.wttc.org/-/media/files/reports/policy-research/coping-with-success—managing-overcrowding-in-tourism-destinations-2017.pdf

Méndez, R., Abad, L. D., & Echaves, C. (2015). *Atlas de la crisis. Impactos socioeconómicos y territorios vulnerables en España*. Valencia: Tirant Humanidades.

Moranta, J., & Valdivielso, J. (2019). The social construction of the tourism degrowth discourse in the Balearic Islands. *Journal of Sustainable Tourism*, doi:10.1080/09669582.2019.1660670

Moreno, A. (2010). Justicia ambiental. Del concepto a la aplicación en análisis de políticas y planificación territoriales. *Scripta Nova. Revista Electrónica de Geografía y Ciencias Sociales*, *XIV*, 316.

Murray, I. (2015). Capitalismo y turismo en España. *"Del milagro económico" a la "gran crisis"*. Barcelona: Alba Sud Editorial.

Murray, I., Yrigoy, I., & Blázquez-Salom, M. (2017). The role of crises in the production, destruction and restructuring of tourist spaces. The case of the Balearic Islands. *Investigaciones Turísticas*, *13*, 1–29. doi:10.14198/INTURI2017.13.01

Nel·lo, O. (2012). *Ordenar el territorio. La experiencia de Barcelona y Cataluña*. Valencia: Tirant lo Blanch.

Peck, J., & Tickell, A. (2002). Neoliberalizing Space. *Antipode*, *34*(3), 380–404. doi:10.1111/1467-8330.00247

Peñín, A. (2006). *Urbanismo y crisis. Hacia un nuevo planeamiento general*. Valencia: Ediciones Generales de la Construcción.

Perles-Ribes, J., Ramón-Rodríguez, A., Vera-Rebollo, J. F., & Ivars-Baidal, J. (2017). The end of growth in residential tourism destinations: Steady state or sustainable development? The case of Calpe. *Current Issues in Tourism*, *21*, 1–31.

Princen, T. (2005). *The Logic of Sufficiency*. Cambridge, MA: MIT Press.

Romero, M. J. & Vidal, (2018). Planificación estratégica y territorial y alteraciones del Plan General. *Ciudad y Territorio: Estudios Territoriales*, *XL*(195), 7–20.

Rullan, O. (2005). Una técnica urbanística para contener el crecimiento residencial en espacios con fuerte presión inmobiliaria. *Scripta Nova. Revista electrónica de geografía y ciencias sociales*, *IX*(194), 32

Rullan, O. (2011). La regulación del crecimiento urbanístico en el litoral mediterráneo español. *Ciudad y territorio: Estudios territoriales*, *168*, 279–297.

Russo, A. P., & Scarnatto, A. (2017). Barcelona in common": A new urban regime for the 21st-century tourist city? *Journal of Urban Affairs*, *40*(4), 455–474. doi:10.1080/07352166.2017.1373023

Saarinen, J., Rogerson, C. M., & Hall, C. M. (2017). Geographies of tourism development and planning. *Tourism Geographies, 19*(3), 307–317. doi:10.1080/14616688.2017.1307442

Sachs, W. (2001). Development patterns in the North and their implications for climate change. *International Journal of Global Environmental Issues, 1*(2), 150–162. doi:10.1504/IJGENVI.2001.000975

Scott, D., & Gössling, S. (2015). What Do the Next 40 Years Hold? The Value of Scenarios in Tourism. *Tourism Recreation Research, 40*(3), 269–285. doi:10.1080/02508281.2015.1075739

Simancas, M. (2015). La ordenación territorial del turismo en espacios insulares. *Ciudad y Territorio: Estudios Territoriales, 185*, 445–462.

Sevilla-Buitrago, A. (2015). Capitalist Formations of Enclosure: Space and the Extinction of the Commons. *Antipode, 47*(4), 999–1020. doi:10.1111/anti.12143

Sklair, L. (2000). The transnational capitalist class and the discourse of globalization. *Cambridge Review of International Affairs, 14*(1), 67–85. doi:10.1080/09557570008400329

Slee, T. (2017). *What's yours is mine. Against the Sharing Economy*. London: Scribe.

Soja, E. (1989). *Postmodern Geographies: The Reassertion of Space in Critical Social Theory*. London: Verso.

Streeck, W. (2014). How will capitalism end? *New Left Review, 87*, 35–64.

Vera-Rebollo, J. F., Olcina Cantos, J., & SáinzPardoTrujillo, A. (2019). La incorporación de la infraestructura verde en la ordenación territorial. El plan de acción territorial de la infraestructura verde del litoral de la Comunidad Valenciana, PATIVEL. *Ciudad y Territorio. Estudios Territoriales, LI*(201), 467–490.

Vera, F., & Ivars, J. A. (2003). Measuring Sustainability in a Mass Tourist Destination: Pressures, Perceptions and Policy Responses in Torrevieja, Spain. *Journal of Sustainable Tourism, 11*(2-3), 181–203.

Vera, F., & Rodríguez, I. (Eds.) (2012). *Renovación y reestructuración de destinos turísticos en áreas costeras. Marco de análisis, procesos, instrumentos y realidades*. València: Publicacions de la Universitat de València.

Vives-Miró, S., Rullan, O., & González, J. M. (2018). *Understanding geographies of home dispossession through the crisis. Evictions Palma Style*. Barcelona: Icaria.

Wachsmuth, D., & Weisler, A. (2018). Airbnb and the Rent Gap: Gentrification Through the Sharing Economy. *Environment and Planning A: Economy and Space, 50*(6), 1147–1170. doi:10.1177/0308518X18778038

Wang, J., & Banzhaf, E. (2018). Towards a better understanding of Green Infrastructure: A critical review. *Ecological Indicators, 85*, 758–772. doi:10.1016/j.ecolind.2017.09.018

Wanner, T. (2015). The New 'Passive Revolution' of the Green Economy and Growth Discourse: Maintaining the 'Sustainable Development' of Neoliberal Capitalism. *New Political Economy, 20*(1), 21–41. doi:10.1080/13563467.2013.866081

Yrigoy, I. (2015). La urbanización turística como 'solución espacial'. Agentes, planeamiento y propiedad en la Playa de Palma y Magaluf (Mallorca) (PhD Thesis). Universitat de les Illes Balears.

Yrigoy, I. (2016). Financialization of hotel corporations in Spain. *Tourism Geographies, 18*(4), 399–421. doi:10.1080/14616688.2016.1198829

Growth machines and social movements in mature tourist destinations: Costa del Sol-Málaga

Enrique Navarro-Jurado, Yolanda Romero-Padilla, José María Romero-Martínez, Eduardo Serrano-Muñoz, Sabina Habegger and Rubén Mora-Esteban

ABSTRACT

The purpose of this study is to analyse the new processes of tourism growth and its conflicts from the perspective of social movements. First, the urban growth machine analysis model is applied by the systematisation of six projects. Second, the resistance movements against those projects and whether this resistance could be the start of local tourism degrowth policies are examined. The methodology is qualitative, based on documentary analysis, participatory observation, discussion groups and interviews. The case study is the destination of Costa del Sol-Málaga. The results enable the development of the urban growth machine model in tourist destinations. Meanwhile, social movements demystify the argument based on neoclassical economic progress. The social movements condemn the effects of large-scale top-down projects, and implement alternative bottom-up proposals. Although the social movements do not reject tourism, they call for greater control over its impact, denounce unlimited growth, overtourism and the loss of urban quality of life. These movements advocate a lifestyle linked to the everyday space, which they believe is threatened by excessive urban-tourism growth. They are a symptom of the need to devise a proposal using the principles of degrowth.

Introduction

The development of tourism activities worldwide is linked to the logic of capitalist expansion and urban agglomerations (Büscher & Fletcher, 2017; Fletcher, 2011; Hall, 2009; Murray & Blázquez-Salom, 2009). In order to understand the unlimited growth of many coastal destinations, it is necessary to analyse other global phenomena in the contemporary world (Borja & Castells, 2004; Harvey, 2013): a reduction in the temporal space of communication, the extension of urban life, and demographic and economic concentration. These three factors have had a particular impact on coastal areas, known as coastalisation, where there has been a progressive concentration of people, infrastructures and economic and financial activities (Pié Ninot & Rosa Jiménez, 2014; Romero, Romero, & Navarro-Jurado, 2015). These aspects constantly feed the *urban growth machines* (Logan & Molotch, 1987) and explain the dynamic of the evolution of coastal destinations, such as those on the Spanish Mediterranean (Romero, Romero, & Navarro-Jurado, 2017). With this growth dynamic in destinations, the potential of "degrowth" has been an unpopular alternative for challenging the expansion of mass tourism because it questions the bases of the capitalist economic system, its myths and the imperative for growth. However, there are multiple symptoms of saturation in some tourist destinations, and limits on growth are being proposed (Saarinen, 2006). At present, doubts are beginning to arise about the virtues of tourist growth and social movements are being organised that oppose projects to enable the growth of destinations. These resistance groups are part of the new social movements and they encourage projects that work from the bottom up, viewing participation as crucial to growth management. The Spanish case is an example of the contradictions that exist between the dominant mentality of growth and the need to apply sustainability measures to more mature and saturated destinations (Pié Ninot & Rosa Jiménez, 2014). The reclassification plans that were launched subject to Spanish and European funding programs (e.g. *Qualifica Costa del Sol)* have in practice resulted in more construction projects (new builds or restoration) and in growth targets (more tourists and more competitiveness) (Navarro-Jurado, 2014).

The study has a twofold objective; first, to put forward an analysis model for urban growth machines in tourist destinations, categorising their characteristics; this aspect highlights the social agreement that aims to justify all of the projects relating to tourism and its new phase of growth. Second, to analyse the resistance movements against those projects and whether this resistance could be the start of local tourism degrowth policies.

The study area is one of the most important mature coastal tourist destinations in the Mediterranean, the Costa del Sol, with a tourism model based on the classic "sun and sea" style holidays of the late 1950s. However, since the 1980s its growth has gone beyond this, making it a modern, cosmopolitan, innovative and creative territory, but also an unlimited urban growth machine (Riechmann, 2001); a territory subjected to huge anthropic pressure with high-impact socio-ecological transformations, and high levels of political and business corruption (Diez Ripollés & Gómez-Céspedes, 2009).

The study begins by defining a theoretical-conceptual basis around the theory of urban growth machines and the approach of new local social movements. Subsequently, the methodology used is detailed and the results in the case study on the Costa del Sol are presented. The study ends with a discussion linking the results and the theoretical framework, outlining the future lines of work.

Literature review

Tourist destinations as urban growth machines in the current crisis

Mature coastal tourist destinations have acquired a special role in the accumulation of capital in eras of great global liquidity, because their property crises are one of the triggers of the great global crises (Harvey, 2013). This role was first established in Florida and the Southwest Coast of the United States before the crisis of 1929, and continued in the recent global crisis of 2007 in Florida itself and the Southwest Coast and spread to other tourist spaces, such as the Spanish Mediterranean (Harvey, 2013; Romero et al., 2015). The restructuring of many destinations has also been carried out via policies that encourage a new growth phase based on more tourists and increased construction of accommodation, facilities and infrastructure. In general, this growth has been based on large processes of urban land expansion carried out via megaprojects (Harvey, 2013) and urban regeneration (Soja, 2008), and both have a negative impact on the environmental crisis, the crisis of social inequality and the political crisis of a lack of democracy (Naredo, 2010; Riechmann, 2001). These growth processes are analysed within the framework of the theory *of urban growth machines* (Cain, 2014; Lang & Rothenberg, 2016; Logan & Molotch, 1987).

The urban growth machine (UGM) is a "class alliance" or agreement between the economic and political stakeholders in a specific territory devised through shared interests with the aim of developing a space. The UGM bases economic activity on investment in urban land (renovation or new buildings), the creation of expectations regarding property construction, and the demographic expansion of the population (Kimelberg, 2011; López & Rodríguez, 2010). There are four key stakeholders in this agreement (Logan & Molotch, 1987; López & Rodríguez, 2010): politicians, business people, developers and bankers; technicians and professionals, and a wide range of media. Consequently, the growth of tourist destinations is linked to the evolution of the construction sector, altering the development, planning and management of its classical variables of offer and demand (Fletcher, 2016).

This thesis, situated within a broader theory on the commodification of space, has been criticised for reflecting a situation that is particular to the United States (Rodgers, 2009). However, it offers an ideal analytical framework for studying the policies of urban-tourism expansion (that is geographically and sociologically rooted), contextualised in a peripheral region of late capitalism - the southern Mediterranean. It is important to bear in mind that the class alliances of the 21st century are subtler and more discreet than in the North American cities of the 1970s (Boyle, 1999).

Three dimensions have been put forward in order to analyse the UGMs: ideas, rules and projects (Romero et al., 2017), that coincide with the proposal of Lefebvre on understanding the space of power or perceived space), the space of knowledge (representation of space or conceived space) and daily space (space as practised or lived space) (Lefebvre, 2013; Soja, 2008). These three dimensions range from the intangible nature of ideas, to the tangible nature of the lived territory, and from global territorial scales to their materialisation in building and urban regeneration projects. The dimensions are:

1. The overall dimension of ideas issued by international bodies (IMF, WB, WTO, UNWTO, etc.). In the case of tourist destinations, projects are justified as a service towards tourism, which enjoys a positive image in the collective imagination as an economic driving force.
2. The dimension of regulations encompasses programmes, plans and laws. Infrastructure plans may be linked on a national and regional level with the strategies of specific megaprojects.
3. Projects make these dimensions tangible at a local level, i.e. capital is transformed into development-renovation. On this level, value is placed on the development of more land and it is decided which part of the city is to be regenerated in order to speculate, contributing to forming part of the secondary circuit of the accumulation of fixed capital (Logan & Molotch, 1987; López and Rodríguez, 2010).

In summary, the *theory of urban growth machines* provides an analysis framework for understanding the growth dynamic of Spanish coastal tourism destinations and the continuity of discourses of growth, even during times of crisis (Murray, Yrigoy, & Blázquez, 2017; Romero et al., 2015), as well as concerns over their saturation from the approaches of carrying capacity and sustainability (Navarro-Jurado et al., 2012). Using this theory, it is possible to show how the growth of destinations is not linked to the classic variables of tourism, and nor does it reflect a sustainable development plan or take into account the environmental and social impact. Within this ideological context based on development, civil society accepts the idea that it is necessary to grow in order to attain wealth and wellbeing, and sociocultural and environmental externalities can be accepted because they will be subsequently resolved. This is compounded by a widespread distrust of alternative development models. In the face of this growth, local resistance groups opposing specific projects emerge.

Local resistance to projects: new local social movements in tourist destinations

The population that is affected and aware of the impact of tourist growth, and mobilises and organises actions to defend and protect its habitable space. The sociological approach of *new social movements* and their recent evolution (Touraine, 2006), shows that unlike the counter-movements of previous decades, current resistance movements present different changes, which are essential to understanding their vision of growth: a social change, a change from formal and hierarchical organisations towards informal and autonomous movements (Castañeda, 2012; Flesher, 2015); a cultural change, moving from dominant ideological thinking and general grievances, towards plurality, integration and specific grievances (Fuster Morell, 2012; Ingrassia, 2013; Soja, 2008); and lastly, a spatial change, from global grievances to local grievances, putting the focus of concern on the spaces that have a more direct impact on daily life (Lefebvre, 2013; Soja, 2008). For this reason, many movements have to define themselves as a means of "defence", "protecting and looking after their own habitat", because they are aware of their circumstances. They are the result of living in the risk society (Beck, 2000) with a tendency towards dispersion (Ingrassia, 2013) and of living in a liquid society (Bauman, 2013). These movements call for the right to the city and spatial justice (Soja, 2008).

There are studies that have analysed the social movements from different perspectives applied to tourist destinations, although they are still limited (Kousis, 2000). One example is the analysis of the impact that the protests of social movements have on the image of a tourist destination, especially when they are violent protests (Monterrubio, 2017). Social movements are also analysed as facilitators of positive change in destinations, such as the case of crafts (McGehee, Kline, & Knollenberg, 2014). Of greater interest are the studies focused on the analysis of networks and stakeholders and their perception on the carrying capacity (Navarro-Jurado, Damian, & Fernández-Morales, 2013), as well as studies of conflicts and local resistance to projects with a major environmental impact (Kousis, 2000), or more recently the studies on "tourism-phobia" (Huete & Mantecón, 2018).

At present, there are social movements that express discontent with tourism growth because it affects their daily life (Fernández Medrano & Pardo Rivacoba, 2017), and the idea of *tourism-phobia* has been disseminated (Huete & Mantecón, 2018; Murray, 2014) in the media (La Opinión de Malaga, 2018). Among other factors, it is necessary to consider the progressive processes of gentrification and touristization, with different levels of intensity, in Barcelona, Venice, Dubrovnik… (Vives-Miro & Rullán, 2017). Social reactions to touristification have gone from being a local concern of destination management to being a global concern. The overtourism report published by the World Tourism Organization; Centre of Expertise Leisure, Tourism & Hospitality; NHTV Breda University of Applied Sciences; and NHL Stenden University of Applied Sciences (2018) analyses this problem and proposes recommendations that range from traditional strategies of seasonal adjustment (time), alleviation of congestion (space) or the use of technologies, to strategies that place an emphasis on the participation of all the stakeholders in the destination. In the case of coastal destinations such as the Spanish Mediterranean, some of these measures have begun to be implemented through different reclassification plans which also committed to improving tourism sustainability. However, in practice, reclassification strategies have focused on growth, on new builds or renovation in order to improve infrastructures or public spaces of tourism interest. Meanwhile, strategies focused on environmental or social sustainability, which have taken the form of containment actions (for example, in the range of accommodation) and management actions (tourist taxes) have been few in number and controversial for tourism entrepreneurs (Pié Ninot & Rosa Jiménez, 2014).

Academic debate has also seen an increase in analysis and reflections on the exhaustion of the dominant global tourism model based on growth, to the extent that concepts like tourism degrowth are being considered (Andreoni & Galmarini, 2014; Bourdeau & Berthelot, 2008; Hall, 2009). As Hall (2009) summarises, general degrowth involves a paradigm shift based on a social change where the predominant values would among others be quality of life instead of the quantity of consumption (non-materialistic), satisfying basic human needs, fairness, a participatory democracy, respect for human rights, a sense of community and coexistence, the reduction of the dependence on economic activity and an increase in free time. However, in tourism it is still a concept that has barely been studied, with the exception of other concepts that may be very closely related, such as carrying capacity.

In short, the theory of urban growth machines and the study of new social movements place stakeholders at the centre of the analysis. Bearing in mind the developments in tourism studies over the last 15–20 years that Russo analyses (Russo, 2016), there is a trend for authors to focus on finding out what happens around tourism within a context of daily life, i.e. integrated into sociocultural, economic and political processes. It also aims to find out the subjectivities of the stakeholders involved in tourism, their relationships, the technologies they use and how tourism takes place in the everyday sphere.

The diversity of the stakeholders and their relationships in a destination is complex (Bramwell & Sharman, 1999) and their knowledge is crucial in order to establish a proper basis for planning and strategic management in a tourist destination. The creation of a shared vision (consensus) is the basis of collaborative planning processes (Huxham, 2003; Jamal & Getz, 1995). Furthermore, the existence of a shared vision is crucial for the coordination of resources, conflict management and future strategic planning (Bramwell & Sharman, 1999). However, its application in the context of tourism is relatively recent (Casanueva, Gallego, & García, 2016) despite the fact that the governance of tourist destinations appears to be the main means of working in the face of social malaise (Milano, 2018).

Methodology and case study

In line with the proposed objectives, this study has two parts. On one hand, the direct consequences of urban growth machines have been studied through the comparison and systematisation of six projects. On the other hand, the resistance caused by these projects has been analysed.

The methodology of the study is essentially qualitative, based on documentary analysis, participant observation, discussion groups and interviews. Qualitative methods are acquiring an increasing importance in tourism studies, as they are considered essential for finding out about tourist spaces and their stakeholders (Beard, Scarles, & Tribe, 2016).

On the other hand, the results shown here constitute a part of the process and have followed the philosophy of autonomous or action research (Balcazar, 2003). Social stakeholders were invited to participate in the research process in order to transform their social reality. This approach made it possible to approach conflicts from the perspective of the stakeholders and external researchers. A dialogue was conducted with the members of the resistance movements, with participation as observer researchers in the actions organised by these movements. The discussion groups were important for conveying individual thoughts at a group level, and creating a dynamic of conflict analysis and common challenges. These results helped to reinforce the strengths of the participating stakeholders and to develop a sense of belonging to the research process. Via this method, social movements transform the research, and at the same time, they obtain a return because they are able to find out which practices are most effective, and take advantage of the experiences of other movements.

Table 1. Methodological tools.

Tools	Areas of work
Participant observation and documentary analysis (January 2017 – July 2018) Applied to: UGM projects and resistance movement analysis	• Identification of case studies - large UGM projects - in the Costa del Sol-Málaga • Creation of the UGM model for adaptation to the case studies. • Review of documentary sources for the analysis of the UGM dynamic, according to the model created, applied to the selected projects • Identification of developer stakeholders and resistance groups and establishing contact • Review of social networks (Twitter), articles, statements and other documents published by the resistance movements. • Creation of data sheets for UGM projects, reasons for conflict and resistance.
Discussion group 1 (30 November 2017) Applied to: resistance movement analysis 8 participants: 6 men and 2 women	Areas covered: • Characteristics of the resistance movement • Stakeholders: those that they support, those that they oppose, those that are missing and those that they would like to involve • Success stories and areas of improvement
Discussion group 2 (21 February 2018) Applied to: resistance movement analysis 7 participants: 5 men and 2 women 6: with university education 5: between 50–60 years of age 2: between 35–45 years of age	Areas covered: • Reporting on results of 1st Discussion Group. • Validation of data sheets for each project that they oppose • Relationship between the intervention that each movement opposes to the development of tourism and the tourist destination. • Relationship between the intervention and the economy and demographic and urban growth. Perception of the concept of degrowth in relation to what each movement calls for. • Internal management of each movement (short-term tactics and long-term strategies)
Interviews (November 2017 – July 2018) Applied to: resistance movement analysis 6 participants: 5 men and 1 woman	Areas covered: • Further examination of the characteristics and internal management of each movement (genealogy; evolution of tactics and strategies, main milestones reached). • Further examination of the map of agents (degree of importance of the stakeholder developers, decisive people within the resistance movement, other groups that it is linked to and its influences). • Tourism and urban policy (relationship between the city model and the tourist model to the project that they oppose, perception of the questioning of benefits of tourism).

Source: prepared by the authors.

Table 1 shows the methodological tools used to check the theory in the case of the study on the Costa del Sol.

In order to select the projects to study, the fulfilment of four criteria was taken into account:

1. New build projects or rehabilitation of urban space;
2. Projects located in places of interest for tourism development;
3. Projects that incorporate services, facilities or similar attributes of a tourist nature;
4. Projects that have generated social resistance reactions as a response.

The six projects selected were analysed using technical and dissemination documentation published by the promoters of each project. In order to create the analysis model of the UGMs, the starting point was three dimensions proposed by Romero et al. (2017). As a result, new analysis categories were developed for this study (Table 2).

Table 2. Categories that develop the analysis model of UGMs.

Dominant Ideas	• Progress
	• Economic reductionism
	• Indefinite growth in quantity and extension
	• Tourism as an economic engine and main conditioner
Rules and Laws	• Cases of exceptional treatment in current legislation
	• Financial weakness of the councils
	• Incompliance with rules/laws
	• Institutional autism relating to citizens
Projects	• Physical environment
	• Negative social impacts
	• Distant decision-making authorities and top-down processes
	• Public administration forms part of the urban growth machines
	• Rentier economy and land speculation
	• Medium and long-term strategy for the creation and profitability of fixed capital

Source: prepared by the authors.

Social movements and their grievances regarding the projects were analysed based on partici-patory observation of their activities, the results of discussion groups, interviews and the material provided by the movements during field work (publications on social networks, articles, state-ments and similar). As a result, two discussion groups and six interviews were carried out in order to further examine the characteristics of their movement and activities, whose participants were selected as representative leaders of each of the six movements. The profiles of the partici-pants and the issues addressed can be consulted in Table 1, and as with the systematisation of the analysis and the results, they have been organised according to the UGMs model shown in Table 2.

The Costa del Sol-Málaga: urban growth machines and resistance movements in tourist destinations and its area of influence

The Costa del Sol (CS) is the largest urban agglomeration in southern Spain, and has been one of the most important tourist destinations in the Mediterranean region since the 1960s. It is undoubtedly a prime example of an urban growth machine in a semi-peripheral region of late capitalism. However, the CS has a very large area of influence and includes other different types of tourists. Along with the sun and sea form of tourism, based on the construction of urban spaces for temporary stays, the area of influence stretches for more than 50 km over the inland mountains to Ronda, with golf courses, luxury hotels, large resorts, etc., and ultimately has the same growth model. In addition to Ronda being a cultural destination and the Serranía de Ronda a rural destination, they are therefore attractions for a constant flow of day-trippers from the CS, who subsequently want to invest in a second property inland. On the other hand, growth in the city of Malaga cannot be understood without the CS. The airport is located in Malaga (the most important in the south of Spain), and the terrestrial communications hub (train and roads) goes through Malaga. Although Malaga is now a cultural destination, some of its projects are metropolitan and Malaga is beginning to rival Marbella in terms of investors, proj-ects, hotels, etc.

Tourism is the most important productive sector and has completely transformed this terri-tory, its society and its economy. The result is the urban development of 75% of the beachfront of the coastline; greater growth in the range of unregulated tourist places (836,880) in relation to regulated ones (146, 207). With regard to demand, the figures are constantly increasing. In 2017, the CS enjoyed the best year of tourism in its history with 12.5 million visitors, with an overall economic impact in the province of 13.83 billion Euros (Turismo y Planificación, 2018).

This territory has not stopped growing and the various administrations (European, central and regional) have continued to invest in infrastructure (Romero et al., 2015). This is not exclusive to the CS, but instead takes place in other well-established coastal tourist destinations like the

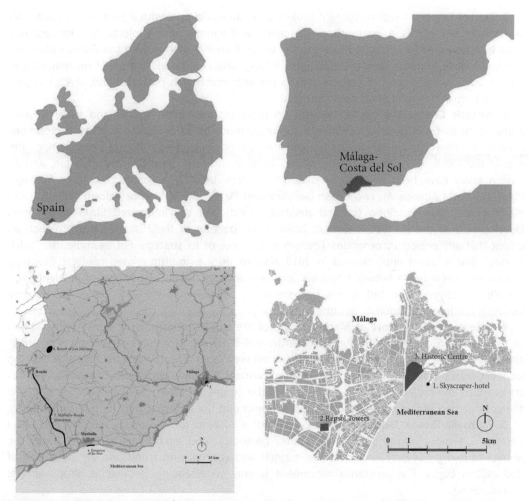

Figure 1. CASE STUDY: Costa del Sol-Málaga. Source: Prepared by the authors based on the IECA (Institute of Statistics and Cartography of Andalusia) and the IdeAndalucía.

Costa Blanca, Costa Dourada and the Balearic Islands, with an important role of second homes (Murray et al., 2017; Rovira & Antón-Clavé, 2014). In fact, the growth in Spanish coastal destinations during the crisis has been characterised by: (1) the encouragement of new public policies to stimulate growth (Romero et al., 2017); (2) the configuration of a scenario of precarious employment associated with the loss of jobs and labour reform (Cañada, 2015); (3) the promotion of tourism as a successful sector and a solution for economic recovery (Murray et al., 2017); and (4) the emergence of technologies that facilitate peer-to-peer relationships (Airbnb, HomeAway, Niumba, etc.).

Within this context of growth, the direct consequences of urban growth machines are studied in specific places and projects, via the comparison and systematisation of six projects, and the resistance movements they have caused (Figure 1). The future development of all the interventions is directly linked to tourism and property development:

1. Skyscraper-hotel in the port of Malaga: this would be the tallest building in the city, located in the dock of the port furthest from the coast and developed by an investment group from Qatar that has no experience in tourism. The resistance movement was formed in 2017 as the *Plataforma Defendamos Nuestro Horizonte* (Let's Defend Our Skyline Platform) with the support of 30 organisations.

2. Repsol Towers: a redevelopment project of an industrial area with a park with 4 residential skyscrapers and offices, a leisure-shopping centre and various hotel projects. It is located very close to a new area for attracting tourism, the western area of Malaga with the Russian Museum, the Automobile Museum, and the traditional fishing neighbourhood. The social movement, created in 2015 (Urban Forest of Malaga-UFB), is the only one that is proactive and which has produced an urban environmental consciousness.

3. Historic Centre: the conflict focuses on touristification, gentrification and social degradation. At present, the greatest problem is the coexistence of residents and tourists in properties used for tourism that are advertised on websites. We have included this case because since the end of the 1980s, the aim of the council has been to increase the resident population, and 75 million euros have been invested in multiple projects (Urban Plan of the EU, three Strategic Plans, the Local Agenda 21, two Urban Development Plans, Special Interior Reform Plan, Housing Plans, Master Plan for Soho (cultural neighbourhood) and the Integrated Sustainable Urban Development of the EU (SUD-strategy), Tourism has penetrated the Historic Centre to such an extent that any project incorporates Tourism as the core of its strategy. For example, the "SUD-strateg" that is being implemented in 2019 aims to resolve tourism-related conflicts (housing, restaurants, coexistence between tourists and residents, etc.). The association of residents was established 25 years ago but it has become more belligerent since 2015, when coexistence between residents and tourists became intolerable.

4. Extension of the Port of Marbella: one of the largest megaprojects, because in addition to the extension of the fishing port (860 berths and a dry dock for 360 boats) there is commercial development and the construction of a hotel-skyscraper. The investment capital is coming from a Qatari property developer. The social movement is mainly comprised of women and has transcended the project to channel the voice of the people for other conflicts, e.g. they opposed the construction of five more skyscrapers in Marbella and the felling of trees in the city centre.

5. Marbella-Ronda Motorway: the project for a 32.8 km toll motorway crossing the Sierra Bermeja - a mountain range of high scenic, geological and environmental value - with the impact caused by several land clearings, tunnels and earthmoving works and an initial cost of 350 million Euros. The resistance movement is very wide-ranging because it affects several municipalities.

6. Resort of Los Merinos (Ronda): the construction of 800 properties, 3 5-star hotels and 2 golf courses in 890 hectares in land that was previously protected. The social movement arose among residents of Ronda in the 1990s.

The initiatives for the developments arise out the relationship between private and public stakeholders. The Administration facilitates each intervention, and there is always one of the three levels involved: state, regional, local. With regard to the current situation, several of the developments have not begun construction, but all have begun different administrative proceedings in order to be carried out. The judicial authorities are also involved, and there are projects with court rulings against them (the Resort of Los Merinos and the Extension of the Port of Marbella), and others are subject to legal action (Urban Centre, Hotel-skyscraper in the port and the Repsol Towers of Malaga). In short, the Costa del Sol and many mature tourist destinations on the Spanish Mediterranean have various peculiarities that are characteristic of the theory of urban growth machines: a strong private sector (especially the banking sector), an autonomous local public sector with extensive powers for urban and tourist development, a large corporate influence on local politics, which is in many cases associated with political-business corruption.

Results: growth and degrowth on the Costa del Sol

The results are divided into two parts. The first part develops the analysis model for UGMs in the case studies in the Costa del Sol, proposing 15 categories classified in three dimensions. The second compares the attitude towards tourism of promoters and resistance groups, as well as the implications of the proposals of resistance groups in terms of degrowth.

In the Dominant Ideas, the reasoning used by developers to justify projects is grounded in the idea of progress based on modernity, the market, employment, economic growth and the abundance of material goods as a necessary condition for the improvement of human quality of life. For the developers, there is a sense of moral urgency, as they state that *"modern times will oblige us to build the tower"* (Architect of the Skyscraper-hotel in the port), *"cities need to constantly evolve" [...] we should think about whether Malaga deserves to lose an investment of this nature"* (President of the Confederation of Businesspeople of Andalusia on Los Reporteros (2018, television program). For the resistance movements, building a skyscraper, cutting down trees or removing green areas is not progress. They argue that *"they have changed our entire urban landscape, [...] for no reason, they simply said it was because the city needed to be modernised"* (Discussion group DG1).

Economic reductionism can be seen in the reasoning of the developers, based around two beliefs: (1) the market is the most efficient mechanism for production and distribution, and the best model for regulating social relations; (2) private sector initiatives are what create wealth. The public administration must therefore be at the service of the private sector. As a result, the future of the territory is decided on the property market, and remains outside the control of citizens. The idea of no employment meaning no growth is the strongest argument of developers, who consider indefinite growth to be necessary. However, the resistance movements express doubts about this argument, given that details are never provided about the *"quality of employment, its temporariness or duration and distribution"* (Discussion group DG2).

The Rules and Laws that support the dominant ideas are applied in all the projects with cases of exceptional treatment in the current legislation. In jurisdictional spheres with specific legislation (roads, coasts, etc.), operations that breach current legislation are allowed. Social movements note this difference and argue that there are two types of administrative procedures: the ordinary, regulated one for ordinary citizens and small business owners; and the special, flexible and quick procedure for key actions in the territory, which is also often carried out behind the backs of citizens. Four of the six movements have denounced planning-administrative controversies due to irregularities in some of the processes. This is the only route that manages to stop projects and the most relevant case is that of the Los Merino macro-resort, where *"the victory was via the contentious-administrative route [...]. And the other route that we took was the criminal proceedings route [...] we spoke to the Anti-Corruption Prosecutor's Office [...] and an investigation was launched that concluded with the arrest of the Mayor and four more councillors in 2011"* (Discussion group DG1).

This exceptional situation is explained by the financial and political weakness of the councils. The lack of participation of municipalities in national public spending (between 12–15%) makes it necessary to seek alternatives in property construction, where taxes and licences are the almost exclusive means of funding (Diez Ripollés & Gómez-Céspedes, 2009). Tourist areas also have the spending from their increased population in summer (it multiplies by 2 or 3). In the case of the city of Malaga, urban regeneration initiatives are only concentrated in the centre of cities, while non-tourist neighbourhoods are neglected (Marín Cots, Guevara Plaza, & Navarro-Jurado, 2017). With the implementation of the SUD-strategy the conflicts are not resolved, and instead are being exacerbated as outlined in the document produced by the association of residents in which they denounce *"tavernisation"* (Document of the Association of Residents presented at the work group of Perchel-Lagunillas SUD-strategy, 2019). This takes place alongside the complexity of urban planning legislation in the Spanish system (unique in relation to the rest of Europe) and it results in a significant municipal urban planning problem: *à la carté* urban development, (Seguido & Hernández, 2015)

There are two conflicts in this category: incompliance with rules/laws and the institutional autism relating to citizens. In the first case, social movements perceive arbitrariness from the institutions because compliance with regulations is not promoted, and the legal provisions of the European Union on municipal legislation are ignored (such as the lack of civic participation in environmental projects in the case of UFB, excessive noise in the Historic Centre of Malaga, etc.). What is even more serious - the legislation is not applied either because of ignorance or a lack of political will - is the case of incompliance with the planning standards that prevent the implementation of businesses in residential buildings (Marín Cots et al., 2017). The resistance movements in the centres of Malaga and Marbella denounce high levels of noise, occupation of the public highway, preference for commercial and hospitality uses as opposed to residential uses, and the most radical proposal, the change from residential to tourism uses in the entire historic centre of Malaga: *"the few residents who have not been thrown out have to withstand the impunity of the #Noise and the mayhem #MálagaCiudadGenial (MalagaFantasticCity)"* (Association of Residents of the Historic Centre of Malaga via @vecinosmalaga).

In the second case, institutional autism, the public participation processes in projects are reduced to mere formalities. Often, the public administration is both "judge and interested party" in contentious issues, with the sole option of appealing to the judicial authority. This is the case of the annulment of the public consultation on the UFB and the reduction of the public exhibition periods for the skyscraper-hotel. A wall of silence is created and technical language, including legal jargon, is overused. For this reason, in all the resistance movements there is a perception of defencelessness and distrust of the political class, and they state that *"Citizens count. We have an opinion, critical spirit and even proposals"* (Let's Defend Our Skyline Platform via @noalrascacielos). It is alleged that the so-called "governance" is not put into practice, despite being the "objective" in all the planning documents. According to them, *"the plans do not protect at all"* (Discussion group DG2) therefore *"civic participation takes place in the courts"* (Discussion group DG2).

The Ideas and Rules facilitate the urban growth machine through large projects and urban regeneration. These projects are designed with notable effects on the physical environment, and the damage increases exponentially with the size of the project. Some examples are the loss of ecosystems in the case of Los Merinos, located in a space declared a Biosphere Reserve or the case of the Marbella-Ronda Motorway, *"for two reasons, firstly, the volume involved with the earth-moving works […] and secondly, because the peridotites go hand-in-hand with biodiversity values that are extremely high on a global level"* (Discussion Group DG1). Other impacts concern the vulnerability of the coastline, pollution and the loss of green spaces in the case of the UFB and the felling of trees in Marbella. There is a particular sensitivity towards the degradation of the natural, rural and urban landscape. The negative impact on the landscape is the strongest argument of the movement against the skyscraper in the port of Malaga, and it has been supported by ICOMOS, which has recommended cancelling the project based on the *"permanent irreversible impact of the building on nature, on the two scales analysed: the landscape heritage of Malaga and that of its port. In both cases, both from a visual and objective point of view, as well as from a subjective and symbolic perspective, the impact would damage the image and the exceptional value of the landscape in the city, and in particular the scenic heritage"* (ICOMOS, 2018).

The negative social impacts are also notable. The main impacts affect the quality and life and daily space of citizens, with the clearest examples being those that take place in neighbourhoods. In the case of the UFB, there are *"two districts that are very affected by overcrowding, due to population density and very precarious urban planning conditions"* (Discussion Group DG1), in the Historic Centre of Malaga, where the residents complain that *"in the centre that right to live in onés neighbourhood in peace has been lost a little, and so has the right not be photographed from the moment you get up"* (Discussion Group DG1). The results are clear: in the Historic Centre of Malaga, the processes of gentrification and touristification have resulted in the expulsion of half the population (a decline from 8,968 residents in 1981 to 4,720 in 2015). The conflict is clear and ongoing: while there are residents who feel *"that the investments that have been made in the historic centre of Malaga, unlike those made in any other neighbourhood, have not been aimed at improving the quality of life of residents in the area, but rather have sought to evict them"* (La Opinión de Malaga, 2018), some councillors in the local government state publicly that *"the Centre must no longer be residential first and foremost"* (in Sau & Muñoz, 2018).

The following category of projects is the reliance on distant decision-making authorities and top-down processes. The projects are backed externally, by speculative international investment funds (as well as tour operators and hotel companies), as in the case of the port of Marbella and the Skyscraper-hotel. The social movements argue that a city model that differs to the approved plans is imposed on them. As a result of all this, they call for "the right to the city and the territory": *"we began to think ... in Marbella are we, the citizens, ever going to have the right to the city or will we remain under the control of Gil* (a former local ruler associated with an era of political-business corruption), *and the investors of the sheikh* (investors in the Port extension project ... *?* (Discussion group DG1). In turn, decisions that reduce the power of local action are taken in Madrid by the national government; this is the case with the SUD-strateg, which in Spain mainly goes towards funding new building works, in the Centre of Malaga construction it is 72% of the budget of 11.8 million Euros (OMAU, 2015).

The desire to attract investment means that the public administration forms part of the urban growth machines; public facilities are granted in order for private investors to implement urban planning and create infrastructures, and always justified by the creation of employment. In the case of the extension of the Port of Marbella, the Council of Marbella forms part of the joint venture that is implementing the project. The citizens in the movements are clear about this: *"It is necessary to call a spade a spade [...] that is to say, when we talk about investment we are talking about the get-rich-quick culture, easy money"* (Discussion group DG1).

Various resources are put at the service of UGMs. Developers use the powerful social networks of public institutions and their authority, as well as other commercial and financial companies, the local media, etc., in order to create a good image of themselves to present to society. On the contrary, although resistance movements are supported by numerous groups, they depend on the voluntary work of a few people, and a minimum provision of resources, *"in the clearly unequal battle, because we are talking about opposing the power of money using volunteer work"* (Discussion Group DG1). Media coverage of the project is through press and image campaigns in order to boost social receptiveness, and attract groups that have an influence on local public opinion. A good example is Los Merinos, which has already been prosecuted and documented, where media outlets and social groups were bought with surreptitious advertising and free activities. Around €500,000 was invested in different payments and contracts such as the *"Charri Channel which was given €12,000€a year for a three-year renewable period, another TV channel Bel was given €3,000 a month for a period renewable for three years. [...] Another local newspaper, La Gaceta de Ronda [...] received more than €125,000 in two years [...] it was owned by the mayor, the one from 2006, who promoted the entire project [...] all that is shown in the contracts."* (Discussion group DG1).

Another trait that characterises several of the case studies is that they are based on a rentier economy and land speculation, where institutions participate with their land in the speculative process (e.g. Los Merinos and UFB). There is an absence of municipal policies against the inflation of land and property prices. This attitude is logical if the driving force of the local economy consists solely of the continuous growth of the added value of land via the transformation of the existing city (in Malaga), and the creation of new urban settlements (on the coastline) in any part of the municipality, creating an unsustainable urban structure. Spain, and especially its tourist areas, form part of the secondary circuit of the accumulation of global capital in fixed capital, with excessive property investment based on the constant increase in the price of land. Each project forms part of a long-term plan, which takes advantage of the price revaluations of land close to the previous project. Even if a project is stalled due to economic or legal problems, the magnitude of the capital involved and the large future profits mean that the development will start up again when those obstacles have been overcome, even if it is many years later. The case of Los Merinos in Ronda is paradigmatic, as it is the oldest of the cases studied, and there is extensive analysis over time, with twelve transactions before and after reclassifications which gradually increased the value of the land (Diez Ripollés & Gómez-Céspedes, 2009).

Attitudes towards tourism of stakeholders involved and degrowth readings of the proposals of resistance groups

Among the dominant ideas, there is also the idea put forward in tourist destinations like the Costa del Sol that tourism is the driving force and determining factor in the collective imagination. It is used by developers in order to justify and defend their actions, such as at the skyscraper-hotel in the Port, where they argue that *"the city has the opportunity to move [...] towards the new 'modernity' offered by its current period of economic, cultural and social boom that its tourism strength provides"* (Seguí, 2017). Resistance movements are certain that the property business is the key to tourism development on the CS, and tourism is a *"mere justification for speculation"* (Discussion Group DG2). They also warn that the economic impact does not seep trickle down to all of society to an equal extent: it is very beneficial for developers and operators, but not always for citizens. The social movements use the data in the Urban Indicators study (National Statistics Institute, 2018) where the municipalities of the CS are among the 20 towns with the most overnight stays by tourists in Spain - on a list of 126 cities - but they are also towards the bottom of the list of 20 cities with the lowest average annual income per household. They also state that tourism can destroy employment in other sectors, *"like a cancer"* (Discussion Group DG2), and it has a significant cost on the opportunity for the development of other areas which could be beneficial for the Costa del Sol-Malaga, *"there is no investment in renewable energy, in R + D, etc., because everything is directed towards tourism"* (Discussion Group DG2).

However, although most resistance movements fight against the negative effects on the physical, urban, social and even economic environment, tourist activity is not questioned. Social movements expressly stress that *"we are not against tourism"* (Discussion group DG2) and *"we are annoyed when people associate us with tourism-phobia (Historic Centre Interview)", "the anti-tourists label is used by developers"* (Discussion group DG2) in order to discredit resistance movements. They feel that tourism on the CS is beneficial, but it is necessary to rectify its excesses and prevent it from imposing itself as an economic monoculture in the area. There is a call for greater planning and regulation in order to prevent tourist saturation, and they even use their own arguments to defend stopping projects and alternative proposals such as the UFB: *"that natural heritage would be sold, which is what happens in other places like London, as attractions relating to tourism"* (Discussion Group DG2). They also believe that in order for the planning to be effective, the process must take into account the full integration of the *"rights of citizens to their city, to participate and express their opinions, and that should be binding on the Administration, that is to say, it should not just be a right to make claims in a process, participation for us should be collaborative"* (Discussion Group DG1).

In this regard, a key issue in the design of this study was to determine the feelings of stakeholders towards strategies of tourism degrowth. From the results of the first discussion group and the documentary analysis, it was deduced that the proposals of the resistance movements are aligned with the degrowth approach, although not explicitly. The second discussion group was asked if the concept of degrowth could represent the six resistance groups. All the representatives concurred affirmatively in their personal stance, and believed that this stance also coincided with the group in five of the six cases, with the exception being the Skyscraper. All the resistance groups understand the criteria associated with degrowth (reduction of needs, consumption, of construction in general, of the sizes of infrastructures, the redistribution of resources, prioritising the local over the global), which is also linked to a demand for more information, more rigour and the democratisation of forms of governance, always from the bottom-up, because as they point out *"we have lost the Welfare State, [...] and therefore it is at a local level where it is possible to have greater strength and that is where we emerge"* (Discussion group DG1).

Discussion

The study has looked at the new processes of tourist growth and the conflicts that arise from the perspective of local social movements. In the literature review, it was observed that in tourist destinations, tourism is used to feed urban growth machines (Kimelberg, 2011; Lang & Rothenberg, 2016; Logan & Molotch, 1987), while the application to the case study confirms that social movements feel that tourist development is associated with speculative building and property development.

The study proposes an analysis model of UGMs applied to tourist destinations, which that uses the analysis of projects and the resistance movements they produce as its basis. The first idea that is put forward is the demystification of the belief that economic growth is progress, in the way that it is measured at present. The developers of UGM projects use the common arguments of neoclassical economics - modernity, market and economic growth - for human welfare. However, as the report by the National Statistics Institute (2018) shows, this does not happen on the CS. In the dominant ideas, the public sector is also seen to be at the service of private enterprise.

With regard to the dominant ideas, it may be considered that the approaches of the resistance movements to projects adopt a position closer to the premises of degrowth (Hall, 2009). Social resistance movements defend the tangible, the specific and the everyday, i.e. lived space (Lefebvre, 2013; Soja, 2008). In turn, they advocate stopping projects, reducing their effects and carrying out alternative proactive proposals from a civic level with positive environmental effects.

In the dimension of norms and laws, the national and regional levels are linked, which is what happens with the infrastructure projects (Romero et al., 2017), and the local scale is also key for the implementation of *"à la carte"* urban planning for the developers of UGMs. This is what makes the uniqueness of urban planning in the Spanish case possible (Seguido & Hernández, 2015); it is liquid urban planning that coincides with the conceptual lines of Bauman (2013). Exceptional treatment in the application of regulations is common in tourist destinations in developing countries, located on the fourth pleasure periphery, as shown in cases in the Caribbean and Central America, and this increases unequal geographical development (Harvey, 2013) and so-called neo-colonialism. In turn, institutional autism, the lack of civic participation processes and decisions taken from the top-down have a negative influence on the governance of the tourist destinations, they prevent a shared vision and hinder conflict management (Bramwell & Sharman, 1999; Milano, 2018). Proper governance practices are known, but are not applied.

With regard to tourism, no rejection is observed despite the fact that all the cases are justified using the benefits of tourist activity. Two reflections stand out in this respect. On one hand, there is the assimilation of tourist activity as part of the socio-economic and cultural "DNA" of the CS, which is a limitation on thinking creatively about the future of the region. On the other, the attraction towards greater control and a reduction of the quantitative dimensions of tourist development affects its classic variables and the way of evaluating its positive evolution, based on unlimited growth (number of tourists and facilities). What emerges is that despite the restructuring and rejuvenation measures that have been launched in mature coastal destinations such as the Qualifica Plan on the Costa del Sol, the improvements in sustainability are not noted by citizens. Meanwhile, in cities such as Malaga, the results of the different tourism strategies have increased tourist activity, generating new conflicts which are perceived by residents.

There is a conflict in the dichotomy of interests between the growth promoters and those affected by its impact. From the perspective of developers, the cases analysed constitute a representation of the tacit pro-growth urban-tourism agreement between the four groups of key stakeholders. From the perspective of those affected, the existence of this agreement is confirmed, and the lack of information and transparency in the processes to implement these projects is something that is repeated in all cases.

Ultimately, in UGMs the relationship between developers and resistance movements displays a pattern of inverse symmetry: (1) consolidated and indisputable arguments, and top-down vs bottom-up arguments that are in the process of being created and questioned; (2) quick vs slow progress times; (3) the concentration of political, economic and media power vs collaborative and voluntary work with a few resources; (4) the exchange value and the domination of space vs the value of use and collective appropriation of space; (5) the production of space vs the creation of the city; (6) attention to the object or project (product) vs attention to the process (daily life); (7) promotion of the private vs defence of what is shared. All of this is linked to the call for the right to the city (Lefebvre, 2013), and when they are understood together on a broader city scale, they can be understood as a collective practice calling for spatial justice (Soja, 2008), as seen in the cases analysed where the resistance movements call for quality of urban life, the right to the landscape, environmental protection, etc. However, above all, the resistance movements call for active and binding participation processes for citizens in order to attain a real right to the city, which is aligned with the need to undertake collaborative planning processes in tourism destinations (Casanueva et al., 2016; Huxham, 2003; Jamal & Getz, 1995).

This study has an essentially qualitative nature applied to a geographic area. Its limitations include the difficulty in obtaining quantitative data that enable a deeper knowledge of the categories identified in the analysis model of the UGMs and a comparison of the model with other areas of study. However, these limitations present opportunities for continuing the work in the future. This study encourages a further examination of other future lines of work, including: (1) identifying comparable quantitative and qualitative comparable indicators associated with the discourse of the UGMs; (2) identifying and checking alternative indicators linked to positive processes in terms of local and sustainable development; (3) further examining the characterisation of resistance movements encouraging the transfer processes characteristic of action research, especially with regard to the options of network working and pooling experiences; (4) increasing knowledge in relation to collaborative planning in tourist destinations, especially on tools for preventing conflicts, and the processes of co-design, co-development and co-implementation of strategies and actions; (5) looking deeper at the conceptualisation of tourist degrowth and the knowledge of applicable measures in saturated tourist destinations.

Disclosure statement

No potential conflict of interest was reported by the authors.

Acknowledgments

The research in this paper was funded by the project "Crisis and restructuring of Spanish coastal tourism areas" (CSO2015-64468-P) and "Overtourism in Spanish coastal destinations. Tourism degrowth strategies An approach from the social dimension" (RTI2018-094844-B-C33) financed by Spanish Ministry of Science, Innovation and Universities (National Plan for R+D+i) the Spanish State Research Agency and the European Regional Development Fund (ERDF).

References

Andreoni, V., & Galmarini, S. (2014). How to increase well-being in a context of degrowth. *Futures*, *55*, 78–89. doi:10. 1016/j.futures.2013.10.021

Balcazar, F. (2003). Investigación acción participativa (iap): Aspectos conceptuales y dificultades de implementación. *Fundamentos en Humanidades*, *IV*(7-8), 59–77.

Bauman, Z. (2013). *Tiempos líquidos. Vivir en una época de incertidumbre* (4a Edición). España: Tusquets Editores SA.

Beard, L., Scarles, C., & Tribe, J. (2016). Mess and method: Using ANT in tourism research. *Annals of Tourism Research*, *60*, 97–110. doi:10.1016/j.annals.2016.06.005

Beck, U. (2000). Retorno a la teoría de la «Sociedad del riesgo». *Boletín de la A.G.E.*, *30*, 9–20.

Borja, J., & Castells, M. (2004). *Local y global. La gestión de las ciudades en la era de la información.* Madrid: Taurus.

Bourdeau, P., & Berthelot, L. (2008). *Tourisme et Décroissance: de la critique à l'utopie?* Paper presented at the First International Conference on Economic De-Growth for Ecological Sustainability and Social Equity, Paris, April 18–19, 2008.

Boyle, M. (1999). Growth machines and propaganda projects: A review of readings of the role of civic boosterism in the politics of local economic development. In A. E. G. Jonas & D. Wilson (Eds.), *The urban growth machine: Critical perspectives two decades later* (pp. 55–70). Nueva York. State University of New York Press

Bramwell, B., & Sharman, A. (1999). Collaboration in local tourism policymaking. *Annals of Tourism Research*, *26*(2), 392–415. doi:10.1016/S0160-7383(98)00105-4

Büscher, B., & Fletcher, R. (2017). Destructive creation: Capital accumulation and the structural violence of tourism. *Journal of Sustainable Tourism*, *25*(5), 651–667. doi:10.1080/09669582.2016.1159214

Cain, C. (2014). Negotiating with the growth machine: Community benefits agreements and value-conscious growth. *Sociological Forum*, *29*(4), 937–958. doi:10.1111/socf.12127

Cañada, E. (2015). *Las que limpian los hoteles. Historias ocultas de precariedad laboral.* Barcelona: Edt. Icaria.

Casanueva, C., Gallego, A., & García, M. (2016). Social network analysis in tourism. *Current Issues in Tourism*, *19*(12), 1190–1209. doi:10.1080/13683500.2014.990422

Castañeda, E. (2012). The indignados of Spain: A precedent to occupy wall street. *Social Movement Studies*, *11*(3-4), 309–319. doi:10.1080/14742837.2012.708830

Diez Ripollés, J. L., & Gómez-Céspedes, A. (2009). La corrupción urbanística: estrategias de análisis. *Anuario de la Facultad de Derecho de la Universidad Autónoma de Madrid*, *12*, 41–69.

Fernández Medrano, H. & Pardo Rivacoba, D. (2017). La lucha por el decrecimiento turístico: El caso de Barcelona. *Ecología Política*, *52*, 104–106.

Flesher, C. (2015). Debunking spontaneity: Spain's 15-M/indignados as autonomous movement. *Social Movement Studies*, *14*(2), 142–163.

Fletcher, R. (2016). Tours Caníbales puesto al día: la ecología política del turismo. In M. Blazquez, M. Mir-Gual, I. Murray, & G. Pons (Eds.), *Turismo y crisis, turismo colaborativo y ecoturismo. XV Coloquio de Geografía del Turismo, el Ocio y la Recreación de la AGE.* Mon. Soc. Hist. Nat. Balears, 23. SHNB-UIB-AGE.

Fletcher, R. (2011). Sustaining tourism, sustaining capitalism? The tourism industry's role in global capitalist expansion. *Tourism Geographies, 13*(3), 443–461. doi:10.1080/14616688.2011.570372

Fuster Morell, F. (2012). The free culture and 15M movements in Spain: Composition, social networks and synergies. *Social Movement Studies, 11*(3-4), 386–392. doi:10.1080/14742837.2012.710323

Hall, C. M. (2009). Degrowing tourism: Décroissance, sustainable consumption and steady-state tourism. *Anatolia, 20*(1), 46–61. doi:10.1080/13032917.2009.10518894

Harvey, D. (2013). *Ciudades rebeldes. Del derecho de la ciudad a la revolución urbana.* Madrid: Akal.

Huete, R., & Mantecón, E. (2018). El auge de la turismofobia ¿hipótesis de investigación o ruido ideológico? *PASOS. Revista de Turismo y Patrimonio Cultural, 16*(1), 9–19.

Huxham, C. (2003). Theorizing collaboration practice. *Public Management Review, 5,* 401–423. doi:10.1080/1471903032000146964

Ingrassia, F. (2013). Por todas partes crece la sensación de ser náufragos a la deriva. In A. Fernández-Savater (Ed.), *Fuera de lugar* (pp. 79–94). Madrid: Acuarela-Machado.

ICOMOS. (2018). Evaluación del impacto del hotel-rascacielos en el Muelle de Levante en el paisaje patrimonial de Málaga. España. Retrieved from http://www.icomos.es/wp-content/uploads/2017/02/Icomos.-Evaluaci%C3%B3n-del-impacto-del-hotel-rascacielos-en-en-el-muelle-de-Levante-en-el-paisaje-patrimonial-de-M%C3%A1laga.pdf

Jamal, T., & Getz, D. (1995). Collaboration theory and community tourism planning. *Annals of Tourism Research, 22*(1), 186–204. doi:10.1016/0160-7383(94)00067-3

Kimelberg, S. M. (2011). Inside the growth machine: Real estate professionals on the perceived challenges of urban development. *City & Community, 10*(1), 76–99. doi:10.1111/j.1540-6040.2010.01351.x

Kousis, M. (2000). Tourism and the environment. A social movements perspective. *Annals of Tourism Research, 27*(2), 468–489. doi:10.1016/S0160-7383(99)00083-3

Lang, S., & Rothenberg, J. (2016). Neoliberal urbanism, public space, and the greening of the growth machine: New York City's High Line park. *Environment and Planning A: Economy and Space, 49*(8), 1743–1761. doi:10.1177/0308518X16677969

Lefebvre, H. (2013). [1974]. *La producción del espacio.* Madrid: Capitán Swing.

Logan, J., & Molotch, H. (1987). *Urban fortunes: The political economy of place.* Los Angeles: University of California Press.

López, I., & Rodríguez, E. (2010). *Fin de ciclo. Financiarización, territorio y sociedad de propietarios en la onda larga del capitalismo hispano (1959-2010).* Madrid: Traficantes de Sueños.

Los Reporteros. (2018, June 23). La torre malagueña de la polémica (documentary). *Canal Sur TV.* Retrieved from http://www.canalsur.es/television/programas/los-reporteros/detalle/55.html?video=1293684&sec=

Marín Cots, P., Guevara Plaza, A., & Navarro-Jurado, E. (2017). Renovación urbana y masificación turística en la ciudad antigua: Pérdida de población y conflictos sociales. *Ciudad y Territorio. Estudios Territoriales, 193,* 458–468.

McGehee, N. G., Kline, S., & Knollenberg, W. (2014). Social movements and tourism-related local action. *Annals of Tourism Research, 48,* 140–155. doi:10.1016/j.annals.2014.06.004

Milano, C. (2018). Overtourism, malestar social y turismofobia. Un debate controvertido. *Pasos. Revista de Turismo y Patrimonio Cultural, 16*(3), 551–564. doi:10.25145/j.pasos.2018.16.041

Murray, I. (2014). Bienvenidos a la fiesta: turistización planetaria y ciudades-espectáculo (y algo más). *Ecología Política, 47,* 87–91.

Murray, I. & Blázquez-Salom, M. (2009). El dinero, la aguja del tejido de la globalización capitalista. *Boletín de la Asociación de Geógrafos Españoles, 50,* 43–80.

Murray, I., Yrigoy, I., & Blázquez, M. (2017). The role of crises in the production, destruction and restructuring of tourist spaces. The case of the Balearic Islands. *Revista Investigaciones Turísticas, 13,* 1–29. doi:10.14198/INTURI2017.13.01

Monterrubio, C. (2017). Protests and tourism crises: A social movement approach to causality. *Tourism Management Perspectives, 22,* 82–89. doi:10.1016/j.tmp.2017.03.001

Naredo, J. M. (2010). El modelo inmobiliario español y sus consecuencias. En Coloquio sobre urbanismo, democracia y mercado: Una experiencia española (1970–2010), Institut d'Urbanisme de Paris, Université de Paris, 15 y 16 de marzo de 2010. Retrieved from http://habitat.aq.upm.es/boletin/n44/ajnar.html

National Statistics Institute (INE). (2018). *Urban Indicators.* Retrieved from https://www.ine.es/dynt3/metadatos/es/RespuestaDatos.htm?oe=30256

Navarro-Jurado, E. (2014). La reestructuración de los destinos litorales. Entre la Retórica y la Len-Titud de Los Cambios. In L. Palomeque & C. Valiente (Eds.), *Turismo y Territorio Innovación, Renovación y Desafíos* (pp. 37–72). Valencia: Edt. Tirant lo Blanc.

Navarro-Jurado, E., Damian, M., & Fernández-Morales, A. (2013). Carrying capacity model applied in coastal destinations. *Annals of Tourism Research, 43,* 1–19. doi:10.1016/j.annals.2013.03.005

Navarro-Jurado, T., Almeida, C., Cortés, D., Fernández, G., Luque, M., Marcenaro, ... Solís, (2012). Carrying capacity assessment for tourist destinations. Methodology for the creation of synthetic indicators applied in a coastal area. *Tourism Management, 33*, 1337–1346.

OMAU. (2015). Estrategia Urbana Integrada Sostenible "Perchel Lagunillas". Ayuntamiento de Málaga. Retrieved from http://static.omau-malaga.com/omau/subidas/archivos/4/1/arc_7714.pdf

Pié Ninot, R., & Rosa Jiménez, C. J. (2014). La cuestión del paisaje en la reinvención de los destinos turísticos maduros: Málaga y la Costa del Sol. *ACE: Architecture, City and Environment, 9*(25), 303–326.

Riechmann, J. (2001). *Todo tiene un límite: Ecología y transformación social.* Madrid: Debate SA.

Rodgers, S. (2009). Urban growth machine. In R. Kitchin & N. Thrift (Eds.), *International encyclopedia of human geography* (pp. 40–45). Oxford: Elsevier

Romero, J. M., Romero, & Navarro-Jurado, E. (2017). Growth machine en destinos turísticos maduros. Zona Metropolitana Costa del Sol (Málaga). *Ciudad y Territorio. Estudios Territoriales, 194*, 661–678.

Romero, J. M., Romero, & Navarro-Jurado, E. (2015). Atributos urbanos contempor aneos del litoral mediterr aneo en la crisis global: caso de la Zona Metropolitana de la Costa del Sol. *Scripta Nova. Revista Electrónica de Geografía y Ciencias Sociales Universidad de Barcelona, 19*(515), 1–10. 10.1344/sn2015.19.15119

Rovira, M. T., & Antón-Clavé, S. (2014). De destino a ciudad. La reformulación urbana de los destinos turísticos costeros maduros. El caso de la Costa Daurada central. *ACE: Architecture, City and Environment, 9*(25), 373–392.

Russo, P. (2016). Las nuevas fronteras del estudio del turismo: retos conceptuales y epistemológicos. *Revista CIDOB d'Afers Internacionals*, (113), 15–32. doi:10.24241/rcai.2016.113.2.15

Saarinen, J. (2006). Traditions of sustainability in tourism studies. *Annals of Tourism Research, 33*(4), 1121–1140. doi: 10.1016/j.annals.2006.06.007

Sau and Muñoz. (2018, February 12). El Ayuntamiento retrasa la moratoria de licencias de bares para buscar consenso. La Opinión de Málaga. Retrieved from https://www.laopiniondemalaga.es/malaga/2018/02/12/ayuntamiento-suspende-moratoria-licencias-bares/986428.html

Seguí, J. (2017, August 9). Las 'miradas' desde la Torre del Puerto. Diario Sur. Retrieved from https://www.diariosur.es/malaga-capital/jose-segui-20170809215540-nt.html

Seguido, A. F. M., & Hernández, M. (2015). Urban sprawl and its effects on water demand: A case study of Alicante, Spain. *Land Use Policy, 50*, 352–362. doi:10.1016/j.landusepol.2015.06.032

Soja, E. W. (2008). *Postmetrópolis. Estudios críticos sobre ciudades y regiones.* Madrid: Traficantes de Sueños.

Touraine, A. (2006). Los movimientos sociales. *Revista Colombiana de Sociología* (27), 255–278.

Turismo y Planificación. (2018). Observatorio Turístico de la Costa del Sol 2017. Diputación de Málaga. Retrieved from https://www.costadelsolmalaga.org/base/ ... /observatorio-turistico-provincia-malaga-2017

Vives-Miro, S., & Rullán, O. (2017). Desposesión de vivienda por turistización? Revalorización y desplazamientos en el Centro Histórico de Palma (Mallorca). *Revista de Geografía Norte Grande, 67*, 53–71. doi:10.4067/S0718-34022017000200004

World Tourism Organization; Centre of Expertise Leisure, Tourism & Hospitality; NHTV Breda University of Applied Sciences; and NHL Stenden University of Applied Sciences, (Eds.) (2018). *'Overtourism'? – Understanding and managing urban tourism growth beyond perceptions.* Madrid: UNWTO.

Overtourism, optimisation, and destination performance indicators: a case study of activities in Fjord Norway

Ove Oklevik, Stefan Gössling ⓘ, C. Michael Hall ⓘ, Jens Kristian Steen Jacobsen, Ivar Petter Grøtte and Scott McCabe ⓘ

ABSTRACT

Many global tourist destinations have experienced growth in arrivals. This has triggered various conflicts in destinations and sparked debates as to how to deal with what is increasingly referred to as 'overtourism'. Most Destination Marketing Organisations (DMOs) pursue strategies to stimulate arrivals even further. Pro-growth discourses are reinforced by lead bodies such as the World Tourism Organisation (UNWTO). However, maximisation strategies based on higher numbers of tourists increasingly cause conflicts with local residents, whereas simultaneously undermining climate change mitigation pledges as negotiated in the Paris Agreement. New approaches to destination management based on optimisation are therefore warranted. Drawing on a survey of international tourists ($n = 5,249$) in south-western Norway, this article discusses whether 'activities', i.e. the development of local, small-scale and ideally more sustainable experiences, can contribute to economic growth without necessarily increasing numbers of arrivals. Results confirm that destinations should seek to better understand their markets, including length of stay, spending, and/or activity intention, to identify profitable markets. Ultimately, such knowledge may help addressing overtourism conflicts while building tourism systems that are more economically, socially, and environmentally resilient.

Introduction

Since the beginning of mass tourism in the 1960s, most destinations in the world have sought to increase numbers of tourist arrivals (Hall, 2008). Even where early 'caps' set out to place limits on inbound tourist numbers, as in the Seychelles, Bhutan, or Grand Cayman, these have subsequently been lifted (Gössling et al., 2002; Johnson, 2002; Nyaupane & Timothy, 2010). However, in recent years, continued rapid growth in tourist arrivals in popular destinations, and associated problems of crowding, localised inflation and/or pressure on residential housing, have created substantial public debates regarding the desirability of a tourism system based on a growth model. Crowding, or 'overtourism' (UNWTO, 2017), as a result of a disproportionally large influx of tourists has become an issue for residents as well as tourists in destinations as diverse as New York City, Amsterdam, Reykavik, the Isle of Skye, Koh Phi Phi, Thailand, and Palawan, Philippines. In comparing population to overnight visitors per year to highlight crowding pressure (1: 360 in Venice; 1: 33 in Dubrovnik; 1: 8 in Paris), the World Economic Forum (2017) suggests that destinations will increasingly turn to caps, citing Santorini (Greece) and Cinque Terre (Italy) as examples. In response to crowding problems, the UNWTO called for destinations to better manage tourism, though without questioning the underlying assumption of a continuation in growth strategy. The World Travel Market 'Minister's Summit', co-organised by UNWTO in London in November 2017, reflects this perspective: 'Overtourism: growth is not the enemy, it is how we manage it' (UNWTO, 2017).

Recent increases in tourism in some destinations has often been fuelled by a combination of heightened accessibility involving low cost carriers and declining airfares (e.g. Lawton, 2017), the global relevance of social media and evaluation platforms in streamlining opinion and influencing demand, also as a result of mobile travel applications offering cheap and convenient services to enhance destination experiences, such as language translation, city guides, and maps; as well as new and inexpensive accommodation offers through AirBnB and other online platforms (Guttentag, 2015). All of these developments have resulted in profound changes in visitor composition, length-of-stay, place-of-stay, tourist expectations, and resident perceptions, especially where AirBnB has caused severe disruptions in residential housing supply (Gutiérrez, García-Palomares, Romanillos, & Salas-Olmedo, 2017). These processes have also resulted in more critical perspectives on the desirability and quality of growth by some destination stakeholders, including businesses and residents, as well as tourists. In the current climate, and with widespread media-reporting on 'overtourism', overcrowding, and anti-tourist sentiment (e.g. Independent, 2017; Skift, 2017; Telegraph, 2018), destination marketing organisations, particularly in Europe have begun to openly and critically discuss the desirability of continued growth-focused perspectives for tourism. These critical perspectives are also prevalent in Norway, where they have emerged on social media, national media, and in multiple stakeholder debates, such as those surrounding the evaluation of UNESCO World Heritage Sites, to which 'Fjord Norway' belongs (Hawkins et al., 2009).

Given global growth in tourist arrivals and notions of tourism systems reaching their limits, an emerging question emerges whether mature or rapidly growing destinations should continue to pursue volume growth strategies (Gössling, Ring, Dwyer, Andersson, & Hall, 2016; Hall, 2009)? Alternative options may include caps or limits, de-marketing, and/or the application of air passenger duties and departure taxes to increase revenue and limit arrivals growth (Hall, 2014), i.e. initiatives that have so far been mostly applied in the context of single, highly frequented sites (such as Machu Picchu, Peru), not entire destinations. Neuts and Nijkamp (2012, p. 2149) concluded that 'prevention of tourist visitation during periods of high use by season spreading of tourist flows might prove a workable solution in order to decrease crowding pressure'. This, however, may acquiesce to perceptions that the economic potential of a tourism system is not fully realised, resulting in resistance from stakeholders seeking to profit from continued arrival growth. An alternative is to optimise tourism systems, i.e. to increase the value obtained from maintaining or even decreasing visitor numbers (Dwyer, Pham, Forsyth, & Spurr, 2014; Gössling et al., 2016). This article discusses optimisation on the basis of a survey of international tourists in south-western Norway, with a focus on price perceptions, length of stay (LOS), and interest in activities. Results are put in the context of calls for further growth, as issued by UNWTO, and with regard to their wider destination management implications.

Crowding and 'overtourism'

Growth in tourist arrivals is a key objective of destination marketing organisations, to maximise tourism's contribution to GDP and employment (Dwyer, Forsyth, & Dwyer, 2010). Even though economic contributions are related to various aspects of the tourism production system, such as transportation, accommodation, attractions, or activities, the general view is that growth in numbers of arrivals is the pathway to economic benefit. For example, Hall (2008) concluded that the most common approach to destination development is 'boosterism', and there is a widespread understanding that tourism development is embedded in wider neoliberal discourses of growth (see also Dwyer et al., 2007; 2012; Hall, 2014). This perspective is fostered by supranational organisations such as UN World Tourism Organisation (UNWTO), World Economic Forum (WEF), or World Travel and Tourism Council (WTTC), which advocate volume growth, framing successful tourism development against indicators of arrival numbers, employment, revenue, or market shares (Blanke & Chiesa, 2013; UNWTO, 2014) as opposed to more humanistic indicators of performance, such as quality of life (e.g. Ridderstaat, Croes, & Nijkamp, 2016). Since the term 'sustainability' is seemingly ubiquitous in the public discourses of these international organisations, growth has become a 'distinctly environmental project' (McCarthy & Prudham, 2004, p. 276). Yet, an awakening to alternative viewpoints is now palatable in many destinations around the world: tourism has become regarded as too dominant a sector in many regions, and in such cases its negative impacts seem to increasingly overshadow its benefits. Specifically, where the influx of tourists has begun to dominate local economies and townscapes, or where large numbers of tourists attempt to visit individual sites, more critical perceptions of 'crowdedness' appear to have emerged.

Crowding effect was originally developed as a concept describing emotions arising out of perceived human density and resulting constraints (Stokols, 1972). Crowding as an issue for destinations and in particular tourist sites has been a recurrent topic in tourism research since the early 1970s, i.e Turner and Ash's (1975) reference to 'golden hordes' and popularised through Doxey's (1975) 'Irritation Index'. Later, Social Exchange Theory (Emerson, 1976) became the starting point for tourism studies focused on issues of human interaction and exchange specifically in leisure contexts, highlighted that tourist numbers can become a source of 'incompatibility' between residents and outsiders (Ap, 1992; Neuts & Nijkamp, 2012; Ward & Berno, 2011). With regard to tourist perceptions, there is general agreement that crowding is situational and depends on individual norms and values, as well as the perceived characteristics of other tourists. Tourists associate crowding with waiting, stress, or specific (negative) destination qualities (Patterson & Hammitt, 1990; Perdue et al., 1999; Riganti & Nijkamp, 2008; Stewart & Cole, 2001). It has been highlighted that crowding can also be positive (Choi, Mirjafari, & Weaver, 1976). This insight, which Neuts and Nijkamp (2012) emphasise has been mostly overlooked, is potentially of growing relevance in tourism (see also Popp, 2012). Notions of 'being in the right place' in the wider context of 'following' trends have gained importance because of information cascades and the concentration of news flows in the age of social media (Turkle, 2015), as well as an increasing focus by consumers on the acquisition of unique experiences, rather than material possessions as markers of identity (Addis & Holbrook, 2001). Specific sites may become increasingly attractive as a result of discussions in social media channels, or as recipients of high numbers of 'like' or positive evaluations on platforms such as TripAdvisor. Table 1 illustrates annual resident to tourist ratios in a number of popular destinations around the world. Note that these mostly represent cities and smaller countries, as perceptions of crowding will be influenced by the concentration of people in time and space, as well as other factors, such as resident/tourist attitudes and comfort thresholds, LOS, weather patterns, season, or the popularity of specific attractions.

In comparison, residents' attitudes to tourists and crowding have also been investigated in various cultural and geographical contexts. Early works discussed, for example, that residents were confronted with high infrastructure use including traffic congestion as a result of tourism, as well as second home purchases (Lankford, 1994; Sheldon & Var, 1984). However, negative perceptions of crowding were not confirmed in all contexts (Mok, Slater, & Cheung, 1991) and were shown to also depend on economic involvement in tourism (Andereck, Valentine, Knopf, &Vogt, 2005). Host irritation, Ward and Berno (2011) affirm, can be mediated by factors such as positive perceptions of tourism impacts, more satisfying intercultural contacts and more positive stereotypes.

Table 1. Popular destinations and resident to annual tourist arrival ratios, 2015.

Destination	Residents000	Tourists '000	Ratio	Source
Bangkok	10,000	18,735	1:1.8	Euromonitor 2017
London	8,788	18,580	1:2.1	Euromonitor 2017
Kuala Lumpur	1,589	12,153	1:7.6	Euromonitor 2017
Maldives	344	1,234	1:3.6	UNWTO/World Bank 2017
Saint Lucia	165	345	1:2.0	UNWTO/World Bank 2017
Amsterdam City	851	6,826	1:8.0	UNWTO 2017
Amsterdam	1,500	17,300	1:11.5	UNWTO 2017
New York City (int.)	8,175	12,700[a]	1:1.6	NYC & Company 2017
New York City (dom.)	8,175	47,800[a]	1:5.9	NYC & Company 2017
New York City (all)	8,175	60,500[a]	1:7.4	
Barcelona	1,608	9,862	1:6.1	Barcelona Tourism 2017
Venice	261	4,280[b]	1:16.3	Citta di Venezia 2014
Paris	2,220	15,468[b]	1:7.0	Office du Tourisme et des Congrès 2017
Grand Paris	6,800	22,177	1:3.3	Office du Tourisme et des Congrès 2017
Croatia	4,190	14,500[c]	1:3.4	Ministry of Tourism 2016, Euromonitor 2017
Florence	379	3,702	1:9.8	HVS - Provincia di Firenze 2017
Malta	436	1,966[a]	1:4.5	UNWTO/World Bank 2017

Source: Compilation by authors; referring to year: a. 2016, b. 2014, c. 2017.

Crowding is perceived as a problem in Norway, a country mostly renowned for its vast landscapes and a tourism product largely based on associations of remoteness and 'solitude'. Between 2010 and 2016, commercial overnight stays grew from 28.5 million to 33.1 million (Innovation Norway, 2017), while the cruise sector saw passenger numbers increase from 0.41 million in 2010 to 0.66 million in 2015. With arrivals concentrated in summer and focused on a limited number of popular sites, debates on crowding have become more prominent. These have mostly emerged in the context of day visitors arriving on cruise ships, dividing locals over the desirability of cruises (Brennpunkt, 2017; Travel News, 2017), as well as at the most popular sites, where large tourist numbers accumulate. This includes several Fjords, specifically Naeroyfjord and Geiranger Fjord, as well as popular sites, such as Trolltunga, Trollstigen, or Preikestolen. Notably, these are also sites receiving high rankings by TripAdvisor, and self-reinforcing processes of recommendations and high visitation rates may here result in 'overtourism'. As an example, a tourist on the 'Norway in a Nutshell' package describes his experiences during a tour to some of the most 'significant' sites in the country, using the platform TripAdvisor:

> "[...] on arrival at our final railway station there were not enough buses to take us to our "fiord cruise". [...] There were at least five full buses unloading passengers (so probably in excess of 300 people) onto a RoRo car ferry that was probably built to take 12 to 15 cars. Everybody was directed upstairs to the passenger lounge which was already full to bursting, being meant for probably no more than 50 people. We ended up spending the whole trip to Flam standing on a very empty and very wet car deck, missing most of the highlights of the fiord because we couldn't see over the sides of the ferry" (TripAdvisor, 2015).

Given the growing importance of traveller opinion, online reputation change is another aspect of overtourism if which destinations need to be aware. Crowding effects have also gained attention in more rural spots, where high visitor numbers have been attributed to a 'Frozen effect', i.e. growing interest in Norwegian landscapes as a result of the Disney movie, released in 2013. In order to counter these trends, Norway has already pursued campaigns to market different parts of the country as year-round destinations (Fjord Norway, 2016). Data from Innovation Norway (2017) suggests, however, that the summer remains the most popular time to visit, with 65% of the new growth between 2015 and 2016 occurring in the warmest months, and hence adding to already high summer tourist numbers.

Optimisation and activities

An alternative to the maximisation of tourist numbers is optimisation, which is, in the context of this article, defined as any destination management strategy that seeks to stabilise – or even reduce

– tourist numbers and to increase yield (value) through other mechanisms, such as new spending opportunities. Research that can be characterised as optimisation related has sought to identify markets that are more profitable (Weaver & Oppermann, 2000), more economically stable (Schiff & Becken, 2011), longer LOS (Alén et al., 2014), incurring a lower carbon cost (Gössling et al., 2015), or having favourable price perceptions and an interest in staying longer or visiting during another season (Gössling et al., 2016). All of these approaches to optimisation are essentially market seg-mentation exercises (Dolnicar, 2014), with the difference that optimisation would explicitly seek to increase financial returns while maintaining or even decreasing international arrival numbers.

Research in Sweden confirms that tourist spending is not necessarily constrained, with 45–90% of visitors from diverse countries reporting flexible, i.e. not principally limited, holiday budgets (Gössling et al., 2016). This is of particular relevance in the Scandinavian context, as Denmark, Iceland, Sweden, and Norway all represent high-value destinations, attracting wealthier visitor segments. Analysis for Sweden suggests, however, that within nationalities, specifically advantageous markets may be identified, based on favourable price perceptions, budgetary resources, and an expressed willingness to increase LOS (Gössling et al., 2016). In particular the latter may be of importance, as it has been linked to various destination challenges, such as shorter term tourists focusing their visits on the main attractions; or capacity limits at airports, with Norway requiring almost nine times as many international arrivals as Martinique to generate the same number of guest nights, a result of the island's significantly longer average LOS (Gössling, Scott, & Hall, 2019). Where destinations can induce tourists to stay longer, they are likely to be able to sell additional activities or to reduce operational costs in the destination (e.g. room cleaning). Despite some evidence showing that shorter stays can result in higher spending per day (Alegre & Pou, 2006; Barros & Machado, 2010; Thrane & Farstad, 2012), encouraging lon-ger stays may positively influence distribution across the destination – i.e. tourists visiting more peripheral attractions or regions and have positive effects for climate change mitigation, given that fewer arrivals ultimately reduces emissions associated with transportation.

Activities – i.e. any experience related to organised tours, cultural visits, or outdoors – may thus have the potential to contribute to an interest in staying longer and, vice versa, longer stays are likely to increase the interest in experience consumption. Destinations should ensure that offers are sustainable, for instance with regard to energy use or other environmental impacts, to safeguard against greater activity participation leading to increased negative externalities.

Methodology

To understand tourists' spending patterns, LOS, as well as their interest in activities, a survey of inter-national leisure tourists was conducted in south-western Norway. The region comprises the counties Sogn og Fjordane, Hordaland, and Rogaland, with a population of about 1.1 million (SSB, 2017) and is internationally branded as 'Fjord Norway'. In 2011, the last year for which data are available, the region was visited by ~970,000 international tourists during the summer (June–August). The most important markets include Germany, the Netherlands, France, Denmark, Sweden, the United States, and the United Kingdom. Summer leisure tourists spend on average 11.9 nights in Norway and 6.7 nights out of this in south-western Norway (Dybedal, 2014). 'Activities' in Norway include a wide range of offers, usually nature-based or cultural, and organised by small and medium-sized enterprises.

Data were collected between 25 May and 15 September 2016, over 153 data collection days. Tourists were interviewed by a company specialising in surveys, Faktum Analyse AS. Questionnaires were administered to tourists in English and German, to adequately capture arriv-als by different transport modes. No language issues were encountered by visitors of other nationalities in completing the questionnaire. Interviews were carried out in six locations includ-ing the airport in Bergen, the ferry terminals in Kristiansand, Hella, and Lavik, as well as the centre of Bergen. This non-probability sampling technique was employed because no specific probability structure was expected, though varying survey days across weeks was adopted to reduce potential sampling bias (temporally stratified sampling; Hurst, 1994). Sampling also covered two central exit points from the area that is, passengers waiting for departure at Bergen airport (38 days, response rate 43%) and Kristiansand seaport (16 days, response rate 66%). To cover visitors exiting in the northern part of the region, questionnaires were handed out to travellers waiting for departure at Hella (29 days, response rate 70%) and Lavik (15 days, response rate 58%). These are two ferry terminals at Sognefjord. A screening question confirmed that respondents were leisure travellers who did not reside in Norway. As the Kristiansand seaport is outside the study region, an additional screening question was used there to identity passengers who had visited the counties Sogn og Fjordane, Hordaland, and/or Rogaland. Hence, a combination of an *in situ* and *en route* approach was used. In addition to these locations, questionnaires were randomly distributed to foreign vacationers in Bergen city centre (55 days, response rate 45%).

Response rates varied between 43 and 70%, in line with airport exit surveys (Rideng & Christensen, 2004), and interviews typically lasted between 10 and 15 minutes. In total, 5,249 questionnaires were completed and returned to the interviewers. Questions addressed perceived expensiveness of the country (Likert 1–10, with 10 representing a very expensive destination), LOS, participation, and potential interest in 33 types of activities, spending and expenses, as well as the type of accommodation used, information behaviour (e.g. use of TripAdvisor), holiday budgets, gender, age, income, and country of residence. Activity types were based on the official distinction used by Fjord Norway, with travellers reporting on the type of activity they participated in, and not the frequency of participation. To visit three museums would consequently be counted as one activity. 'Intention to participate in activities' consequently refers to those activities travellers had not actually participated in.

Table 2 shows the distribution of respondents by gender, age, and nationality, indicating that about half of the respondents are male (50.4%) and female (49.6%). The age distribution includes in particular a large share (24.2%) of younger tourists (25–34 years old). Other age brackets are evenly distributed. Nationalities include, in particular, Germans (26.3%), British (11.0%), and US citizens (10.7%). Note that the nationality distribution in the survey cannot be compared to national arrival statistics, as this survey focuses on leisure tourists, while national data include leisure and business travellers.

With regard to spending, 2,557 (48.7%) of respondents reported their expenditures in Norwegian Crowns (NOK) or national currencies, as well as personal net incomes and the number of days spent travelling. Where national currencies were reported, currency tables by the Bank of Norway were used to calculate NOK. In this article, values are provided in Euro to allow for comparison in a more widely established currency (1 NOK: 0.10575 Euro; November 2017).

Data analysis focused on the identification of markets with a potential to increase participation in activities. Spending outliers (NOK >200,000/trip; $n = 11$) were removed from all analyses. Means between groups of tourists were tested with t-tests for a wide range of parameters, including spending and income by nationality and accommodation type, price perceptions, participation in activities during the stay as well as per day (by nationality and accommodation type), as well as expressed interest in (further) participation in activities and nationality. Correlations were tested between some of the variables. Where these were found to be significant, results are reported. The analysis also derived spending per activity type, to allow conclusions regarding the activities that can make the most significant contributions to increase spending. Results are presented in the following sections and discussed with regard to their relevance for crowding/overtourism, as well as destination planning and marketing under scenarios of climate and global socioeconomic change. As a limitation, the article does not discuss where money was spent or by whom. Norway is a country with a more even distribution in incomes, however, where economic growth benefits large parts of society.

Various limitations characterise the survey. First of all, the questionnaire does not distinguish the proportion of money spent on transport. This is of importance, as local revenue is of interest

Table 2. Sample demographics.

	#	%
Gender		
Male	2 555	50.4
Female	2 516	49.6
Total	5 061	100.0
Age		
–18	196	3.9
19–24	722	14.3
25–34	1 221	24.2
35–44	722	14.3
45–54	844	16.7
55–64	777	15.4
65–	563	11.2
Total	5 045	100.0
Nationality		
Sweden	136	2.6
Denmark	202	3.8
Finland	17	0.3
Netherlands	378	7.1
France	235	4.4
Spain	200	3.8
Italy	195	3.7
Germany	1 389	26.3
Switzerland/Austria	227	4.3
UK	581	11.0
Ireland	8	0.2
Eastern Europe	188	3.6
Other countries in Europe	191	3.6
US	567	10.7
Asia	327	6.2
Other countries	408	7.7
Total	5 249	100.0

in the context of optimisation approaches as discussed in this article. Yet, this survey focused on overall spending to increase response numbers as well as the reliability of answers. This raises the question as to whether spending by some nationalities contains a higher share of transport-related cost. Another dataset for Sweden distinguishing transport cost shares (Gössling et al., 2016; $n = 1,914$) was analysed to determine the relevance of these effects. It indicates that the cost of transportation varies between 8% and 21% for the 14 countries studied (transport cost share per day of stay; for countries with a sample size of $n > 20$). There is no indication that this share is higher for long-haul visitors, apparently because they tend to stay longer. For instance, the transport cost share is 10% for Chinese and 16% for Australians, and 18% for Austrians and 21% for British visitors. For Finland it is 8% and for Poland 9%. This suggests that transportation cost can only explain about 10% of spending differences between countries.

A second limitation is that tourists were asked about their LOS in Norway. In particular long-haul tourists may visit several international destinations during one trip (Gössling et al., 2019), which could cause bias. While this cannot be ruled out, tourists may rather have chosen not to answer the question, which clearly referred to the cost associated with the trip to Norway. The fact that more than half of all tourists did not answer the question on the cost of the trip would seem to confirm that those who were uncertain about this aspect chose to pass the question.

Prospects and potential strategies for optimisation: Insights from Norway

Current spending and price perceptions

Revenue generation is a key performance indicator for tourism destinations. The survey consequently investigated spending patterns as well as price perceptions among tourists. Spending is of relevance to determine the relative amount of money introduced in the Norwegian economy by visitors, while price perceptions are an indicator of resilience. Where countries are perceived as too expensive, this may deter visitation, particularly in a situation of economic downturn.

Figure 1 illustrates spending by tourist nationality, as an indicator of the overall contribution made by these groups to revenue generation, and in relation to income levels. US travellers (M = €3,782) were found to spend the most per person per trip, followed by travellers from Switzerland/Austria (M = €3,043), i.e. for these groups spending was significantly higher ($p < 0.05$) than for all other nationalities. Together with tourists from Italy, France, The Netherlands, Asia, and these nationalities are the highest spenders. Reported income data show that high spending is not necessarily related to income, with for instance Irish tourists reporting the third highest income and the third lowest spending levels. In particular visitors from Asia and the USA are disproportionately wealthy, reporting net annual personal incomes averaging €105,000 and €120,500, respectively (Figure 2). This is considerably higher than the survey average of €59,000, which already represents a very high value. The European Union reports that the EU28 median net income is €16,500 (in 2016; Eurostat, 2017). Only visitors from Eastern Europe reported income levels close to European averages (€18,200). Tourists in south-western Norway, with three to four times the average European Union net income, consequently belong to a very wealthy share of global society.

Overall spending patterns are confirmed in the analysis of per person per day spending patterns (Figure 2). US-residents, Asian, and Italian visitors spend the most per day, up to €214 per person ($p < 0.01$; USA). Spending per day consequently shows a difference of almost a factor four between nationalities, with the lowest spenders being Danes at €79. High spending per day was also found to be significant for Asian tourists (M = €192, $p < 0.01$), as well as visitors from Italy (M = €161; $p < 0.05$). These results are largely aligned with earlier spending studies in Norway.

Figure 3 shows spending patterns by accommodation type, indicating that tourists staying in hotels deliver more money in the economy than those using AirBnB services, bed and breakfast, or private accommodation. More specifically, results indicate that hotel guests spend €187 per person per day ($p < 0.01$), 40% more than those staying in AirBnB accommodation (M = €126, $p < 0.01$). Findings also indicate that first time visitors spend significantly more than repeat visitors ($M_{first\ time} = €132$; $M_{repeat} = €104$, $p < 0.01$). Results were also controlled for use of TripAdvisor, showing that tourists using TripAdvisor spent significantly more than others ($M_{TripAdvisor} = €162$; $M_{nonTripAdvisor} = €114$; $p < 0.01$).

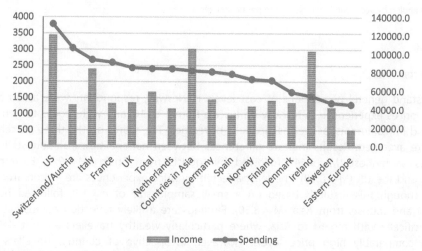

Figure 1. Total spending in relation to income, by nationality (in Euro).

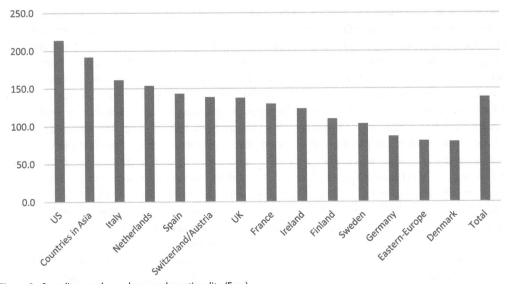

Figure 2. Spending per day and person, by nationality (Euro).

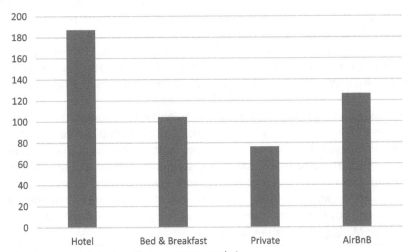

Figure 3. Spending by accommodation type (Euro per person per day).

Price perceptions

To understand general perceptions of cost levels in Norway, respondents were asked how they rated the prices experienced in Norway on a scale from 1 to 10, and with regard to general price levels, food in restaurants, as well as alcoholic beverages. The scores on the three perceived price items were averaged. Results indicate differences between nationalities, Irish tourists experiencing prices as highest (M = 9.44), followed by tourists from Spain (M = 9.0), Eastern Europe (M = 9.0), and the UK (M = 8.98). The least affected by price experiences are visitors from Finland (M = 8.0; though this result is based on a small sample size of $n = 17$), followed by Swedes (M = 8.28) and tourists from Asia (M = 8.50). Findings are a likely reflection on market composition, specifically with regard to Asia, where particularly wealthy travellers are not deterred by Norway's comparably high price levels. However, irrespective of country, travellers consider Norway's price levels as high.

No significant differences in price perceptions were found between holiday types, i.e. cruise, visiting friends and relatives, sports, nature-experiences, adventure holidays, sun & sea, or countryside stays. Analysis, however, reveals that tourists booked on packages perceive prices as lower than the average tourist ($M_{packages} = 8.61$; $M_{individuals} = 8.75$, $p < 0.01$), a likely outcome of pre-payments and a comparably low cost within the country. For package tourists, there is a negative correlation between their actual and their expected spending ($r = -0.08$, $p < 001$). However, there is a positive correlation for visitors who planned and organised their trip individually between their actual and expected spending ($r = 0.08$, $p < 0.01$). A possible conclusion is that it may be easier to market additional offers, also in the form of activities, to package holidaymakers, and in the country. This may require co-operation with travel agents and tour guides, as such spontaneously booked activities may require a degree of flexibility on the side of these tourists.

Activities

Activities are at the core of this analysis, as they have considerable importance for local spending, because money is more often directly injected in the local economy. This hypothesis is supported by the data set, as a significant relationship was found between activities and total spending ($r = 0.04$, $p < 0.05$). Activities may also be organised by smaller companies, with comparably large employment-generating potential. On average, tourists had engaged in 3.72 activities during the 6.7 days of their stay. However, about one third (30.9%) had not participated in any activities at all, while there is a statistically significant, but very small difference in perceptions of expensiveness between those participating and not participating in activities ($M_{ParticpateInActivities} = 8.76$; $M_{Nonparticipants} = 8.66$, $p < 0.01$). Hence, nonparticipation in activities cannot be explained with price perceptions. Further insights can be derived from the analysis of nationality to trip participation ratios (Figure 4). Results indicate considerable differences, with tourists from Eastern Europe ($M = 4.73$), Ireland ($M = 4.63$), Switzerland/Austria ($M = 4.29$), and Spain (=4.28) participating disproportionally often in activities (all significant higher than the average; $p < 0.05$). In comparison, tourists from Denmark ($M = 2.97$), Sweden ($M = 2.54$), and Finland ($M = 1.94$), as well as Asian tourists ($M = 3.00$) were the least interested in activities (all significant lower mean than other tourists, $p < 0.01$). These results are largely identical if measured on a relative basis, i.e. if measured as activities per day (see Figure 5). Again, Irish, and East-European tourists are the most active at 0.65 activities per day, compared to, e.g. 0.2 activities per day for visitors from Finland. Given earlier findings regarding price perceptions, there

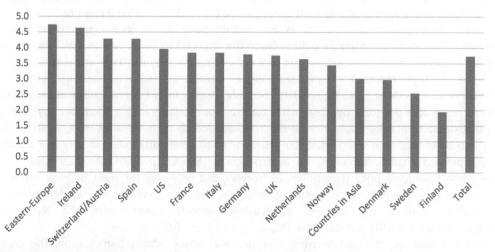

Figure 4. Total number of activities by nationality.

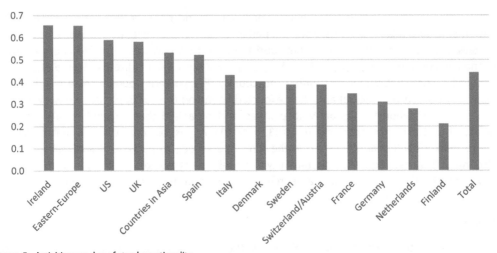

Figure 5. Activities per day of stay by nationality.

appears to be some evidence that the tourists experiencing prices as highest are also those that are participating in most activities. Activity-participation may thus contribute to an understanding that Norway is expensive.

Analysis of activity groups reveals only small and nonsignificant differences. One potentially relevant finding is that cyclists and hikers experienced Norway as more expensive than other tourists ($M_{cyclists} = 8.87$; $M_{hikers} = 8.79$, $p < 0.05$). These are the main groups targeted by DMOs to develop new and potentially more sustainable tourism products in south-western Norway. Culturally interested tourists (architecture, culture, museums), another potentially more sustainable group of tourists, also experienced prices higher than others ($M_{architecture} = 8.83$, $M_{culture} = 8.83$, $M_{museums} = 8.79$, all with a significant higher mean than other tourists at $p < 0.05$). However, as differences are small, price experiences in these segments does not necessarily make these tourists less relevant for Norway.

Activity levels were also investigated in relation to accommodation choices. For instance, it has been speculated that travellers staying in comparably cheap accommodation, such as pensions or AirBnB, will spend more money locally. While no statistically significant correlations were identified to support such a hypothesis, AirBnB guests were found to participate in more activities than other visitors ($M = 0.62$ activities per day, $p < 0.01$; compared to the average of $M = 0.44$). Campers were found to be the least active ($M = 0.32$, $p < 0.01$) (Figure 6).

Finally, an important question is as to whether participation levels in activities can be increased. Data show considerable differences in the *intention* to participate in activities, depending on country (Figure 7). Tourists from Finland ($M_{Finland} = 6.05$, $p < 0.01$) and Eastern Europe ($M = 5.38$, $p < 0.01$) reported a significantly higher interest in (additional) activity participation than other tourists ($M_{Others} = 3.94$, $p < 0.01$). Notably, visitors from Eastern Europe already participate in many activities (0.65 per day), while tourists from Finland are not (0.28 per day), indicating that desirable activity levels may be different, depending on nationality. Here, Asian markets may also be of interest – while Asian tourists reported to have participated in very few activities, they expressed a considerable interest in experiences ($M = 4.6$; $p < 0.01$). As these visitors also have more favourable price perceptions of Norway, but only stay for short periods, marketing may have to make activity opportunities more visible, also with a view to increase length-of-stay. Nationalities with a low interest in activities include visitors from the Netherlands ($M_{activities} = 2.94$, $p < 0.01$) and Denmark ($M_{activities} = 3.13$, $p < 0.05$).

Figure 8 illustrates the gap between intended and actual activity participation. The greater the negative value, the greater is participation intention in comparison to actual participation.

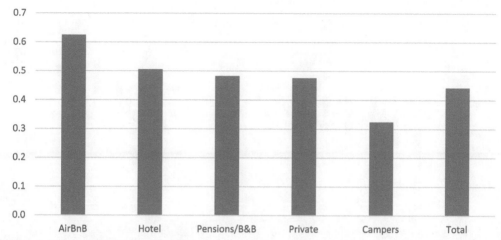

Figure 6. Activity per day by type of accommodation.

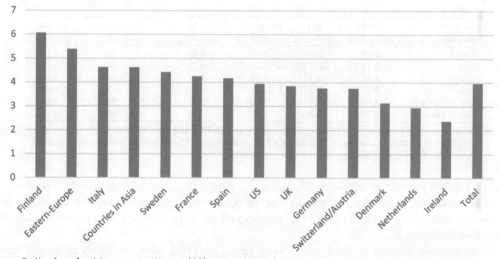

Figure 7. Number of activity types tourists would like to participate in.

A positive values indicate that tourists already participate in high activity numbers compared to their intention to participate in further activities. Especially, tourists from the Nordic countries (Finland, Sweden, and Norway) tend to have higher intentions than actual participation rates for activities. In contrast, tourists from Ireland, Netherlands, Switzerland/Austria already participate in high numbers of activities, with limited interest in further participation.

Yet another group of interest for the marketing of activities are AirBnB guests, who reported a significantly higher intention to participate in activities than other tourists ($M_{AirBnB} = 5.32$; $M_{others} = 3.85$, $p < 0.01$), while hotel guests ($M_{HotelGuests} = 3.17$; $M_{others} = 4.28$, $p < 0.01$) reported low intentions. Notably, AirBnB guests also reported to have spent less money than planned, even though they already participate in higher activity numbers than other tourists. They consequently need to be considered a suitable group for marketing efforts in the context of activities, even though their price perceptions are less favourable, as are their overall spending patterns (Table 3). As AirBnB interferes with the residential housing market, the desirability of AirBnB guests will depend on the organisation of this platform, i.e. whether cities allow year-round rentals, or whether homes can only be made available temporarily, i.e. when permanent residents stay elsewhere. Notably, all tourists using the Internet to find information reported a significantly

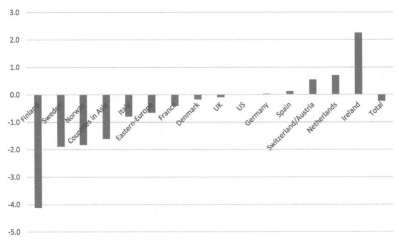

Figure 8. Differences between actual number and intended number of activities.

Table 3. Markets identified as suitable for the marketing of activities.

Segment for marketing	Price perception[a]	Net income (€)[b]	Length of stay[c]	Activities, # per day[d]	Spending per day (€)[e]	Activity intention[f]
AirBnB	8.77	49,183	8.60	0.62	126	5.32
Asia	8.49	104,687	8.07	0.53	192	4.61
USA	8.55	120,517	8.61	0.59	214	3.94
Italy	8.58	83,767	10.21	0.43	161	4.63
The Netherlands	8.78	40,974	15.20	0.28	154	2.94
Survey average	*8.73*	*58,942*	*11.00*	*0.44*	*139*	*3.95*

Note: a: measured on a scale 1–10, where 1 is very cheap and 10 is very expensive; b: Annual net income. c: Number of days in Norway. d: Number of activities per day. e: Total spending per day and person; f: number of activities considered attractive for participation.

higher level of interest in activities ($M_{InternetTourists} = 4.09$; $M_{others} = 3.37$, $p < 0.01$). This, then, is another important insight for destination marketers, as they need to identify the channels used to identify activities, specifically in light of ongoing efforts to develop a Norway-specific platform for activities (Figure 9).

In comparison, tourists booked on package tours, who had been identified as having more favourable price perceptions of Norway, are considerably less interested in activities ($M_{PackageTourist} = 2.64$; $M_{others} = 4.26$, $p < 0.01$). A significantly lower interest in participation in activities was also expressed by repeat visitors in comparison to first time visitors ($M_{RepeatVisitors} = 3.51$; $M_{FirstTimeVisitors} = 4.12$; $p < 0.01$). These findings are validated against their actual participation in activities ($M_{RepeatVisitors} = 3.56$; $M_{FirstTimeVisitors} = 3.79$; $p < 0.01$). These latter findings are of importance because they indicate that a potential return visit may not be the best opportunity to market activities. Rather, it seems important that first time visitors become aware of the spectrum of opportunities, or that activities are marketed pro-actively. More knowledge is needed regarding the timing of booking activities, however.

In summary, the survey results were analysed on the basis of the assumption that activities are best suited to make a contribution to increasing LOS, to increase spending, to stimulate local economic development and hence to create employment. Results were framed against various parameters of relevance, including price perceptions, lower than expected spending, and interest in activities. These were again tested against nationality, holiday type, and accommodation choice. Results would support that AirBnB guests, two long-haul markets (Asia, USA), as well as two European markets (The Netherlands, Italy) may be the most relevant for the marketing of activities. This does not further distinguish the characteristics of the specific activities consumed by these tourist groups, an issue that should be considered in the future research.

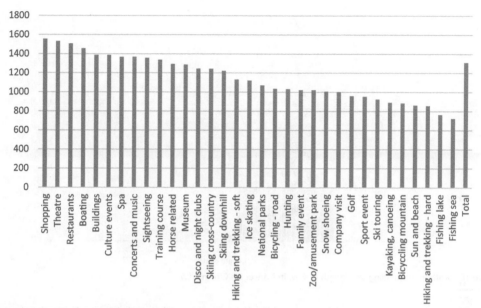

Figure 9. Spending per day for different activities, in Norwegian Crowns.

Furthermore, a number of caveats need to be considered. First, visitors from The Netherlands are high spenders in terms of overall trip expenditure, but they expressed very limited interest in activities. It remains unclear whether pro-active marketing could convince Dutch visitors to spend more on activities, particularly since these visitors already have unfavourable price perceptions. On the other hand, AirBnB visitors are low spenders overall, also with unfavourable price perceptions, while they participate in many activities and expressed a strong intention to participate in more activities. This is of relevance given that this group reports to have spent less for the holiday than planned. Asian and Italian visitors also expressed considerable interest in activities, with Italians currently participating in fewer activities than the survey average. Here, it may be considered if language issues are a barrier to participation. US visitors are characterised by high incomes and favourable price perceptions, but only an average interest in additional activities.

These results provide many opportunities for DMOs to develop their product base. Two additional factors may be considered: Spending for different activities was found to vary, with some activities yielding considerably lower spending levels than others (Figure 10). In the future, price optimisation of activities and their relative relevance for revenue generation may also be considered by DMOs, in consideration of tourist demand.

Discussion

This research studied a large sample of international leisure tourists with regard to price perceptions, net income, LOS, activities per day, spending per day, and activity intention.

This study suggests that it is advisable to focus on the development of specific segmented markets to optimise the Norwegian tourism system, i.e. those with more favourable price perceptions, high net incomes (as a proxy for spending options and market stability), high spending per day, greater LOS, and activity intention. These markets should make a greater contribution to destination development than others, though this may also involve trade-offs. Visitors from Asia and the USA (long-haul markets) as well as Italy (short-haul markets) were found to spend more on average, have significantly higher incomes, and more favourable price perceptions than the average tourist (Table 3). They also show greater interest in activity participation (Asia and

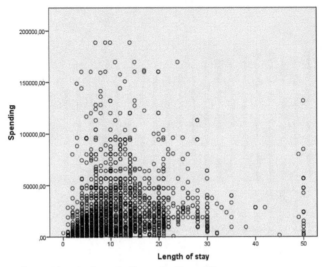

Figure 10. Scatterplot spending and length of stay, in Norwegian Crowns/day.

Italy). Hence, it may be advisable to develop these markets. Visitors from the Netherlands could be another favourable market segment. They have lower net incomes, more negative price perceptions, and less favourable activity intentions, but they stay for significantly longer periods than other guests, and it may be possible to increase these visitors' interest in activities. Trade-offs involve the carbon cost of each tourist. Visitors from Asia and the USA will travel far greater distances, and their contribution to climate change is greater. Increasing their LOS can help reduce carbon footprints per day in Norway. Currently, these markets stay for significantly shorter periods in Norway, possibly as a result of multiple destination visits.

This raises the question as to whether it is possible, and advisable, to increase LOS. As Barros and Machado (2010, p. 702) highlighted, 'high-spending tourists stay for shorter lengths of time', while Grigolon, Borgers, Kemperman, and Timmermans (2014, p. 166) affirmed that '[...] in general, longer lengths of stay are at first sight responsible for higher profits (i.e. regarding tourist accommodations), but shorter lengths of stay allow an increased number of tourists to visit a destination and make a larger contribution to tourism revenues, especially in the higher seasons'. These conclusions do not adequately capture the complexity of LOS. To illustrate this, LOS was analysed with regard to reported spending (Figure 10). As the figure illustrates, there appears to be an increase in spending over time up to a certain point, the median split of the sample, which is 10 days, where it is possible to distinguish between visitors staying for this period of time as well as those staying longer. Correlation analysis between total spending and LOS does show unique patterns for the two groups, though both correlations are weak. While the correlation between LOS and total spending is positive and significant ($r = 0.21$, $p < 0.01$) for the shorter stay visitor group, it is close to zero and not significant in the longer-time visitor group ($r = 0.04$, $p > 0.10$). Hence, the economic contribution by visitors staying for longer periods is not necessarily determined, indicating opportunities for optimisation.

More generally, market segmentation to capture shorter staying, high spending *vis-a-vis* long-staying, moderate spending visitors (*sensu* Grigolon et al., 2014) is not a question of 'either/or', unless all accommodation is booked at capacity. Hence, increasing the average number of guest nights may be viable for most destinations during most of the year. Moreover, even for longer staying guests, there may be opportunities to increase spending. In the specific case of Norway, all four 'recommended' markets, i.e. Asia, USA, Italy, and The Netherlands spend more per day than the average tourist. If LOS was extended for visitors from Asia, USA, and Italy, average spending per day may decline. Yet, as the Dutch market illustrates, longer staying guests can still spend more than the average tourist. It should also be noted that AirBnB guests, who stay almost two and a half days shorter than the average tourist, spend *less* per day than the average visitor. Last, shorter stays incur a cost that should be considered. For instance, more arrivals require additional transport infrastructure, which is usually subsidised (Gössling, Fichert, & Forsyth, 2017), or additional staff, for instance to handle a greater number of room changes and cleaning. Long-distance visitors, if spending more time in Norway, may shorten their LOS in other destinations, which will be unfavourable for these destinations. However, they may also increase their overall stay or focus their visit exclusively on Norway: These are scenarios warranted from a viewpoint of climate change mitigation.

With regard to the rapidly emerging importance of online platforms, research indicates that AirBnB guests have less favourable price perceptions of south-western Norway, as well as net incomes considerably lower than the average tourist. They also stay for shorter periods and spend less money per day than the average visitor. This finding contradicts claims by some analysts (Jumpshot, 2016; Morgan Stanley, 2017). AirBnB guests are, however, the most frequent consumers of activities on a per day basis, and they are by far the most important visitors in terms of activity intentions (interest in further activities). While a focus on AirBnB guests is thus somewhat ambiguous from a destination viewpoint and should perhaps not be actively pursued in light of problems associated with the business model (e.g. Gutiérrez et al., 2017), it is meaningful to highlight activity opportunities to these travellers. Notably, AirBnB guests reported to have underspent their budgets, and it is thus likely that they be encouraged to engage in more activities. AirBnB guests also spent more per day than tourists staying in bed and breakfast, or private accommodation.

These findings are illustrated in Figure 11, which demonstrates how destination managers may seek to develop various markets with regard to maximisation (more/fewer arrivals) as well as optimisation (marketing of activities). While all markets can be optimised with regard to activity consumption, focus should be placed on sustainable activities that will not increase perceptions of crowding. For instance, nature-based activities can attract travellers that stay longer (recreational fishing: M = 13.60 days; $p < 0.01$) or shorter (hunting: M = 8.40, $p < 0.05$), though both can generate very significant revenue.

Destinations may use these results to more systematically develop markets on the basis of economic benefits, environmental impacts, and market resilience; and in consideration of each market segments' relative importance. This is shown in Table 4, where maximisation and optimisation priorities are specified in the context of market segments and market size. Where the

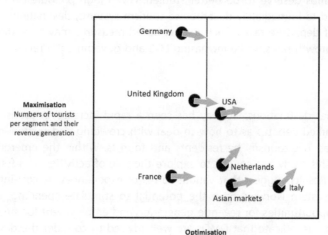

Figure 11. Pathways to optimisation by market.

Table 4. Overview of maximisation versus optimisation attributes.

Market segment	Market size	Maximisation attributes				Optimisation attributes		
		Revenue generation				Revenue distribution		Environmental footprint
		Existing spending	Price perception	Online reputation	Length of stay	Spending by accommodation type	Activity participation	Distance market has to travel

relative size of a market is to change, maximisation attributes related to revenue generation may be considered (existing spending, price perceptions, holiday budgets, LOS), while optimisation attributes may focus on parameters related to revenue distribution (spending by accommodation type, activity participation levels) as well as environmental outcomes (distance market to destination).

Results also support the more general view that 'maximisation' is a concept in need of reconceptualisation in view of 'overtourism', questions of economic distribution, and climate change; all of which demand new approaches to destination management (cf. Dwyer & Kim, 2003; Gössling et al., 2016). Currently, UNWTO (2017) and national DMOs measure and compare 'performance' on the basis of indicators such as the share of global arrivals received, total arrival numbers and arrival growth, tourism employment, sector contribution to GDP, or tourism revenue. In light of challenges related to overtourism and climate change, destinations may rather seek to reduce tourist volumes, and to increase the benefits associated with each arrival, taking account of a broader range of performance criteria. These benefits need to be distributed, generating viable incomes and making a contribution to the circular economy. They need to be generated with environmental footprints that are small, and in line with climate change mitigation goals (ETC, 2018; Scott et al., 2016).

Some recommendations for DMOs may be deduced from the findings. First of all, 'future' indicators for destinations seeking to optimise the tourism system will require a more detailed understanding of tourist spending, interests, and other system characteristics, such as the development of LOS (leisure/business) and/or the carbon intensity of each arrival. Based on such data, destinations will be empowered to better target their marketing efforts at specific markets and segments, to develop new and attractive tourism products, and to reduce emissions from the tourism system. Where crowding is a problem, increasing LOS may represent a solution, though such interrelationships deserve to be better studied. Given high pressure on many destinations, as well as the need to immediately decarbonise tourism systems, destinations may also consider the introduction of departure taxes. Such market-based measures may have the triple advantage of reducing high growth rates, while increasing LOS and governmental revenue (ETC, 2018).

Conclusions

As with many other destinations, Norway has seen a rapid increase in tourist arrivals in recent years. This has sparked debates as to how to deal with crowding and related impacts, in what is widely perceived as 'overtourism' by residents and tourists. Within the emerging critical debate on maximisation, this study has sought to explore the role of activities as a form of tourism system optimisation. Results suggest that various forms of experiences, as cost-intense aspects of a holiday in south-western Norway, have the potential to stimulate spending, with positive side effects including opportunities for revenue generation and employment for small enterprises and in rural areas. Findings indicate that DMOs are well-advised to consider the development of new products in the context of spending and LOS by market. This also has repercussions for online reviews and reputation, with indications that tourists already perceive sites as unacceptably crowded.

In Norway, activity development may appeal to visitors from Asian markets, the USA, Italy and, potentially, The Netherlands in particular. These nationalities have the greatest economic value for Norway as a result of a combination of high relative net incomes, high spending patterns, more favourable price perceptions, or long periods of stay. Italy and The Netherlands have smaller environmental footprints, as a result of more limited amounts of energy needed for transportation. They also stay for longer periods and can thus reduce air transport infrastructure capacity demand. For this reason, any change in marketing should begin with these European markets. In comparison, the development of long-haul markets will increase the energy intensity of the Norwegian tourism system, for which there is little room under international decarbonisation agreements. Travellers who booked through AirBnB, as a specific tourist segment, were found to be less favourable with regard to any of the indicators of optimisation discussed in this article, but they reported the highest interest in activities. Overall, the insights are of considerable importance in terms of generating more stable and valuable tourism systems. They indicate that as destinations evolve, so does the need to consider more complex management approaches. New sets of indicators for DMOs should be developed that more adequately reflect emerging local and global challenges, such as the carbon intensity of tourism systems, as well as emerging issues of overtourism and revenue distribution. Optimisation of tourism systems can make an important contribution in this regard, for which data availability will be a key issue. DMOs are thus advised to more appropriately collect data from tourists, for instance when reservations are made or activities booked, so as to more systematically evaluate these for destination management against criteria for optimisation. They will also need to segment their markets differently and apply appropriate communications to reflect an optimisation strategy.

Disclosure statement

No potential conflict of interest was reported by the authors.

ORCID

Stefan Gössling (iD) http://orcid.org/0000-0003-0505-9207
C. Michael Hall (iD) https://orcid.org/0000-0002-7734-4587
Scott McCabe (iD) http://orcid.org/0000-0002-9807-9321

References

Addis, M., & Holbrook, M. B. (2001). On the conceptual link between mass customisation and experiential consumption: An explosion of subjectivity. *Journal of Consumer Behaviour: An International Research Review, 1*(1), 50–66.
Alegre, J., & Pou, L. (2006). The length of stay in the demand for tourism. *Tourism Management, 27*(6), 1343–1355.
Alén, E., Nicolau, J. L., Losada, N., & Domínguez, T. (2014). Determinant factors of senior tourists' length of stay. *Annals of Tourism Research, 49*, 19–32.
Andereck, K. L., Valentine, K. M., Knopf, R. C., & Vogt, C. A. (2005). Residents' perceptions of community tourism impacts. *Annals of Tourism Research, 32*(4), 1056–1076.
Ap, J. (1992). Residents' perceptions on tourism impacts. *Annals of Tourism Research, 19*(4), 665–690.
Barros, C., & Machado, L. (2010). The length of stay in tourism. *Annals of Tourism Research, 37*(3), 692–706.
Barcelona Tourism (2016). Estadístiques de turisme. Barcelona: Ciutat I entorn. L'Ajuntament de Barcelona, la Diputació de Barcelona i el Consorci Turisme de Barcelona. *Barcelona.* Retrieved from http://www.barcelonaturisme.com/uploads/web/estadistiques/2016OTB2.pdf
Blanke, J., & Chiesa, T. (Eds.) (2013). *The travel & tourism competitiveness report 2013: Reducing barriers to economic growth and job creation.* Davos: Author.
Brennpunkt. (2017). *Shit O'hoi.* Retrieved from https://tv.nrk.no/serie/brennpunkt
Choi, S. C., Mirjafari, A., & Weaver, H. B. (1976). The concept of crowding: A critical review and proposal of an alternative approach. *Environment and Behavior, 8*(3), 345–362.
Croatia Ministry of Tourism (2016). Tourism in Figures 2015. Republic of Croatia.
Dolnicar, S. (2014). Market segmentation approaches in tourism. In S. McCabe (Ed.), *The Routledge handbook of tourism marketing* (pp. 197–208). London: Routledge.
Doxey, G. V. (1975). A causation theory of visitor-resident irritants, methodology and research inferences. The impact of tourism. Sixth Annual Conference Proceedings of the Travel Research Association, San Diego, pp. 195–198.
Dwyer, L., & Kim, C. (2003). Destination competitiveness: Determinants and indicators. *Current Issues in Tourism, 6*(5), 369–414.
Dwyer, L., Pham, T., Forsyth, P., & Spurr, R. (2014). Destination marketing of Australia: Return on investment. *Journal of Travel Research, 53*(3), 281–295.
Dwyer, L., Forsyth, P., & Dwyer, W. (2010). *Tourism economics and policy.* Clevedon: Channel View.
Dwyer, L., Forsyth, P., Fredline, L., Jago, L., Deery, M., & Lundie, S. (2007). Yield measures for Australia's special interest inbound tourism markets. *Tourism Economics, 13*(3), 421–440.
Dybedal, P. (2014). *Profiles of foreign summer season tourism in Western Norway 2011.* Oslo: Institute of Transport Economics.
Emerson, R. M. (1976). Social exchange theory. *Annual Review of Sociology, 2*(1), 335–362.
ETC (European Travel Commission) (2018). *Tourism and climate change mitigation. Embracing the Paris Agreement.* Retrieved from http://www.etc-corporate.org/advocacy-sustainability
Euromonitor 2017. *Top 100 City Destinations Ranking.* Euromonitor International. Retrieved from http://blog.euromonitor.com/2017/01/top-100-city-destination-ranking-2017.pdf
Fjord, N. (2016). *Topp attraksjoner.* Retrieved from www.no.fjordnorway.com
Gössling, S., Hansson, C. B., Hörstmeier, O., & Saggel, S. (2002). Ecological footprint analysis as a tool to assess tourism sustainability. *Ecological Economics, 43*(2-3), 199–211.
Gössling, S., Ring, A., Dwyer, L., Andersson, A.-C., & Hall, C. M. (2016). Optimizing or maximising? A challenge to sustainable tourism. *Journal of Sustainable Tourism, 24*(4), 527–548.
Gössling, S., Scott, D., & Hall, C. M. (2015). Inter-market variability in CO_2 emission-intensities in tourism: Implications for destination marketing and carbon management. *Tourism Management, 46*, 203–212.
Gössling, S., Fichert, F., & Forsyth, P. (2017). Subsidies in aviation. *Sustainability, 9*(8), 1295, http://www.mdpi.com/2071-1050/9/8/1295
Grigolon, A. B., Borgers, A. W. J., Kemperman, A. D. A. M., & Timmermans, H. J. P. (2014). Vacation length choice: A dynamic mixed multinomial logit model. *Tourism Management, 41*(0), 158–167.
Gutiérrez, J., García-Palomares, J. C., Romanillos, G., & Salas-Olmedo, M. H. (2017). The eruption of Airbnb in tourist cities: Comparing spatial patterns of hotels and peer-to-peer accommodation in Barcelona. *Tourism Management, 62*, 278–291.

Guttentag, D. (2015). Airbnb: disruptive innovation and the rise of an informal tourism accommodation sector. *Current Issues in Tourism, 18*(12), 1192–1217.

Hall, C. M. (2008). *Tourism planning* (2nd ed.). Harlow: Pearson.

Hall, C. M. (2009). Degrowing tourism: Décroissance, sustainable consumption and steady-state tourism. *Anatolia, 20*(1), 46–61.

Hall, C. M. (2014). *Tourism and social marketing*. Abingdon: Routledge.

Hawkins, D. E., Chang, B., & Warnes, K. (2009). A comparison of the National Geographic Stewardship Scorecard Ratings by experts and stakeholders for selected World Heritage destinations. *Journal of Sustainable Tourism, 17*(1), 71–90.

Hurst, F. (1994). En route surveys. In J. R. B. Ritchie & C. R. Goeldner (Eds.), *Travel, tourism, and hospitality research* (pp. 453–472). New York, NY: Wiley.

Independent. (2017). *Eight places that hate tourists the most*. Retrieved from http://www.independent.co.uk/travel/news-and-advice/places-hate-tourist-the-most-countries-ban-visitors-venice-thailand-amsterdam-japan-onsen-santorini-a7733136.html

Innovation Norway. (2017). *Key figures for Norwegian travel and tourism 2016*. Retrieved from http://www.innovasjonnorge.no/contentassets/0d32e3231c0a4367a96838ee3bb5b294/key-figrues-2016.pdf

Johnson, D. (2002). Environmentally sustainable cruise tourism: A reality check. *Marine Policy, 26*(4), 261–270.

Jumpshot. (2016). *Airbnb infographic: Who uses Airbnb and why*. Retrieved from https://www.jumpshot.com/airbnb-infographic-who-uses-airbnb-and-why

Lankford, S. V. (1994). Attitudes and perceptions toward tourism and rural regional development. *Journal of Travel Research, 32*(3), 35–43.

Lawton, T. C. (2017). *Cleared for take-off: Structure and strategy in the low fare airline business*. London: Routledge.

McCarthy, J., & Prudham, S. (2004). Neoliberal nature and the nature of neoliberalism. *Geoforum, 35*(3), 275–283.

Mok, C., Slater, B., & Cheung, V. (1991). Residents' attitudes towards tourism in Hong Kong. *International Journal of Hospitality Management, 10*(3), 289–293.

Morgan Stanley (2017). *Surprising Airbnb Adoption Slowdown in US/EU, and What it Means for Hotels and OTAs*. Retrieved from: http://www.fullertreacymoney.com/system/data/files/PDFs/2017/November/16th/ARCOST2017 1023211633_73976052-b8-11e7-863e-cb02ae2926cb_DigitalPremium.pdf

Neuts, B., & Nijkamp, P. (2012). Tourist crowding perception and acceptability in cities: An applied modelling study on Bruges. *Annals of Tourism Research, 39*(4), 2133–2153.

Nyaupane, G. P., & Timothy, D. J. (2010). Power, regionalism and tourism policy in Bhutan. *Annals of Tourism Research, 37*(4), 969–988.

Patterson, M. E., & Hammitt, W. E. (1990). Backcountry encounter norms, actual reported encounters, and their relationship to wilderness solitude. *Journal of Leisure Research, 22*(3), 259–275.

Perdue, R. R., Long, P. T., & Kang, Y. S. (1999). Boomtown tourism and resident quality of life: The marketing of gaming to host community residents. *Journal of Business Research, 44*(3), 165–177.

Popp, M. (2012). Positive and negative urban tourist crowding: Florence, Italy. *Tourism Geographies. An International Journal of Tourism Space, Place and Environment, 14*(1), 50–72.

Ridderstaat, J., Croes, R., & Nijkamp, P. (2016). The tourism development–Quality of life nexus in a small island destination. *Journal of Travel Research, 55*(1), 79–94.

Rideng, A., & Christensen, P. (2004). En route surveys. *Scandinavian Journal of Hospitality and Tourism, 4*(3), 242–258.

Riganti, P., & Nijkamp, P. (2008). Congestion in popular tourist areas: A multi-attribute experimental choice analysis of willingness-to-wait in Amsterdam. *Tourism Economics, 14*(1), 25–44.

Schiff, A., & Becken, S. (2011). Demand elasticity estimates for New Zealand tourism. *Tourism Management, 32*(3), 564–575.

Scott, D., Hall, C. M., & Gössling, S. (2016). A report on the Paris Climate Change Agreement and its implications for tourism: Why we will always have Paris. *Journal of Sustainable Tourism, 24*(7), 933–948.

Sheldon, P. J., & Var, T. (1984). Resident attitudes to tourism in North Wales. *Tourism Management, 5*(1), 40–47.

Skift. (2017). *Summer of overtourism: 4 lessons for the travel industry*. Retrieved from https://skift.com/2017/08/16/summer-of-overtourism-4-lessons-for-the-travel-industry

SSB. (2017). *Folkemengd 1 januar. Heile landet, fylke og kommunar*. Retrieved from https://www.ssb.no/befolkning/statistikker/folkemengde/aar-per-1-januar

Steen Jacobsen, J. K. (2003). *Utenlandske turisters forbruk i Norge sommeren 2002. TØI rapport 636/2003*. Oslo: Transportøkonomisk institutt.

Stewart, W. P., & Cole, D. N. (2001). Number of encounters and experience quality in Grand Canyon backcountry: Consistently negative and weak relationships. *Journal of Leisure Research, 33*(1), 106–120.

Stokols, D. (1972). A social-psychological model of human crowding phenomena. *Journal of the American Planning Association, 38*(2), 72–83.

Telegraph. (2018). *Is Greece on the brink of an overtourism crisis?* Retrieved from https://www.telegraph.co.uk/travel/destinations/europe/greece/articles/greece-overtourism-santorini

Thrane, C., & Farstad, E. (2012). Nationality as a segmentation criterion in tourism research: The case of international tourists' expenditures while on trips in Norway. *Tourism Economics, 18*(1), 203–217.

Travel News. (2017). *Innfører cruise-tak.* Retrieved from http://travelnews.no/nyheter/innforer-cruise-tak/amp

TripAdvisor. (2015). *Norway in a Nutshell from Oslo to Bergen. Review of Fjord Tours.* Retrieved from https://www.tripadvisor.com/ShowUserReviews-g190502-d1173124-r277589280-Fjord_Tours-Bergen_Hordaland_Western_Norway.html

Turkle, S. (2015). *Reclaiming conversation.* New York, NY: Basic Books.

Turner, L., & Ash, J. (1975). *The "golden hordes": International tourism and the pleasure periphery.* London: Constable Limited.

UNWTO. (2014). *Why tourism?* Retrieved from http://www2.unwto.org/content/why-tourism

UN World Tourism Organization (UNWTO) (2017). *Yearbook of Tourism Statistics.* Madrid, UNWTO.

Ward, C., & Berno, T. (2011). Beyond social exchange theory: Attitudes toward tourists. *Annals of Tourism Research, 38*(4), 1556–1569.

Weaver, D., & Oppermann, M. (2000). *Tourism management.* New York, NY: John Wiley.

World Economic Forum. (2017). *Wish you weren't here: What can we do about over-tourism?* Retrieved from https://www.weforum.org/agenda/2017/09/what-can-we-do-about-overtourism

World Bank (2017). *Population.* Retrieved from https://data.worldbank.org/indicator/SP.POP.TOTL

Tourism as a right: a "frivolous claim" against degrowth?

Jordi Gascón

ABSTRACT

Social movements and academic sectors gather information on the negative consequences of tourism development. These consequences affect the rights of the local population, and favour global processes such as Climate Change. In light of this situation, numerous voices are calling for a slowdown in the growth of tourism. They are even calling for its degrowth. The strategy of the tourism sector has been to put forward discourses and actions aimed at preventing the application of limitations to its activity. This article focuses on an action promoted by the UNWTO: the aim to turn tourism into a human right. First, the text offers a critical analysis of what this idea is based on and the debate it has generated. It then investigates its motives. The work concludes that by legitimizing tourism as a supposed human right, it would allow the debate to centre on a conflict of rights (the right of the citizen as a tourist against the rights of the citizen as a resident of a territory or as a worker). Because a debate between rights always ends up in stalemate. This way, degrowth proposals in tourism would be neutralized.

Introduction

Degrowth is a trend of political thought that has emerged from social movements and academia close to Political Ecology. Recovering marginal thinkers such as Ivan Illich and Nicholas Georgescu-Roegen, critics of development of the likes of Vandana Shiva and Arturo Escobar, and also partly proposals to limit growth such as those of E.F. Schumacher and the Meadows Report, Degrowth advocates a controlled decrease in economic activity. Economic activity has to be aimed at meeting needs, because growth for growth's sake, as fostered by capitalist economics, consumes the resources of a finite planet. Degrowth has to be accompanied by a fair distribution of wealth to prevent the decrease in economic activity from increasing structural poverty (Latouche, 2006; Taibo, 2009).

The demand for a "socially sustainable economic degrowth" (Martínez-Alier, 2009) has permeated the requirement for sustainability in different economic sectors. The tourism sector, however, appears to be immune to this influence. The academic works that speak of or propose degrowth in tourism are few and far between (cf. Andriotis, 2018; Bourdeau & Berthelot, 2008; Luis Blanco, 2011; Panzer-Krause, 2018; Paquot, 2016). There are even texts, among this scant literature, that consider that Degrowth consists of maintaining the tourism structure while reducing the use of natural and energy services thanks to the improvement of technological efficiency (Hall, 2009, 2011). But it is precisely the statement that the problems of economic unsustainability can be solved by technological improvements that has been criticized by Degrowth (Latouche, 2006; Sempere, 2008). The principal refutation is that increases in efficiency create the Jevons Paradox: the greater the efficiency in the use of a resource, so the price of the resource falls, and this price fall triggers consumption of it that is greater than the savings obtained thanks to the technological improvement (Alcott, Giampietro, Mayumi, & Polimeni, 2012). The case of air travel is an example: as energy efficiency has improved (efficient engines and designs, better air traffic control), so the price has fallen, and this has allowed a sharp increase in the number of flights. In the end, the use of fossil fuel is higher than the energy saving per flight obtained from the technological improvements (Gascón & Ojeda, 2014; Scott, Peeters, & Gössling, 2010; Williams, Noland, Majundar, Toumi, & Ochien, 2007).

However, without speaking strictly of degrowth, in recent decades, the voices calling for the limitation or control of tourism development, and even for a reduction in its volume, have increased. Social conflicts in the area of tourism have multiplied: land expropriation (Aledo, 2008); appalling employment conditions (Cañada, 2015); inflationary processes (Gascón & Cañada, 2016; Mowforth & Munt, 2016); climate change vector (IPCC, 2014). Büscher and Fletcher (2017) state that tourism combines various forms of structural violence. They are increasingly more evident situations that explain the growing anti-tourism (Bourdeau & Berthelot, 2008; Milano, 2018).

This, however, is contradicted by another phenomenon: the desire to travel for leisure has grown among the middle and working classes. The tourism sector knows that it has many growth options. Therefore, its main dilemma is no longer increasing the market in light of the fear of stagnation. Today, its main dilemma is counteracting the voices that are calling for its limitation and even its reduction. Because these demands are no longer limited to social movements and specific academic sectors. They are demands that are beginning to have an influence in the political arena, as shown by the attempts to tax air travel with ecological taxes, and the success of municipal candidates that call for a reduction in the number of visitors and stricter regulation of the tourism sector (Barcelona, Amsterdam, Rome, etc.).

Tourism is a sector that is fed by the continued growth of the activity. Therefore, the calls to reverse this growth affect its corporate interests. What should it do? The strategy of the tourism sector has been to develop discourses and propose actions aimed at preventing the application of limitations to its activity (Milano, 2018). For example, the air transport sector(International Air Transport Association IATA, International Civil Aviation Organization ICAO) claims that it is possible to maintain the growth of air travel while reducing its contribution to climate change to zero, even though there are numerous research projects that show that this is not possible (Gössling & Peeters, 2007; Peeters & Eijgelaar, 2014). Or that the application of self-regulation mechanisms by the tourism business sector (sustainability certificates, corporate social responsibility policies) will enable unsustainable practices to be neutralized, which has also been doubted (Mowforth & Munt, 2016; Wall, 2005). The strategies proposed by the UNWTO to contribute to achieving the Sustainable Development Goals (SDGs), approved by the United Nations in 2015, are significant (UNWTO & UNDP, 2017). The UNWTO's contribution is based on a growth in activity. At no time does it propose its reduction or limitation, even when it may have a negative effect on ecosystems, populations or other economic sectors. Uncritically, tourism always appears as an opportunity for sustainable development that can be made the most of by improving the efficiency of the tourism structure, increasing the skills of its players, or through public subsidies to the business sector "to influence the behaviour of tourism enterprises and financiers" (UNWTO & UNDP, 2017: 66).

One of these strategies is to turn tourism into a right, because if tourism is seen as a right, any policy to reverse its growth loses legitimacy. This article seeks to analyse how tourism came to be conceived of as a right and how the idea has spread and subsequently to scrutinize the interests hidden behind it. The article aims to show that the principal agent defending and disseminating this idea is the UNWTO. However, it does not do so explicitly. As a United Nations agency (an institution guaranteeing Human Rights), this statement would be very risky. This is why the UNWTO does not propose what type of right the right to tourism would be (human or fundamental, collective or individual, social and cultural, or civil, etc.). It leaves it to the good understanding of the listener. However, the use of cryptic language and its status as a United Nations agency allows the insinuation that it refers to human rights. Insinuating without stating is, after all, the strategy of the UNWTO in disseminating the supposed human right to tourism.

This article is based on the analysis of the primary documentation drafted by the agents that take part in the phenomenon, especially the UNWTO. In the first two sections, we will see how the idea arose and examine the academic debate it has generated. The following sections will argue that the designation of tourism as a right seeks to legitimize the role of the UNWTO within the United Nations system and, especially, to defend the interests of the tourism industry, to which the UNWTO is linked. Turning tourism into a human right is a strategy aimed at undermining any policy or any discourse that proposes or calls for reducing tourist activity.

Tourism as a right

For several decades, the World Tourism Organization (UNWTO) has promoted the idea that tourism is a right. This long campaign began in 1980, when the Manila Declaration on World Tourism Document stated:

> Tourism is considered an activity essential to the life of nations (…) and its development is linked to the social and economic development of nations and can only be possible if man has access to creative rest and holidays and enjoys freedom to travel (World Tourism Organization, 1980, p. 1).

This philosophy began to take shape with the UNWTO General Assembly's approval of the Tourism Bill of Rights and Tourist Code (1985). It asserts:

> The right of everyone to rest and leisure periodic leave with pay and freedom of movement without limitation, within the bounds of law, is universally recognized. The exercise of this right constitutes a factor of social balance and enhancement of national and universal awareness (World Tourism Organization, 1985, p. 2).

With the Global Code of Ethics for Tourism in 1999, the idea was finally consolidated. In its debated and cited Article 7, titled "Right to Tourism", this document states:

> The universal right to tourism must be regarded as the corollary of the right to rest and leisure, including reasonable limitation of working hours and periodic holidays with pay, guaranteed by Article 24 of the Universal Declaration of Human Rights and Article 7.d of the International Covenant on Economic, Social and Cultural Rights (World Tourism Organization, 1999, p. 6).

Finally, in September 2017, at the 22nd General Assembly, the UNWTO approved the directives to turn the Code into a Convention, without changing its text (Ruling A/RES/678-XXII). In the words of the UNWTO president, Taleb Rifai, this decision:

> It is also a strong sign that countries are committed to make tourism a force for a better future for all. It reinforces UNWTO's institutional outreach in the UN system (UNWTO, 2017).

Today, the final part of the procedure remains to be completed: the approval of the UNWTO Framework Convention on Tourism Ethics by the United Nations General Assembly. If the General Assembly does not approve it, the Code will become a multilateral treaty, which can be ratified or not by the different countries: they are sovereign to accept it or not. As of that moment, the work of the UNWTO will be to convince countries to sign it. Countries that sign the Convention will have to adapt their legislative system to this treaty.[1]

But what type of right is tourism? The UNWTO does not appear willing to answer this question, at least not formally and explicitly. This is slippery terrain because the organization is an agency of the United Nations, the institution that guarantees the Universal Declaration of Human Rights. Article 7 of the Global Code mentions the universal right to tourism. The United Nations uses the word "universal" in its Universal Declaration of Human Rights, but it does not qualify the rights contained in the Declaration in this manner. Is this wordplay? It would seem that the UNWTO is seeking to confuse. Curiously, the Spanish version of the Global Code translates "universal right to tourism" into the equally confusing "right to tourism for all" ("*derecho al turismo para todos*") (Organización Mundial del Turismo, 1999, p. 6).

The UNWTO avoids explicitly stating that tourism is a human right,[2] but it does insinuate as much. For example, in a brief prologue to a book on social tourism, Taleb Rifari (2011), the secretary general of the UNWTO, alludes to Article 7 and ends by calling for the "Right to Tourism" (note the use of capitalization; in the rest of the prologue, neither "right" nor "tourism" is capitalized this way). The cleverest insinuation, however, is found in Article 7 of the Global Code, which defends tourism as a right based on the Universal Declaration of Human Rights. If the right to tourism is rooted in recognized human rights, it can be intuited that tourism too is considered a human right.

The designation of tourism as a human right has been adopted by many political organizations. In 2013, ministers and top tourism authorities in South America concluded in a meeting in Quito that tourism should be promoted as a human right within international organizations because of its importance and its effects on people and their development (Ministerio de Turismo – Ecuador, 2013). One year later, Uruguay's Chambers of Senators and Representatives implemented legislation declaring tourism to be a human right.[3] Notably, Tourism and Sports Minister Liliam Kechichián stated that this new law, by recognizing tourism as a human right, was "in accordance with what the World Tourism Organization has promoted since 1980" (Presidencia de la República Oriental de Uruguay, 2014). If the UNWTO's objective was to promote tourism as a human right without having to explain its reasons, it has undoubtedly been successful.

In the academic realm as well, tourism as a human right has become a topic of analysis and debate. While some authors deny that it is a human right, others consider it as such.

Breakey and Breakey (2013) sum up the position of the latter camp. These authors believe that designating tourism as a human right is the natural result of Articles 13 and 24 of the Universal Declaration of Human Rights. Article 13 makes reference to the right to freedom of movement, and Article 24 discusses the right to leisure and paid holidays. It has been reiterated that the right to tourism arises from these two human rights (e.g., Moncada Jiménez, Sosa Ferreira, Martínez, Beltrán Pérez, & Domínguez Estrada, 2015), and we will analyse this later. For now, what interests us is that Breakey and Breakey assert that states have a responsibility to uphold tourism as a right. They also believe that public investment in defending the right to tourism will result, as a positive secondary effect, in the promotion of the tourism industry. From a slightly less extreme perspective, McCabe and Diekmann (2015) suggest that one should speak of tourism as a "social right" rather than a "human right", but they also arrive at the conclusion that tourism should be guaranteed in public budgets.[44]

Also defending tourism as a right, but from an entirely different perspective, are authors who focus on the analysis of social tourism (e.g., Hazel, 2005; Minnaert, Maitland, & Miller, 2011). Higgins-Desbiolles is perhaps most representative of this trend. Along the lines of the International Social Tourism Organisation's (ISTO) Montreal Declaration of 1996 (Bélanger & Jolin, 2011), she believes that the right to tourism legitimizes the creation of an institutional social tourism agenda. Unlike Breakey and Breakey, however, she believes that, precisely because tourism is a right, it must be decommodified (Higgins-Desbiolles and Russell-Mundine, 2008). Higgins-Desbiolles (2006, 2011) states that tourism can be an instrument of change, but only if it exists outside of market structures and is designed to satisfy human development needs – that is, considered a public good rather than merchandise. Until this is so, the right to tourism cannot be universally enjoyed.

Critiques

The academic literature disagreeing with the notion of tourism as a general right, and specifically as a human right, raises various concerns, the most common being that no consideration is given to how tourism affects host populations. Bianchi and Stephenson (2013, 2014), and Hernández-Ramírez (2018) states that the right to tourist mobility can limit mobility of the local population as well as the use and enjoyment of their resources (right to tourism vs. right to the city). Simpson and Simpson (2007, 2010) state that Article 7 of the Global Code is contradictory because it prioritizes the (supposed) rights of tourists over those of the local population, and it is not always possible to harmonize these interests.

Kingsbury (2005) refines this reasoning by pointing out that the Global Code presents a democratic approach, claiming that everyone, as a tourist, should be able to enjoy the planet and its resources. However, behind this stated intention lies the objective of putting local resources, which are often scarce, at the disposal of the tourism industry. In this sense, Higgins-Desbiolles and Whyte (2015: 107) state that, although tourism is seen "as a violator of human rights", the discourse regarding human rights and tourism has focused on the rights of tourists and the tourism industry and not on those of local populations. This is what some authors, adapting the concept from Harvey (2003), refer to as accumulation by dispossession in tourism (Benjaminsen & Bryceson, 2012; Blázquez, Cañada, & Murray, 2011; Bojórquez & Villa, 2014). Higgins-Desbiolles and Whyte state that, while the right to tourism is based on the Universal Declaration of Human Rights, its advocates do not appear to consider Article 25.1, which asserts the rights of local populations.

It has been stated that the Global Code seeks to harmonize the right to enjoy tourism with the rights of local societies (Faure & Arsika, 2015). Certainly, it would be erroneous to suggest that the Global Code does not consider the needs of host populations. For example, Article 5.2 states:

Tourism policies should be applied in such a way as to help to raise the standard of living of the populations of the regions visited and meet their needs.

Meanwhile, Article 4.4 states:

Tourism activity should be planned in such a way as to allow traditional cultural products, crafts and folklore to survive and flourish, rather than causing them to degenerate and become standardized.

However, these needs are positioned not as rights but rather as factors to be taken into consideration. Let us examine the use of verbs. Regarding the right to tourism in the aforementioned Article 7, the verb "must" is used, along with the present tense, thereby endorsing its obligatory and established nature. In the more recently cited passages, the verbs are more circumstantial ("should be", "to help", "to plan") and are conjugated in the future simple or the infinitive, suggesting that these objectives are desirable but not guaranteed.

Finally, D'Sa (1999) notes that in many southern countries, tourism is characterized by an insulting socio-economic disparity between tourists and hosts, leading to racism, discrimination, and a disregard for the economic and social rights of the local population. The Global Code does not confront this reality but rather distracts from it, because it does not address the root of the problem: tourism is an industry motivated by profit and does not take into account the social costs of its development.

Another type of critique, in this instance metaphysical in nature, is put forward by Castañeda (2012). This anthropologist states that the consideration of tourism as a human right stems from an ontological confusion in which the tourist is thought of as a concrete type of person. Tourists are human beings, and human beings have rights; thus, tourists have rights. This is undeniable, but this is because of their condition as human beings, not as tourists. "Being a tourist" is a circumstantial state, experienced for a fixed time. Therefore, it is not a human category, such as being indigenous or a woman, and it cannot be the object of specific human rights.

A third type of critique analyses the genesis of tourism as a human right. As we have stated, it arises from a combination of two rights recognized in the Universal Declaration of Human Rights: those expressed in Articles 13 and 24 (Breakey & Breakey, 2013; Castañeda, 2012). Article 13 makes reference to the right to freedom of movement:

1. Everyone has the right to freedom of movement and residence within the borders of each State. 2. Everyone has the right to leave any country, including his own, and to return to his country.

Article 24 alludes to the labour rights obtained after long and costly union struggles to achieve more just working conditions:

Everyone has the right to rest and leisure, including reasonable limitation of working hours and periodic holidays with pay (United Nations, 1948).

Using these two articles as a premise, Aristotelian logic is applied: All human beings have a right to freedom of movement; All human beings have a right to leisure; Therefore, all human beings have a right to tourism (the sum of leisure and mobility).

However, the syllogism is poorly conceived and is, in fact, a sophism. From the point of view of the Aristotelian method, it falls into the "error of precipitated generalization" by considering tourism to be the sum of leisure and mobility. Not all forms of leisure are tourism (for example, a football game among friends), nor do all forms of mobility qualify as tourism (for example, emigration).

The syllogism also suffers from the "questionable premise fallacy". The reasoning is based on a biased reading of the articles of the Universal Declaration that are used as premises. When the Universal Declaration mentions "holidays with pay" in Article 24, it is referring to the right of the worker to continue receiving a salary during vacation periods, not to receive funds for lavish leisure activities (Gascón, 2016).

At this stage, it is necessary to question what interests may be involved in considering tourism a human right. This is an easy question to pose but a difficult one to answer, because the agents that participate in this process generally conceal these interests; the process is illegitimate because behind the assertion of rights lie other objectives that are not altruistic or related to the desire for justice. Therefore, we are forced to take a speculative approach, in the philosophical sense of the term – that is, an interpretation that cannot reach reliable conclusions but that does present reasonable approximations.

Interests (I): legitimize the UNWTO

While the history of the UNWTO can be traced to the interwar period, as a UN agency it is a young institution; it joined in 2003. Since then, it has been a specialized agency of the United Nations Economic and Social Council. One of the United Nations' main objectives is the safeguarding and promotion of human rights (Heyns & Viljoen, 2002; Jessup, 1968). Therefore, membership in the United Nations obliged the UNWTO to consider this aspect.

The UNWTO could address the relationship between human rights and tourism from different perspectives. For example, it could seek to ensure the rights of local populations that are violated by tourism development. There are empirical cases that show that tourism can improve the living conditions of the local population (Carr, Ruhanen, & Whitford, 2016). However, it is also true that often, tourism promotes gentrification; the marginalization of social sectors; increased costs of living; the loss of natural resources; and even other, more direct, forms of violence (Andrews, 2014; Cole, 2014; Gascón & Cañada, 2017; Mowforth & Munt, 2016). Conflicts of this type have increased as the tourism industry has expanded (Cañada, 2013; Gascón, 2012).

The response of the UNWTO to these situations has been scant, null or contradictory. When possible, it avoids these issues. When it does address such issues, it practices a triple strategy. First, it makes general reference to these problems, but without denouncing specific situations in which the rights of local populations have been violated. Second, it fails to expose and analyse the processes that generate these violations of rights. (For example, what is the role of tourism in processes of urban gentrification? When and how does tourism increase inflation?) Third, the UNWTO notes the supposed benefits that tourism generates in the local economy, which counteract the negative effects. This is what Hall (2005) calls boosterism: a simplistic attitude according to which tourism development is good and generates benefits for the local population in a way that is automatic and natural.

As an example, let us take a reference text published by the UNWTO: its *Sustainable Tourism for Development* guide. Its executive summary states:

> Tourism has many characteristics that make it especially valuable as an agent for development. As a crosscutting sector, it stimulates productive capacities from trade and the provision of jobs linked to the tourism value chain. In particular, it thrives on assets, such as the natural environment, a warm climate, rich cultural heritage and plentiful human resources, in which developing countries have a comparative advantage. However, tourism can also be a source of environmental damage and pollution, a heavy user of scarce resources and a cause of negative change in society. For these reasons, it is imperative for it to be well planned and managed, embracing the principles of sustainable tourism, defined as "tourism that takes full account of its current and future economic, social and environmental impacts, addressing the needs of visitors, the industry, the environment and host communities" (UNWTO, 2013b, p. 11).

The text does not deny the negative impacts of tourism. In a document on sustainability, it would be impossible to avoid the issue. However, a) the positive effects are prioritized and considered inherent to tourism development ("**it stimulates** productive capacities from trade and the provision of jobs linked to the tourism value chain"); b) the negative effects are presented as circumstantial consequences that are not inherent to the sector ("tourism **can also** be a source of environmental damage"); and c) the solution consists of improving tourism management rather than limiting or halting the development of tourist activity ("for these reasons, it is imperative for it to be well planned and managed").

Another perspective connecting tourism with human rights is that of the labour conditions of workers in the sector, in terms of compliance with the economic and social rights established by the United Nations in 1966. This is a concerning topic (Cañada, 2015). Studies by another United Nations agency, the International Labour Organization (ILO), affirm that tourism is one of the economic sectors in which labour rights are most frequently violated (International Labour Organization, 2010). On its website, the ILO states:

> (…) the sector has a reputation of poor working conditions due to a number of factors: it is a fragmented industry with a majority of employers small and medium sized enterprises with low union density, and work characterized by low wages and low levels of skill requirements, shift and night work and seasonality (International Labour Organization, 2019).

The Global Code, in Article 9, addresses the issue of labour rights:

> The fundamental rights of salaried and self-employed workers in the tourism industry and related activities should be guaranteed under the supervision of the national and local administrations, both of their States of origin and of the host countries, with particular care given the specific constraints linked in particular to the seasonality of their activity, the global dimension of their industry and the flexibility often required of them by the nature of their work (World Tourism Organization, 1999, p. 6).

Nevertheless, the UNWTO has no campaign or programme of action regarding the quality of work and labour rights. The UNWTO and ILO signed an agreement in 2008 (UNWTO & ILO, 2008a). It established, among other objectives, the coordination of an agenda supporting dignified work and promoting the application of international conventions on labour. The following year, this agreement was ratified in a brief joint declaration (UNWTO & ILO, 2009). However, beyond declarations of good intentions, few results have emerged from this collaboration. Only in 2014 did the agencies jointly edit a guide designed to calculate tourism-based employment (UNWTO & ILO, 2014). This guide complemented an earlier one, which also had statistical objectives (UNWTO & ILO, 2008b). However, these publications merely establish a quantitative instrument to measure employment created by tourism. This is a complex issue, as tourism is a fragmented industry (hospitality, restaurants, transportation, construction, etc.) and thus closely linked to other sectors. Establishing these statistical systems was one of the objectives of the

2008 agreement between the two agencies, and to date, it is the collaboration's only result. The agreements regarding the quality and rights of tourism work have not borne fruit.

It would be false to state that the UNWTO has never proposed a view of human rights focused on the consequences of tourism development on local populations or labour conditions. For example, in 2006 it signed an agreement with the Prince of Wales International Business Leaders Forum, a foundation created by multinational companies to develop a set of human rights principles to be applied in the tourism sector (Hospitalitynet, 2006). However, twelve years later, no document or programme has emerged as a result.

As we have seen, the UNWTO has chosen to connect tourism and human rights issues by considering this leisure activity to be a right. The designation of tourism as a human right or an economic, social and cultural right (ESCR) helps legitimize the role of the UNWTO within the United Nations. However, so too would defending the rights of local populations violated by tourism or establishing programmes to monitor complaints about a lack of compliance with labour rights. The UNWTO's choice is explained by its strong link with the tourism sector; turning tourism into a right favours this sector. To denounce rights violations caused by tourism would do the opposite. It could even force the UNWTO to defend the limitation or degrowth of tourist activity in some destinations or means of transport.

Interests (II): support for the business sector

Several authors have already highlighted the close ties between the tourism industry – especially transnational organizations – and the UNWTO, and the ways these links work in favour of the industry (Bramwell & Lane, 2011; Duterme & Pleumaron, 2006; Hall, 2007; Schilcher, 2007). In the middle part of the last decade, Pleumaron (2006) stated that, although the UNWTO was part of the United Nations, its procedures continued to be anti-democratic and to favour the business sector.

In 2016, the UNWTO had six specialized committees. These advisory committees are designed to make recommendations regarding the management and content of the UNWTO's programmes. Each is composed of public representatives from seven to eleven countries and a representative of the Affiliate Members, which in mid-2015 was the Spanish Institute for Quality Tourism (*Instituto para la Calidad Turística Española* or ICTE). The ICTE is a certification entity for quality systems managed and controlled by the Spanish trade association (*Confederación Española de Hoteles y Alojamientos Turísticos, Asociación Empresarial de Agencias de Viajes Españolas, Asociación de Mayoristas de Viaje Españolas, Federación Española Empresarial de Transporte de Viajeros*, etc.). Also participating were the State Secretariat for Tourism of Spain and several autonomous communities (Instituto para la Calidad Turística Española, 2017). In practically none of these committees do we find labour unions or social organizations that could represent local/host populations. In fact, only in the World Committee on Tourism Ethics is there a union presence. However, even in this case the business presence is greater, with three representatives (UNWTO., 2019).

This over-representation by the business sector on some committees that determine the institutional policies of the UNWTO is explained by the fact that nearly 500 affiliate members of the organization are business associations (travel agencies, the hotel sector, transportation, etc.) or mixed (public-private). (See Table 1).

This situation allows Cheong and Miller (2000) and Hannam (2002) to claim that the UNWTO is an essential player in the institutionalization of tourism. This institutionalization confers legitimacy on supposedly neutral ideas that are derived from ethical codes but that in reality defend the interests of the tourism industry. It is not surprising, then, that the UNWTO's explicit objective is to promote the growth of the sector rather than to regulate o to limit it, which would perhaps be more appropriate for a United Nations agency.

Here we find another motive for considering tourism to be a right: it legitimizes opposition to proposals that limit tourism activity or reduce corporate profits. The UNWTO's policies regarding climate change are one example. We should remember that the responsibility of air transport for the emission of greenhouse gases is, scientifically, increasingly more evident (IPCC, 2014). This is one of the reasons why a limitation or degrowth of tourist activity is being called for. On the one hand, the efforts of the UNWTO are aimed at downplaying the role tourism plays in climate change. On the other hand, it claims that it is possible to reduce tourism's contribution to greenhouse gas emissions by improving technical efficiency, promoting the use of biofuels or applying voluntary mechanisms, such as the purchase of CO_2 emission allowances. However, it always affirms that this reduction is possible without limiting the growth of the air transportation sector or taxing it with environmental fees (UNWTO, 2008, 2009).

This is not the place to analyse whether it is feasible to mitigate the contribution of air transportation to climate change without shrinking the industry or limiting its growth. However, we will state that it is a debated issue and that a substantial portion of the academic literature considers it unfeasible (e.g., Gascón & Ojeda, 2014; Hall et al., 2015; Scott et al., 2010; Stroebel, 2015). What interests us here is how the UNWTO defends the sector and how it uses the designation of tourism as a right to do so.

The document prepared by the UNWTO for the XV United Nations Climate Change Conference in Copenhagen (December 2009) is a good example of this strategy. It begins by defending the importance of the sector:

> Tourism and travel is a vital contributor to the global economy and especially important for many developing countries. Tourism is an effective way of redistributing wealth and a catalyst for gender equality, cultural preservation and nature conservation (UNWTO, 2009, p. 2).

The document accepts that air transportation plays a role in climate change. However, the above paragraph is a declaration of the UNWTO's intentions at the Conference, which have been demonstrated by various authors (e.g., Buades, 2009; Mangalassery, 2012).

> As tourism is so important to poverty reduction and economic development in developing nations, any policies aimed at mitigating and reducing greenhouse gas emissions should be formulated and implemented in a considered way in order not to disadvantage these countries. The transportation sector, so fundamental to tourism, will form a critical aspect of national and international mitigation policy negotiations. UNWTO has called for **preferential treatment for air services** that support the development of tourism in the least developed countries (UNWTO, 2009, p. 2. Emphasis added).

The consideration of tourism as a right legitimizes opposition to any attempt at control or restriction. The document of reference for UNWTO policy regarding climate change is *Climate Change and Tourism: Responding to Global Challenges*, published in 2008. Here, the UNWTO explicitly interconnects climate change, the need to avoid regulatory – o degrowth - measures and the conception of tourism as a right.

Table 1. Affiliate members of the UNWTO in 2016.

Type of affiliate	Number	Percentage
Private businesses and associations, business platforms or foundations	256	52.2%
Public and mixed (public-private) regional/national tourism agencies, companies, associations and institutions	46	9.4%
Town councils and municipal tourism businesses or entities (public and mixed)	24	4.9%
Other mixed entities (public-private)	8	1.6%
Workers' union platforms	2	0.4%
Schools and university or educational foundations	126	25.7%
Other foundations	9	1.8%
Entities difficult to categorize	19	3.9%

Source: "UNWTO Affiliate Members – Directory". Website of the UNWTO (Accessed on 7 June 2016).

Mitigation is thus of particular importance in tourism; however, mitigation policies need to consider a number of dimensions, such as the need to stabilize the global climate, the right of people to rest and recover and leisure, and attaining the United Nations Millennium Development Goals (UNWTO, 2008, p. 34).

When the text mentions "the right of people to rest and recover and leisure", it refers in a footnote to the aforementioned Article 7 of the Global Code.

Conclusion

Philip Alston is a human rights specialist who served as United Nations Special Rapporteur. In the mid-1980s, he published an article titled "Conjuring up New Human Rights: A Proposal for Quality Control". Alston was concerned by the surge in supposed new human rights. One of the proposals he identified and took a negative view of was the UNWTO's attempt to consider tourism a human right. He called this a "frivolous claim" (Alston, 1984, p. 611). For Alston, it was a worrisome occurrence because it trivialized the concept of human rights.

Alston did not detect hidden ambitions behind the proposal. However, the designation of tourism as a right is not ornamental. It has political and economic objectives. In this text, we have analysed two: to legitimize the presence of the UNWTO in the United Nations structure and to defend the interests of the tourism industry in a context where the demand is to limit and even reverse its growth. This second objective is especially important for the issue that concerns us: the consolidation of a supposed right to tourism would permit the counteracting of any call for degrowth of the sector due to its consequences on the rights of the host population or its impact on the global environment. This second objective has or can have consequences. One is equating the supposed rights of tourists with the rights of the local population to their own resources. In Article 4, the Global Code exemplifies this statement:

(...) particular care should be devoted to preserving and upgrading monuments, shrines and museums as well as archaeological and historic sites which **must be widely open to tourist visits**; encouragement **should be** given to public access to privately-owned cultural property and monuments, with respect for the rights of their owners, as well as to religious buildings, without prejudice to normal needs of worship (World Tourism Organization, 1999, p. 5. Emphasis added).

Note, once again, the use of verb tenses. The Global Code uses "must be" to refer to free tourist access to patrimonial goods. When it presents limits to that free access, it uses "should be".

It is an ethical code. In fact, some authors argue that its presentation as an ethical code and not as a law (soft law) aims to facilitate the agreement of a greater number of countries (Faure & Arsika, 2015). Therefore, although it is presented with an imperative tone, it is not an imposition. It is, however, a code that arises from a United Nations agency, and thus it has heightened authority and legitimacy – authority and legitimacy that is used by the business sector and the UNWTO itself in its lobbying policies, to stop any proposal to limit the growth of the sector. It is not an unusual process. Cousin (2008) observes how the "cultural tourism" concept, fostered by the UNESCO (another United Nations agency), although presented as "good tourism", an alternative to mass tourism, in fact serves the same business interests.

The interest in turning tourism into a right lies in that it allows the debate to be side-tracked. The debate would no longer be about whether the negative impacts of tourism should be tackled through technological development and self-regulation measures (the viability of which is disputable) or, by contrast, through institutional intervention and degrowth policies. The debate would become about how to manage the conflict between rights: the right of the citizen as a tourist against the rights of the citizen as a resident of a territory or as a worker; the right of the tourist to travel the planet against the rights aimed at ensuring the resilience of ecosystems. This way, the debate would move from a political "arena" into another of a legal-philosophical nature; and this arena is much less dangerous to the tourism sector. This is partly due to its more reflective and rhetorical nature than a practical one, but especially because when legitimate (we should say "legitimized") rights are opposed, it normally ends up in stalemate. In other words, the calls for the "sustainable degrowth" of tourism would be neutralized.

Disclosure statement

No potential conflict of interest was reported by the author.

Notes

1. In the United Nations General Assembly 2018 sessions period, the UNWTO Framework Convention on Tourism Ethics was not approved. We speak of the Code, and not the Convention, as it has not yet been ratified by this agency at the time this article was written.
2. Human rights are those considered inherent to all human beings, with no distinction whatsoever by race, colour, sex, language, religion, political or any other type of opinion, national or social origin, economic position, birth or any other condition. These rights are interrelated, interdependent and indivisible and are made explicit in the United Nations General Assembly's Universal Declaration of Human Rights.
3. "To the extent that tourism constitutes a human right, the universality of its enjoyment must be ensured, both from the economic point of view and in terms of its infrastructure" (República Oriental del Uruguay – Poder Legislativo, 2014, Art. 3).
4. Social rights aim to manage and correct social inequalities with the intention of protecting people. Labour or migration rights are forms of social rights.

References

Alcott, B., Giampietro, M., Mayumi, K., & Polimeni, J. (2012). *The Jevons paradox and the myth of resource efficiency improvements*. London: Earthscan.

Aledo, A. (2008). De la tierra al suelo: La transformación del paisaje y el nuevo turismo residencial [From the land to the ground: The transformation of the landscape and the new residential tourism]. *Arbor, 184*(729), 99–113.

Alston, P. (1984). Conjuring up new human rights: A proposal for quality control. *The American Journal of International Law, 78*(3), 607–621. doi:10.2307/2202599

Andrews, H., (Ed.). (2014). *Tourism and violence*. Surrey: Ashgate Publishing.

Andriotis, K. (2018). *Degrowth in tourism: Conceptual, theoretical and philosophical issues*. Oxfordshire: CABI.

Bélanger, C. E., & Jolin, L. (2011). The International Organisation of Social Tourism (ISTO) working towards a right to holidays and tourism for all. *Current Issues in Tourism, 14*(5), 475–482. doi:10.1080/13683500.2011.568056

Benjaminsen, T. A., & Bryceson, I. (2012). Conservation, green/blue grabbing and accumulation by dispossession in Tanzania. *Journal of Peasant Studies, 39*(2), 335–355. doi:10.1080/03066150.2012.667405

Bianchi, R., & Stephenson, M. (2014). *Tourism and citizenship: Rights, freedoms and responsibilities in the global order*. London: Routledge.

Bianchi, R. V., & Stephenson, M. L. (2013). Deciphering tourism and citizenship in a globalized world. *Tourism Management, 39*, 10–20. doi:10.1016/j.tourman.2013.03.006

Blázquez, M., Cañada, E., & Murray, I. (2011). Búnker playa-sol: Conflictos derivados de la construcción de enclaves de capital transnacional turístico español en El Caribe y Centroamérica [Beach-Sun Bunker: Conflicts arising from the construction of enclaves of Spanish transnational tourism capital in the Caribbean and Central America]. *Scripta Nova: Revista Electrónica de Geografía y Ciencias Sociales, 15*, 368.

Bojórquez, J., & Villa, M. A. (2014). Expansión turística y acumulación por desposesión: El caso de Cabo San Lucas, Baja California Sur (México) [Tourist expansion and accumulation by dispossession: The case of Cabo San Lucas, Baja California Sur (Mexico)]. *Cuadernos de Geografía: Revista Colombiana de Geografía, 23*(2), 179–202.

Bourdeau, P., & Berthelot, L. (2008). La décroissance pour repenser le tourisme [Degrowth to rethink tourism]. *L'autre Voie, 5*, 1–14.

Bramwell, B., & Lane, B. (2011). Critical research on the governance of tourism and sustainability. *Journal of Sustainable Tourism, 19*(4–5), 411–421. doi:10.1080/09669582.2011.580586

Breakey, N., & Breakey, H. (2013). Is there a right to tourism? *Tourism Analysis, 18*(6), 739–748. doi:10.3727/108354213X13824558470943

Buades, J. (2009). *Copenhague y después: El turismo y la justicia climática global [Copenhagen and after: Tourism and global climate justice]* (Opiniones en Desarrollo 4). Barcelona: Alba Sud.

Büscher, B., & Fletcher, R. (2017). Destructive creation: Capital accumulation and the structural violence of tourism. *Journal of Sustainable Tourism, 25*(5), 651–667. doi:10.1080/09669582.2016.1159214

Cañada, E. (2015). *Las que limpian los hoteles: Historias ocultas de precariedad laboral [Those who clean the hotels: Hidden stories of job insecurity]*. Barcelona: Icaria.

Cañada, E. C. (2013). *Turismos en Centroamérica: Un diagnóstico para el debate [Tourisms in Central America: A diagnosis for the debate]*. Managua: Enlace.

Carr, A., Ruhanen, L., & Whitford, M. (2016). Indigenous peoples and tourism: The challenges and opportunities for sustainable tourism. *Journal of Sustainable Tourism, 24*(8-9), 1067–1079. doi:10.1080/09669582.2016.1206112

Castañeda, Q. (2012). The neoliberal imperative of tourism: Rights and legitimization in the UNWTO Code of Ethics for Tourism. *Practicing Anthropology, 34*(3), 47–51. doi:10.17730/praa.34.3.w0251w655647750j

Cheong, S.-M., & Miller, M. L. (2000). Power and tourism: A Foucauldian observation. *Annals of Tourism Research, 27*(2), 371–390. doi:10.1016/S0160-7383(99)00065-1

Cole, S. (2014). Tourism and water: From stakeholders to rights holders, and what tourism businesses need to do. *Journal of Sustainable Tourism, 22*(1), 89–106. doi:10.1080/09669582.2013.776062

Cousin, S. (2008). L'Unesco et la doctrine du tourisme culturel: Généalogie d'un «bon» tourisme [Unesco and the cultural tourism doctrine: Genealogy of a "good" tourism]. *Civilisations: Revue Internationale D'anthropologie et de Sciences Humaines, 22*(1–2), 41–56.

D'Sa, E. (1999). Wanted: Tourists with a social conscience. *International Journal of Contemporary Hospitality Management, 11*(2–3), 64–68.

Duterme, B., & Pleumaron, A. (2006). Expansion du tourisme international: Gagnants et perdants [Expansion of international tourism: Winners and losers]. *Alternatives Sud, 13*(3), 7–22.

Faure, M. G., & Arsika, I. M. B. (2015). Settling disputes in the tourism industry: The global code of ethics for tourism and the world committee on tourism ethics. *Santa Clara Journal of International Law, 132*, 375–415.

Gascón, J. (2012). Introducción: Apuntes para un análisis crítico del turismo [Introduction: Notes for a critical analysis of tourism]. In J. Buades, E. Cañada, & J. Gascón (Eds.), *El turismo en el inicio del milenio: Una lectura crítica a tres voces* (pp. 11–21). Madrid: Foro de Turismo Responsable.

Gascón, J. (2016). Deconstruyendo el derecho al turismo [Deconstructing the right to tourism]. *Revista CIDOB D'afers Internacionals, 113*, 51–69. doi:10.24241/rcai.2016.113.2.51

Gascón, J. & Cañada, E. (Eds.). (2016). *Turismo residencial y gentrificación rural* [Residential tourism and rural gentrification]. Tenerife & Xixón: PASOS & Foro de Turismo Responsable.

Gascón, J., & Cañada, E. (2017). El mundo es finito, también para el turismo: Del multiplicador turístico al conflicto redistributivo [The world is finite, also for tourism: From the tourist multiplier to the redistributive conflict]. *Oikonomics, 7*, 28–34. doi:10.7238/o.n7.1705

Gascón, J., & Ojeda, D. (2014). *Turistas y campesinado: El turismo como vector de cambio de las economías campesinas en la era de la globalización [Tourists and peasantry: Tourism as a vector of change of peasant economies in the era of globalization]*. Madrid & Tenerife: Pasos & Foro de Turismo Responsable.

Gössling, S., & Peeters, P. (2007). It does not harm the environment!': An analysis of industry discourses on tourism, air travel and the environment. *Journal of Sustainable Tourism, 15*(4), 402–417. doi:10.2167/jost672.0

Hall, C. M. (2005). *Tourism: Rethinking the social science of mobility*. Essex: Pearson Education.

Hall, C. M. (2007). Editorial: Por-poor tourism: Do tourism exchanges benefit primaly the countires of the South? In C. M. Hall (Ed.), *Pro-poor tourism: Who benefits? Perspectives on tourism and poverty reduction* (pp. 1–8). Bristol: Channel View Publications.

Hall, C. M. (2009). Degrowing tourism: Décroissance, sustainable consumption and steady-state tourism. *Anatolia, 20*(1), 46–61. doi:10.1080/13032917.2009.10518894

Hall, C. M. (2011). Policy learning and policy failure in sustainable tourism governance: From first-and second-order to third-order change? *Journal of Sustainable Tourism, 19*(4-5), 649–671. doi:10.1080/09669582.2011.555555

Hall, C. M., Amelung, B., Cohen, S., Eijgelaar, E., Gössling, S., Higham, J., … Scott, D. (2015). On climate change skepticism and denial in tourism. *Journal of Sustainable Tourism, 23*(1), 4–25. doi:10.1080/09669582.2014.953544

Hannam, K. (2002). Tourism and development. I: Globalization and power. *Progress in Development Studies, 2*(3), 227–234. doi:10.1191/1464993402ps039pr

Harvey, D. (2003). *The New Imperialism*. London: Oxford University Press.

Hazel, N. (2005). Holidays for children and families in need: An exploration of the research and policy context for social tourism in the UK. *Children & Society, 19*(3), 225–236. doi:10.1002/chi.838

Heyns, C. H., & Viljoen, F. (Eds.). (2002). *The impact of the United Nations human rights treaties on the domestic level*. Boston: Martinus Nijhoff Publishers.

Hernández-Ramírez, J. (2018). La voracidad del turismo y el derecho a la ciudad [The voracity of tourism and the right to the city]. *Revista Andaluza de Antropología, 15*, 22–46. doi:10.12795/RAA.2018.15.02

Higgins-Desbiolles, F. (2006). More than an 'industry': The forgotten power of tourism as a social force. *Tourism Management, 27*(6), 1192–1208. doi:10.1016/j.tourman.2005.05.020

Higgins-Desbiolles, F. (2011). Resisting the hegemony of the market: Reclaiming the social capacities of tourism. In S. McCabe, L. Minnaert, & A. Diekmann (Eds.), *Social tourism in Europe: Theory and practice* (pp. 53–68). Bristol: Channel View Publications.

Higgins-Desbiolles, F., & Russell-Mundine, G. (2008). Absences in the volunteer tourism phenomenon: The right to travel, solidarity tours and transformation beyond the one-way. In K. D. Lyons & S. Wearing (Eds.), *Journeys of discovery in volunteer tourism: International case study perspectives* (pp. 182–194). Oxfordshire: CABI.

Higgins-Desbiolles, F., & Whyte, K. P. (2015). Tourism and human rights. In G. Burns (Ed.), *Ethics in tourism: The Routledge Handbook of Tourism and Sustainability* (pp. 105–116). Abingdon: Routledge.

Hospitalitynet. (2006, March 22). UNWTO and International Business Leaders Forum Announce A New Human Rights Initiative for the Tourism Industry. *Hospitalitynet.* Retrieved from http://www.hospitalitynet.org/news/4026791.html

Instituto para la Calidad Turística Española. (2017). Miembros [Members] [Web page]. Retrieved from http://www.icte.es/ESP/e/13/El-ICTE/Miembros

International Labour Organization. (2010). Sectoral Activities Programme Developments and challenges in the hospitality and tourism sector: Issues paper for discussion at the Global Dialogue Forum for the Hotels, Catering, Tourism Sector. (Report GDFHTS/2010). Geneva: ILO.

International Labour Organization. (2019). *Hotels, catering and tourism sector* [Web page]. Retrieved from http://www.ilo.org/global/industries-and-sectors/hotels-catering-tourism/lang–en/index.htm

IPCC. (2014). *Climate Change 2014: Synthesis Report. Contribution of Working Groups I, II and III to the Fifth Assessment Report of the Intergovernmental Panel on Climate Change* [Core Writing Team, R. K. Pachauri & L. A. Meyer (Eds.)]. Geneva: Intergovernmental Panel on Climate Change.

Jessup, P. C. (1968). *A modern law of nations: An introduction.* Hamden, CT: Archon Books.

Kingsbury, P. (2005). Jamaican tourism and the politics of enjoyment. *Geoforum, 36*(1), 113–132. doi:10.1016/j.geoforum.2004.03.012

Latouche, S. (2006). *Le pari de la décroissance [The bet for degrowth].* Paris: Fayard.

Luis Blanco, A. D. (2011). Una aproximación al turismo Slow: El turismo Slow en las Cittaslow de España [An approach to tourism Slow: Slow tourism in the Cittaslow of Spain]. *Investigaciones Turísticas, 1,* 122–133.

Mangalassery, S. (2012). Regulator or Facilitator?: Redefining the Role of Governments. In C. Kamp (Ed.), *Beyond greening: Reflections on tourism in the Rio-process* (pp. 57–62). Bonn: EED.

Martínez-Alier, J. (2009). Socially sustainable economic de-growth. *Development and Change, 40*(6), 1099–1119. doi:10.1111/j.1467-7660.2009.01618.x

McCabe, S., & Diekmann, A. (2015). The rights to tourism: Reflections on social tourism and human rights. *Tourism Recreation Research, 40*(2), 194–204. doi:10.1080/02508281.2015.1049022

Milano, C. (2018). Overtourism, malestar social y turismofobia: Un debate controvertido [Overtourism, social unrest and turismophobia: A controversial debate]. *Pasos. Revista de Turismo y Patrimonio Cultural, 16*(3), 551–564. doi:10.25145/j.pasos.2018.16.041

Ministerio de Turismo – Ecuador. (2013). *Sudamérica propone que el turismo sea considerado un derecho humano* [South America proposes that tourism be considered a human right] [Web page]. Retrieved from http://www.turismo.gob.ec/sudamerica-propone-que-el-turismo-sea-considerado-un-derecho-humano/

Minnaert, L., Maitland, R., & Miller, G. (2011). What is social tourism? *Current Issues in Tourism, 14*(5), 403–415. doi:10.1080/13683500.2011.568051

Moncada Jiménez, P., Sosa Ferreira, A. P., Martínez, C., Beltrán Pérez, M. L., & Domínguez Estrada, F. (2015). El caso de Cancún a los 20 años de la Carta de Turismo Sostenible de Lanzarote de 1995: Visión de los actores clave [The case of Cancún at 20 years of the Charter of Sustainable Tourism of Lanzarote of 1995: Vision of the key actors]. *Pasos Revista de Turismo y Patrimonio Cultural, 13*(6), 1463–1476. doi:10.25145/j.pasos.2015.13.102

Mowforth, M., & Munt, I. (2016). *Tourism and sustainability: Development, globalisation and new tourism in the third world* (4th ed.). Abingdon: Routledge.

Organización Mundial del Turismo. (1999). *Código Ético Mundial para el Turismo [Global Code of Ethics for Tourism].* Madrid: OMT.

Paquot, T. (2016). Tourisme urbain: à quand la décroissance? [Urban tourism: When will the degrowth?]. *Esprit, 7,* 86–89. doi:10.3917/espri.1607.0086

Panzer-Krause, S. (2018). Networking towards sustainable tourism: Innovations between green growth and degrowth strategies. *Regional Studies,* Advance online publication. [doi:10.1080/00343404.2018.1508873]

Peeters, P. M., & Eijgelaar, E. (2014). Tourism's climate mitigation dilemma: Flying between rich and poor countries. *Tourism Management, 40,* 15–26. doi:10.1016/j.tourman.2013.05.001

Pleumaron, A. (2006). Tourisme, mondialisation, consumérisme et développement durable en Asie du Sud-Est [Tourism, globalization, consumerism and sustainable development in Southeast Asia]. *Alternatives Sud, 13*(3), 133–148.

Rifari, T. (2011). Foreword. In B.Buhalis & S. Darcy (Eds.), *Accessible tourism: Concepts and issues*. Bristol: Channel View Publications.

Presidencia de la República Oriental de Uruguay. (2014, August 21). Nueva ley crea Consejo Nacional de Turismo y fondo para el fomento de la actividad [The National Tourism Council creates a new law and a fund for the promotion of the activity] [Press release]. Retrieved from http://presidencia.gub.uy/comunicacion/comunicacionnoti-cias/nueva-ley-crea-consejo-nacional-de-turismo-y-fondo-para-el-fomento-de-la-actividad

República Oriental del Uruguay – Poder Legislativo. (2014). Ley N° 19.253 sobre actividad turística [Law No. 19.253 on tourism activity] [Law]. Retrieved from http://faolex.fao.org/docs/pdf/uru138821.pdf

Schilcher, D. (2007). Growth versus equity: The continuum of pro-poor tourism and neoliberal governance. In C. M. Hall (Ed.), *Pro-poor tourism: Who benefits? Perspectives on tourism and poverty reduction* (pp. 56–83). Bristol: Channel View Publications.

Scott, D., Peeters, P., & Gössling, S. (2010). Can tourism deliver its "aspirational" greenhouse gas emission reduction targets? *Journal of Sustainable Tourism, 18*(3), 393–408. doi:10.1080/09669581003653542

Simpson, B., & Simpson, C. (2007). The End of Tourism, the Beginning of Law? In P. M. Burns & M. Novelli (Eds.), *Tourism and politics: Global frameworks and local realities* (pp. 369–388). Oxford: Elsevier.

Simpson, B., & Simpson, C. (2010). *From heritage to terrorism: Regulating tourism in an age of uncertainty*. London: Routledge.

Stroebel, M. (2015). Tourism and the green economy: Inspiring or averting change? *Third World Quarterly, 36*(12), 2225–2243. doi:10.1080/01436597.2015.1071658

Taibo, C. (2009). *En defensa del decrecimiento: Sobre capitalismo, crisis y barbarie* [In defense of the Degrowth: On capitalism, crisis and barbarism]. Madrid: Los Libros de la Catarata.

United Nations. (1948). Universal Declaration of Human Rights. Retrieved from http://www.ohchr.org/EN/UDHR/Documents/UDHR_Translations/eng.pdf

UNWTO. (2008). *Climate change and tourism: Responding to global challenges*. Madrid: World Tourism Organization.

UNWTO. (2009). From Davos to Copenhagen and Beyond: Advancing Tourism's Response to Climate Change: UNWTO Background Paper [Background Paper]. Retrieved from http://sdt.unwto.org/sites/all/files/docpdf/fromda-vostocopenhagenbeyondunwtopaperelectronicversion.pdf

UNWTO. (2013b). *Sustainable tourism for development*. Madrid: UNWTO. Retrieved from http://cf.cdn.unwto.org/sites/all/files/docpdf/devcoengfinal.pdf

UNWTO. (2016). UNWTO Affiliate Members – Directory. Retrieved from http://www2.unwto.org

UNWTO. (2017). Historical decision: Approval of the UNWTO Framework Convention on Tourism Ethics [Press release]. Retrieved from https://media.unwto.org/press-release/2017-09-15/historical-decision-approval-unwto-framework-convention-tourism-ethics

UNWTO. (2019). Committees [Web page]. Retrieved from http://www2.unwto.org/en/node/17

UNWTO & ILO. (2008a). Agreement between the World Tourism Organization (UNWTO) and the International Labour Organization (ILO) [Press release]. Retrieved from http://www.ilo.org/wcmsp5/groups/public/—ed_norm/—relconf/documents/meetingdocument/wcms_090566.pdf

UNWTO & ILO. (2008b). *Sources and Methods: Labour Statistics – Employment in the Tourism Industries*. Madrid & Geneve: UNWTO & ILO. Retrieved from https://www.e-unwto.org/doi/pdf/10.18111/9789284412334

UNWTO & ILO. (2009). *ILO/UNWTO Statement on Tourism and Employment* [Press release]. Retrieved from http://www.ilo.org/wcmsp5/groups/public/—ed_dialogue/—sector/documents/statement/wcms_162290.pdf

UNWTO & ILO. (2014). *Measuring Employment in the Tourism Industries: Guide with Best Practices*. Madrid & Geneve: UNWTO & ILO.

UNWTO & UNDP. (2017). *Tourism and the Sustainable Development Goals: Journey to 2030*. Madrid: UNWTO.

Wall, G. (2005). Sustainable Tourism – Unsustainable Development. In J. J. Pigram & S. Wahab (Eds.), *Tourism, development and growth: The challenge of sustainability* (pp. 33–49). Abingdon: Routledge.

Williams, V., Noland, R., Majundar, A., Toumi, R., & Ochien, W. (2007). Mitigation of climate impacts with innovative air transport management tools. In P. M. Peeters (Ed.), *Tourism and climate change mitigation: Methods, greenhouse gas reductions and policies* (pp. 91–104). Breda: NHTV.

World Tourism Organization. (1980). Manila Declaration on World Tourism Document [Declaration]. Retrieved from http://ethics.unwto.org/sites/all/files/docpdf/unwtoresolutiona-res-406xiii1999.pdf

World Tourism Organization. (1985). Tourism Bill of Rights and Tourist Code [Declaration]. Retrieved from http://www.univeur.org/cuebc/downloads/PDF%20carte/67.%20Sofia.PDF

World Tourism Organization. (1999). Global Code of Ethics for Tourism. Retrieved from http://cf.cdn.unwto.org/sites/all/files/docpdf/gcetbrochureglobalcodeen.pdf

Post-growth in the Tropics? Contestations over *Tri Hita Karana* and a tourism megaproject in Bali

Made Adityanandana and Julien-François Gerber

ABSTRACT

This study looks at a socio-environmental conflict over a tourism mega-project in the Benoa Bay in Bali, Indonesia. This conflict is interesting because it crystallizes key questions about the future of the island. Intriguingly, all the conflicting groups of actors mobilize the same philosophy of *Tri Hita Karana* (THK), which can be translated as the "three causes of well-being" and which is said to guide the development policies of the island. Our objective is to investigate how THK relates to the conflict and to what extent some of its interpretations are growth-critical. Using political ecology as a theoretical lens and qualitative methods, we find that the conflicting groups do not oppose each other through different languages of valuation, but *within* them. Likewise, THK is only superficially "one" idiom of valuation. In reality, THK covers different visions of development, depending on the actors involved. We identify three broad ways of interpreting THK in this conflict: (i) a marketable way, (ii) an equity-oriented way, and (iii) a radical-integral way, which bears similarities with post-growth views. This article is a contribution to the emerging debates on post-growth thinking from the "global South" and to the radical critique of tourism industry in developing regions.

Introduction

The development of tourism has, over the past one hundred years, been one of the main global forces for drastic social and environmental change. The share of the tourism market commanded by the "developing world" has grown from 30% in 1980 to 45% in 2015 and is forecasted to reach 60% by 2030 (UNWTO, 2016). Asia, in particular, experienced an annual average of 7% increase in international arrivals between 2005 and 2016, higher than the worldwide 4% increase (UNWTO, 2018). During this same period, South Asia (11% increase) and South-East Asia (8%) were the sub-regions with the fastest arrival growth globally (UNWTO & GTERC, 2017). Tourism is also the main contributor of foreign direct investment for a third of the developing world and for half of the "least developed countries" (UNCTAD, 2010). In some countries, it can contribute up to 50% of total employment (UNEP & UNWTO, 2012).

But the colossal expansion of tourism has also been criticized for its negative impacts, including environmental degradation, labor exploitation and cultural erosion, as well as for the frequent foreign control over the sector (Brown & Hall, 2008; Mowforth & Munt, 2016; Telfer &

Sharpley, 2016). In particular, studies coming from the field of political ecology have provided solid critical analyses of the growth of tourism (Stonich, 1998; Gössling, 2003; Mostafanezhad et al., 2016; Nepal & Saarinen, 2016). A handful of political ecologists have recently started to explore how tourism has become a cornerstone of capitalist growth (Büscher & Fletcher, 2017) and to investigate the link between tourism and post-growth approaches (Bourdeau & Berthelot, 2008; Hall, 2009). Higgins-Desbiolles (2018), for instance, explicitly calls for tourism to transition away from the "growth fetish", through "a clear-eyed engagement with notions of limits that the current culture of consumerism and pro-growth ideology precludes" (2010, p. 125).

The present article seeks to further probe the relationship of post-growth and tourism by focusing on an important resistance movement against a tourism development megaproject in the Benoa Bay in Bali, an island that has been described as an ideal "tourism laboratory" for social science research (Cole, 2012, p. 1223). Introduced to the European world during Dutch colonization and then advertised as a mass tourist destination by President Soeharto's New Order regime, Bali remains the cash cow of the Indonesian tourism industry. In 2017, the small island of Bali recorded more than 5.6 million foreign tourist arrivals, which represented 40% of all the arrivals in Indonesia, a number that nearly tripled since 2008 (BGTO, 2018a; BGTO, 2018b; Statistics Indonesia, 2018).[1] Accommodation and restaurants contribute 22% of the province's GDP and 30% of its employment (Statistics Indonesia, 2017a, 2017b).

Although the Balinese are sometimes portrayed as "apolitical islanders" who have been successful in harmonizing tourism growth and cultural preservation (Roth & Sedana, 2015), the resistance movement against the Benoa Bay Revitalization project is yet another proof that such accounts are invalid. This movement sheds useful light, we will argue, on the tourism, development and post-growth nexus. Our objectives will be to highlight how opposing actors have mobilized the philosophy of *Tri Hita Karana* (hereafter THK) as an attempt to justify their positions, and to what extent some of the interpretations of THK are compatible with post-growth views. THK can be translated as the "three sources of wellbeing" and is commonly regarded as the traditional guiding principle of Balinese life as well as a foundational inspiration for development policies in the province. According to the THK cosmology, the self's pursuit of happiness must establish a harmonious relationship with fellow humans, nature and the divine (Agung, 2005; Peters & Wardana, 2013; Roth & Sedana, 2015). These three fundamental relationships correspond to different languages of valuation that are used by all the conflicting actors, but, as we will see, in contradictory ways.

The next section outlines our theoretical framework and is followed by the research methods. A section expanding on the THK framework is then presented and followed by empirical detail on the case study. We then analyse how THK has been interpreted and mobilized in the conflict, before ending with some policy implications and a conclusion.

Theoretical framework

Political ecology offers a unique vantage point for understanding the relationship between society and ecology in the context of unequal power relationships (Forsyth, 2003; Nepal & Saarinen, 2016). It allows the kind of multi-level, multi-framing and multi-stakeholder analysis that the study requires. We will particularly focus on four interconnected political-ecological concepts: the different narratives of "development", languages of valuation, environmental conflicts, and post-growth. In short, we will problematize how power relationships are re/produced through specific narratives of development and well-being – i.e., specific interpretations of THK –, and how these narratives are contested in an environmental struggle expressed through a variety of languages of valuation, namely through a variety of value systems expressing what should be prioritized in decision-making.

Political ecology shows that environmental struggles do not only emerge due to conflicting interests over natural resources, but also due to clashes in value systems and in visions of what constitutes a "good life". In particular, conflicting groups may value nature differently, be it in the same standard of valuation or across a variety of valuation languages, as explained by Martínez-Alier (2002). While powerful actors tend to favor monetary valuation and use a modernist (i.e., pro-growth and technocratic) languages of valuation, local communities, indigenous groups and activists often express their views within other languages of valuation, such as the idioms of human rights, livelihood or sacredness. Such clashes may exemplify a weak comparability of values, or even a fundamental incommensurability of values (Martínez-Alier, 2002; Gerber et al., 2009).

However, grassroots languages of valuation are increasingly being appropriated and commodified by governments or the corporate sector with the purpose of taming conflicts or adding value to standardized products (Heller, 2010, pp. 101–110). Jackson (2017), for instance, documented how Australian water management authorities simplistically framed indigenous values on water within their own policies, and how this had serious consequences on minority groups' access to water. Her study revealed a clash of ontological perspectives on water. Similarly, the commodification of indigenous valuation languages has been recurrent in the tourism industry, responding to market saturation by transforming standardized package tours into various niche tourisms offering "heritage experiences" and "authenticity" (Coupland & Coupland, 2014). Büscher and Fletcher (2017) suggest that those processes of tourism-based commodification create structural violence in the forms of production of inequality, ecological damage and "spaces of exception". Nonetheless, these authors argue that it is not tourism per se that commodifies culture and nature, but the capitalist structure within which it operates. From a post-capitalist perspective, then, tourism could be part of a post-growth future, but how this will actually look like remains an open question.

Accordingly, an increasing number of political ecologists are working on the impacts of growth and on the possible post-growth alternatives. In this article, we define "post-growth" as the academic and activist quest for alternatives to the current global model promoting Western-type growth-driven economies (Latouche, 2009; Gerber & Raina, 2018a; 2018b). Post-growth problematizes the fact that GDP growth is not just a "neutral" developmental objective; GDP growth reflects a particular way of defining the "good society" based on the belief that more market exchanges means that more needs are met. Consequently, an economy centered on GDP growth "naturally" tends to value processes of commodification, privatization and mass consumption of "stuff". Replacing GDP growth with another vision thus implies a fundamental rethinking of what "we" value in the economy, for whom, and using what language of valuation. This cannot just be a technical project but a political and a sociocultural one.

Post-growth encompasses a variety of currents and views, the main ones being degrowth, agrowth, steady-state economics and post-development (Gerber & Raina, 2018a; 2018b). Degrowth has both academic and activist roots and promotes a radical politico-economic transformation towards a smaller and more equitable global metabolism (Latouche, 2009; D'Alisa & Demaria, 2014). Agrowth, on the other hand, is agnostic about growth: it suggests that welfare and sustainable targets should be carefully defined, but whether these targets require "growth" is seen as irrelevant (van den Bergh, 2011). Steady-state economics, for its part, promotes non-growing societies based on a stable material and energy throughput (Daly, 1991). Finally, post-development argues that the concept and practice of "development" fundamentally reflects a capitalist and Western hegemony over the rest of the world and should be abandoned (Kothari et al., 2019). Gerber & Raina (2018a) identified three main orientations within post-development theory that are especially relevant to post-growth, namely: (i) the various forms of solidarity or community economies (Gibson-Graham et al., 2013), (ii) post-extractivism, which calls for a societal change away from economies guided by extractive industries (Acosta, 2017), and (iii)

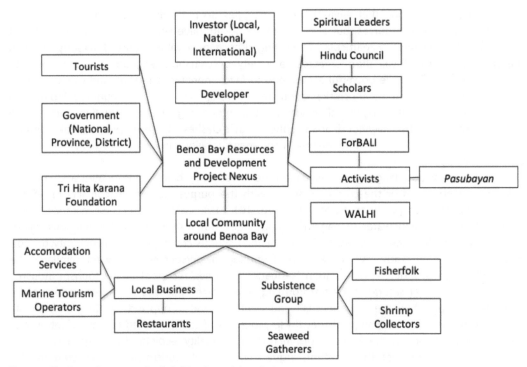

Figure 1. The Benoa Bay nexus of stakeholders (own elaboration).

culturally-specific conceptions of the "good life" as alternative models for social flourishing. It is this last orientation that will be especially relevant here.

Studies across various disciplines have indeed shown that there are various conceptions of the "good life" that do not seem to place endless chrematistic growth as a desirable objective. Examples of these cosmologies include *Buen Vivir* from the Andean region, where "to live well" ("buen vivir") is preferred over "to live better", *Ubuntu* ("human mutuality") in Southern Africa, *Swaraj* ("self-rule") in India, *Kyōsei* ("human welfare") in Japan or Gross National Happiness (GNH) in Bhutan (Gudynas, 2014; Kothari et al., 2019). However, scholars have also found that those cosmologies remain contested and are subject to different interpretations. Gerber & Raina (2018a) distinguish different interpretations of GNH, ranging from one that is close to (capitalist) green growth to one that includes sufficiency threshold beyond which growth should stop. Likewise, Gudynas (2014) suggests three interpretations of *Buen Vivir* – a generic, a restricted and a substantive use – and argues that only the last one bears a similarity with the concept of post-growth. In this article, we will examine whether there are also distinct interpretations of THK by looking at a socio-environmental conflict that involves various actors and various languages of valuation.

Methods

This paper results from a two-month fieldwork conducted in the Benoa Bay in Bali from July to August 2017. Following Cole (2012) who conducted a political-ecological study of water on the island, we first mapped the different stakeholders around the Benoa Bay's tourism megaproject (Figure 1). One of us carried out 12 interviews of a broad spectrum of key stakeholder representatives, namely the Bali Provincial Secretary, the development company's Executive Director, the Tri Hita Karana Foundation head, the Bali Hindu Council head, one of the coordinators of the Bali Against Reclamation ("ForBALI") movement, one key activist of the Indonesian Forum for the Environment (Walhi Bali), one representative of *Pasubayan*,[2] one Hindu high priest, one marine tourism operator, one fisherman and two shrimp collectors.

We selected participants who were substantially involved and influential in the conflict. The priest we interviewed, for example, was one of the spiritual leaders who had been invited to comment on the Benoa Bay conflict during a meeting organized by the Balinese Hindu Council. We also relied on the help of one key informant (a small-scale marine tourism operator) who helped us establish contact with local fishermen and shrimp collectors. All participants voluntarily participated in the study and were asked permission before any recording was made. Participants from vulnerable groups preferred to remain anonymous in any publication resulting from this study, while the others openly agreed to be mentioned by name.

We used a semi-structured interview method, which allowed us to follow up on different angles deemed important by interviewees, while still maintaining an active role in focusing the conversation (Brinkmann, 2018, pp. 1002–1007). Questions were mostly open-ended, inquiring about the participants' views on the development project as well as about their lived experience in relation to the conflict and to Bali's tourism industry. We followed one of Yin's (2014, pp. 136–138) analytic strategies by working on the data "from the ground up". We first created a table based on the narratives told by the participants and classified their key answers into separate columns, namely: (i) their stance in the conflict (supporting or opposing the megaproject), (ii) their perception of the development project and its forthcoming impacts, (iii) their views on the project in relation with THK, as well as (iv) their own conception of the "good life" and "good development". We then cross-checked and complemented our interview data with secondary sources from academic research, NGO reports, media articles and internet resources, including the project's feasibility study.

While conducting the data collection and the analyses, our own value premises and positionality as male middle-class academics were constantly interrogated. Both of us being sympathetic to post-growth ideas, our research did not seek to be "value-free" but to problematize how our own biases could influence our interpretation of the data. We conducted our research in spirit of what Borras (2016, p. 1) called "scholar-activism", namely "rigorous academic work [...] which is explicitly and unapologetically connected to political projects". One of us is a Balinese, which facilitated the collection of data – language-wise as well as in building rapport with "gatekeepers" (Hammersley & Atkinson, 2007, pp. 49–52). However, it did not necessarily help with the activists who were at first wary of our intentions. After a few meetings detailing our own position in the conflict, the activists finally agreed to participate in the study and possibilities for future collaboration were envisaged.

The THK framework

Although its root can be traced back to Vedic texts and the Bhagavad Gita, the modern formulation of THK is relatively recent and took place in the 1950s during the years following independence (Roth & Sedana, 2015). Neither Muslim nor strictly secular, the Indonesian constitution is guided by the ideological foundation of *Pancasila* – the five *silas* or principles – with the first principle stipulating adherence to a monotheistic God. This, in effect, required the Balinese to reframe their spiritual-religious practices, which were regarded as too close to animism by the majority of Muslim officials, in order to have Balinese Hinduism recognized as one of the five official religions of the country (Picard, 2011, p. 124; Ramstedt, 2014, p. 64; Roth & Sedana, 2015, pp. 164–165). In this context, THK conveniently reinforced the Balinese religious identity and was subsequently introduced in the policy arena as the foundation for development in the island (Peters & Wardana, 2013, p. 68). It gained its official recognition as the "life philosophy" of the Balinese in 1969, during a meeting chaired by the Bali Provincial Board of Planning that was set up as part of Soeharto's Five Year Development Plan policy.

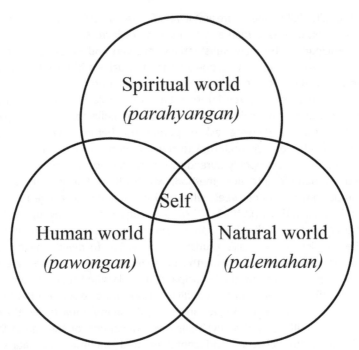

Figure 2. The three interrelated worlds in *Tri Hita Karana* (own elaboration).

THK means a harmonious integration of three interrelated realms, i.e., the human world (*pawongan*), the natural world (*palemahan*), and the spiritual world (*parahyangan*) (Figure 2). Briefly speaking, two traditional Balinese institutions – namely the customary community (*banjar*) and the irrigation system (*subak*) – are key in understanding the conception of the human world in THK. Rural communities traditionally organize collective work at the sub-village level and make decisions more or less collectively on land use, religious rituals, security, as well as on important life-cycle events such as wedding and funeral ceremonies. As a common, the Balinese irrigation system is central in enabling rice production and connects each customary community as well as peasant families. The disruption of the irrigation system following the "green revolution" ended up disastrous, cutting total rice supply on the island by half (Santos, 2007, p. 73). Both the customary community and its irrigation system have spatial and membership boundaries that are governed by regulations and dispute resolution mechanisms (Agung, 2005, p. 297).

The Balinese notions of macrocosm (*bhuwana agung*) and microcosm (*bhuwana alit*) can help explain the THK conception of the natural world. Unlike the assumption of a nature-culture divide proposed by early Western anthropologists, the above-mentioned concepts suggest that the self (microcosm) is not separate from the universe or nature (macrocosm) and that both are composed of the same elements. Accordingly, the THK framework suggests that violence towards nature means harm against oneself. Furthermore, in Balinese Hinduism, nature is regarded as the embodiment of the Supreme Being, hence seen as essentially sacred. Such a view implies that nature is not an object that must be ruled and dominated by humans, but deserves reverence, as captured in a passage of the *Śvetāśvataropaniṣad*: "Bow to God for God is inside the fire, inside the air, inside the whole universe, inside the plants that are on trees" (quoted in Agung, 2005, p. 298).

Finally, the THK conception of the spiritual world is linked to the more general Hindu-Balinese view of entelechy (Agung, 2005). This doctrine is classically elaborated in the *Puruṣārtha* (the objects of human pursuit), which consists of moral (*dharma*), economic (*artha*), sensual (*kama*) and spiritual values (*moksha*). While all are considered important, one's pursuit of economic and sensual desires should never neglect moral values in order to attain spiritual fulfillment – the ultimate end (Flood, 1997). The path towards *moksha* (or liberation from suffering, inherent in the rebirth cycle) unfolds through several lifetimes depending on one's action (*karma*) and on the soul's ripeness to detach itself from the physical world. Throughout one's lifetime, but also across several lifetimes, the expansion of consciousness results in less attachment to ego-driven material pleasures and more investment in a soul-driven sense of (immaterial) care and services for others.

In this sense, the THK philosophy of the "good life" is rooted for the common wo/men in the search for a harmony between material and immaterial concerns, while ultimate ends will largely be post-material. These ideas correspond to the fundamental human desire/need for balance, integration and wholeness. They have counterparts in other cultural settings, including in the West as in Jungian psychology. In many ways, these ideas could converge with a degrowth ethics of sharing, caring, conviviality, voluntary simplicity or frugal abundance (D'Alisa & Demaria, 2014). We will now present the conflict case study, with special reference to the diverging languages of valuation used, before analyzing how THK has been interpreted by the various actors.

The conflict case of Benoa Bay

The Benoa Bay is an area of almost 2000 ha located in the southern tip of Bali. Falling into the three districts of South Denpasar, Kuta, and South Kuta, the intertidal zone is a reservoir of five sub-drainage basins with an average depth of two meters during high tide (Conservation International, 2013, p. 15). The area was classified as a conservation zone (PD, 2011) and is surrounded by about 1400 hectares of mangrove, making it the largest mangrove ecosystem in the island. It is part of a larger biome, which also comprises seagrass and coral ecosystems (Sudiarta & Sudiarta, 2011). Together, the coastal ecosystems are home to a variety of terrestrial and intertidal fauna, including 94 bird species and 290 species of fish, reptiles and primates, as well as edible and economically valuable species of shrimps, crabs, oysters, rabbitfish and barramundi (Allen & Erdmann, 2011; Conservation International, 2013). The bay and its biodiversity have for some years suffered from problems of pollution and of siltation caused by a previous reclamation project on Serangan Island, harbor activities, and the construction of a toll road.

In 2012, Governor Pastika granted Tirta Wahana Bali Internasional (hereafter TWBI) the right to develop 838 hectares of the bay (GD, 2012). TWBI is part of the Artha Graha Network, a leading business empire owned by the Indonesian tycoon Tomy Winata, which operates in banking, tourism, agriculture, retail, mining, telecommunication and entertainment. The company's proposed development is called "Nusa Benoa" and was planned as a 30 trillion rupiah "revitalization" project that includes the creation of 12 new islands and the establishment of luxury resorts, apartments, a yacht marina, a theme park, a botanical garden and other urban-residential facilities (Adityo, 2014; Nusa Benoa website, 2018). The decree immediately drew criticism from activists and the public who complained about the lack of transparency (Hasanudin, 2013). However, after a number of twists, TWBI had still not, at the time of writing (May 2019), carried out any land reclamation activities at Benoa Bay.

The project was first questioned by Walhi, the oldest and largest environmental justice network in Indonesia. In August 2013, a group of local people – including Walhi activists – identifying themselves as "ForBALI" (the Balinese Forum Against Reclamation) gathered at the regional people's assembly office and demanded the government to revoke the bill, on the grounds that the law-making process was unilateral and non-democratic (Erviani, 2013). ForBALI has since then grown and can now be described as an alliance of activists, students, scholars, artists and local inhabitants from different class backgrounds who oppose the "revitalization" project. The movement gained stronger grassroots legitimacy after 39 customary villages signed a collective agreement (*pasubayan*) opposing the project. Ten out of eleven customary villages encircling the bay were part of the agreement.

In May 2014, President Yudhoyono officially opened the zone for commercial activities, effectively stripping its conservation status (PD, 2014). This decision was received as a shock by sections of the local population. Protests sporadically followed, ranging from a few hundreds to tens of thousands of participants (Tribunnews, 2014; Suriyani, 2016). These marches were in some ways historical as they represented by far the largest social mobilization critical of tourism in Bali. At least six activists were arrested under different charges (Ismayana, 2017; Ulum, 2014).

In August 2018, TWBI lost the location permit of the land reclamation project because the company failed to get the project's feasibility study approved by the Ministry of Environment and Forestry before the permit's expiration date. The feasibility study was delayed due to the resistance of local communities, which influenced the socio-cultural assessment of the project (Tempo, 2018). However, what was thought as victory by local communities and activists quickly turned into a disappointment when the Ministry of Maritime Affairs issued a new permit for TWBI in November 2018. As long as the original decree (PD, 2014) remains operative, the area of the Benoa Bay designated for the project remains outside of protective zoning, and the future of the bay thus remains uncertain.

In the following sections, we will describe three main languages of valuation that have been used by the various actors in justifying their positions in the Benoa Bay conflict. The three valuation idioms are the languages of "ecological sustainability", "economic gains/losses", and "heritage and spirituality". They respectively correspond to the THK conception of the natural, human and spiritual worlds.

Contestations within the valuation language of ecological sustainability

The proponents of the "revitalization" project claim that it is in accordance with the THK conception of human-nature relationship. They argue that revitalization is meant for ecological ends, specifically for saving the mangrove ecosystem, which has been degraded due to the severity of pollution and siltation. The government warned that efforts to solve the waste issue have been financially burdensome for the province, which had allocated 10 billion rupiah (about USD 700,000) in a year to collect five to seven tons of garbage in the bay daily (C.N. Pemayun, Bali Provincial Secretary, personal communication, July 24, 2017). The government had also organized annual mangrove replanting programs as part of the Bali Clean and Green project, which was launched in 2013. However, the program was stopped four years later because most saplings did not survive. The government concluded that some form of "revitalization" is therefore needed and that those who contest the plan not complying with the THK principles:

> Those who oppose the project are not following *Tri Hita Karana*. Where is the human-nature relationship? The mangrove ecosystem is very polluted. When the tide is low, one can even find condoms and underwears there. Or carcasses of dogs and chickens. It is filthy. Now that Artha Graha [i.e. the project's consortium] has stepped in, the ecosystem will be cleaned [...]. This is what we want for South Bali – not killing and cutting the mangroves. (C.N. Pemayun, Bali Provincial Secretary, personal communication, July 24, 2017, our translation)

In agreement with mainstream neoliberal policies, the "revitalization" project as a form of public-private partnership is said to crucially relieve the state both in a financial and a managerial sense (Wardana, 2017). Packaged as a green development concept, "revitalization" is endorsed as a model of sustainable tourism development. TWBI, for instance, suggests that Nusa Benoa is an ecologically sound development project because the company employs consultants with "A-grade in sustainability" credentials (H.B. Wasesa, TWBI's executive director, personal communication, July 21, 2017). This concerns its overall spatial design, building materials, waterways system, energy source, as well as its waste management. Finally, the megaproject is said to solve the bay's siltification problem, as the process of creating new lands would involve the dredging of the bay's sediments. Following this line of arguments, the proponents of "revitalization" presents Nusa Benoa as a win-win solution, which allows the growth of the tourism industry without converting more of Bali's agricultural and forested lands, while solving various environmental problems at the same time.

Opponents of the "revitalization" project, in sharp contrast, contest each one of those claims. For them, the project does not only involve land-use change but it is essentially a form of *landscape*-use change considering the size of the area that must undergo physical and functional alterations (S. Darmoko, Walhi Bali activist, personal communication, August 5, 2017). They worry about the subsequent ecological disasters, such as backwater, floods, and coastal erosion that may come with the development project since the bay's capacity as a reservoir will diminish. Furthermore, instead of preserving the environment, the process of land reclamation is expected to cause biodiversity loss in two ways. Firstly, it will disrupt the migratory route of shorebirds since the bay is a feeding stopover for many bird species. Secondly, the process of land reclamation will produce huge amounts of debris that will be harmful for the coral ecosystems. As local small-scale tourism operator noted:

> I have myself written a statement rejecting the reclamation project. I care about the coral reefs […]. If the reclamation project takes place, the coral reefs will be damaged. Moreover, the village of Tanjung Benoa is already prone to floods whenever the tide is high. The reclamation project will surely have an effect on the volume of water. Learning from the previous reclamation project of the [nearby] Serangan island, [one can be sure that] this project will worsen coastal degradation. (I. M. Tromat, marine tourism entrepreneur, personal communication, July 19, 2017, our translation)

Contestations within the valuation language of economic gains/losses

According to the promoters of the "revitalization" project, the THK principle of the harmonious human world is in no way violated by the project. The latter is indeed said to create economic opportunities for the locals and for Bali in general. Jobs will be provided and growth will be stimulated amid global competition in the industry. The "revitalization" is forecasted to generate 300 trillion rupiah (USD 21 billion) when multiplier effects are taken into account (H.B. Wasesa, TWBI's executive director, personal communication, July 21, 2017) and taxes from tourist activities are estimated to hit 10 billion rupiah (about USD 700,000) daily (I.M.M. Pastika, Bali Governor, CNN Indonesia, September 1, 2016). As such, a more ambitious development agenda for the province can be achieved in the future. In the words of the Governor:

> Development in Bali is based on its own philosophy. While at national level, development abides by three elements – pro-growth, pro-job and pro-poor, Bali also considers pro-environment and pro-culture principles. We would not accept [a given development project] if one were not fulfilled. The environmental and cultural elements are prerequisite, and development must bring welfare for the people. […] Our population grows, our needs grow, hence growth is mandatory. (I.M.M. Pastika, CNN Indonesia, September 1, 2016, our translation)

The "revitalization" of the Benoa Bay is anticipated to generate 250,000 jobs, 70% of which will be reserved for Balinese. TWBI claims that it will train locals in order to ensure that they will match the requirements for the new positions, especially those related to luxury hotel management. Furthermore, the proponents of the "revitalization" project suggest that the venture will benefit fishermen and water-sport businesses in terms of productivity. The canal system of Nusa Benoa will allow them to engage in their activities at any time, in contrast to the current situation limited by the tidal cycle. Additionally, as explained by TWBI's Executive Director:

> We are working with the THK Foundation. They will be our advisor […]. We will establish a Fisherman's Wharf, which will benefit local fishermen. The people who will live there [at Nusa Benoa] will purchase fish with higher price. They will only need to make one phone call to the Fisherman's Wharf from their home to

make the transaction! That is the human-human relationship [of THK]. (H.B. Wasesa, TWBI's executive director, personal communication, July 21, 2017, our translation)

Nonetheless, many are not convinced by the promises of the company and government representatives who guarantee the waterways will remain accessible to the public. The opponents of the "revitalization" worry that the project will instead lead to a new form of enclosures of the bay and its resources, which are currently held in common. For the opposition groups, the issue of "access" cannot be reduced to "entry" as framed by the elites (Walhi coordinator, personal communication, 5 August, 2017). One should not ignore, they argue, that the project would turn nearly half of the bay, including some of the fishing and shrimp collecting ground, into permanent lands. Additionally, the productivity claims of project proponents simply ignore subsistence groups that actually depend on the tidal cycle to collect shrimps. Transforming the intertidal zone into permanent deep water means dispossession of their source of livelihood. A shrimp collector expressed such concern to one of us:

There will be no more places where to catch shrimps, just like what happened after the development of Serangan Island. The water at the edge of the island became too deep to fish. People from Serangan also come here now. Sometimes they collect seaweeds. Those are our only sources of livelihood. There is no other source of income for us small fisherfolk. (male shrimp collector, personal communication, July 22, 2017, our translation)

Ultimately, some opponents argue that the Nusa Benoa project will worsen the price war on hotel rooms[3] in addition to intensifying traffic congestion and exacerbating waste and pollution problems in South Bali – adding more psychological and socioeconomic pressures to what is already borne by local inhabitants.

Contestations within the valuation language of heritage and spirituality

The promoters of the "revitalization" project proclaim that it will promote Balinese cultural heritage and spirituality. This will be mainly achieved, they argue, through the restoration of the Pudut Island, an eroded one-hectare isle regularly visited by locals for religious rituals. Titled "Pudut Cultural Island", this sub-project is planned to become a new art and cultural center of Bali while the temples that used to stand on the island will be rebuilt.

However, the resisting groups argue that the "revitalization" plan, in essence, disregards Balinese cultural and spiritual values. According to them, the project will erase the local custom of collecting edible crustaceans and mollusks during low tide (*makekarang*) because the construction project targets the seabed mounds where the practice traditionally takes place. The "revitalization" is also perceived as disrespectful towards the bay's historical value as it is said to be the site where Shivaism-Buddhism was first introduced in the island and acculturated with local spiritual practices (I.W. Swarsa, *Pasubayan* representative, personal communication, July 22, 2017).

Finally, the opponents also mobilize the language of sacredness in rejecting the development proposal. They contend that the construction of new temples cannot simply establish a harmonious human-spirits relationship when the development project, in fact, ignores locals' spiritual belief. Based on a research conducted by student activists, ForBALI issued a map locating 70 sacred points in the Benoa Bay area (BaleBengong, 2016). For local people, sacred places can take different forms:

In the Balinese teachings, sacred places do not only take the form of magnificent temples. Any point on this earth – be it on land or in the ocean – that reverberates spiritual energy would be revered. Accordingly, such places would be regarded as sacred sites. (I.W. Swarsa, *Pasubayan* representative, personal communication, July 22, 2017, our translation)

In summary, these narratives show that actors speak similar languages of valuation despite their conflicting positions in the conflict. Contrary to the original formulation of the idea by

Martínez-Alier (2002), the Benoa Bay struggle is not expressed as a clash *between* languages of valuation, but as a series of conflicts *within* multiple languages of valuation. Each language of valuation becomes a battle ground. The government and the corporate sector mobilize the languages of ecological sustainability, economics, as well as heritage and spirituality to justify the "revitalization" of Benoa Bay. Likewise, local community, activists, and spiritual leaders speak similar languages of valuation in resisting the same project. Such seemingly identical expressions blur the boundary between supposedly different valuation of Benoa Bay and its natural resources. We therefore had to formulate the conflict not as a clash of valuation languages but as a clash of 'paradigms' (or 'visions') over Bali's future.

The different uses of THK in the conflict

Based on our analysis, we identify three major ways of interpreting THK in the Benoa Bay conflict. Each interpretation corresponds to a particular paradigm/vision about how the future of Bali should look like. Unlike what we could observe with languages of valuation, these different interpretations were not contested within them, but the conflict occurred between them. The three THK paradigms are "marketable THK", "equity-oriented THK", and "radical-integral THK".

Marketable THK

Marketable THK is mobilized by the governmental, corporation and ecolabel representatives who all support the "revitalization" project. This first version of THK resembles the "green economy" concept proposed by mainstream intergovernmental organizations and its two main normative strategies could be described as the "ecologization of the economy" and the "economization of nature" (Wichterich, 2015, p. 72). Within the first strategy, it is suggested that tourism-based economic growth in Bali is inevitable and "natural" instead of "historical". Such idea is similar to the views defended by the UNWTO Secretary-General Taleb Rifai (2017) when he asserted that growth is "the eternal story of mankind", hence "not the enemy", but what counts is "how we manage it". Marketable THK proposes shifting from "business as usual" to techno-engineering innovations able to lessen the environmental impacts of tourism, while maintaining growth as its ultimate objective. While criticism against the tourism industry is rising for its damages to nature and society, the "greening" of the tourism sector is not only intended to soften such impacts, but also necessary to revitalize the conditions for capital accumulation through new markets, investments and clienteles (like the globalized upper class who can afford top luxury accommodation and "green" consumer niches). As explained by TWBI's executive director:

> For us, to conform to the THK principles is not a handicap. Quite the opposite, it benefits us as we explain it to our investors who get more excited. In this way, our project can gain additional value. (H.B. Wasesa, personal communication, July 21, 2017, our translation)

Accordingly, THK is exhibited on different pages of the company's website and explicitly linked to "development"; it is also included in the company's mission statement: "to preserve and honor Bali's local value of *Tri Hita Karana*" (TWBI, 2018).

Within the second strategy (economization of nature), the marketable take on THK implies that the solution to the bay's ecological problems, as externalities, lies in their internalization in the price system. This requires some institutional adjustments, such privatization and commodification, in order to enable the market to include what was outside its domain. The project and its surroundings (including its mangrove ecosystems) are assessed through monetary cost/benefit analysis in order to make visible its tourism and economic potential as well as the need for its conservation. Granting property rights to TWBI over the bay and its resources is presented as the solution for the bay's "tragedy of the commons".

Finally, marketable THK mystifies distributional conflict through the deployment of ecolabel and certification. Although the founders of the "THK Award" initially launched the label out of concern for the impacts of mass tourism, especially the inequality it creates, the awarding committee is far from being critical about resource control by the tourism sector (Peters & Wardana, 2013, pp. 92-99). The Award, instead of encouraging alternative forms of tourism in Bali, exacerbates the main-stream growth of the tourism sector because obtaining certification has now merely become part of corporate branding strategy. This is not surprising, however, because the THK Foundation (from which the Award stems) eventually shares the same view as the UNWTO regarding "sustainable tourism". The two organizations even committed to "synergize" THK and the Global Code of Ethics of Tourism.

While at times the THK Foundation claims to be neutral in the Benoa Bay conflict, it certainly opposed the resistance movement:

> How could we conclude that the project will bring negative impacts when it has not even started yet? We are supposed first to make an assessment and then conclude whether the project corresponds with THK or not, before completely opposing it. After all, the developer intends to adjust the project to meet the principles of THK, which are also compatible with the UNWTO's Global Code of Ethics of Tourism. (W. Wardana, THK Foundation's Head, personal communication, August 2, 2017, our translation)

Equity-oriented THK

The equity-oriented THK is mobilized by the local communities living around the Benoa Bay. They include the marine tourism operator, the shrimp collectors and the fishermen we inter-viewed, who are all part of the larger stakeholders group opposing the "revitalization" project. Unlike the first type of THK, the equity-oriented use of THK is more critical toward tourism devel-opment. This second type of THK is comparable to the programs of true social-democratic parties, or to Gudynas' (2014, p. 201) description of *Buen Vivir* in its "restricted use". It does not question the notion of growth per se but sees the inequality generated by the tourism industry as an important problem.

The mobilization of this type of THK seeks political-economic transformation of tourism toward redistributive justice but does not problematize the soundness of the use of nature, par-ticularly its utilitarian use (O'Neill, 1993, pp. 98-117). In short, it mainly focuses on the issue of ownership and/or redistribution. As such, the proponents of "revitalization" often regard the activism of those who mobilize equity-oriented THK as non-environmental. As a result, the broader environmental justice movement that they are part of is also delegitimized.

Those who mobilize this second type of THK argue that the "revitalization" project is not THK because it ignores subsistence groups and local communities, which are also part of the "human world" in the THK framework. They oppose the privatization of Benoa Bay because it removes access rights from marginalized groups in order to allow particular groups of people to profit. They therefore defend the Benoa Bay as a common. As expressed by a fisherman we interviewed:

> The communities do not want this project. It is not useful for us because people are likely to lose their jobs and livelihood. Of course, the project might be good, but only for a handful of individuals [...]. There is no harmonious relationship between the developer and the community. THK does not manifest itself here. There is no harmony between humans. (Fisherman, personal communication, July 19, 2017, our translation)

Radical-integral THK

Like equity-oriented THK, this third way of interpreting THK also calls for a fundamental rethink-ing of the institutions governing ownership and development in Bali. However, this interpret-ation of THK also seeks to include its ecological and immaterial (spiritual) dimensions, at times advancing a non-utilitarian conception of nature (which dissociates nature's value from its economic worth). It is typically mobilized by the environmental justice activists and the representatives of the Hindu Council.

Based on four points we will elaborate below, we argue that radical-integral THK is the only interpretation that contains elements of a post-growth program as it envisages another conception of the "modern good life", a conception that is not troubled to tackle existential and "ultimate end" questions.

First of all, we found out that those who mobilize radical-integral THK explicitly criticize GDP as an indicator of progress and as a guideline for development policies in Bali. Their focus on socio-environmental justice highlights instead that the impacts of "development" are typically borne by the majority of community members while some selected benefits may be gained by a few – hence the non-integral nature of most development projects and their biased interpretations of THK. A prominent ForBALI leader questioned the Nusa Benoa project in the following terms:

> What if accumulation of capital takes place but other aspects are degraded? How much is the cost of backwater? How much is the cost of biodiversity loss in the Benoa Bay? What about the loss of corals, coastal erosions, erasures of local customs, damages toward sacred places? Could it be measured only in GDP? We reject measuring development only with GDP. (W. Suardana, personal communication, August 4, 2017, our translation)

Second, radical-integral THK challenges the current regime of mass-tourism development in Bali, which underlies an addiction to unequal and unsustainable growth. It is particularly concerned with the overdevelopment of the tourism sector in South Bali, which has shown a colossal physical growth (in the form of real estate, hotels and touristic facility developments, but also in terms of the high number of workers and visitors involved). This has required vast amounts of resources, from fossil fuels to freshwater, and it has generated enormous volumes of waste. Proponents of radical-integral THK seem at times to favor a stabilization of tourism at a sustainable level, as in the form of "steady-state tourism" targeted at a viable level of material and energy throughput. To quote the *Pasubayan* representative:

> We are not being unreceptive toward people who come to Bali to find a living. However, we must consider the capacity of the island. Tourism facilities, including condotels and thousands of hotel rooms will be built on those reclaimed lands. There will be human and economic activities going on over there, which also come with various impacts, such as production of garbage, wastewater, and also more exploitation of freshwater. Is that compatible with the government and corporate claims of saving the environment? And wouldn't these workers need a place to live? (I.W. Swarsa, personal communication, July 22, 2017, our translation)

Third, the radical-integral THK contains an alternative conception of the "good life" that is not identical to the capitalist modernity of Western(ized) growth-driven societies. It implies a critique of modernity associated with mass consumption and commodification. Instead, the pursuit of existential fulfillment of all actors involved in tourism (both on the production and consumption sides) requires some balance between the three interrelated realms of THK. For radical-integral THK, the concept of *palemahan* (natural world) does not simply materialize in the establishment of botanical garden or mangrove replanting schemes, and the complexities of *pawongan* (human world) cannot be reduced into producer-consumer relationships as between fishermen and their prospective buyers. Similarly, the restoration of Pudut Island and the refurbishment of temples would not suffice to establish a healthy *parahyangan* (spiritual world) when the "revitalization" project would essentially take places on areas considered sacred by many local inhabitants.

Finally, radical-integral THK recognizes the non-utilitarian value of nature. As explained in the Sabha Walaka text proposed by the Hindu Council (2015, our translation):

What is no less important is [to ask] what is the relationship between humans and nature? Is nature created for the pleasure of human (nature for exploitation), or are humans created together with nature, hence an integral part of nature (maintaining each other)? Without any philosophical basis, everyone can manipulate and use THK to justify particular economic interest, which in essence can jeopardize life.

These four points briefly discussed above indicate that it would make sense to start a dialogue between, on one hand, the radical-integral interpretation of THK and, on the other hand, comparable approaches/cosmologies developed elsewhere such as *Buen Vivir*, *Ubuntu*, eco-*Swaraj*, *Kyōsei* or GNH. These models all seek to interrogate the mainstream notion of the "good life" with, among other things, its defense of material accumulation.

THK, tourism, post-growth and the commons: some preliminary policy implications

While Hall (2009) made a valuable contribution to what a degrowth project for tourism may look like through the idea of "rightsizing", he did not put forward the *commons*. Quite the opposite, the commons would be central to THK-inspired guidelines for post-growth in tourism. Indeed, as we have seen, the commons are one of the key roots of THK, as exemplified in traditional agrarian collective institutions and irrigation systems. Accordingly, a radical-integral interpretation of THK suggests that tourism should also flourish within the commons. But what would that mean concretely?

Following Büscher and Fletcher (2017, p. 664), we would like to investigate what it would mean for tourism to contribute to the commons in both a material and a subjective sense. Materially speaking, commoning must start from processes of collective appropriation/democratization of the resources that are required for tourist activities to take place. This would ensure a fair distribution of the benefits and impacts and could take the form of *cooperatives*. More empirical research on collectively owned tourist facilities in Bali (as in the village of Tenganan) would be required. Furthermore, tourism development must be based on principles of sufficiency and industrial ecology (Ayres & Ayres, 2002), namely on an approach that seeks as much as possible to reuse output flows of materials and energy as input flows. Industrial ecology crucially requires working with *regional wholes* in a holistic and coordinated way – as opposed to working with individualized businesses that all compete in the pursuit of their own profits.

Regarding the links between tourism and the "subjective commons", we argue that THK – seen as a Balinese "common" but also as a contested concept – could provide a subjective substrate in which post-growth tourism could take roots. Radical-integral THK can indeed offer an alternative to the hegemonic narrative of the "good life" based on private property, mass consumption and growth-addiction. Very concretely, any policy related to tourism on the island should integrate the different languages of valuation that are found in a radical-integral interpretation of THK, thereby relying on multi-criteria evaluations instead of cost/benefit analyses. Likewise in Bhutan, a GNH Policy Screening Tool has been implemented to help the GNH Commission – a powerful committee orchestrating the economy's planning process and chaired by the Prime Minister – in assessing policies and projects for their compatibility with the GNH philosophy of development (Gerber & Raina, 2018a). This screening tool plays a significant role in decision-making, like in Bhutan's rejection of World Trade Organization membership or in the country's decision to limit mining activities (Hayden, 2015).

Within a radical-integral THK perspective, however, relating tourism with nature and society will not suffice. Every actor involved in tourism – be it on the production or the consumption sides – is in search of existential fulfillment in one-way or another. On the production side, activities related to hospitality in its noblest sense can be made more rewarding and meaningful. On the consumption side, travels should not just be exterior ("exploring a tropical island") but also interior ("exploring our relationships to ourselves, others, nature and the cosmos"). Such "inner travels" are often deeply at odds with mass consumption and can only flourish within forms of voluntary simplicity. In this sense, tourism need not be a practice that depends on and perpetuates the material gap between the affluent and the less privileged. Instead, drawing on the paradoxes of frugal abundance, tourism must shift into a mutually enriching experience that seeks to address our inner poverties and deficiencies in all their forms.

Conclusion

This article explored the interconnections between THK, languages of valuation and post-growth theory. It did so because these interrelations are at the heart of a prominent conflict over a tourism development megaproject in South Bali, the empirical focus of our study. We argued that this conflict is less expressed through clashing valuation languages as it is expressed through clashing interpretations of THK. Just like *Buen Vivir* (Gudynas, 2014) and GNH (Gerber & Raina, 2018a), THK is therefore not a uniform and coherent idiom in itself, but a fundamental "battle ground" that reflects how the valuation languages of ecological sustainability, economic gains/ losses, and heritage and spirituality are understood by the conflicting actors. Accordingly, the different interpretations of THK generate very different visions of development for Bali.

Our analysis suggests that there are three main interpretations of THK in the conflict, i.e., a marketable, an equity-oriented, and a radical-integral interpretation. In the mainstream narrative, THK is compatible with growth-driven mass tourism and seeks to transform the source of the island's socio-environmental problems into "solutions" (as seen in the idea of "revitalization"). It promulgates a weak "sustainable tourism" agenda similar to the one proposed by the UNWTO through a narrative of productivity and eco-efficiency. On the other hand, "equity-oriented THK" criticizes the material inequalities related to tourism development, but it does not contest the notion of growth in itself. Finally, in its third use, THK implies a non-utilitarian conception of nature and challenges both the privatization regime and the trajectory of the island's tourism sector. This radical-integral THK endorses a conception of well-being that does not depend on chrematistic growth, but that embraces instead interconnectedness between the self, others, nature and the numinous. As such, we argued, it bears clear similarities with post-growth thinking, particularly with degrowth and post-development.

Ultimately, our study demonstrates that post-growth theory is highly relevant to tourism research, not only theoretically in sharpening the socio-ecological critique of tourism and in making sense of social movements that contest it, but also practically in the design of sustainable alternatives. Furthermore, post-growth theory is as relevant to the tourism industry in the global North as it is to the global South, and this is undoubtedly one major finding of our article. We can only stress, however, the need for more growth-critical research in tourism studies in order to hopefully generate some impacts in the real world.

Notes

1. Together with domestic arrivals, tourist inbounds reach more than 14.4 million in 2017. The contribution of tourism to the province's economy is even higher when other businesses are included (e.g., travel and tour packages, transportation, spa and wellness, etc.).
2. The Balinese term for mutual agreement. In the Benoa Bay case, it refers to the union of customary villages in opposition of development project.
3. In 2010, Governor Pastika issued the Letter 570/1665/BPM about the Moratorium on Principal Licenses for Tourism Accommodation Enterprises following a report from the Ministry of Tourism that evidenced an oversupply of hotel rooms in South Bali.

Acknowledgements

We would like to thank Walhi Bali, the Provincial Secretary of Bali, and the other research participants for their availability and for providing essential research materials. We would also like to thank three anonymous reviewers for their invaluable comments on an earlier version of the manuscript.

Disclosure statement

No potential conflict of interest was reported by the authors.

Funding

This study was supported by the Indonesia Endowment Fund for Education (LPDP).

References

Acosta, A. (2017). Post-extractivism: From discourse to practice—reflections for action. *Revue Internationale de Politique de Développement, 9*(9), 77–101. doi:10.4000/poldev.2356

Adityo, E. (2014, October 7). Tomy Winata's property unit continues with Benoa Bay project. The Jakarta Globe. Retrieved from http://jakartaglobe.id/news/tomy-winatas-property-unit-continues-benoa-bay-project/

Agung, A. A. G. (2005). *Bali endangered paradise? Tri Hita Karana and the conservation of the island's biocultural diversity.* Leiden Ethnosystems and Development Program (LEAD).

Allen, G. R., & Erdmann, M. V. (2011). Reef Fishes of Bali, Indonesia. *Bali Marine Rapid Assessment Program 2011: RAP Bulletin of Biological Assessment No. 64.* (pp. 15–68). Denpasar: Conservation International Indonesia

Ayres, R. U., & Ayres, L. (Eds.). (2002). *A handbook of industrial ecology.* Northampton: Edward Elgar Publishing.

BaleBengong. (2016, March 1). Letter from Bali to the world. Retrieved from https://balebengong.id/lingkungan/a-letter-from-bali-to-the-world.html?lang=id

Bali Government Tourism Office (BGTO). (2018a). The Number of Foreign Tourist Arrival to Bali By Month. Retrieved from Bali Government Tourism Office website: http://www.disparda.baliprov.go.id/en/Statistics2

Bali Government Tourism Office (BGTO). (2018b). The Growth of Domestic Tourist Arrival to Bali in 2017. Retrieved from Bali Government Tourism Office website: http://www.disparda.baliprov.go.id/en/Statistics2

Borras, S. M. (2016). *Land politics, agrarian movements and scholar-activism.* Inaugural lecture, 14 April 2016. The Hague: International Institute of Social Studies.

Bourdeau, P., & Berthelot, L. (2008). Tourisme et décroissance: De la critique à l'utopie? *First International Conference on Economic De-Growth for Ecological Sustainability and Social Equity,* Paris, France, 78–86.

Brinkmann, S. (2018). The interview. In N. K. Denzin & Y. S. Lincoln (Eds.), *The SAGE handbook of qualitative research* (5th ed.) (pp. 997–1038). London: SAGE Publications Ltd.

Brown, F., & Hall, D. (2008). Tourism and development in the global south: The issues. *Third World Quarterly, 29*(5), 839–849. doi:10.1080/01436590802105967

Büscher, B., & Fletcher, R. (2017). Destructive creation: Capital accumulation and the structural violence of tourism. *Journal of Sustainable Tourism, 25*(5), 651–667. doi:10.1080/09669582.2016.1159214

CNN Indonesia. (2016, September 1). Insight with Desi Anwar – polemik reklamasi Teluk Benoa, Bali. Retrieved from https://www.youtube.com/watch?v=H1p9c9zimio

Cole, S. (2012). A political ecology of water equity and tourism: A case study from Bali. *Annals of Tourism Research, 39*(2), 1221–1241. doi:10.1016/j.annals.2012.01.003

Conservation International. (2013). *Kajian Modeling Dampak Perubahan Fungsi Teluk Benoa untuk Sistem Pendukung Keputusan (Decision Support System) dalam Jejaring KKP Bali.* Conservation International Indonesia Report *(pp. 1-47).* Denpasar: Conservation International Indonesia.

Coupland, B., & Coupland, N. (2014). The authenticating discourses of mining heritage tourism in Cornwall and Wales. *Journal of Sociolinguistics, 18*(4), 495–517. doi:10.1111/josl.12081

D'Alisa, G., & Demaria, F. & (2014). *Degrowth: A vocabulary for a new era.* Kallis, G. (Eds.). London: Routledge.

Daly, H. E. (1991. [1977]). *Steady-state economics.* Washington, DC: Island Press.

Erviani, N. K. (2013, August 29). Musisi Bali teriakkan penolakan reklamasi Teluk Benoa lewat lagu. Mongabay. Retrieved from http://www.mongabay.co.id/2013/08/29/musisi-bali-teriakkan-penolakan-reklamasi-teluk-benoa-lewat-lagu/

Flood, G. (1997). The meaning and context of the Purusarthas. In J. Lipner (Ed.), *The fruits of our desiring: An enquiry into the ethics of the Bhagavadgītā for our times* (pp. 11–27). Calgary: Bayeux

Forsyth, T. (2003). *Critical political ecology: The politics of environmental science.* London: Routledge.

Gerber, J.-F., & Raina, R. S. (2018a). Post-growth in the global South? Some reflections from India and Bhutan. *Ecological Economics, 150,* 353–358. doi:10.1016/j.ecolecon.2018.02.020

Gerber, J. F., & Raina, R. S. (Eds.). (2018b). *Post-growth thinking in India.* New Delhi: Orient BlackSwan.

Gerber, J.-F., Veuthey, S., & Martínez-Alier, J. (2009). Linking political ecology with ecological economics in tree plantation conflicts in Cameroon and Ecuador. *Ecological Economics, 68*(12), 2885–2889. doi:10.1016/j.ecolecon.2009.06.029

Gibson-Graham, J. K., Cameron, J., & Healy, S. (2013). *Take back the economy*. Minneapolis: University of Minnesota Press.

Gössling, S. (2003). *Tourism and development in tropical islands: Political ecology perspectives*. Cheltenham: Edward Elgar Publishing Ltd.

Gubernatorial Decree 2138/02-C/HK (GD). (2012). *Granting of permits and rights for the utilization, development and management of coastal area of Benoa Bay Bali Province*. Denpasar: Bali Provincial Government.

Gudynas, E. (2014). Buen vivir. In G. D'Alisa, F. Demaria & G. Kallis (Eds.), *Degrowth: A vocabulary for a new era* (pp. 201–204). London: Routledge.

Hall, C. M. (2009). Degrowing tourism: Décroissance, sustainable consumption and steady-state tourism. *Anatolia*, *20*(1), 46–61. doi:10.1080/13032917.2009.10518894

Hammersley, M., & Atkinson, P. (2007). *Ethnography: Principles in practice* (3rd ed.) London: Routledge.

Hasanudin, M. (2013, August 2). Tolak reklamasi, warga Bali demo di tengah laut. *Kompas*. Retrieved from https://regional.kompas.com/read/2013/08/02/1522169/Tolak.Reklamasi.Warga.B%20ali.Demo.di.Tengah.Laut

Hayden, A. (2015). Bhutan: Blazing a trail to a postgrowth future? Or stepping on the treadmill of production? *The Journal of Environment & Development*, *24*(2), 161–186. doi:10.1177/1070496515579199

Heller, M. (2010). The commodification of language. *Annual Review of Anthropology*, *39*(1), 101–114. doi:10.1146/annurev.anthro.012809.104951

Higgins-Desbiolles, F. (2018). Sustainable tourism: Sustaining tourism or something more? *Tourism Management Perspectives*, *25*, 157–160. doi:10.1016/j.tmp.2017.11.017

Hindu Council. (2015). *Keputusan Pesamuhan Sabha Walaka Parisada Hindu Dharma Indonesia Nomor: 06/KEP/SW PARISADA/X/2015 tentang Rekomendasi Kawasan Suci Teluk Benoa [Policy Recommendation]*. Denpasar: Parisada Hindu Dharma Indonesia.

Ismayana, I. M. A. (2017, February 14). Penahanan dua aktivis ForBALI ditangguhkan. Tribun-Bali. Retrieved from http://bali.tribunnews.com/2017/02/14/penahanan-dua-aktivis-forbali-ditangguhkan

Jackson, S. (2017). How much water does a culture need? Environmental water management's cultural challenge and indigenous responses. In A. Horne, J. Webb, M. Stewardson, M. Acreman, and B. D. Richter (Eds.), *Water for the environment: From policy and science to implementation and management* (pp. 173–188). Cambridge, MA: Academic Press.

Kothari, A., Salleh, A., Escobar, A., Demaria, F., & Acosta, A. (Eds.). (2019). *Pluriverse: A post-development dictionary*. New Delhi: Tulika Books.

Latouche, S. (2009). *Farewell to growth*. Cambridge: Polity.

Martínez-Alier, J. (2002). *The environmentalism of the poor: A study of ecological conflicts and valuation*. Cheltenham: Edward Elgar.

Mostafanezhad, M., Norum, R., & Shelton, E. J. & (2016). *Political ecology of tourism: Community, power and the environment*. Thompson-Carr, A. (Eds.). Abingdon: Routledge.

Mowforth, M., & Munt, I. (2016). *Tourism and sustainability: Development, globalisation and new tourism in the third world* (4th ed.). Abingdon: Routledge.

Nepal, S., & Saarinen, J. (Eds.). (2016). *Political ecology and tourism*. Abingdon: Routledge.

Nusa Benoa website. (2018). http://nusabenoa.com

O'Neill, J. (1993). *Ecology, policy and politics: Human well-being and the natural world (Environmental philosophies)*. London: Routledge.

Peters, J. H., & Wardana, W. (2013). *Tri Hita Karana: The spirit of Bali*. Jakarta: Kepustakaan Populer Gramedia (KPG).

Picard, M. (2011). From 'Agama hindu bali' to 'Agama hindu' and back toward a relocalization of the balinese religion? In M. Picard & R. Madinier (Eds.), *The politics of religion in Indonesia: Syncretism, orthodoxy, and religious contention in Java and Bali* (pp. 117–140). Hoboken: Taylor & Francis.

Presidential Decree No. 45 (PD). (2011). *Spatial plan of urban area Denpasar, Badung, Gianyar, and Tabanan*. Jakarta: State Secretariat of the Republic of Indonesia.

Presidential Decree No. 51 (PD). (2014). *Amendment of Presidential Decree 45/2011 on Granting of Permits and Rights for the Utilization, Development and Management of Coastal Area of Benoa Bay Bali Province*. Jakarta: State Secretariat of the Republic of Indonesia.

Ramstedt, M. (2014). Discordant temporalities in bali's new village jurisdictions. *The Journal of Legal Pluralism and Unofficial Law*, *46*(1), 60–78. doi:10.1080/07329113.2014.893722

Rifai, T. (2017, August 15). Tourism: Growth is not the enemy; it's how we manage it that counts. UNWTO. Retrieved from http://media.unwto.org/press-release/2017-08-15/tourism-growth-not-enemy-it-s-how-we-manage-it-counts

Roth, D., & Sedana, G. (2015). Reframing *Tri Hita Karana*: From 'Balinese culture'to politics. *The Asia Pacific Journal of Anthropology*, *16*(2), 157–175. doi:10.1080/14442213.2014.994674

Santos, B. (2007). Beyond abyssal thinking: From global lines to ecologies of knowledges. *Review (Fernand Braudel Center)*, *30*(1), 45–89.

Statistics Indonesia. (2017a). *Produk Domestik Regional Bruto Provinsi Bali Menurut Lapangan Usaha 2012-2016*. Jakarta: Statistics Indonesia.

Statistics Indonesia. (2017b). *Statistik Ketenagakerjaan Provinsi Bali 2016*. Jakarta: Statistics Indonesia.

Statistics Indonesia. (2018). *Perkembangan Pariwisata dan Transportasi Nasional Desember 2017*. Jakarta: Statistics Indonesia.

Stonich, S. C. (1998). Political ecology of tourism. *Annals of Tourism Research, 25*(1), 25–54. doi:10.1016/S0160-7383(97)00037-6

Sudiarta, I. K., & Sudiarta, I. G. (2011). Status kondisi dan identifikasi permasalahan kerusakan padang lamun di bali. *Jurnal Mitra Bahari, 5*(2), 104–126.

Suriyani, L. D. (2016, July 17) Aksi Desa Sanur menyambut putusan Susi Pudjiastuti. *Mongabay*. Retireved from http://www.mongabay.co.id/2016/07/17/aksi-desa-sanur-menyambut-putusan-susi-pudjiastuti/

Telfer, D., & Sharpley, R. (2016). *Tourism and development in the developing world* (2nd ed.). Abingdon: Routledge.

Tempo. (2018, August 24). Benoa Bay reclamation scrapped, says Bali Governor-elect. Retrieved from https://en.tempo.co/read/news/2018/08/24/056921083/Benoa-Bay-Reclamation-Scrapped-Says-Bali-Governor-elect

Tirta Wahana Bali International (TWBI) website. (2018). http://twbi.co.id.

Tribunnews. (2014, August 8). Ribuan warga Denpasar turun ke jalan tolak reklamasi Teluk Benoa. Retrieved from http://www.tribunnews.com/regional/2014/08/08/ribuan-warga-denpasar-turun-ke-jalan-tolak-reklamasi-teluk-benoa

Ulum, M. (2014, March 24) Ditangkap polisi, 4 aktivis lingkungan raih penghargaan. Sindonews. Retrieved from https://daerah.sindonews.com/read/847208/27/ditangkap-polisi-4-aktivis-lingkungan-raih-penghargaan-1395655845

United Nations Conference on Trade and Development (UNCTAD). (2010). *The contribution of tourism to trade and development. Note by the UNCTAD secretariat.* TD/B/C.I/8. UNCTAD, UN, New York and Geneva.

United Nations Environment Programme and World Tourism Organization (UNEP & UNWTO). (2012). *Tourism in the Green Economy – Background Report*, UNWTO, Madrid.

van den Bergh, J. (2011). Environment versus growth – a criticism of "degrowth" and a plea for "a-growth. *Ecological Economics, 70*(5), 881–890. doi:10.1016/j.ecolecon.2010.09.035

Wardana, A. (2017). Neoliberalisasi kawasan perairan Teluk Benoa: Sebuah catatan kritis atas praksis perlawanan di Bali. *Wacana, 35*, 55–90.

Wichterich, C. (2015). Contesting green growth, connecting care, commons and enough. In W. Harcourt, & I. L. Nelson (Eds.), *Practicing feminist political ecology: Moving beyond the 'Green economy'* (pp. 67–100). London: Zed Books.

World Tourism Organization (UNWTO). (2016). *UNWTO Tourism Highlights, 2016 Edition*, UNWTO, Madrid.

World Tourism Organization (UNWTO). (2018). *UNWTO Annual Report 2017*, UNWTO, Madrid.

World Tourism Organization and Global Tourism Economy Research Centre (UNWTO & GTERC). (2017). *UNWTO/GTERC Annual Report on Tourism Trends, 2017 Edition – Executive Summary*, UNWTO, Madrid.

Yin, R. (2014). *Case study research: Design and methods.* (5th ed.). Thousand Oaks, CA: Sage Publications.

Overtourism and degrowth: a social movements perspective

Claudio Milano ⓘD, Marina Novelli ⓘD and Joseph M. Cheer ⓘD

ABSTRACT

Overtourism is a contemporary phenomenon, rapidly evolving and underlined by what is evidently excessive visitation to tourist destinations. This is obvious in the seemingly uncontrolled and unplanned occurrence of urban overtourism in popular destinations and arguably a consequence of unregulated capital accumulation and growth strategies heavily associated with selling cities as tourism commodities. The vested interests of social movements has converged into growing protests against overtourism and associated degrowth campaigns have emerged out of this activism that calls for alternative governance and management measures that eschew touristic monoculture and simplistic economic growth-oriented models. Accordingly, we explore the evolution of the tourism degrowth discourse among social movement activists in Barcelona, and in particular, where this is related to claims associated with overtourism and the extent to which this might be influencing a paradigm shift from 'tourism growth' to 'tourism degrowth'. Methodologically, we draw from an overarching framework that leverages long-term ethnographic research in Barcelona. Here, we employ in-depth semi-structured interviews, participant observations, informal conversations and retrospective evaluation of field diary entries.

Introduction

During the 1950s and 1960s, embedded liberalism policies delivered high rates of economic growth to only a handful of national economies, thus raising concerns regarding equality and inequality (Harvey, 2007). This period was marked by a firm belief that growth was synonymous with development and this train of thought has been employed widely since the 1950s as an economic paradigm associated with the push for more prosperous conditions in non-industrialized economies (Escobar, 2014). Indeed, that growth does not necessarily equate to sustainable development is a well-established truism (Hall, 2010; Novelli, 2015), with some critics addressing 'degrowth' as the antithesis of growth itself (Latouche, 2014; 2009). Over the last decade, there has been a boom in the sheer numbers of international conferences, peer-reviewed publications and reports on degrowth and particularly, sustainable degrowth (Martínez-Alier, Pascual, Vivien, & Zaccai, 2010; Schneider, Martinez-Alier, & Kallis, 2011).

Evidently, there is increasing grassroots activism and the development of research networks concerning degrowth such as the Research & Degrowth (R&D) Association (Kallis, Demaria, & D'Alisa, 2014). The ensuing degrowth debate has overlapped with the leap from modernity to postmodernity and has coincided with the shift from embedded liberalism to neoliberalism (Harvey, 1990). Together with the 1970's neoliberal city boom, urban spaces have witnessed intensive land improvement and real estate speculation, higher population densities and increased levels of economic activity (Molotch, 1976).

Tourism is considered the fastest growing and most widespread industry worldwide (UNWTO, 2018) and has arguably made a considerable contribution to the proliferation and functioning of the capitalist world system (Fletcher, 2011). It is within this milieu that tourism and the degrowth agenda intersects and underlined by the spread of global mass tourism that has inevitably attracted mounting criticism, particularly regarding the controversial relationship between tourism, growth and development, and the extent to which it builds resilience and adaptive capacities (Cheer, Milano, & Novelli, 2019; Cheer & Lew, 2018; Lew & Cheer, 2018).

The heightened interest in selling cities as authentic commodities for tourism purposes has proliferated to become a fast-evolving and alternative form of capital accumulation (Harvey, 2007). Contrary to popular opinion that the term was invented recently, the term overtourism appears to have been first mentioned in the Sydney Morning Herald in 2001 where reference was made to tourism growth in Pompei and how destination management was hampered by underfunding and overtourism (Petersen, 2001). Urban overtourism elaborations that have emerged more recently are largely related to visitation growth that has led to overcrowding in areas where residents suffer the consequences of temporary and seasonal tourism peaks, enforcing permanent changes to their lifestyles, and impinging their access to amenities and the realisation of optimum well-being (Milano, Cheer, & Novelli, 2019).

Notwithstanding, the contemporary debate on the effects of over-visitation and over-crowding of tourism destinations, general concerns and related theoretical discourses addressing the problems of excessive tourism growth are not new and were flagged more than forty years ago by Turner and Ash (1975) and Doxey (1975), followed by Butler (1980), UNWTO (1983), O'Reilly (1986), Boissevain (1996) and more recently by Colomb and Novy (2016), Koens, Postma, and Papp (2018) and Milano and Mansilla (2018). In more recent times, the debate has shifted toward overtourism and the emergence of the degrowth discourse in tourism studies (Andriotis, 2018; Hall, 2009).

This article offers a critical examination of the controversial debates linking overtourism, social movement activism and degrowth in the city of Barcelona. While the city has experienced exponential increases in visitor arrivals, and overall economic activity, the tourism degrowth discourse has emerged, underlined by the political agenda of social movements. Over the last decade, Barcelona has become emblematic of tourism growth that has come to be resisted by social movements. By assessing the activities of grassroots movements such as the ABTS (*Assemblea de Barris per un Turisme Sostenible* – Assembly of Neighbourhoods for Sustainable Tourism) and SET (*Red de ciudades del Sur de Europa ante la Turistización* – Network of Southern European Cities against Touristification), we emphasise how social movements align with the degrowth discourse.

The *Barcelona Strategic Tourism Plan for 2020'* that estimates 30 million visitors annually, of which half are overnight visitors, the remainder being day-trippers (Barcelona City Council, 2016) underlines the ABTS and SET Network's tourism degrowth campaigns against what they consider to be unsustainable and socially disruptive growth. The ABTS and SET Network propose an alternative model of governance, agitating for shifts away from a touristic monoculture and simplistic economic growth-oriented approach, to one that encourages tourism degrowth characterised by steady-state tourism theory and rooted in protection of local resident quality of life and well-being (Hall, 2009). More recently, the focus of social movements has shifted to directly campaigning against overtourism, with ABTS the forerunner. Although such activism is by no means unprecedented with various Barcelona neighbourhoods having experienced protests against overtourism, hotel development projects and HUT (housing for touristic use) (Blanco-Romero, Blázquez-Salom, & Cànoves, 2018; Cócola-Gant, 2016; Mansilla, 2018; Milano, 2017b; 2018; Russo & Scarnato, 2018).

Since ABTS was established in November 2015, as a grassroots organisation initially formed by thirty-five Barcelona-based social movements, associations and entities, it has shaped the tourism degrowth agenda and has become central to public events, stakeholder meetings, debates and campaigns focusing on city rights, cost of living, housing affordability, reduction in the numbers of tourists arriving in the city and incoming flights, and other practices that heighten the proliferation of unmanageable and unsustainable tourism flows. Based on a commitment to forging a more socially and environmentally fair city, designed by and for its residents, ABTS has been pivotal in reinforcing their agenda, both in the mass media and within local political arenas. The appointment of Ada Colau as Mayor has helped foster a more open debate on tourism-related issues and legitimized grassroots movements in the Barcelona Tourism and City Board.

Building upon sparse degrowth literature in tourism (Andriotis, 2014; 2018; Hall, 2009, Canavan, 2014), the 2000s saw the intensification of tourism related social movements and degrowth advocacy (Demaria, Schneider, Sekulova, & Martinez-Alier, 2013), and investigations into the disruptive effects of the Barcelona model (Capel, 2005; Delgado, 2007; Milano & Mansilla, 2018; Russo & Scarnato, 2018). In this light, ABTS' activism and the extent to which this has influenced a shift, from "growth for development" to "degrowth for liveability" is explored. By drawing upon ethnographic research conducted in Barcelona between 2015 and 2018, and employing a Rapid Situation Analysis (RSA) participatory method based on in-depth and semi-structured interviews, informal conversations, participant-observations and retrospective evaluations of field diary entries to identify emergent themes, this study adds to the unfolding critical literature regarding the links between overtourism, social movements and tourism degrowth.

Degrowth and social movement in the age of overtourism

A number of theoretical perspectives form the scaffold upon which empirical findings of this paper are discussed. As a phenomenon, overtourism can be viewed from a range of theoretical lenses including political economy, human geography, social anthropology, cultural studies, urban, rural and coastal planning, tourism marketing (and de-marketing) and destination management, to name just a few. In particular, the approach to the study of overtourism taken draws upon the juxtaposition of two key framing perspectives: degrowth (Kallis et al., 2018) and social movements theory (Castells, 1983). In both cases, the literature is diverse and longstanding, but rather than addressing these in minute detail, we acknowledge, integrate and investigate those dimensions relevant to critically assessing the relationship between overtourism, grassroots activism and the evolution of tourism degrowth campaigns. Importantly, the argument for degrowth is, to a large degree, driven from the bottom-up by advocates, activists and civil society groups for whom growth has proved to be disruptive, marginalising and has led to largely adverse outcomes. Overtourism is emblematic of the processes and outcomes of tourism growth, oftentimes rapid and unsustainable expansion, and in many cases, exogenously driven and embedded in the global travel supply chain that mostly operates outside the purview of destination communities (Milano, Cheer, & Novelli, 2018). Degrowth is largely a reaction to economic growth, where processes of consumption and production have become largely divorced (Kallis et al., 2018) and where supply chains proliferate through increasing extraction of underlying resources for productive gain, while costs of production are borne by communities and resource guardians.

As key proponents of degrowth, Kallis et al. (2018) contend, it is worth considering how reducing production and consumption might be possible without diminishing prosperity or well-being. Promoters of growth, mostly international agencies, government and private sector actors, characteristically spurn thoughts of economic contraction citing that expansion and resources exploitation is vital to maintaining standards of living and increasing incomes, and that overall, productivity is vital to economic stability (Beckerman, 1975). Indeed, productivity is considered the benchmark of what underpins a vibrant economy in much the same way that profitability is used to distinguish the performance and prospects of corporations – clearly emphasising economic indicators as the marker of prosperity. Yet, when growth takes little stock of non-economic considerations, this creates fertile ground for opponents of economic growth, especially civil society groups who find themselves on the periphery of the growth nexus, and often excluded from policy and planning processes or academic discourses.

In theorizing degrowth, Kallis et al. (2018) draw on political economy, political ecology and sustainable development concerns that underpin the clarion call for economic degrowth as a corollary toward more sustainable and just outcomes. This also speaks to growing global advocacy questioning consumptive patterns underpinned by economic growth and whether the pace and rate of change undermines the natural endowments for future generations. Kallis (2011) has been particularly vehement that sustainable degrowth should be foregrounded and given urgency within policy and planning discourses. Furthermore, he emphasises that "sustainable degrowth is not only an inevitable hypothesis, but also a potent political vision that can be socially transformative" (2011, p. 873). The coalescing of economic policy with social-ecological concerns is central to the degrowth thesis, calling for a commensurate focus to be given to the non-economic perturbations that are a direct result of economic growth.

Serge Latouche (2009), a key proponent in the development of degrowth scholarly discourses conceptualises that the thematic of delineating consumption growth and the extent to which this is enhancing human well-being or not is fundamental to degrowth advocacy. The question as to whether productivity gains are actually fostering human well-being or undermining prospects for the future is resonant in the degrowth putsch and is also echoed in the overtourism uprising as well. D'Alisa et al (2014, p. 25) throws into stark relief notions of degrowth and contends that "the idea of economic degrowth and of the construction of a society of sharing, frugality and conviviality continue to strengthen" is fundamental. However, although the limits to growth (Meadows, Meadows, Randers, & Behrens, 1972) and the antigrowth movement were rooted into the political agendas of large cities in the 1970s (Molotch, 1976), whether degrowth advocacy has made material changes to policymaker and business attitudes to economic expansion orientations remains doubtful.

Social movements theory, as advanced by Castells (1983) and Touraine (1981) over four decades ago and new social movements theory by Buechler (1995) and Anyon (2014) suggests that the mobilisation of grassroots actors and activists in organised activism is a vital response to problematic economic, socio-political and environmental changes that marginalise and undermine ecological endowments. The shift from proletarian movements toward collective action for a wider array of motivations underlines the progression of social movement theory (Buechler, 1995). McCarthy and Zald (1987) make the important distinction that while social movements were described as spontaneous banding of individuals, it is now a more common mobilisation in response to socio-political, economic and environmental grievances. This is evident in the rise of social movements in opposition to political (Yellow Umbrella Movement and the Anti-Consumerism Movement), economic (Occupy Wall Street), social (LGBTIQ rights) and environmental (Sea Shepherd/Greenpeace) causes seeking redress and/or reform to institutional inertia. The progression to what may be argued to be new "new social movements" is underlined in the Information Age where "networked social movements" (Castells, 2015) highly organized, share information and enact unprecedented digital strategies with more ease toward greater and more rapid impact.

Political and economic processes that have diminished agencies and wellbeing of particular populaces is especially pertinent, and more so where these have proved to be disruptive to public and private spaces or have undermined the commons. Social movement theory has a deep and diverse trajectory (Diani, 1992) and while it is beyond the remit of this paper to take a deep dive into what are evidently divergent perspectives, especially the binaries that exist between what it is and isn't, and the disciplinary leanings that prevail. Notwithstanding, social movement theory considers social movements as bottom-up activism predicated on rectifying problematic disjunctures that emerge in accordance with socio-political, economic and environmental transformation. This is in harmony with the links Zald and McCarthy (2017, p. 17) make with the term resource mobilization where "an increase in the extent or intensity of grievances or deprivation and the development of ideology occur prior to the emergence of social movement phenomena". Moreover, this is especially discernible in the present where although global economic prosperity has reached unprecedented heights, sizeable cohorts remain adrift of such developments creating fertile grounds for discontent and grievances.

Castells (1983, p. xv) frames social movement making as "purposive social action" that is predicated on reform and rectifying perceived system failures that have impinged on the rights and wellbeing of interest groups. Diani (2007) refers to advocacy groups as "social movement networks" made up of individuals and networks with common aspirations around attaining positions of social justice, democratic reform, fairness and redress for circumstances often characterised by mismanagement, deficient planning and poor governance. In essence, Castells (1983, xvi) underlines that social movements are driven by "a reaction to a crisis created by an economically determined structural logic". Similarly, Escobar and Alvarez (1992, p. 4) outline: "Social action is understood as the product of complex social processes in which structure and agency interact in manifold ways and in which actors produce meanings, negotiate, and make decisions".

Social movements are essentially counterpoised against incumbent authority and socio-political and economic structures that have led to actors within such collectives baying for change that halts and to some degree, unwinds enduring and emergent institutional marginalisation and injustice. This disruption is exemplified by Owens (2008) who argues that very often, social movements are created by tensions from below that use, as their inspiration, the dissonance between government and business lobby interests and what they see as overriding imperatives of economic growth that leave them on the outer. These are common themes in social movement theory where thresholds of disempowerment and disenfranchisement spurs collective action aimed at remedying longstanding grievances that have slowly led to widespread injustices and expropriation of legacies from which actors within movements have enjoyed, leveraged, or inherited. This is exemplified in practice where displacement, exploitation and transformation have served to alienate and disadvantage members of movements.

Linking degrowth with social movements might be the aftereffect of how some contemporary social activism is predicated on growth and transformation that is disproportionately justified upon overarching economic rationale to maintain productivity, employment and income growth. This feeds into social movement opposition against neoliberal and globalization agendas that are framed by keeping financial markets stable and production and supply chains continuously in 'production mode'. The aversion to degrowth stokes fears of economic recession and threats to political longevity of governments and business viability of corporations, making ensuing contentions prone to politicisation and fear mongering.

In conflating overtourism with the dual theoretical underpinnings of social movement theory and principles of degrowth, what is evident is that social movements and degrowth are intertwined in the struggles that have ensued where host community tolerances and wellbeing have been breached by the collectivized actions of visitor economy growth (Owens, 2008). The displacement and alienating effects central to the angst that drives overtourism is intimately connected to calls for tourism degrowth. However, whether destination managers and the global travel supply chain can countenance such moves is questionable. Travel consumption is emblematic of wider consumptive trends underlined by economic prosperity and driven by the desire for greater mobility. What this means for social movements aligned against touristic endeavours suggests that there may be little for activists to be sanguine about.

Social movements' touristification and tourism activism on the rise

The fact that tourism requires political stability, security and public safety in order to flourish is firmly established in extant literature (Espiner, Orchiston, & Higham, 2017; Stephenson & Bianchi,

2014). In this context, activism in the form of social movements protests, demonstrations and/or strikes represent an anti-tourist element (Cordero Ulate, 2006). The relationship between tourism and the engagement with urban social movements is diverse and complex and needs to be investigated not only from the perspective of "exploitation and resistance to tourism", but rather as a dialectic process between all of the parties involved (Owens, 2008).

The twin domains of tourism and social movements studies have rarely been linked in scholarly investigations with the exception of Colomb and Novy (2016). However, in recent years, there has been a noticeable rise in activism driven by social movements and in their struggles and denunciations against tourism expansion, they have shifted concerns from the local to the global, with this convergence leading to reciprocal exchanges between tourism industry and social movements (Milano, 2017a). For instance, tourism can be both a target and a result of activism and, the latter can become a tourist attraction. For example, social movements have been employed for the promotion of tourism including political tourism, revolutionary tourism or Zapatourism in Mexico (Coronado, 2008; Garza Tovar & Sánchez Crispín, 2015), militant and brigade tourism in Central America and as seen in Brazil's Landless Workers Movement's (MST) (Gascón, 2009), volunteer tourism in Palestine (Belhassen, Uriely, & Assor, 2014; Isaac & Platenkamp, 2010) and in volunteer tourism (McGehee, 2002; McGehee & Santos, 2005), as well as NGO (non-government organisations) study tours and rights-based tourism (Spencer, 2008). Conversely, tourism has become the subject of what might be referred to as the touristification of social movements agendas, particularly in relation to tourism activism where overtourism has become a catch cry (Milano, 2018). In all, social movements have appropriated a critical discourse and spawned tourism-centred activism.

Historically, social movements have been centred on the struggle of workers against precarious working conditions, gender inequality, sex discrimination, healthcare services, social exclusion and the privatization of education (Cohen & Rai, 2000). However, in recent decades, critical discourses specifically related to tourism and the wider visitor economy have become central to social movement narratives as evidenced in debates and at assemblies that appeal for action. At the same time, mainstream media discourses have provided wide coverage of overtourism describing evidently adverse impacts of tourism in cities. In emphasising urban settings, social movements have tended to gloss over tourism development in rural and coastal regions. However, the latter is not at all a new or less important area of concern. While in Southern Europe local environmental activism against tourism development emerged in the mid 1970s (Kousis, 2000), in Latin America there are many cases of popular mobilizations against tourism development in rural areas (Almeida & Cordero Ulate, 2015), including actions of environmental groups related to climate change protests in Costa Rica (Cordero Ulate, 2015), local clashes to preserve native land rights in Panama (Maney, 2001), resistance to tourism mega-projects in indigenous territories in Northeast Brazil (Lustosa & de Almeida, 2011) and denunciation of displacement, precarious labour and real-estate speculation in Mexico and Central America (Blázquez & Cañada, 2011; Cañada, 2010; Hiernaux-Nicolas, 1999; Horton, 2007, Bonilla & Mortd, 2008).

In urban settings specifically, the overtourism debate is embedded in growing criticism of tourism development models characterised by privatization and saturation of public spaces, inflationary effects on house prices and the resulting diminishment of resident purchasing power, outsourcing of employment leading to precarious working conditions and the transformation of the commercial fabric of cities that undermine essential characteristics of places. These have been instrumental in the "touristification of social movements" (Milano, 2018) agenda and of "urban tourism politicisation from below" in international tourist hotspots in Europe, North America, South America and Asia" (Colomb & Novy, 2016, p. 5). In the 1990s Boissevain (1996) emphasised the disjunctures resulting from mass tourism in various southern European destinations and how local communities used tourism as a source of dispute through covert resistance, hiding, fencing, rituals, organized protests and aggression. More recently, mainstream media sensationalism and preoccupation with overtourism has legitimized critical discourses regarding

Table 1. Historical Milestones, 2004–2018.

Year	Milestone Event
2018	2nd *Fòrum Veïnal sobre Turisme – Reflexions sobre turisme a Barcelona i el Sud d'Europa*
2018	SET Network press conference in Barcelona
2018	Meeting: Neighbourhood Life - Tourist Tours. Can we share the space?
2018	Meeting: Port-city: towards what model are we adopting?
2017	Protest against the opening of the first Gaudí work "Casa Vincens"
2017	Protest against the arrival of the biggest cruise ship of the world "Symphony of the Seas"
2017	Demonstration against the opening of a new Port Terminal
	A group of youths' slashes tyres on sightseeing bus and rental bikes in Barcelona
2016	1st *Fòrum Veïnal sobre Turisme - Crítica, anàlisi i proposte*
2015	Constitution of ABTS
2008	*El País* newspaper publishes an article titled "*Turistofobia*", written by Manuel Delgado
2004	Universal Forum of Cultures held in Barcelona provokes discontent among residents

tourism development and the relationship between social movements and tourism development cities. Conversely, academic discourses have been slower to undertake critical examinations.

Lastly, the interrelationships between urban social movements and tourism can be seen as practice-based predicated on a twofold rule of engagement; firstly, by established social movements pointing to tourism as the cause of existing discontents and inequalities due to gentrification, displacement and/or housing crises, and secondly through the *ad hoc* constitution of social movements specifically aimed at tourism activism, such as the ABTS. It is worth noting that the actors participating in such activism are distinct from the classic revolutionary factory workers commonly referred to in Keynesian discourses and instead, are associated with middle-class urbanities struggling to maintain and preserve their quality of life amidst contemporary post-industrial neoliberal contexts (Mayer, 2012).

Research context

Barcelona has become one of the globe's most visited tourist cities with the initial tourism growth spurt taking place during the urban transformations that ensued prior to the summer Olympics Games in 1992 and the establishment in 1993 of the public-private Consortium of *Turisme de Barcelona,* a tourism marketing agency of the city. The nineties marked a point from which Barcelona embarked on the trajectory to become one of the urban tourism capitals of Europe (Lópoz-Palomeque, 2015; Palou, 2011). This is unsurprising given the breadth and spread of tangible and intangible culture and the historic backdrop that underpins the city. In particular, the city's inimitable architecture and design (Borja, 2010) together with the spread of services, technology, urban marketing and tourism placemaking (Lew, 2017; Mansilla, 2016; Mansilla & Milano, 2019) catapulted it into the European practice of commodifying cities. The so-called "Barcelona Model" (Capel, 2005; Delgado, 2007) and the intensifying city tourism growth is central to upsurge in grassroots activism.

Concerning social movements' activism against tourism, the summer of 2017 is remembered as a watershed of protests against mass tourism that occurred in several Spanish cities (Hughes, 2018). However, the root cause of such discontent is arguably found in much earlier debates at events such as the *Universal Forum of Cultures,* an international event that took place in Barcelona in 2004; it had three main themes including cultural diversity, sustainable development and conditions for peace. This event is arguably a milestone (see Table 1) of the controversial relationship between Barcelona's citizens and tourism, concerned about the city's capacity to absorb more tourists, and wanting to strike a balance between residents' everyday life and tourism (Suñol, 2016). Since then, the focus of social movements against tourism has shifted and is now characterised by activism with ABTS at the helm. ABTS has concentrated on mobilising voices of neighbourhood cohorts on issues such as reversing the triumphalist tourism discourse rooted in production and consumption growth models, the alleviation of pressures from real estate speculation and rising housing costs, as well as emphasizing tourism degrowth.

On July 1st 2016, the first Neighbourhood Forum on Tourism (*Foro Vecinal sobre Turismo*) was hosted in Barcelona and resulted in acknowledgement of the need to address overtourism and facilitate closer ties with counterparts in Venice, Mallorca, Camp de Tarragona and Malaga. Two years later, on May 18th and 19th 2018, neighbourhood associations, social movements and activist groups from 14 southern European cities convened in Barcelona for the second Neighbourhood Forum on Tourism (*Foro Vecinal sobre Turismo*) under the theme "Tourism reflections on Barcelona and South Europe". This resulted in the constitution of the Network of Southern European Cities against Touristification (SET Network*)*. SET initially comprised of social movements from sixteen places - Venice, Valencia, Sevilla, Pamplona, Palma de Mallorca, Malta, Málaga, Madrid, Lisbon, Florencia, Ibiza, Girona, San Sebastián, Canarias, Camp de Tarragona and Barcelona. By adopting a synergic approach, SET's main goal is to engage in joint actions of protest against the "growth centred model" of urban tourism and apply pressure on national governments to promote degrowth.

Methodology

This study is comprised of a team of three researchers including an established "insider" (who has been a resident in Barcelona since 2008) and two "outsiders" (Beebe, 2001). The value of having long-term field research conducted by an "insider" with extensive research experience in the destination provided a high level of trust with local communities, allowed unique access to key stakeholders and enabled the employment of snowball sampling. Critical reflections on the evolution of social movements discourses were gleaned from the first Neighbourhood Forum on Tourism (*Foro Vecinal sobre Turismo*) in 2016, by the "insider" and was instrumental in identifying key historical milestones (see Table 1) and in tracking the evolution of social movements. Importantly, however, these reflections were mediated and reviewed through probing questions by "outsider" counterparts, who had more "distance" from the effects of overtourism and social movements based in other geographical locations.

Drawing upon evidence emerging from ethnography conducted in Barcelona between 2015 and 2018, this article reports on fieldwork undertaken in informal settings using Rapid Situation Analysis (RSA) as an overarching research approach. RSA is a tried and tested (Novelli, Morgan, Mitchell, & Ivanov, 2016) "hybrid, participatory, bottom-up [qualitative and interpretative] research approach" (Koutra, 2010, pp. 1016). The analysis of participants *in situ* allows for a more nuanced and critical investigation of the complex dynamics associated with overtourism and social movements and their promotion of degrowth in Barcelona. RSA interprets and consolidates feedback from local participants which, when shared with the community, allows for reflection, ownership and transformation (Koutra, 2010). The research in this case consisted of four stages realized between 2015 and 2018:

- Stage 1 – Desk research of secondary data sources including government statements, social movements manifestos and websites, city council reports and plans, press releases, social media network discourses
- Stage 2 – In depth semi-structured interviews with social movement agents in Barcelona
- Stage 3 – Overt participant observations and informal conversations during workshops, stakeholder consultations, assemblies and meetings
- Stage 4 – Retrospective analysis of field diary entries based on fieldwork and informal conversations with respondents

The main intention was to employ participatory research methods with social movement actors to explore their attitudes toward overtourism and degrowth. Concurrent to the participatory research undertaken in Barcelona, fieldwork was conducted during social movements events in other places as part of the SET Network. These included the 'Social movements facing tourism' event in Mallorca in June 2017 (*Moviments socials davant el turisme. Una lluita compartida a diferents territoris i ciutats*) and in San Sebastian in May 2018 – 'The effects of tourism on San Sebastian inhabitants daily life' (*Los efectos del Turismo en la vida de las donostiarras*). Further fieldwork interviewing stakeholders with differing levels of influence and interest, and with a geographical spread across various neighbourhoods of Barcelona commenced in July 2016 during the first Neighbourhood Forum on Tourism (*Foro Vecinal sobre Turismo*) and throughout the period that led to the second Neighbourhood Forum on Tourism (*Foro Vecinal sobre Turismo*) in May 2018, through to August 2018.

While reflexive analysis of field diary entries to identify emergent themes and participant observation records framed evidence of social movements activities during the period under investigation, in-depth semi-structured interviews allowed participants to provide deep insights into their experience with tourism activism. This allowed data triangulation with field diary entries and participant's observational findings.

Initial focus was on research questions that contribute to understanding how and why events occurred and evolved, rather than testing a hypothesis with theory derived from generated data (Hart, 1998; Robson, 2011). The interpretation of overtourism by social movements lends itself to a holistic inductive research design focused on the adoption and evolution of the degrowth concept in Barcelona as a series of complex inter-related components rather than assessing individual parts (Armstrong, 2008). Interviews were conducted between 2016 and 2018 with residents (n = 7 and coded R1 to R7) and social movement activists from Barcelona international activists from SET Network members (n = 8 and coded SMA1 to SMA8). In addition, field diary notes were compiled during participant observation and fieldwork (coded FD1).

Targeted research participants were recruited at assemblies, demonstrations and specific events for interviews, with an indication of the focus provided beforehand comprised of guiding questions. Although a set of predetermined questions had been identified, and was aimed at determining the participants' connection with tourism activism in Barcelona, the priority was to enable research participants to guide conversations and to provide insight into their own experiences. Participants were encouraged to engage through open conversations that aided the establishment of a healthy rapport and trust, which proved invaluable when analysing, interpreting and contextualizing the interview transcripts. To aid the data recording process, participants' permission was sought to tape-record interviews and undertake notetaking. Although most of the participants did not ask for anonymity, all were coded for consistency. The interviews were transcribed and analysed using direct content analysis to "identify core consistencies and meanings", which guided the identification of themes (Patton, 2002, p. 453). Direct content analysis was employed in the evaluation of the personal diary entries, which supplemented the data collection process. Photographic evidence supplemented interviews providing visual evidence and record of events. Interviews lasted between thirty minutes to an hour and were conducted in Spanish, Portuguese and Italian in line with the nationalities of social movements.

Findings: the tourism degrowth campaign

The ensuing findings highlighted how tourism degrowth had evolved and how it entered social movement discourses led by the ABTS in Barcelona and the subsequent spread internationally through the SET Network. Overarching findings suggest that hitherto, the tourism degrowth campaign was strictly related to deep-rooted social unrest associated to overtourism concerns.

(1) Tourism growth, overtourism symptoms and social unrest

In Barcelona, recent decades have been characterized by tourism growth-oriented policies that have fostered foreign investment, tourism-oriented infrastructure development, city branding policies and proliferation of housing for touristic use (HUT). The related transformations have fed social unrest and the diminishment of Barcelonans liveability and wellbeing related to housing and cost of living pressures, congestion of public transport and the exclusivity of tourist-related shops.

While overtourism concerns are usually related to the transformations caused by tourism massification, transformation in cities is unavoidable and occurs irrespective of tourism. For instance, as stated by a resident: "the reality of a city is the transformation and the only immutable thing in a city or in an urban space is change (...) but what has happened in the Gothic Quarter is brutal, what happened in Barceloneta is brutal and what is happening in Sant Antoni can only be dangerous" (R1). In mid-May 2018, the Sant Antoni Market reopened after nine years of renewal works and the official unveiling was met with protests and concerns against gentrification processes that the refurbishment of the market provoked. Furthermore, the issue of how overtourism may affect residents' sense of belonging emerged social movement activist statements: "we are talking about residents with the ability to create a community. Everything changes but it's not about nostalgia. We are Mediterranean, we are used to physical relationships with spaces as we need a place to have coffee or a beer. We need our neighbourhoods" (SMA2).

Importantly, social movement claims are not just related to tourism-related concerns: 'the main objective is to combat gentrification and for the defence of more inclusive neighbourhoods" (R2). According to a social movement activists, the social unrest in Barcelona is not as recent as one may think. It started in 2000 with "a concern about the purchase of [residential] apartments, which were turning into tourist accommodations (...) and in that moment it was more a concern of coexistence about the different lifestyles of people who come for tourism purpose and people who have a daily routine" (SMA2). Currently, criticism and social unrest has evolved, as exemplified in a resident's statement: "I can see a change in the ideological proclamations and the combative struggle of an elite with an alternative rebel attitude, still I don't know if for everyone is clear what gentrification or touristification means" (R1).

(2) It's not tourismphobia - this is just an attempt to discourage critical discourse

More recently in 2015, ABTS encouraged a more consistent narrative and awareness about the overtourism social unrest, both in the media and in the political arena. Its most significant discourse revolves around tourism degrowth in the city of Barcelona (Figure 1). ABTS agenda have become more visible also as a result of academic and activists' collaborations (Cócola-Gant & Pardo, 2017), press exposure, through the dissemination of scientific publications (Medrano & Pardo, 2016) and as a result of the formation of a research group on degrowth tourism that meshes the participation of researchers, activists and residents.

During the meeting Neighbourhood Life - Tourist Tours. Can we share the space? held in Barcelona the 9th of February, 2018 with some fifty participants, including tourist guides and residents, the discussion addressed the congestion of public space in the Gothic Quarter due to the proliferation of independent and guided walking tours. A member of AGUICAT (Association of Tourist Guides of Catalonia) highlighted that only a small number of tour guides were practicing sustainable ways to guide tours that did not contribute to the congestion of public spaces (FD1). The AGUICAT code of good practice for walking tours that minimize annoyances to local residents includes: keep small groups and avoid busy areas, use the wireless whispers audio system to avoid noise pollution, do not interfere with daily local life of locals by taking photos and respecting privacy and safety as well as avoiding long explanations in congested areas.

Figure 1. Tourism degrowth event organized in Barcelona, 12 March, 2017 (Source: ABTS Photoreporters).

By inferring to the need for tourism degrowth associated with the emergence of intolerant behaviours towards tourists, a respondent concluded, "there is no tourismphobia, but [there is] an aggression to the public space and civic coexistence, which requires immediate attention" (FD1). Furthermore, a social activist stated: "tourismphobia has been an invention of the tourism industry, which stigmatized dissidences. There have been attempts to discourage the critical discourse with the conception of a negative new term. The problem is not tourism, but all the circumstances surrounding that [the phenomenon]" (SMA3).

Activism in Barcelona related to overtourism social unrest maintains a controversial dualism. While on one hand, overtourism criticism has been tainted by media sensationalism (see Figure 2) and has promoted the use of the word tourismphobia deflecting attention from genuine social movement concern. For instance, the social media bubble on tourismphobia, that exploded during the summer of 2017 coincided with the denouncements for improved labour rights in the hotel sector by housekeepers' unions and professional associations (Cañada, 2015; 2018), thus directing attention elsewhere. Conversely, tourismphobia has given greater visibility to the struggles of service workers and fostered the introduction of tourism degrowth into political debates and urban planning agenda. According to social movement respondents, their focus on tourism started in Barcelona in the middle of the last decade and is used to refer to their 'specialization in tourism issues' (SMA1; SMA3). It is this specialization that has facilitated the introduction of degrowth as a potential solution to the objections of social movements.

(3) Tourism degrowth is not just a technical solution

On many occasions, Barcelona's social movements, led by ABTS, have criticised public policies aimed at addressing overtourism as simplistic through their 'one size fits all' technical approach, rather than dealing with the underpinning causes in a more strategic manner. As a result, degrowth became their preferred way forward. In this regard, the individual use of the 5D's - Deseasonalization, Decongestion, Decentralization, Diversification and Deluxe tourism have been criticised as neoliberal strategies that do not address the many factors that have led to overtourism (Milano, 2018). This reductive and simplistic approach is considered (SMA2 and SMA3)

Figure 2. Front Page El Periódico 6 August 2017 (Source: El Periódico).

inadequate on the basis that each of the 5Ds, if taken in isolation, remain short-term solutions that does not sufficiently deal with the underlying complexity of urban tourism governance.

Overwhelming sentiments from respondents is that to achieve tourism degrowth and a paradigm shift in the way tourism success is measured can't be addressed with isolated technical solutions. Overtourism is not only a tourism issue and is part of a wider urban planning agenda. While the 5D's technical approach might not epitomise a profound change. According to the ABTS and SET Network, any technical solution needs encompass degrowth as part of the political landscape. Degrowth has been widely promoted by the ABTS in several instances (i.e. stakeholders meeting, neighbourhood associations, assemblies and in peaceful demonstrations). The first example of synergic social movements intervention promoting tourism degrowth was the *1st*

Table 2. ABTS' ten key principles towards tourism degrowth (Source: adapted from ABTS, 2016).

ABTS' ten key principles towards tourism degrowth
(1) Identify specific data that validates that tourism impacts in Barcelona are understood
(2) Develop an index that enables the measurement of the quality of life in cities
(3) Foster a debate on tourism between different critics' actors and stakeholders
(4) Run campaigns to raise awareness of tourism's impacts
(5) Establish local representation on the Barcelona Port Authority Administration Board
(6) Propose alternative models to Port management
(7) Establish a tourist tax to address the negative impacts of tourism in the city
(8) Promote a public platform to endorse legislation for the management of areas close to the Port not currently controlled by the City Council
(9) Develop an integrated Port Plan
(10) Promote better coordination among social movements, and internationalize initiatives

Table 3. Measures aimed at tourism degrowth in Barcelona (Source: SMA1).

Measures aimed at tourism degrowth in Barcelona
(1) Remove funds for the promotion of tourism toward destination de-marketing
(2) Remove public funds dedicated to to the public/private consortium *Turisme de Barcelona*.
(3) Replace *Turisme de Barcelona* with a public tourism agency that manages and plans the sector rather than promoting it
(4) Withdraw subsidies, tax relief, grants and transfer of public funds to the tourism industry private sector
(5) Implement more restrictive urban planning legislation than the current Special Urban Planning Plan for Tourist Accommodation (PEAUT).
(6) Establish resident representation on the management boards of both the Port and Airport
(7) Revise the legislation to improve working conditions of workers in the tourism industry
(8) Increase a process of democratization to implement and establish a public debate and analysis on the city's tourism development.

Neighbourhood Forum on Tourism, held in Barcelona in 2016, that gathered international social movements such as *No Grandi Navi* from Venice. The event addressed controversial issues such as the employment of residential properties and public space for tourism, the proliferation of growth oriented economic models, and poor governance of cruise tourism as seen in the administration of Barcelona Port. At the Forum, the ABTS identified a number of challenges and proposed ten key principles to effectively engage in tourism degrowth. These are summarized in Table 2.

These were identified as urgent actions to be tackled by various stakeholders (R4, SMA2, SMA3; SMA4; SMA5), and these principles were further elaborated into a set of measures aimed at tourism degrowth in Barcelona by ABTS and SET Network members (SMA1) (See Table 3).

Overall, the aforementioned tourism degrowth principles and measures appear as the only acceptable ways to tackle overtourism. As emphasized by respondents: 'The only solution is degrowth (...) we must stop financing tourism promotion with public funds, abolish any public subsidy, direct and indirect, to the tourism industry and the famous taxes needs to be multiplied in a broader sense of responsibility and sustainability and not just as a greenwashing. Those are polluting companies, just as the rest" (SMA2).

(4) The campaign went global: the SET network

ABTS led activities in Barcelona and the tourism degrowth campaign (*#Decreixement turístic*), was accompanied by the summer of 2017 campaign *#CapMésEstiuComAquest* (No more summers like this), that denounced the effects of tourism continuing to grow at an increasing rate. In 2017, these campaigns went beyond Barcelona's boundaries with the constitution of the SET Network convoyed through several international meetings, such as the June 2017 "Social movements against tourism – a battle shared between different regions and cities" in Mallorca that gathered different social movements from European cities to discuss overtourism concerns. The event was attended by *Comitato No Grandi Navi* from Venice, *Oficina de Urbanismo Social* from Lavapiés neighbourhood in Madrid, *Sindicato de Inquilinos* from Madrid, *Assemblea Ciutat per qui l'Habita* from Mallorca, *Morar em Lisboa* from Lisbon, *Entre Barris* from Valencia and the *Assemblea de Barris per un Turisme Sostenible* (ABTS) from Barcelona.

The ABTS tourism degrowth campaign provoked a snowball effect among southern European social movements, resulting in the constitution of the SET Network to cope with a growing global phenomenon. During the first press conference of the 26th April 2018 event, the SET manifesto (SET, 2018) highlighted pressing issues such as: the decrease of available housing for residents; the transformation of local trade patterns (i.e. souvenirs shops replacing local food shops); the congestion of public space (i.e. streets and square) and public transport; the specialization of the city's economy on servicing tourism (i.e. mushrooming of restaurants); the precariousness of working conditions; the generation of high pollution (i.e. increased arrival of airplanes, cruise ships and coaches) and waste; the unintended usage of public infrastructure (i.e. roads, ports, airports, etc.) and the stereotyping of both urban and natural destinations.

The SET network is emblematic of a social movements network emerging from the interactions of different nodes and actors (Diani, 2007; Castells, 2015). These synergies and networks have also meant a coordination of actions between various social movements that have led the awakening of social unrest associated with overtourism in southern European cities. In Italy there were two national meetings in 2018 that were attended by several Italian cities that make up the SET Italian Network. During interviews and informal conversations with activists from Venice (SMA4), Madrid (SMA5), Lisbon (SMA6), Florence (SMA7; SMA8) and Naples (FD1), the need for tourism degrowth and a deceleration of tourism promotion were emphasised.

Conclusions

Overtourism is conceived by respondents to this study as a shared responsibility among the various stakeholders, and in particular, city administrators and destination managers can have a considerable influence. The tourism value chain involves a complex urban governance system based on urban transport and mobility, housing, public health, public space, direct and indirect employment and other daily social practices. In Barcelona, social movements fostering an interventionist approach to overcome the overtourism phenomenon has evolved into the ABTS and its intensive programme of resistance, as well as the advancement of a SET Network agenda aimed at a tourism degrowth based on tighter regulation of the tourism sector.

Evidently, while a 'one size fits all' approach is regarded as not creating any useful and enduring change, dealing with overtourism remains a complex endeavour, requiring strategic deliberations and decision making that is necessarily contentious. The tourism degrowth discourse is claimed by social movements interviewed and observed in this research as the only way forward. However, the implementation of suggested measures (see Tables 1 and 2) would represent an unprecedented scenario and may remain largely aspirational, as inciting a tourism crisis will mean substantial economic repercussions for those who rely directly and indirectly on the tourism sector.

What is also clear is that strategies based only on tourism degrowth may not be sufficient to fully shift from a sector engrained with the 'growth for development' paradigm, to a 'degrowth for liveability' one, and it may be too optimistic to think that such an approach could cope with the underlying complexity of urban tourism settings. The complementarity of the degrowth approach with 5D's - Deseasonalization, Decongestion, Decentralization, Diversification and Deluxe tourism (Figure 3), may therefore, provide a more context-adaptable and effective tool to deal with overtourism, but only if approached within the wider urban political agenda. Tourism is a vital vehicle for creating the conditions of production and reproduction of capital, as well as only one of the forces that configure a contemporary city within new urban mobilities.

Figure 3. 5Ds.

Further research in this regard would advance understandings of the controversial inter-relationship between overtourism, degrowth and grassroots organization resistance. A social movements perspective and mass media communication analysis can help future research to shed light on the reasons why overtourism has become a contemporary issue in most tourist cities. Beyond the sensationalist journalism, tourism degrowth campaigns offer the opportunity to re-open a pressing debate on the exploitation of finite resources, limits to growth, the looming climate emergency and the recent emergence of flight shaming that questions the ethics of flying.

To achieve a substantive paradigm shift in urban tourism governance, both technical solutions and political will to act against overtourism are required. Tourism is one of many intrinsic components of the daily life of cities such as Barcelona and any degrowth potentially threatens the status quo the challenge for policy makers, academics, private stakeholders and grassroots organizations remains understanding how to live with the hypermobility of contemporary societies and the capital accumulation processes of inner cities characterized by a wider range of social actors such as regular and temporary residents, tourists, digital nomads, daily visitors, cruise passengers, international students, commuters, which are all seeking experiences and claiming different rights to the city. Encouraging a dialogue on the inclusiveness of our cities is of paramount importance and the current tourism degrowth campaign led by the ABTS in Barcelona and by the SET Network internationally is helping to facilitate a recharged debate on the limits of acceptable tourism growth internationally.

ORCID

Claudio Milano (iD) http://orcid.org/0000-0003-4349-367X
Marina Novelli (iD) http://orcid.org/0000-0003-4629-4481
Joseph M. Cheer (iD) http://orcid.org/0000-0001-5927-2615

References

ABTS - Assemblea de Barris per un Turisme Sostenible (2016). *Conclusions del I Fòrum Veïnal sobre Turisme.* [Conclusions of the I Neighborhood Forum on Tourism] Retrieved from: https://assembleabarris.files.wordpress.com/2016/08/conclu.pdf

Almeida, P., & Cordero Ulate, A. (Eds.). (2015). *Handbook of social movements across Latin America.*Dordrecht: Springer.

Alvarez, S. E., & Escobar, A. (1992). Conclusion: Theoretical and political horizons of change in contemporary Latin American social movements. In A. Escobar, (Ed.), *The making of social movements in Latin America* (pp. 317–331). New York, NY: Routledge.

Andriotis, K. (2014). Tourism development and the degrowth paradigm. *Turisticko Poslovanje, 2014*(13), 37–45. doi:10.5937/TurPos1413037A

Andriotis, K. (2018). *Degrowth in Tourism: Conceptual, Theoretical and Philosophical Issues.* Oxfordshire: CABI.

Anyon, J. (2014). *Radical possibilities: Public policy, urban education, and a new social movement.* London: Routledge.

Barcelona Strategic Tourism Plan for 2020. Barcelona: Tourism Department Manager's Office for Enterprise and Tourism.

Beckerman, W. (1975). *Two Cheers for the Affluent Society: A spirited defense of economic growth.* New York, NY: Saint Martin's Press.

Beebe, J. (2001). *Rapid assessment process: An introduction.* Altamira: Rowman.

Belhassen, Y., Uriely, N., & Assor, O. (2014). The touristification of a conflict zone: The case of Bil'in. *Annals of Tourism Research, 49*, 174–189. doi:10.1016/j.annals.2014.09.007

Blanco-Romero, A., Blázquez-Salom, M., & Cànoves, G. (2018). Barcelona, Housing Rent Bubble in a Tourist City. Social Responses and Local Policies. *Sustainability, 10*(6), 2043. doi:10.3390/su10062043

Blázquez, M., & Cañada, E. (Eds.). (2011). *Turismo placebo: nueva colonización turística del Mediterráneo a Mesoamérica y el Caribe, lógicas espaciales del capital turístico.* [Tourism placebo: New tourist colonization of Mesoamerica and the Caribbean, space logic of tourist capital] Managua: EDISA.

Boissevain, J. (Ed.). (1996). Coping with tourists: European reactions to mass tourism (Vol. 1). Providence, RI: Berghahn Books.

Bonilla, A., & Mortd, M. (2008). *Turismo y conflictos territoriales en el Pacífico de Nicaragua: El caso de Tola, más allá de los titulares.* [Tourism and territorial conflicts in the Nicaraguan Pacific: The case of Tola, beyond headlines]. San Salvador: Fundación Prisma.

Borja, J. (2010). *Luces y sombras del urbanismo de Barcelona.* [Lights and shadows of Barcelona's urbanism] Barcelona: UOC Edicions.

Buechler, S. M. (1995). New social movement theories. *The Sociological Quarterly, 36*(3), 441–464. doi:10.1111/j.1533-8525.1995.tb00447.x

Butler, R. W. (1980). The concept of a tourist area cycle of evolution: Implications for management of resources. *The Canadian Geographer/Le Géographe Canadien, 24*(1), 5–12. doi:10.1111/j.1541-0064.1980.tb00970.x

Canavan, B. (2014). Sustainable tourism: Development, decline and de-growth. Management issues from the Isle of Man. *Journal of Sustainable Tourism, 22*(1), 127–147. doi:10.1080/09669582.2013.819876

Cañada, E. (Ed.). (2010). *Turismo en Centroamérica: nuevo escenario de conflictividad.* [Tourism Central America: New scenario of conflict] Managua: Enlace Editorial.

Cañada, E. (2015). *Las que limpian los hoteles. Historias ocultas de precariedad laboral.* [Those who clean the hotels. Hidden stories of job insecurity] Barcelona: Icaria/Antrazyt.

Cañada, E. (2018). Too precarious to be inclusive? Hotel maid employment in Spain. *Tourism Geographies, 20*(4), 653–674. doi:10.1080/14616688.2018.1437765

Capel, H. (2005). *El Modelo Barcelona: Un examen crítico.* [The Barcelona model: A critical examination] Barcelona: Ed. Del Serbal.

Castells, M. (1983). *The city and the grassroots: A cross-cultural theory of urban social movements (No. 7).* Berkeley: Univ. of California Press.

Castells, M. (2015). Networks of outrage and hope: Social movements in the Internet age. New York, NY: John Wiley & Sons.

Cheer, J. M. & Lew, A. (Eds.) (2018). *Tourism resilience and sustainability: Adapting to social, political and economic change.* London: Routledge.

Cheer, J. M., Milano, C., & Novelli, M. (2019). Tourism and community resilience in the Anthropocene: Accentuating temporal overtourism. *Journal of Sustainable Tourism, 27*(4), 554–572. doi:10.1080/09669582.2019.1578363

Cocóla Gant, A. (2016). Holiday rentals: The new gentrification battlefront. Sociological Research Online, 21(3), 1–9. doi:10.5153/sro.4071

Cócola-Gant, A., & Pardo, D. (2017). Resisting tourism gentrification: The experience of grassroots movements in Barcelona. *Urbanistica Tre, Giornale Online di Urbanistica, 5*(13), 39–47.

Cohen, R., & Rai, S. M. (2000). *Global social movements.* Athlone Press.

Colomb, C., & Novy, J. (Eds.) (2016). *Protest and resistance in the tourist city.* London: Routledge.

Cordero Ulate, A. (2006). *Nuevos ejes de acumulación y naturaleza. El caso del turismo.* [New aspects of accumulation and nature. The tourism case]. Clacso: Buenos Aires.

Cordero Ulate, A. C. (2015). Forest, water, and struggle: environmental movements in Costa Rica. In Almeida, P., & Cordero Ulate, A. (Eds.). *Handbook of social movements across Latin America* (pp. 255–271). Dordrecht: Springer.

Coronado, G. (2008). Insurgencia y turismo: Reflexiones sobre el impacto del turista politizado en Chiapas. [Insurgence and tourism: Reflections on the impact of politicized tourist in Chiapas]. *Pasos Revista de Turismo y Patrimonio Cultural, 6*(1), 53–68. doi:10.25145/j.pasos.2008.06.005

D'Alisa, G., & Demaria, F., & Kallis, G. (Eds.). (2014). *Degrowth: A vocabulary for a new era.* London: Routledge.

Delgado, M. (2007). *La ciudad mentirosa. Fraude y miseria del "Modelo Barcelona".* [The lying city. Fraude and misery of the "Barcelona Model"] Madrid: Los libros de la Catarata.

Demaria, F., Schneider, F., Sekulova, F., & Martinez-Alier, J. (2013). What is degrowth? From an activist slogan to a social movement. *Environmental Values, 22*(2), 191–215. doi:10.3197/096327113X13581561725194

Diani, M. (1992). The concept of social movement. *The Sociological Review, 40*(1), 1–25. doi:10.1111/j.1467-954X.1992.tb02943.x

Diani M. (2007). Social movements, Networks and". In Ritzer G. (Ed.) Blackwell Encyclopedia of Sociology. (pp. 4463–4466). Oxford: Blackwell.

Doxey, G. V. (1975). A causation theory of visitor/resident irritants: Methodology and research inferences. *Proceedings of the Travel Research Association 6th Annual Conference* (pp. 195–198). San Diego, CA: Travel Research Association.

Escobar, A. & Alvarez, S. E., (1992). Introduction: Theory and Protest i n Latin America Today. In A. Escobar, (Ed.), *The making of social movements in Latin America* (pp. 1–8). New York, NY: Routledge.

Escobar, R. (2014). Development, critiques of. In G. D'Alisa, F. Demaria & G. Kallis (Eds.), *Degrowth: A vocabulary for a new era* (pp. 29–32). New York, NY: Routledge.

Espiner, S., Orchiston, C., & Higham, J. (2017). Resilience and sustainability: A complementary relationship? Towards a practical conceptual model for the sustainability–resilience nexus in tourism. *Journal of Sustainable Tourism, 25*(10), 1385–1400. doi:10.1080/09669582.2017.1281929

Fletcher, R. (2011). Sustaining tourism, sustaining capitalism? The tourism industry's role in global capitalist expansion. *Tourism Geographies, 13*(3), 443–461. doi:10.1080/14616688.2011.570372

Garza Tovar, J. R., & Sánchez Crispín, Á. (2015). Estructura territorial del turismo en San Cristóbal de las Casas, Chiapas, México. [Tourism territorial structure in San Cristobal de las Casas, Chiapas, Mexico]. *Cuadernos de Turismo,* (35), 185–209. doi:10.6018/turismo.35.221571

Gascón, J. (2009). *El turismo en la cooperación internacional: De las brigadas internacionalistas al turismo solidario.* [Tourism in international cooperation: Internationalist brigades for solidarity tourism] Barcelona: Icaria.

Hall, C. M. (2009). Degrowing tourism: Décroissance, sustainable consumption and steady-state tourism. *Anatolia, 20*(1), 46–61. doi:10.1080/13032917.2009.10518894

Hall, C. M. (2010). Changing paradigms and global change: From sustainable to steady-state tourism. *Tourism Recreation Research, 35*(2), 131–143. doi:10.1080/02508281.2010.11081629

Hart, C. (1998). *Doing a literature review.* London: Sage.

Harvey, D. (1990). *The condition of postmodernity: An enquiry into the conditions of cultural change.* Malden, MA: Blackwell.

Harvey, D. (2007). *A brief history of neoliberalism.* New York: Oxford University Press

Hiernaux-Nicolas, D. (1999). Cancun Bliss. In D. Judd, & S. Fainstein (Eds.), *The Tourist City* (pp.124–139) New Haven, CT, Yale University Press.

Horton, L. (2007). *Grassroots struggles for sustainability in Central America.* Boulder: University of Colorado Press.

Hughes, N. (2018) 'Tourists go home': anti-tourism industry protest in Barcelona, Social Movement Studies, 17(4) 471–477, doi:10.1080/14742837.2018.1468244

Isaac, R. K., & Platenkamp, V. (2010). Volunteer tourism in Palestine: A normative perspective. In O. Moufakkir, & I. Kelly (Eds.), *Tourism, progress and peace* (pp. 148–161). Wallingford: CABI International.

Kallis, G. (2011). In defence of degrowth. *Ecological Economics, 70*(5), 873–880. doi:10.1016/j.ecolecon.2010.12.007

Kallis, G., Demaria, F., & D'Alisa, G. (2014). Introduction: Degrowth. In G. D'Alisa, F. Demaria, & G. Kallis (Eds.), *Degrowth: A vocabulary for a new era.* (pp. 1–17). New York, NY: Routledge.

Kallis, G., Kostakis, V., Lange, S., Muraca, B., Paulson, S., & Schmelzer, M. (2018). Research on Degrowth. *Annual Review of Environment and Resources, 43*(1), 291–226. doi:10.1146/annurev-environ-102017-025941

Koens, K., Postma, A., & Papp, B. (2018). Is overtourism overused? Understanding the impact of tourism in a city context. *Sustainability, 10*(12), 4384. doi:10.3390/su10124384

Kousis, M. (2000). Tourism and the environment: A social movements perspective. *Annals of Tourism Research, 27*(2), 468–489. doi:10.1016/S0160-7383(99)00083-3

Koutra, C. (2010). Rapid situation analysis: A hybrid, multi-methods, qualitative, participatory approach to researching tourism development phenomena. *Journal of Sustainable Tourism, 18*(8), 1015–1033. doi:10.1080/09669582.2010.497221

Latouche, S. (2009). *Farewell to growth.* Cambridge: Polity.

Latouche, S. (2014). Imaginary, decolonization of. In G. D'Alisa, F. Demaria, & G. Kallis (Eds.), *Degrowth: A vocabulary for a new era* (pp. 117–120). New York, NY: Routledge.

Lew, A. A. (2017). Tourism planning and place making: Place-making or placemaking? *Tourism Geographies, 19*(3), 448–466. doi:10.1080/14616688.2017.1282007

Lew, A. A., & Cheer, J. M. (Eds.). (2018). *Tourism resilience and adaptation to environmental change.* London: Routledge.

Lustosa, I. M. C., & de Almeida, M. G. (2011). Turismo em terras indígenas: Auto-gestão e novo colonialismo no nordeste do Brasil. [Tourism in indigenous territories: Self and new colonialism in Northeastern Brazil]. *Revista Geográfica de América Central, 2,* 1–15.

Maney, G. M. (2001). Rival transnational networks and indigenous rights: The san blas kuna in Panama and the Yanomami in Brazil. *Research in Social Movements, Conflicts and Change, 23,* 103–144.

Mansilla, J. A. (2016). Urbanismo, privatizacion y marketing urbano. La Barcelona neoliberal a traves de tres ejemplos. [Urbanism, privatization and urban marketing. The neoliberal Barcelona through three exemptions]. *Encrucijadas-Revista Crítica de Ciencias Sociales, 11,* 1–18.

Mansilla, J. A. (2018). Vecinos en peligro de extinción. Turismo urbano, movimientos sociales y exclusión socioespacial en Barcelona. [Neighbors in danger of extinction. Urban tourism, social movements and socio-spatial exclusion in Barcelona]. *PASOS Revista de Turismo y Patrimonio Cultural, 16*(2), 279–296.

Mansilla, J. A. & Milano, C. (2019) Becoming centre: tourism placemaking and space production in two neighborhoods in Barcelona, *Tourism Geographies,* doi:10.1080/14616688.2019.1571097

McCarthy, J. D., & Zald, M. N. (Eds.). (1987). Social movements in an organizational society: Collected essays. New York: Transaction Books.

McGehee, N. G. (2002). Alternative tourism and social movements. *Annals of Tourism Research, 29*(1), 124–143.

McGehee, N. G., & Santos, C. (2005). Social change, discourse, and volunteer tourism. *Annals of Tourism Research, 32*(3), 760–779. doi:10.1016/j.annals.2004.12.002

Martínez-Alier, J., Pascual, U., Vivien, F. D., & Zaccai, E. (2010). Sustainable de-growth: Mapping the context, criticisms and future prospects of an emergent paradigm. *Ecological Economics, 69*(9), 1741–1747. doi:10.1016/j.ecolecon.2010.04.017

Mayer, M. (2012). The "right to the city" in urban social movements. In N. Brenner, P. Marcuse, & M. Mayer (Eds.), *Cities for people, not for profit* (pp. 63–85). New York, NY: Routledge.

Meadows, D., Meadows, D., Randers, J., & Behrens, W. W. III, (1972). *The limits to growth. A report for the Club of Rome's project on the predicament of mankind.* New York, NY: Universe Books.

Medrano, H. F., & Pardo, D. (2016). La lucha por el decrecimiento turístico: El caso de Barcelona. [The fight for tourist degrowth: The case of Barcelona]. Ecología Política, 52, 104–106.

Milano, C. (2017a). Turismofobia: Cuando el turismo entra en la agenda de los movimientos sociales. [Tourismphobia: When tourism enters the social movements agenda]. *Marea Urbana, 1,* 5–8.

Milano, C. (2017b). *Overtourism and tourismphobia. Global trends and local contexts.* Barcelona: Ostelea School of Tourism & Hospitality.

Milano, C. (2018). Overtourism, malestar social y turismofobia. Un debate controvertido. [Overtourism, social unrest and tourismphobia. A controversial debate]. *Pasos. Revista de Turismo y Patrimonio Cultural, 16*(3), 551–564. doi: 10.25145/j.pasos.2018.16.041

Milano, C., & Mansilla, J. A. (2018). *Ciudad de vacaciones. Conflictos urbanos en espacios turísticos.* [City of vacations. Urban conflicts in tourist spaces]. Barcelona: Pol·Len Ediciones.

Milano, C., Cheer, J. M., & Novelli, M. (2018). Overtourism: A growing global problem. Retrieved from https://theconversation.com/overtourism-a-growing-global-problem-100029

Milano, C., Cheer, J. M., & Novelli, M. (2019). *Overtourism: Excesses, discontents and measures in travel and tourism.* Wallingford: CABI.

Milano, C., Novelli, M., & Cheer, J. M. (2019). Overtourism and tourismphobia: A journey through four decades of tourism development, planning and local concerns. *Tourism Planning & Development, 16*(4), 353–357.

Molotch, H. (1976). The city as a growth machine: Toward a political economy of place. *American Journal of Sociology, 82*(2), 309–332. doi:10.1086/226311

Novelli, M. (2015). *Tourism and development in Sub-Saharan Africa: Current issues and local realities.* London: Routledge.

Novelli, M., Morgan, N., Mitchell, G., & Ivanov, K. (2016). Travel philanthropy and sustainable development: The case of the Plymouth Banjul challenge. *Journal of Sustainable Tourism, 24*(6), 824–845. doi:10.1080/09669582.2015.1088858

O'Reilly, A. M. (1986). Tourism carrying capacity: Concept and issues. *Tourism Management, 7*(4), 254–258. doi:10.1016/0261-5177(86)90035-X

Owens, L. (2008). From tourists to anti-tourists to tourist attractions: The transformation of the Amsterdam squatters' movement. *Social Movement Studies, 7*(1), 43–59. doi:10.1080/14742830801969340

Palou, S. (2011). *Barcelona, destinació turística. Promoció pública, turismes, imatges i ciutat (1888-2010)*. [Barcelona, tourist destination. Public promotion, tourisms, images and city (1888–2010)]. PhD Dissertation. University of Barcelona.

Petersen, F. (2001). Blast from the past. The Sydney Morning Herald, 15 December. Retrieved from: https://www.smh.com.au/national/blast-from-the-past-20011215-gdf4yo.html?fbclid=IwAR19NzmyUepcDz5AZtWFtn1T6hDCuxiUTd6PQa-BY5JNbMkE2Kar-nEf21g

Lópoz-Palomeque, F. (2015). Barcelona, de ciudad con turismo a ciudad turística: Notas sobre un proceso complejo e inacabado. [Barcelona, from a city with tourism to a tourist city: Notes on a complex and unfinished process]. *Documents d'anàlisi geogràfica, 61*(3), 0483–0506.

Patton, M. Q. (2002). *Qualitative research and evaluation methods*. London: Sage.

Robson, C. (2011). *Real world research: A resource for users of social research methods in applied settings* (3rd ed.). Chichester: Wiley.

Russo, A. P., & Scarnato, A. (2018). "Barcelona in common": A new urban regime for the 21st-century tourist city? *Journal of Urban Affairs, 40*(4), 455–474.

Schneider, F., Martinez-Alier, J., & Kallis, G. (2011). Sustainable degrowth. *Journal of Industrial Ecology, 15*(5), 654–656. doi:10.1111/j.1530-9290.2011.00388.x

SET (2018). SET manifesto press release. Retrieved from https://www.ecologistasenaccion.org/94342/ciudades-y-regiones-del-sur-de-europa-contra-la-turistizacion/

Smith, N. (1992). Geography, difference, and the politics of scale. In J. Doherty, E. Graham, & M. Malek (Eds.) *Postmodernism and the Social Sciences* (pp. 57–79). London: Macmillan

Spencer, R. (2008). Lessons from Cuba: A volunteer army of ambassadors. In S. Wearing, & K. Lyons (Eds.), *Journeys of discovery in volunteer tourism: International case study perspectives*. Oxfordshire: UK: CABI

Stephenson, M. L., & Bianchi, R. (2014). *Tourism and citizenship: Rights, freedoms and responsibilities in the global order*. London: Routledge.

Suñol, X. (2016). Polítiques públiques del turisme al segle XXI. [Public tourism policies in the 21st century]. In S. Palou Rubio (Eds.). *Destinació BCN. Història del turisme a la ciutat de Barcelona*. (pp.140–153). [Destination BCN. History of tourism in the city of Barcelona]. Barcelona: Efadós; Arxiu Històric de la Ciutat.

Touraine, A. (1981). *The voice and the eye: An analysis of social movements*. Cambridge: Cambridge University Press.

Turner, L., & Ash, J. (1975). *The golden hordes: International tourism and the pleasure periphery*. Constable Limited.

UN World Tourism Organization (2018). *UNWTO Tourism Highlights, 2018*. Madrid: Author.

UN World Tourism Organization (1983). *Risks of saturation of tourist carrying capacity overload in holiday destinations*. Madrid: Author.

The social construction of the tourism degrowth discourse in the Balearic Islands

Joaquín Valdivielso (iD) and Joan Moranta (iD)

ABSTRACT

In recent years, overtourism and tourism gentrification have been a central feature of public debate in the Balearic Islands, one of the most touristified regions on the planet. In this context, the discourse of tourism degrowth has thrived, being discussed across the political spectrum and even serving to legitimize a sustainable tourism plan and a new Tourism Act. This article provides a brief analysis of the debate around tourism degrowth in the 2014–2019 period and differentiates between two approaches. On the one hand, tourism degrowth has been used by socio-environmental platforms as a byword for detourisfication and the politicization of the hegemonic consensus on tourism. On the other, degrowth has been adopted as a green washing rhetoric in order to justify public policies aimed at tourist decongestion through deseasonalizing, while promoting tourism expansion. This work brings into focus the social construction of the tourism degrowth narrative by applying critical discourse analysis. We conclude that the debate over tourism degrowth is not just a discrepancy between different approaches to deal with overtourism, tourism pressure and gentrification. It is also a social struggle where the discourse over tourism degrowth has helped new democratic political subjects to coalesce and organize in civil society.

Introduction

In a recent comprehensive review on critical discourse analysis (CDA) related to tourism research, Qian, Wei, and Law (2018) found that relatively few studies succeed compared with CDA studies in other disciplines in social sciences. Moreover, they revealed that little attention is paid to the discourse over tourism degrowth among the five major topics identified in CDA tourism studies (travel motivation, destination image, tourism marketing, sustainable tourism, and social relationship in tourism). At most, degrowth is related to social relationships in tourism as part of the debate around overtourism, defined as the excessive growth of visitors leading to overcrowding and the consequential suffering of residents. As far as overtourism is a rising concern into the debate of the effects of tourism worldwide in the last decade (see Milano, Novelli, & Cheer, 2019, and references cited there in), the demand for degrowth related to tourism has spread out in many destinations (Boluk, Cavaliere, & Higgins-Desbiolles, 2019; Hall, 2011; Panzer-Krause, 2019). Nevertheless, there is absence of research focused on identifying and critically assessing the discourse over tourism degrowth itself.

Critical understanding of discourses is not just a descriptive empiricist tool in social research. CDA is seen also to foster change and extend deliberation as it "denaturalizes" language and makes hidden assumptions and values explicit (Stibbe, 2015). This approach attempts to capture how deliberation in "public spheres" (Torgerson, 2000), under certain procedural conditions, promotes enlarged social reflexivity. Therefore, it aims at enlightening and democratizing public discussion. As a consequence, the challenge of positionality is obvious in critical theory as it takes knowledge as always being situated while, at the same time, aims to critically analyse the stances adopted by social actors (see Stibbe, 2015, pp. 188–192). When analysing discourses, we are also framed by them. In this work, we apply CDA in order to map the tourism degrowth narrative in the Balearic Islands and to dissect the way it has been socially constructed. Tourism degrowth has been adopted at the highest level in political discourses.

The Balearics are a laboratory for observing the impacts and aftermath of exponential growth in a tourist hotspot. Tourism accounts for 45% of Balearic GDP and the bulk of the economy revolves around services linked to tourism and the related property market, which makes the islands a unique case in terms of tourism intensity in the world (Manera & Navinés, 2018, p. 109). Over half of the tourist arrivals, accommodation and overnight stays in the western Mediterranean islands combined are concentrated in the scant 4992 km^2 of the archipelago, with around 25% of these services being offered at what is termed "non-regulated" tourist accommodation (Manera & Navinés, 2018: 47–55, p. 117). The number of visitors this century has doubled from 8 to 16 million, while the current resident population is only 1.1 million; this means the archipelago has the highest air traffic intensity in the EU. Over the near-same period (2000–2015), per capita income at current prices has fallen by an average of −1.2% per year, and the Balearics have dropped from third to seventh position in the ranking of Spanish regions, and from 57th to 121st in the European table (Fundació Impulsa Balears, 2017). There is general agreement that the tourism model is economically inefficient, being dependent on constant rises in activity—visitors; flights; cruises; motorized transport; urbanization; energy and water consumption; waste management.

Since 2012 tourism trends have speeded up as result of the rampant growth in available holiday rentals driven by online platforms such as HomeAway or Airbnb (Murray, Yrigoy & Blázquez-Salom, 2017). Meanwhile, after decades of debate over applying limits to tourism growth, the knock-on effects of the current holiday rental boom have boosted popular resistance and demands for new regulations to put an end to saturation, massification, tourism pressure and gentrification. In this context, the left-wing government enacted the new Tourism Act and tourism degrowth appeared on the horizon. In May 2019, a few days before the local elections, the regional Minister of Tourism for the Balearic Islands, *Consellera* Bel Busquets, announced "the beginning of degrowth". During the election campaign, her political party had used the hashtag *#Decreixement* (degrowth) and she proudly announced that the party had been behind the new Tourism Act that "aims for degrowth". Still, as we will see, this is a rhetoric use of "degrowth" to greenwash a new tourism policy aimed at rationalizing overtourism while at the same promoting tourism growth. This top-down approach is deep inside the institutional response to a bottom-up demand emerging from an autonomous "degrowth public sphere" in civil society.

Several difficulties arise when attempting to analyse the debate around tourism degrowth in the Balearic Islands. Firstly, as in many other similar tourist destinations, overtourism is studied from the perspective of urban gentrification (Cócola, 2016; Colomb & Novy, 2017; Milano, 2018; Milano & Mansilla, 2018); yet the research itself often fails to mention whether degrowth has been analysed in relation to urban tourist gentrification, including those studies on the Balearic Islands (Morell, 2018b). Moreover, in our case, debate has moved beyond the problem of urban tourism gentrification and, in part, cannot be explained as an urban logic.

Another difficulty lies in the concept of tourism degrowth. The scientific literature does not share a common understanding of either the *who* or the *what* (Andriotis, 2018; Hall, 2009, 2010). It is said that tourism degrowth requires a moral shift to "rightsize growth", but public debate and policy-making are missing in the shift from personal ethics to rightsizing. The *who* of degrowth are meant to be morally enlightened individuals. In turn, tourism degrowth is believed to be compatible with "limited growth" and to not necessarily mean contraction in terms of income as measured by GDP. For this reason, many critics of the ideology of growth prefer the term post-growth to degrowth (Dobson, 2014; Prádanos, 2018). Therefore, when dealing with degrowth, the question of *what* should decrease—if not GDP—remains open.

With these challenges in mind, we present the case of the Balearic Islands with an emphasis on the social construction of tourism degrowth, i.e. its agents and how they have articulated this perspective on tourism (which we terms "discourses"), and what impact they have had on the public agenda. "Popular 'epidemiology' of overtourism" section presents an historical discussion of the events of the 2014–2019 period, when the tourism debate shifted to overtourism and degrowth. Next, we differentiate between two types of approaches to tourism degrowth: "Tourism degrowth as greenwashing: the 'spatial fix' hypothesis" section sets out the official version used to justify a public policy for sustainable tourism that promotes a cap-and-trade model where debate revolves around a tourist "ceiling". This vision is a form of greenwashing that is instrumental to tourism growth in terms of volume. Section three then demonstrates how this use of tourism degrowth is the antithesis of the original version driven by social movements in civil society. Here, degrowth means reducing the quantitative cap, as well as tourism pressure in qualitative terms. Our hypothesis is that this approach aims at the tourism decommodification of society in response to the struggle to determine the tourism frontier.

Our methodology includes CDA with sources from participant observation in events, meetings, protests, public debates and informal talks, as well as a literature review including scientific papers, books and reports, in addition to manifestoes, websites, the media and social networks. Both authors have been engaged in civic platforms and participated in formal meetings with scholars, journalists, political parties, local tourism officials and social activists. We are also academic researchers in the fields of political philosophy and the conservation of natural resources. We have therefore kept positionality in mind at all stages of the research.

Popular "epidemiology" of overtourism

Criticising tourism has historically been taboo in Spanish society. In the Balearic Islands, however, criticism has always accompanied the evolution of tourism expansion and its different boom and bust cycles (Blázquez, 2006; Valdivielso & Riutort, 2004). Led by the environmental movement, the debate has mostly denounced tourism as an agent of territorial urbanization although, in recent years, there has been a shift towards a criticism of overtourism with the term "degrowth" coming to the fore.

The year 2014 marked a milestone with the publication by the emergent *Tot Inclós* (All-inclusive) collective of the first issue of a homonymous magazine on "Damages and consequences of tourism in our islands" (Pallicer & Blázquez, 2016). Since this time, there have been increasing signs of protest against overtourism and the issue has caught public opinion. One turning point that shocked public opinion came in early 2016, when graffiti messages such as "Refugees Welcome, tourists go home", "stop guiris" (*guiri* is a derogatory term for foreign tourists), "eat the guiri" or "tourism destroys the city" appeared in the historic centre of Palma. The media then began opening daily programmes with news on successive record tourism figures and their negative side-effects on overloaded infrastructures and natural resources, the privatization of public space and the impact of holiday rentals on housing prices. These issues began to be expressed in terms of massification and saturation.

The political milieu seemed to open a window of opportunity to respond to the case for overtourism. Since June 2015, coalitions of left-wing parties have been in power in the regional government (*Govern*), the island governments (*Consells*) and the main city governments, including Palma. These coalitions comprise the social democratic PSIB-PSOE, the eco-sovereignist *Més per Menorca* and *Més per Mallorca*—which include the "green" *Els Verds* party—and *Podemos*, which emerged from the anti-austerity 15-M *indignados* movement brandishing a "new politics" label. The new self-proclaimed "government of the people" drafted "Agreements for Change", which included "modification of the Tourism Act to regulate holiday rentals", the creation of a tourism tax and other measures in pursuit of "quality" tourism. *Més* took over the regional Department for Tourism and launched "welcome sustainable tourism" and a "better in winter" deseasonalizing campaigns.

The *Govern* then began to draft and negotiate changes to the Tourism Act in 2016. While the new act was being drafted, the regional *Vicepresident* and minister for Tourism at the time, Biel Barceló, stated that "tourism saturation is a subjective but important sensation". Environmental groups interpreted this as a denial of massification and in response, *Tot Inclós* used infographics to publicize the evolution of tourism figures with a picture of Barceló at the centre of the image. The message was clear: massification is objective. A decisive moment came in March 2017 when *Terraferida* (Wounded Land—an ecologist group with a wide social media impact by means of critical memetics) used data from InsideAirbnb to launch its #*DesmontantAirbnb* (Dismantling Airbnb) campaign. It revealed the concentration of Airbnb multi-listings, including an interactive map of the platform's holiday rentals in Majorca in 2016. Though the data were not new, the map became iconic for showing how tourism had conquered new niches: urban centres and the rural inland area.

In the months that followed, a wildfire of social response and public debate ensued, catalysing a collection of initiatives, social protest and *artivism* on social networks critiquing tourism, including the *Sense límits no hi ha futur* (There is no future without limits) platform launched in September 2016. Neighbourhood associations in Palma galvanized and the *Ciutat per a qui l'habita, no per a qui la visita* (A city for residents, not for visitors—we refer as *Ciutat Habita* hereafter—) platform emerged in October 2016 to claim the right to the city and to denounce how residential use of housing was being replaced by short-term holiday rentals. Under the slogan "Tourism kills the city", *Ciutat Habita* used public performances and protests to reclaim the city from on-going airbnbfication. The conflict drew in historical conservationist groups such as the GOB (Group for Ornithology and the Defence of Nature) and in September 2017, a demonstration was held in Palma under the slogan *Fins aquí hem arribat* (This far and no further). Public opinion in the entire archipelago was focused on the debate surrounding massification and a lack of residential housing. Consequently, the idea "degrowth" began to take on momentum. The term "degrowth" had already started to gain traction within progressive activism thanks to the 15-M movement in 2011 (Asara, 2016; Prádanos, 2018), with "tourism degrowth" emerging from Catalan activists and platforms (Fernández & Pardo, 2016; Meana, 2016).

After this, academe began to pay notice: in response to the *Terraferida* maps and discourse, neo-classical economists published an extensively circulated report defending the benefits of the "sharing economy" in Majorca (Groizard & Nilsson, 2017). Airbnb, not known for its transparency (Molas, 2017), does not share any data so they were purchased from the company Airdna, thanks to funding from the Tourism Agency of the *Govern* (Nilsson, Leoni, & Figini, 2016), which also funded a survey to show public support for holiday rentals in 2016. The report, distributed by the local holiday rentals lobby *Aptur* (now *Habtur*) as "scientific" evidence on the "sharing economy", was soon confronted with research produced by the geographers Vives-Miró, Rullan, and Gónzalez (2018). Their work demonstrated a high correlation between touristification via Airbnb and the gentrification of neighbourhoods in Palma. Yrigoy (2017) established a similar pattern in Ciudadela, Minorca.

The dispute over tourist numbers focused the debate. *Terraferida* has regularly published new online maps for the entire Balearic archipelago based on data from web scraping, in collaboration with platforms such as *DinsAirbnb* (the local version of InsideAirbnb). The maps reveal an exponential year-on-year increase in tourist places available through Airbnb. However, the main

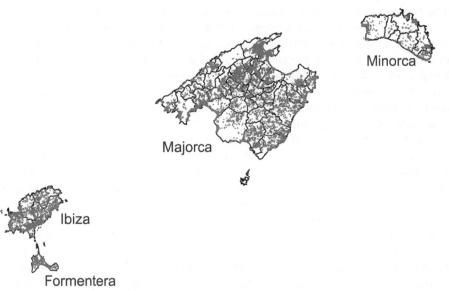

Figure 1. Map of the Balearic Islands showing the dissemination of available Airbnb homes in May 2019. Data published by Terraferida and DinsAirbnb (http://www.dissidentbits.cat/).

commercial platform in the Balearic Islands in 2017 was not Airbnb but HomeAway, with 23,968 listed homes corresponding to 145,000 bed places. The ten largest companies behind HomeAway ads provided 39.1% of its listing; one "super-host" alone listed 4,923 homes (30,000 beds). Thus, activists denounced the sector as being highly professionalized and concentrated. More recent data from *Terraferida* and *DinsAirbnb* show that available offers on Airbnb continue to expand, reaching 141,213 beds in May 2019 (Figure 1). The relative magnitude of holiday rentals in Palma, Ibiza, Majorca or the Balearics as a whole is much higher than other well-known gentrified spots such as San Francisco or Barcelona (Cócola, 2016; Milano & Mansilla, 2018, p. 58; Opillard, 2016).

Deciphering the total tourism offer—holiday rentals plus hotel accommodation—was another focal point in the debate. *Terraferida* has termed it the "mystery of the tourism holy trinity". The calculation is made along these lines: the resident population, alongside the number of people who could occupy legal tourism bed places, is subtracted from the total population at the summer peak—calculated from the human pressure index to be around two million people. The remainder is the "mystery": almost half a million individuals at the August peak in 2016. Although a fraction of these numbers corresponds to the floating population of workers, the bulk could only be second-home tourism, illegal holiday rentals and hidden hotel availability. Overall, the data reveal a striking lack of public control over the tourism business.

From a statistical standpoint, the platforms—*Tot Inclós*, *Terraferida*, *Ciutat Habita*—were mapping the volume of available tourist bed places. This "popular" tourism mapping has forced the regional authorities to update their statistics to include the legal supply of holiday rentals. The results for total authorized tourist places for the 2012–2018 Airbnbification period show increases of 36% in Majorca, 51% in Minorca, 28% in Ibiza and 155% in Formentera, although there are still no official data for the latter two islands. The total stands at 587,000 tourist bed places. Although tourism lobbies and officials were sceptical about the expertise of these citizen platforms, current official data match what the platforms initially asserted. Therefore, social movements have played the role of a "popular" epistemic community. Moreover, the platforms were also mapping a series of tourism externalities: pressure on residential housing; population displacement; substitution of non-tourism economic activities and land uses; (*r*)*urbanalization* and the weakness of the state. This process can be compared to what the 1970s environmental

Table 1. Evolution of main tourist indicators in the Balearic Islands.

		Authorised tourist bed places	Tourist arrivals (millions)
First boom	1959	14,609	0.32
	1974	227,406	3.17
Second boom	1978	226,883	3.80
	1989	348,019	6.42
Third boom	1993	381,108	6.88
	2008	423,054	12.58
Fourth boom	2011	421,782	12.29
	2015	424,663	14.01
New Tourism Act	2017	552,680	16.33
	2018	575,196	16.59
Tourist cap	2019	623,624	

Data adapted from Murray et al. (2017) and updated from the Tourist Strategy Agency of the Balearic Islands (AETIB); http://www.caib.es/govern/organigrama/area.do?lang=ca&coduo=475.

justice movement in the United States labelled as "popular epidemiology" (Bullard, 1998). At that time, it referred to the research undertaken by mothers in racialized neighbourhoods out of concern for their children, who were being exposed to toxic waste. In our context, it refers to activists and neighbours who research exposure to the hidden costs of tourism, so the "epidemic" is metaphorical. It is about a form of overtourism "slow violence" (Nixon, 2011) that "kills the city" and "destroys the territory".

The new Balearic Tourism Act *6/2017* then came into force. It set a one-year moratorium on new tourist accommodation permits. Meanwhile, each island had to establish a cap or "ceiling" for total authorized tourist bed places, based on existing authorized tourist accommodation, along with a reserve stock "pool" for potential growth. New licences would be subject to zoning based on environmental and territorial criteria used to determine the types of accommodation—apartments, houses, primary residences, secondary residences and also hotels—that can be marketed: in which area, at what times of year and for how long. Future permits would face new requirements including energy efficiency. Nonetheless, zoning is only applicable to new tourist places, thereby excluding the bulk of the pre-existing legal offer. At the same time, the law legalized the rental of apartments for tourism purposes, which had been prohibited since 2012. So far, only Majorca has approved the zoning plan, allowing for an additional 43,000 authorized tourism bed places shared between two different "pools" for hotels and holiday rentals. The local government in Palma has opted for a somewhat different approach, where holiday rentals in multi-family units have remained banned. After a moratorium, new licences are being requested as of August 2018, although the total number of legal tourist accommodation places is only expanding in Majorca. The total cap for the archipelago would be around 623,000 if the reserve stock in Majorca is granted (Table 1).

Over the 2012–2017 period and until the enactment of the new law, both conservative and left-wing governments tolerated most of the illegal activity and paved the way for it to be legalized. Indeed, the lack of a moratorium before the enactment of the new law—even in the context of a contentious public debate—made it possible. Environmental organizations term it an "open bar" policy while for the coalition parties in the *Govern*, the legalization of the activity has been justified as a "come to the surface" policy for an activity that distributes "shared prosperity". Meanwhile, those entrusted with the top three tourism posts in the *Govern*, including *Vicepresident* Barceló, have had to resign amid accusations of favouritism. Tourism officials now argue that the law will cut up to 120,000 tourist bed places in the long-term over several decades, since it establishes new requirements that will not enable licences first granted as exceptions to be renewed. This is why *Consellera* Busquets declared the beginning of a new era of degrowth. Nevertheless, according to Terraferida, the number of holiday rentals on Airbnb is still expanding in 2019 on the islands, with at least 38% being illegal. The Department for Tourism, however, argues that degrowth has begun since the tourist cap in Mallorca has already declined by 5,439 tourist beds thanks to the new legislation.

These disputes have upset the socio-political spectrum somewhat and fragmented former alliances. On one side, the demand for tourism degrowth has been written off as tourism-phobia by conservatives and even by certain sectors within the left-wing parties in the *Govern*. They avoid the term "degrowth" in relation to tourism. The conservative People's Party (PP) accused Francina Armengol, *Presidenta* of the regional government (*Govern*), of "working hand in hand with irresponsible people who square-on speak of tourism degrowth"; they used the term tourism-phobia (Goodwin, 2017) to deride these "irresponsible people". On the other, part of the electoral base of those left-wing parties—mostly *Més* and *Podem*—participate in *milieux* that are critical of their management of tourism massification. *Podem* remained silent on degrowth until the 2019 election campaign, though they had forced the new legislation to be reformed to include a mechanism to freeze new licences in the event of a "housing emergency". *Més* has defined itself as "the political ecology that adopts the debate of social ecology". So, the mayor of the city of Palma—where half the population of Majorca lives—pointed out that "to be a city for its residents, visitors […] the great business of the tourist city have to stop". Along similar lines, an emerging party rooted in citizen platforms, *Crida per Palma*, championed: "We have to stop being a theme park […] tourism degrowth and the diversification of the economy are the only possible way forward." Still, *Més* did attempt to co-opt environmental groups into a citizens' platform to reclaim local management of the airport from the central government, while failing to regulate tourist flows through accommodation supply management. In turn, the hotel industry also attempted to involve those groups in a platform to restrict tourism and holiday rentals. Both co-opting strategies failed, as the organizations refused to participate. Meanwhile, a new lobby emerged around *Habtur* to represent the interests of owners who, in general, cross party dividing lines. *Habtur* has also endorsed degrowth, although only for hotel beds, so that the holiday rentals can expand. Finally, the pro-degrowth constellation has taken an ecological-political turn to a new cleavage of social-cum-environmental demands that distances itself somewhat from more traditional conservationist environmentalism.

Tourism degrowth as greenwashing: the "spatial fix" hypothesis

The debate on constraint and even decrease of available tourist accommodation is not new in the Balearic Islands. "Limits to growth", "zero growth", the reduction of the number of bed places for tourist accommodation and even the number of visitors have been discussed in previous tourism booms. Indeed, according to the literature on the geography and political economy of tourism in the Balearic Islands, the different tourism cycles start as a "boom", followed by a policy of restriction for certain tourist accommodation (Murray et al., 2017, p. 20).

Rullan (1998) established a typology centred on the "territorial model" of each boom. The first (1959–1974) involved intensive urbanization and vertical hotel construction at specific coastal locations. The second (1978–1989) expanded across coastal areas with the horizontal construction of aparthotels and tourism housing complexes. The third boom (1993–2008) brought residential construction to inland areas and incorporated dispersed rural properties into the tourism business. Nonetheless, the number of authorized tourist bed places on offer remained the same, thanks to earlier restrictive tourism planning (Table 1). At the same time, the Balearic model became transnational thanks to local hotel chains like Melià Hotels, Barceló, Riu, Iberostar (Cañada & Blázquez, 2011).

This view highlights the tight correlation between tourism booms, space and capital accumulation cycles in the Balearics. Murray et al. (2017) describe a pattern where crises play a central role in restructuring tourist spaces. For them, tourism serves as a "fix" to capitalist crises through the expansion of the commodity frontier into new spaces where profits are comparatively higher. It takes inspiration from David Harvey's (2003) "spatial fix" and Neil Smith's (1996) "urban frontier" and "rent gap" theories. The gap between present and potential ground rent explains where the urban tourism frontier shifts. This view also informs the general theory of gentrification, applied by Morell (2018a, 2018b) to the city of Palma. Moreover, it also informs the study of rural gentrification in the diffuse urbanization of natural spaces and local peasant landscapes in the Balearics (Murray et al., 2017; Vives-Miró et al., 2018).

Various assumptions sustain this approach. Firstly, the image of the whole territory as a tourism-led urban space. In these terms, Mestre (2016) has described Majorca in its entirety as an island-city. Thus, the rural hinterland is viewed as what Brenner (2018) and Brenner and Schmid (2015) terms an "associate operational landscape" to tourism-led urbanization, capital accumulation and primary commodity production. Secondly, it is also assumed that the role of the state is subordinate and functional to tourism-real estate capital accumulation. The state sets the legal framework, makes available the hardware in infrastructures and urban planning, and undertakes the task of legitimization: it not only smooths the terrain for accumulation in normal times, but also tries to avoid over-supply through policies of restraint and to restore conditions for a new expansive cycle in times of crisis. Finally, both public policy and antagonistic resistance are viewed as functional to capital accumulation. Insofar as environmentalism pushes for tourism growth moratoria, it would promote elitist tourism and forms of "environmental gentrification" (Blanco-Romero, Blázquez-Salom, & Mínguez, 2017, p. 1520; Blázquez, 2006; Pallicer & Blázquez, 2016: 89). Developing Neil Smith's thesis of the "revanchist city", Artigues and Blázquez (2016) speak of a "revanchist conservationism" that protects high-quality environmental spots with increased monopolistic profits for the owner class and transnational elites. So, civil society and the capitalist class may paradoxically coincide in demarcating the tourism commodity frontier (Murray et al., 2017, p. 21).

This functionalist approach helps to explain the current fourth boom. After the financial crisis of 2008 the number of tourists stagnated. Since then, it has skyrocketed and the tourism frontier has expanded in new directions: urban areas (both in cities and villages) and the rural inland (except in Minorca). The expected ground rent in tourism use is much higher than the rent for resident uses (Morell, 2018a, p. 134) and in non-tourism productive uses such as agriculture (Murray, Jover-Avellà, Fullana, & Tello, 2019, p. 16). The "buy to let" formula for tourism purposes is adding an extra expected value to the already lucrative real estate business. Thus, it is no surprise that residents' letter boxes are bombarded with "we buy your house" ads or that travellers arriving at local airports are greeted with signs reading: "Do you have a home to sell? We know a lot of frozen Scandinavians".

In turn, the state has been active in accompanying the process through legal reforms that have cleared the path to making the Balearic Islands the main Spanish Airbnb destination, such as the loosening of Act 4/2013 on Urban Leases and Act 11/2009 on Real Estate Investment Trusts (Blanco-Romero et al., 2017, p. 1517; Morell, 2018b, p. 265; Murray, 2018; Murray et al., 2017: 18). This legal framework has paved the way for what is considered to be the first condition for gentrification: dispossession of the resident population by removing existing tenants (Wachsmuth & Weisler, 2018). Nevertheless, the state is multi-level and comprises sub- and supra-national political bodies, including the active role played by the EU and local authorities. To some extent, the "sustainable tourism" policy and new Balearic Tourism Act 6/2017 laid the groundwork.

The new Balearic tourism law on the one hand sets a cap to avert overproduction (an excess of tourism places and declining prices and profits) while, on the other, promoting a new pathway for further expansion. Thus, the *Govern's* target is to increase tourist numbers in low season. As seasonality and spatial concentration are some of the main features of mass tourism in southern Europe's coastal regions (Bramwell, 2004, chapter 1), the tourism frontier can expand beyond these time-space coordinates. Milano (2018) paints it as a "5-D" strategy for tourism growth: deseasonalization, decongestion, decentralization, diversification and deluxe tourism (elitization). This 5-D strategy is fairly similar to what the *Govern* promotes for the Balearic Islands through its "better in winter" (deseasonalization) and "welcome sustainable tourism" (diversification) campaigns, as well as through the cap on tourist bed places (decongestion). The main difference with past boom cycles is the role of the local state in the fourth boom being secondary in economic and legal terms, as seen in similar destinations (Sequera & Gil, 2018, p. 196). The facilities for accumulation existed in already constructed residential housing, and the legal framework to promote its tourist use and to shrink residential tenant rights was already in place. Thus, decentralization in the new boom came not from the state but from the airbnbfication of tourist accommodation in already built residential units across the region.

The Balearics, however, present several specificities at different levels. Firstly, expansion in rural areas also requires the state to be active in connecting an uneven geography of operational landscapes. In Ibiza, Minorca and Majorca, new major road projects have been launched in recent years. The second is the fact that holiday rentals were already regulated by a regional law in the Balearics, being prohibited in multi-family units. This represented an obstacle when compared to similar over-touristified destinations and is where the role of the *Govern* has been relatively active. In reality, regulations were already in place for this type of accommodation: prohibition; the legal reform opened the door to legalization. The *Govern* is also active in opening up a new frontier through the "better in winter" campaign. As a whole, the plan simultaneously promotes a vertical cap on synchronic tourist accommodation, while attempting to horizontally extend tourism activity throughout the year within the limits of the cap. Moreover, the cap is higher than ever as a consequence of the so-called "open bar" policy, meaning it will be higher for all four seasons of the year.

A further specificity can be seen in terms of legitimization. The Department for Tourism, run by *Més*, has been using the grammar of degrowth in order to justify the new tourism policy. Never before had tourism restraint been referred to as "degrowth". Under the leadership of the Fundació Impulsa, a fraction of progressive economic elites, political parties like the PSIB-PSOE and local stakeholders, such as the CCOO trade union, admit to there being a need for a "paradigm shift" in tourism towards *atemporality*, i.e. deseasonalization. Nevertheless, they avoid the term "degrowth", whose connotations are recession, declining profits, unemployment and the fiscal crisis of the state. *Més* joined the alliance for the paradigm shift, although it adopted the term "degrowth" in the face of pressure from social movements, since the term is also associated with environmental sustainability, decongestion and degentrification. Thus, the subtext of their bivalent approach to degrowth combines ideas of economic and tourism growth, social cohesion and degrowth of ecological footprint. In this light, the *what* of degrowth predicts a win–win scenario.

As stated, tourism degrowth theories are ambiguous in relation to economic degrowth measured by income. This is why Hall (2009, p. 46) defines environmentally sustainable tourism in biophysical terms as "steady state tourism" instead of tourism degrowth. Based on a strong sustainability perspective on tourism degrowth, for Hall "steady state tourism" keeps "a constant flow of throughput at a sustainable (low) level", taking into account the entire consumption and production process of a tourist stay. In these terms, Hall (2010) sees tourism as less sustainable than it has ever been, mostly because of international tourism travel. Aviation, and long-haul international travel in particular, is highly emission-intense and causes substantial global environmental change; therefore, flight degrowth is a must. The Balearics are champions of air traffic due to tourism and local authorities are campaigning to attract tourists from far-flung markets such as China, the USA or Canada. Similarly, deseasonalization means increasing tourist trips and visitors. Moreover, official data for Majorca report that average consumption by tourists is up to 3, 4 times higher in water and 5 in energy to that of residents (GAAT, 2018, pp. 13–18). These figures are included in the report used to draft the zoning plan for Majorca and served to justify a record increase in bed spaces under the cap. It also affirmed that holiday rentals "may" lead to pressure for urbanization and tertiarization in rural areas which would then "lose their original function (agriculture)".

The bivalent sustainable tourism model "aimed at degrowth" is not designed for environmental sustainability nor can it be considered steady state tourism. In this sense, degrowth represents local decongestion. The new tourism agenda is not actually that new, nor does it aim for degrowth in terms of tourist accommodation and visitors, or in the ecological footprint of tourism. All this lends plausibility to the hypothesis of a "spatial fix". Indeed, the fourth and ongoing boom can be explained as a spatial fix to the 2009 crisis through the expansion of the tourism commodity frontier, with a current risk of an oversupply crisis. In this vein, self-constraint in a given spatial domain and the exploration of a new one are required and, in this context, the discourse of degrowth functions as a rhetorical tool to justify tourism regulation that is functional to capital accumulation cycles.

Tourism degrowth as politicization: the "boundary struggle" hypothesis

As a spatial fix, it is capitalism that imposes the "strategies" that tourist administrations implement in a disciplined manner. However, in our case study neither the political system nor the tourism business has had a uniform and consistent response to overtourism and social contention.

The tourism business does not have a single interest: in today's boom, the hotel industry is partially involved in the new holiday rental niche, but on the whole has to compete therein with a new constellation of transnational corporations, small-scale tenants instilled with a sense of popular capitalism, large-scale tenants, homeowner-entrepreneur lobbies and investment funds (Murray et al., 2017, p. 21). Likewise, within the political system some players have shown some sensitivity to pressure from civil society. Tourism inspections face constant scrutiny from public opinion and some multinationals, such as Tripadvisor or Airbnb, have been fined for advertising illegal tourist accommodation. The municipality of Palma—where pressure from residents has been constant—has maintained a ban on holiday rentals in residential apartments. Moreover, official public statistics are more realistic than ever, which can hardly be deemed as functional to the tourism business, though tourism inspections have proven themselves ineffective in halting illegal activity. Additionally, *Més'* move from denial to constraint and finally degrowth speech was forced by civil society agents. Indeed, the party cannibalized a particular concept of tourism degrowth that emerged firstly in public resistance to overtourism outside the economic and political system. In our view, this resistance cannot be explained in functionalistic terms.

Accordingly, we propose a different strategy to analyse the struggle for degrowth in the Balearics. We have opted for a theoretical framework that approaches the standpoint of agents situated in social struggles and how they see themselves: the critical theory of society in line with John S. Dryzek and Nancy Fraser's blueprints. This approach seeks to "clarify the grammar of social struggle and the prospects for social transformation", taking into account, at the same time, the structural-systemic dimension (Fraser & Jaeggi, 2018, p. 123). It is not exclusionary in terms of a functionalist approach, but complementary. Fraser terms it a *structural-ethical* theory. For Dryzek (1997, p. 19), "discourses can constitute institutional software while formal rules constitute institutional hardware".

We will proceed in two stages. First, following Dryzek's (1997; Dryzek & Schlosberg, 1998) approach to environmental discourses, we analyse the discourse of advocates for tourism degrowth in civil society. Degrowth discourse in the Balearics arose from a pre-existing matrix for environmental struggles, so the former can be considered a derivative of the latter. Second, we interpret such discourse as a "boundary struggle". Here, we follow Nancy Fraser's "extended theory of capitalism" as an institutionalized social order in different spheres. Therefore, pro-degrowth demands will be understood as an attempt to reshape the boundaries between spheres such as the market, reproduction, nature and politics.

Dryzek (1997, p. 19) states that a discourse is "a shared way of looking at the world [that] rests on some common definitions, judgements, assumptions and contentions". In its ideal form, the common structure of a discourse comprises: (1) an ontology—basic entities whose existence is recognized or constructed; (2) assumptions about natural relationships; (3) agents and their motives, and (4) key metaphors and other rhetorical devices. Using this template, Dryzek has developed a sophisticated typology of environmental discourses, although tourism is rarely mentioned as a case study (Dryzek, Norgaard, & Schlosberg, 2012, p. 3).

In line with Dryzek's model, Valdivielso (2011) described the discourse in the Balearic Islands in response to previous tourist booms as "territorialist". The main discursive recourses identified "territory" with local "carrying capacity" and "limits", using a pre-tourism imaginary—its ontology—through binary associations of care and esteem versus destruction induced by urbanization. Within the territorialist discourse, subjects were articulated in opposition to the in/out axis: "*lo nostro*" ("ours") versus an external other embodied by tourism. Territory was subjectivized through rhetorical figures as an agent that "dies", "is consumed" and has to be "defended" or "saved" from tourism. As Mercè Picornell (2014) has pointed out, this discourse is based on an urban/rural dichotomy, where the city and suburban tourism spaces represent territorial deformation (Picornell, 2014, p. 230). Accordingly, this representation renders the social dynamics and cultural life of the city invisible. Agency is embodied in the territory, "*sa nostra terra*" (our land), represented by unspoilt landscapes besieged by tourism and tourist-induced urbanization. This explains the so-called "toponymical" emphasis in the local history of environmental struggles, focused on the defence of natural spaces such as the islets of Sa Dragonera and Cabrera, Ses Salines in Ibiza and Formentera, and Es Trenc in Majorca (Rayó, 2004).

However, as in other environmental contentions along the Spanish Mediterranean coastline, the "defence of the territory" in the Balearic Islands has served as a discursive umbrella that encompasses various demands. Territory can refer to a pre-tourist ethno-linguistic community, a tourist-colonized nation that fights for sovereignty, ecological metabolism and to common environmental goods, among others. This polysemy of "territory" made it possible to articulate social and political coalitions that triggered the fall of conservative governments (in 1999, 2007) and paved the way for constraint policies for tourism and urbanism. The discourse then weakened with the onset of the financial crisis, when environmental issues fell off the agenda while tourist numbers continued to increase. In this context, environmental organizations moved beyond their antagonistic approach and began to emphasize what Curato, Niemeyer, and Dryzek (2013) call a "feel-good" or "appreciative" management style, where contestation is avoided. The subsequent holiday rental boom and degrowth debate altered the scenario and socio-environmental antagonism re-emerged.

Degrowth and territorialist discourses differ, although the latter serves as a matrix for the former. The current discourse of tourism degrowth displays a grammar in which the demand for sustainability intersects with the right to the city. In line with Dryzek's discursive template, its *ontology* is centred on the islands as a fragile ecosystem, both at the local level as "territory" and the global level as "climate change", but also including entities such as "capitalism", "city" or "public space". *Relationships* express "massification"; "growth"; "gentrification"; "unsustainability"; "dispossession"; "commodification"; "overload"; "speculation"; "tourism pressure"; "violation of rights"—to the city, housing and the environment—; "colonization"; "invasion"; "gentrification" versus "ceiling"; "limit"; "containment"; "detouristification"; "contraction" and "social cohesion". *Subjects* are "residents", "neighbours" or those who have been "driven out" versus "tourists"; "big tenants"; "rent-seekers"; "lobbies" and "Airbnb". "City", "neighbourhood", "island" or "territory" demonstrate traits of agency. Finally, *rhetorical devices* depict how "tourism kills", "the city is dying", "collapse", "destruction" or "saturation" along with the "tourism boom" imaginary.

According to our theoretical perspective, a sort of discursive "rationalization" (Dryzek, 1997, p. 172) has occurred in relation to territorialist discourse. Now, nature appears mainly as ecosystem, and social, economic and political structures also become relevant. Global unsustainability gains momentum through the argument that tourism contributes to climate change. Furthermore, global capitalism is seen as an active agent in the form of international speculative investment and online platforms. In turn, relationships are informed by the principles of social equity and justice, and a complex view of social interaction, although the resident/tourist dichotomization still persists. Agent motivations are multidimensional, including instrumental strategic as well as morally led motives. Agency in nature is minimized though not necessarily denied. As for rhetorical devices, organic metaphors carry forward—"tourism kills"—but the in/out dualism for the city is eased. Many of these elements could already be found in the territorialist perspective, although now they have become distinctive traits. Territory is still present, but the romantic and communitarian subtext is not prevalent. In the end, urban gentrification has exceeded the spatial imaginary of territorial discourse.

This narrative shares many similar features with the "environmental justice movement" discourse (Bullard, 1998). Both stress the intertwinement of justice and sustainability and distance themselves from conservationism; social class is considered the first pillar of injustice, and the well-being of present and future generations takes preference over defence of the territory. Nevertheless, there are certain differences. The target in our case is not industrial "bads" but tourism externalities. Moreover, the environmental justice movement displays an intersectional view of justice, where the axes of class, gender and race crosscut. The gender axis in gentrification has been denounced by *Ciutat Habita*, and gained visibility in the protests against overtourism thanks to the appearance of "Las Kellys". The Kellys are cleaning workers in the hotel industry, an "invisible" sphere of precarious and overworked female labour (Cañada, 2015). In turn, though "racialized gentrification" has been identified in other contexts (Wachsmuth & Weisler, 2018), it is not present in the tourism degrowth movement, where "tourist classism" is preferred to "tourist racism". Nonetheless, *guiri* has a pejorative sense and the motto "a city for residents, *not for visitors*" risks being deemed exclusionary.

Degrowth discourse is wider in scope than that focused on tourist urban gentrification and the geography of cities. Indeed, it identifies different kinds of negative impacts caused by overtourism:

1. The aggregate effects of physical tourism saturation that overload the carrying capacity of natural spaces, resources and infrastructures
2. The contribution of tourism to climate change and global environmental change
3. Urban tourism gentrification
4. The tertiarization of the countryside and rural tourism gentrification
5. The privatization of public space and the commons.

As we have seen, the rural hinterland has a role as an operational landscape for tourism expansion. However, it does not entail geographical differentiation no longer existing between wilderness, peasant landscapes, coastal tourist spots, and suburban and rural spaces (Brenner, 2018, p. 575). Differential tourism-induced urbanization, then, implies socio-spatial differentiation. This affects the conditions in which movements and struggles can be articulated. In the city of Palma, neighbourhood associations catalysed the resistance against tourism gentrification through *Ciutat Habita*. Nothing comparable has emerged against rural gentrification: environmental organizations like GOB, *Terraferida* and *Tot Inclós* play the role of proxies for socioenvironmental externalities in those spaces (Murray et al, 2019, p. 11). This might be why "territory" still persists in tourism degrowth discourse.

Degrowth also covers demands for global sustainability, such as the very recent climate mobilizations in Palma by the local branches of Extinction Rebellion and Fridays for Future. Many other associations such as the local *Amics de la Terra* (Friends of the Earth) and platforms for Energy Sovereignty are also using the language of degrowth. Together they form what can be termed a coalition for degrowth, which includes tourism degrowth. Some other players, such as the Kellys, participate in protesting against overtourism, although not all of them can be deemed "degrowthers". What they all seem to share is the goal to degrow tourism pressure and for them, tourism degrowth does not just mean reducing the tourist cap, but rather the detouristification of society and shrinking the domain of tourism: this represents a struggle over the boundaries between social spheres.

Fraser defines boundary struggles as those that seek to transform the institutional topography of a capitalist society. For her, the sphere of commodity in capitalism tends to expand against other spheres that are the background conditions to society and the economy itself: namely, reproduction, polity and ecology. The economy penetrates these spheres and extracts various types of values to maximize capital. Over the clash between these domains, struggles emerge that attempt to redraw the boundaries in order to defend the background conditions of society. According to Fraser's typology (Fraser & Jaeggi, 2018: 174), the tourism degrowth struggle presented here could be defined as *defensive* ("aimed at repulsing the invasion") and *affirmative* (of "the given institutional boundary [that] should exist in more or less its present form"). The boundaries to be defended and affirmed are social reproduction—the city, housing, public space—and non-human nature—the ecology of the Earth and the biophysical commons. This paints the tourism degrowth struggle as a resistance against the expansion of the tourism frontier, i.e. touristification. It can be explained as a "double movement for protection" of society from the economy as per Fraser's interpretation of Polanyi's (2001). Therefore, it is a struggle for resistance against tourism commodification.

All the same, a closer look may offer a different interpretation. To some extent, contesting tourism growth is also *offensive* and *transformative*: its goal is to spread a new common sense regarding tourism; to socialize knowledge through the popular "epidemiology" of overtourism; to push the state into monitoring the unfettered tourist industry, and to empower citizens. We would even propose interpreting this struggle in line with what Fraser terms a "'meta-struggle' over the processes through which boundaries should be drawn", a struggle for "the capacity to participate in fundamental decisions about who we are or want to be" (Fraser & Jaeggi, 2018: 174, 131). Thus, tourism degrowth is about democracy and, in this sense, could be considered a "triple movement for emancipation", not just resistance for protection (Fraser, 2013; see also Fraser & Jaeggi, 2018, pp. 190–193).

Concluding remarks: emancipation through tourism degrowth

In recent years, overtourism has played a central role in public debate in the Balearic Islands, one of the most touristified regions of the planet. In this context, degrowth discourse has thrived, being discussed across the political spectrum and even serving to legitimize a sustainable tourism plan. As we have seen, the plan for sustainable tourism "aimed at degrowth" is not new when compared with past tourism planning in phases of oversupply and social contestation. Here, it is a bivalent cap-and-trade plan that seeks deseasonalized tourism growth. In turn, the language of degrowth has been used in platforms and social movements in response to overtourism. For them, tourism degrowth means detourisification and decommodification. Their discourse has emerged from environmental struggles and narratives, and is counter-hegemonic. We thus have two different visions: one used to justify a public policy and the other to form a process of bottom-up politicization. The former updates the greenwashing rhetoric in self-limitation policies of the tourism business while the latter renews an inherited environmental experience and leads it to a higher degree of rationalization. Our conclusion is that the debate over tourism degrowth is not just a discrepancy between different approaches to deal with overtourism and gentrification. It is also a social struggle where the discourse over tourism degrowth has helped new democratic political subjects to coalesce and organize in civil society. Therefore, the discourse over tourism degrowth has a constitutive effect in social action. The performance of tourism degrowth discourse shapes social and political subjects.

Prospects for reflexive potential of the tourism degrowth discourse analysed herein present various challenges. The social map resulting from the struggle around overtourism and tourism degrowth is complex. In studies on overtourism and gentrification, it is often simplified around fundamental social classes—capitalists versus the working poor, "communities versus corporations" (Wachsmuth & Weisler, 2018). In this sense, the Balearic market has been hypothesized as being and continuing to be increasingly in the hands of large-scale stakeholders controlling the value chain (Murray, 2018; Vives-Miró et al., 2018; Yrigoy, 2017). Nonetheless, in our case the demand for tourist use of residential housing has permeated across all social strata. This business model has become pervasive, even among left-wing politics. In this setting, tourism degrowth does not coalesce into a winning coalition, as the defence of the territory has done.

A second challenge concerns the inclusive potential of the counter-hegemonic discourse of tourism degrowth: it remains silent about the economic, political and social consequences of degrowth. Moreover, it has been suggested that present-day critics of tourist gentrification actually benefitted from gentrification in the past, that rejection of overtourism masks rejection of working-class tourists, or that it encourages a "revanchist environmentalism" that is appropriated by large-scale owners (Artigues & Blázquez, 2016). Consequently, a radical approach to tourism degrowth risks becoming a type of self-interested *nimby* (not in my back yard!) movement. Nevertheless, in several contexts there is evidence that conflicts around overtourism and gentrification can lead to solidarity and inter-class multi-thematic *niaby* (not in anyone's backyard!) or even *nope* (not on planet Earth!) coalitions (Camargo, 2016, Opillard, 2016). This may be occurring in the Balearic Islands, where platforms are synergizing with like-minded collectives in other regions and countries. However, as Fraser insists, the question to be addressed is whether they actually move towards emancipation, inclusive values and democratic organizations as well.

Acknowledgments

We are very grateful to Antoni Salvà and Ivan Murray for sharing data and maps, and to four anonymous reviewers for their insightful and constructive observations.

Funding

This research was supported by the Spanish Ministerio de Ciencia, Innovación y Universidades through project "Public Sphere and Emerging Subjects" (FFI2016-75603-R, AEI/FEDER, UE).

ORCID

Joaquín Valdivielso (iD) http://orcid.org/0000-0003-3324-3845
Joan Moranta (iD) http://orcid.org/0000-0002-9814-0735

References

Andriotis, K. (2018*). Degrowth in tourism. Conceptual, theoretical and philosophical issues.* Wallingford, Oxfordshire, UK: CABI.

Artigues, A., & Blázquez, M. (2016). Huidas al paraíso y la realización mercantil del sueño [Escape to paradise and the commercial realization of the dream]. *XIV Coloquio Internacional de Geocrítica. Las Utopías y la Construcción de la Sociedad Del Futuro, Barcelona.*

Asara, V. (2016). The Indignados as a socio-environmental movement: Framing the crisis and democracy. *Environmental Policy and Governance, 26*(6), 527–542. doi:10.1002/eet.1721

Blanco-Romero, A., Blázquez-Salom, M., & Mínguez, C. (2017). Claves de la reestructuración turística de la ciudad [Keys to the city's tourism restructuring], *Naturaleza, Territorio y Ciudad en un Mundo Global. Actas de XXV Congreso de la Asociación de Geógrafos Españoles. AGE/UAM,* 1516–1524.

Blázquez, M. (2006). Calmar, contenir i decréixer: Polítiques provades (1983-2003) i possibles de planificació urbanística' [To calm down, to contain and to degrow: Proven and possible policies of urban planning (1983–2003)]. *Territoris, 6,* 159–172.

Boluk, K. A., Cavaliere, C. T., & Higgins-Desbiolles, F. (2019). A critical framework for interrogating the United Nations Sustainable Development Goals 2030 Agenda in tourism. *Journal of Sustainable Tourism, 27*(7), 847–864. doi:10.1080/09669582.2019.1619748

Bramwell, B. (Ed.). (2004). *Coastal mass tourism. Diversification and sustainable development in Southern Europe.* Clevedon: Channel View Publications.

Brenner, N. (2018). Debating planetary urbanization: For an engaged pluralism. *Environment and Planning D: Society and Space, 36*(3), 570–590. doi:10.1177/0263775818757510

Brenner, N., & Schmid, C. (2015). Towards a new epistemology of the urban? *City, 19*(2–3), 151–182. doi:10.1080/13604813.2015.1014712

Bullard, R. D. (1998). Anatomy of Environmental Racism and the Environmental Justice Movement. In J. S. Dryzek & D. Schlosberg (Eds.) *Debating the Earth. The environmental politics reader* (pp. 471–492): Oxford: Oxford University Press.

Camargo, J. (2016). Movimiento antipetrolífero en Portugal: Del NIMBY al NOPE, del turismo al cambio climático [Anti-oil movement in Portugal: From NIMBY to NOPE, from tourism to climate change]. *Ecología Política, 52,* 93–97.

Cañada, E. (2015). *Las que limpian los hoteles. Historias ocultas de precariedad laboral* [Those who clean the hotels. Hidden stories of job precariousness]. Barcelona: Icaria.

Cañada, E., & Blázquez, M. (2011). *Turismo Placebo. Nueva colonización turística: Del Mediterráneo a Mesoamérica y El Caribe. Lógicas espaciales del capital turístico* [Placebo Tourism. New tourist colonization: From the Mediterranean to Mesoamerica and the Caribbean. Spatial logic of the tourist capital]. Managua: Edisa

Cócola, A. (2016). Holiday rentals: The new gentrification battlefront. *Sociological Research Online, 21*(3), 1–10.

Colomb, C., & Novy, J. (2017). *Protest and resistance in the tourist city.* Abingdon and New York: Routledge.

Curato, N., Niemeyer, S., & Dryzek, J. S. (2013). Appreciative and contestatory inquiry in deliberative forums: Can group hugs be dangerous? *Critical Policy Studies, 7*(1), 1–17. doi:10.1080/19460171.2012.758595

Dobson, A. (2014). *The politics of post-growth.* Weymouth: Green House. Retrieved from https://www.greenhouse-thinktank.org/reports.html

Dryzek, J. S. (1997). The politics of the earth. *Environmental Discourses.* New York: OUP.

Dryzek, J. S., Norgaard, R. B., & Schlosberg, D. (Ed.). (2012). *The Oxford handbook of climate change and society.* Oxford: OUP.

Dryzek, J. S., & Schlosberg, D. (1998). *Debating the Earth. The environmental politics reader.* Oxford: OUP.

Fernández, H., & Pardo, D. (2016). La lucha por el decrecimiento turístico: El caso de Barcelona [The struggle for the tourist degrowth: The case of Barcelona]. *Ecología Política, 52,* 104–106.

Fraser, N. (2013). A triple movement? Parsing the politics of crisis after Polanyi. *New Left Review, 81,* 119–132.

Fraser, F., & Jaeggi, R. (2018). *Capitalism. A conversation in critical theory.* Cambridge, UK: Polity.

Fundació Impulsa Balears. (2017). Cap a una estratègia de competitivitat global per a les Balears. Consignes estratègiques i vies de progrés [Towards a strategy of global competitiveness for the Balearic Islands. Strategic guides and prospects of progress] (Report i|dossiers No 1). Retrieved from http://impulsabalears.org/pdf/idossiers/i_dossier_ca.pdf

GAAT. (2018). *Delimitació provisional de les zones aptes per a la comercialització d'estades turístiques en habitatges d'ús residencial* [Provisional delimitation of the appropriate areas for the commercialization of tourist stays in residential homes]. Palma: Consell de Mallorca.

Goodwin, H. (2017).. The challenge of overtourism. Responsible Tourism Partnership Working Paper 4. Retrieved from http://haroldgoodwin.info/pubs/RTP%27WP4Overtourism01%272017.pdf

Groizard, J. L., & Nilsson, W. (2017). Mito y realidad del alquiler vacacional en las Islas Baleares (o Airbnb para principiantes) [Myths and realities of holiday rentals in the Balearic Islands (or Airbnb for beginners]. DEA WP no. 84 Working Paper Series. Retrieved from http://dea.uib.cat/digitalAssets/430/430024_w84.pdf.

Hall, C. M. (2009). Degrowing tourism: Décroissance, sustainable consumption and steady-state tourism. *Anatolia*, *20*(1), 46–61. doi:10.1080/13032917.2009.10518894

Hall, C. M. (2010). Changing paradigms and global change: From sustainable to steady-state tourism. *Tourism Recreation Research*, *35*(2), 131–143. doi:10.1080/02508281.2010.11081629

Hall, C. M. (2011). Policy learning and policy failure in sustainable tourism governance: From first- and second-order to third-order change? *Journal of Sustainable Tourism*, *19*(4-5), 649–671. doi:10.1080/09669582.2011.555555

Harvey, D. (2003). *The new imperialism*. Oxford: Oxford University Press

Manera, C., & Navinés, F. (2018). La industria invisible, 1950-2016. *El desenvolupament del turisme a l'economia balear [The invisible industry, 1950-2016. The development of tourism in the Balearic economy]*. Palma: Lleonard Muntaner.

Meana, R. (2016). Extralimitación, decrecimiento y turismo: La necesidad de un cambio de modelo [Overshoot, degrowth and tourism: The need for a change of model]. *Ecología Política*, *52*, 8–11.

Mestre, M. (2016). *Ciutat i territori a Mallorca. Una aproximació a la relació entre Palma i el sistema urbà mallorquí [City and territory in Mallorca. An approach to the relationship between Palma and the Majorcan urban system]* (Doctoral Dissertation). Barcelona: Universitat Autònoma de Barcelona. Retrieved from http://hdl.handle.net/10803/400083.

Milano, C. (2018). Overtourism, malestar social y turismofobia. Un debate controvertido [Overtourism, social unease and tourism-phobia. A controversial debate]. *PASOS. Revista de Turismo y Patrimonio Cultural*, *16*(3), 551–564. doi: 10.25145/j.pasos.2018.16.041

Milano, C. J., & Mansilla, J. (2018). Ciudad de vacaciones. *Conflictos urbanos en espacios turísticos [Holiday city. Urban conflicts in tourist spaces]*. (pp. 255–287). Barcelona: Pol·len.

Milano, C., Novelli, M., & Cheer, J. M. (2019). Overtourism and tourismphobia: A journey through four decades of tourism development, planning and local concerns. *Tourism Planning & Development*, *16*(4), 353–357.

Molas, M. (2017). Barcelona lidera el NO a l'economia col·laborativa capitalista [Barcelona leads the NO to the capitalist collaborative economy. *Recerca. Revista de Pensament i Anàlisi.*, *21*, 159–163.], doi:10.6035/Recerca.2017.21.10

Morell, M. (2018a). The class gap in gentrification. A political reading of the rent gap hypothesis. In A. Albet & N. Benach (Eds.) *Gentrification as a global strategy. Neil Smith and Beyond* (pp. 132–141). New York: Routledge.

Morell, M. (2018b). Una casa deshabitada no es en realidad un verdadera casa". Estado y movimiento en el alquiler turístico en Mallorca [An uninhabited house is not really a real home. State and movement in holiday rentals in Mallorca]. In C. Milano & J. Mansilla, *Ciudad de vacaciones. Conflictos urbanos en espacios turísticos* (pp. 255–287). Barcelona: Pol·len.

Murray, I., Jover-Avellà, G., Fullana, O., & Tello, E. (2019). Biocultural heritages in Mallorca: Explaining the resilience of peasant landscapes within a Mediterranean Tourist Hotspot, 1870–2016. *Sustainability*, *11*(7), 1926, 1–22. doi: 10.3390/su11071926

Murray, I., Yrigoy, I., & Blázquez-Salom, M. (2017). The role of crises in the production, destruction and restructuring of tourist spaces. The case of the Balearic Islands. *Revista de Investigaciones Turísticas*, *13*, 1–29.

Murray, I. (2018). La turistización es la muerte de la ciudad [Touristification is the death of the city]. *InfoLibre*, Retrieved from https://www.infolibre.es/noticias/politica/2018/05/30/ivan_murray_turistizacion_muerte_ciudad_82937_1012.html

Nilsson, W., Leoni, V., & Figini, P. (2016). Report on the Airbnb rental market for the Balearic Islands. *Agència de Turisme de Les Illes Balears/Universitat de Les Illes Balears*. Retrieved from http://www.caib.es/sites/estadistiques-delturisme/ca/altres_estudis-85585/

Nixon, R. (2011). *Slow violence and the environmentalism of the poor*. Cambridge, MA: Harvard U.P.

Opillard, F. (2016). From San Francisco's "Tech Boom 2.0" to Valparaíso's UNESCO World Heritage Site: Resistance to tourism gentrification in a comparative political perspective. In C. Colomb & J. Novy (Eds.) *Protest and resistance in the tourist city* (pp. 129–151). London: Routledge.

Pallicer, A., & Blázquez, M. (2016). Turismo y caciquismo hotelero en las Islas Baleares: La publicación Tot Inclòs y la quiebra del consenso social [Tourism and hotel caciquism in the Balearic Islands: The publication of *Tot Inclòs* and the breakdown of social consensus]. *Ecología Política*, *52*, 88–92.

Panzer-Krause, S. (2019). Networking towards sustainable tourism: Innovations between green growth and degrowth strategies. *Regional Studies*, *53*(7), 927–938. doi:10.1080/00343404.2018.1508873

Picornell, M. (2014). Insular identity and urban contexts: Representations of the local in the construction of an image of Palma (Mallorca, Balearic Islands). *Island Studies Journal*, *9*(2), 223–238.

Polanyi, K. (2001). *The great transformation*. Boston: Beacon.

Prádanos, L. I. (2018). *Postgrowth imaginaries. New ecologies and counterhegemonic culture in Post-2008 Spain*. Liverpool: Liverpool U.P.

Qian, J., Wei, J., & Law, R. (2018). Review of critical discourse analysis in tourism studies. *International Journal of Tourism Research*, *20*(4), 526–537. doi:10.1002/jtr.2202

Rayó, M. (2004). *L'ecologisme a les Balears [Ecologism in the Balearics]*. Palma: Documenta.

Rullan, N. (1998). De la cova de Canet al Tercer Boom turístic. Una primera aproximació a la geografia històrica de Mallorca [From the Canet cave to the third tourist boom. An initial approach to the historical geography of Mallorca], DD. AA. *El medi ambient a les Illes Balears. Qui és qui?*, Palma: Sa Nostra, 171–213

Sequera, J., & Gil, J. (2018). Resistencias contra la ciudad turística. Airbnb en Madrid [Resistances against the tourist city. Airbnb in Madrid]. In C. Milano & J. Mansilla (Eds.). *Ciudad de vacaciones. Conflictos urbanos en espacios turísticos* (pp. 189–222). Barcelona: Pol·len.

Smith, N. (1996). *The New Urban Frontier: Gentrification and the Revanchist City*. London: Routledge.

Stibbe, A. (2015). *Ecolinguistics. Language, Ecology and the Stories We Live By*. Oxon: Routledge.

Torgerson, D. (2000). Farewell to the green movement? Political action and the green public sphere. *Environmental Politics*, *9*(4), 1–19. doi:10.1080/09644010008414548

Valdivielso, J. (2011). Les polítiques del lloc a les illes Balears: Identitat, medi ambient i territori [Politics of place in the Balearic Islands: Identity, environment and territory]. *Journal of Catalan Studies*, *13*, 351–372.

Valdivielso, J., & Riutort, B. (2004). Canvi social i crisi ecològica a les Illes Balears [Social change and ecological crisis in the Balearic Islands.]. In J. Valdivielso (Ed.), *Les dimensions socials de la crisi ecològica*, Palma: UIB.

Vives-Miró, S., Rullan, N., & Gónzalez, J. M. (2018). *Understanding geographies of home dispossession through the crisis. Evictions Palma Style*. Barcelona: Icaria.

Wachsmuth, D., & Weisler, A. (2018). Airbnb and the rent gap: Gentrification through the sharing economy. *Environment and Planning A: Economy and Space*, *50*(6), 1147–1170. doi:10.1177/0308518X18778038

Yrigoy, I. (2017). Airbnb en Menorca: ¿Una nueva forma de gentrificación turística? Localización de la vivienda turística, agentes e impactos sobre el alquiler residencial [Airbnb in Minorca: A new way of tourist gentrification? Location of holiday homes, agents and impacts on residential rent]. *Scripta Nova, XXI*, 580. doi:10.1344/sn2017. 21.18573

Community-owned tourism and degrowth: a case study in the Kichwa Añangu community

Sarah Rachelle Renkert

ABSTRACT

Tourism is a booming global industry, seemingly at odds with a degrowth movement seeking to challenge the profit-maximizing model embedded in capitalist expansion. However, the tourism industry is not a homogenous entity, but is instead characterized by diverse forms of distinct tourisms. In Ecuador, the Kichwa Añangu Community has chosen to dedicate their livelihood to community-owned tourism. Añangu owns and operates two lodges, whose management and over-sight are administered through communal governance. As a result, tourism is locally embraced as a vehicle for livelihood wellbeing, cultural reclamation, and environmental stewardship. Community-owned tourism will not provide a cure-all answer to the critiques levied against tourism or to the vulnerabilities inherent in the practice of tourism. However, Añangu's project offers a compelling case study for consider-ing how certain tourisms could become a vehicle for developing a local-ized degrowth society. The Añangu have decentralized the value placed upon profit in the practice of tourism, replacing it with Kichwa forms of communal organizing guided by their goal for *Sumak Kawsay*, or the "good life." For the Añangu, the sustainability of their project cannot be separated from its economic viability, however, success is also measured by how tourism contributes to a number of community-defined goals.

Introduction: Tourism and degrowth

Degrowth as an activist movement, academic focus, and applied practice, emerges from the embedded contradictions of a growth-oriented economic system, which fails to account for capi-talism's dependence on uneven economic opportunities and finite environmental resources (Kallis, 2011). These critiques are seemingly at odds with the so-called tourism industry, which relies on a global market of wealthy consumers, international travel, built infrastructure, and profit. Considering these incongruities, this paper examines how community-owned tourism might serve as an avenue of localized degrowth for small communities whose livelihoods cur-rently depend on local tourism. Specifically, it draws on Gibson-Graham's use of diverse econo-mies (Gibson-Graham, 2006), to consider how community-owned tourism can serve as a vehicle for achieving locally defined goals which go beyond individual income and economic growth.

To explore the relationship between community-owned tourism and degrowth, this paper turns to the case of tourism in the Kichwa Añangu Community, who own and operate ecotour-ism and cultural tourism lodges in the Ecuadorian Amazon's Yasuní National Park. The Añangu have built their tourism project around the Kichwa notion of *Sumak Kawsay*, which has been roughly translated to the "good life," or *"buen vivir"* in Spanish. The philosophy of *Sumak Kawsay* or the related *Suma Qamaña* in Aymara, have been differentially interpreted, applied, and historicized by Amazonian and Andean communities, governments, activists, and academics (Altmann, 2014; Capitán & Guevara, 2014; Recasens, 2014). Drawing from a Kichwa perspective, Mónica Chuji from the Kichwa Community of Sarayaku, explains that, *"Sumak Kawsay* is the alternative to progress, to development, to modernity. It is a notion that wants to recover that harmonious relationship between human beings and their environment. Between humanity and their fellow humans" (Chuji, 2009). By consistently engaging this vision of *Sumak Kawsay* in the management and daily practice of tourism, the Añangu have used their tourism project to strive towards specific, community-defined goals, including the production of local livelihood opportunities, cultural reclamation, and environmental stewardship.

Both degrowth and *Sumak Kawsay* offer compelling critiques of neoliberal capitalism's need for constant economic expansion, by focusing on communal wellbeing, environmental protection, and a reorientation of the economy towards producing greater social good (Thomson, 2011). In a description of *Sumak Kawsay* by Ecuadorian economists Pablo Dávalos, it would be easy to see the two terms as nearly synonymous:

> The good life is a conception of life, distant from the most expensive parameters of modernity and economic growth: individualism, the pursuit of profit, [...], the use of nature, [...], the total commodification of all spheres of human life, the inherent violence of consumer selfishness, etc. (Dávalos, 2008, p. 5)

However, it is important to not equate the Indigenous interpretation of *Sumak Kawsay* to degrowth (Altmann, 2017). How the Añangu engage *Sumak Kawsay* is embedded with cultural and spiritual values which go beyond Western framings of a degrowth society. For this reason, degrowth serves as a useful concept for considering how other small communities could engage Añangu's model of self-determination in the practice of community-owned tourism. Tourism as practiced by the Añangu, focuses on the wellbeing of its people and the environment, over the constant need for capitalist growth and business profitability. There is no guarantee that other tourism projects will inevitably destabilize capitalist practices focused on growth and profit. However, for those community-owned tourism projects which engage a just collective decision-making process and prioritize values beyond economic growth, they will be able to challenge ontologies of hierarchical power structures and the valorization of financial profitability common in a growth economy.

Throughout the remainder of this article, I will first provide a critical overview of the tourism industry, while also introducing community-owned tourism. I will then consider the relationship between tourism and degrowth, by arguing that degrowth requires not only a change in economic practices but also a reorientation of social values and priorities, focusing on shared goals over individual profit. These sections will be followed by an overview of research methods and an introduction to the Kichwa Añangu Community. In turning to the case study, I will examine two themes which demonstrate how community-owned tourism in Añangu can serve as a vehicle of degrowth. First, I will look at the management of the tourism project, with a focus on communal governance. Then, I will examine how tourism is being used to achieve community-defined goals including localized livelihood opportunities, cultural reclamation, and environmental stewardship, rather than solely focusing on profit.

A critical look at the "tourism industry"

Tourism is often viewed as a booming global industry. According to the United Nations World Tourism Organization (UNWTO), in 2016, tourism employed one in ten people across the globe, made up 10% of the world's gross domestic product, and is expected to grow at a rate of 3% to

4% through 2030 (UNWTO, 2017). However, this growth comes with its own challenges. Tourism has been critiqued for contributing to global climate change (IPCC, 1999), ecosystem destruction (Stonich, 1998), and the exclusion of people from their traditional lands and livelihoods (Sirima & Backman, 2013; Vásquez-León, 2012). Economically, the involvement of transnational corporations has often meant that money generated by tourism leaves the host nation (Honey, 2008; Robinson, 2003), while producing primarily low-wage, service-level employment (Honey, 2008). Culturally, tourists have been accused of being indifferent to local norms and oblivious to the processes and potential downsides of cultural commodification and transformation (Greenwood, 1989).

However, the notion of a single "tourism industry" mischaracterizes the complexity of tourism in practice (Higgins-Desbiolles, 2006, 2008). While "mass tourism," and "alternative tourism," have been conceptually used to nuance the perception of two distinct branches of the tourism industry (Honey, 2008; O'Neill, 2002), they both frequently lack bounded definitions (Honey, 2016; Robinson, 2003; Stronza, 2001; Vainikka, 2013). In problematizing 'mass tourism', Vainikka has argued that the label ambiguously serves as a "loose umbrella term" for large-scale popular tourism (2013, p. 280). Mass tourism, as a concept, tells us little about the impact and ethics of distinct tourism enterprises. While "alternative tourism" has been celebrated for offering more responsible, small-scale options, there are no enforceable established practices binding so-called alternative tourisms to ethical norms (Font, Sanabria, & Skinner, 2008; Honey, 2008, 2016; Russell & Wallace, 2004; Salazar, 2012). Notably, alternative tourisms cannot easily be separated from the profit-driven desire to attract new niche markets (Fletcher, 2011). Fletcher argues that these expanding forms of alternative tourisms facilitate capitalism's dependence on constant growth by finding "outlets for excess capital that might otherwise provoke an overproduction crisis" (2011, p. 449). Ultimately, they function to create a diversified tourism marketplace, where excess capital can be spent.

However, given the diversity of alternative tourism market options, it is important to recognize that tourism, in its plural forms, is not inevitably susceptible to the ecological, economic, and cultural critiques levied at the so-called tourism industry more broadly (Higgins-Desbiolles, 2006). Higgins-Desbiolles argues that tourism can be a "powerful social force [...] harnessed to meet human development imperatives and the wider public good," when its practice is separated from neoliberal market logics (2006, p. 1192). Drawing on this proposition, the question then becomes, are there tourism practices which can shift tourism's focus on profit and accumulation to one that allows tourism to serve as a vision of degrowth?

In the case of tourism which involves a host community, community-based tourism (CBT) has been proposed for creating an inclusionary and democratic relationship between the tourism business and the people or "community" who are featured as a part of the tourism experience (Okazaki, 2008). The UNWTO states that the practice of CBT should involve local communities in the "development process" of tourism operations. Community priorities should take precedence in decision-making processes, creating a "catalyst of social cohesion," which is able to advance "sustainable development from the grassroots level" (UNWTO, 2014). Rozemeijer expands on this overview by explaining that CBT should either be run as a joint and equitable partnership between the private sector and local peoples or be owned by one or more communities (Rozemeijer, 2001).

In practice, CBT is not limited to a single type of tourism (e.g. ecotourism or cultural tourism), but instead attempts to reshape how tourism is managed when a local "community," or a self-identifying group of people, is involved. Like other alternative tourisms, CBT has been critiqued for lacking transparency in practice (Blackstock, 2005; Salazar, 2012). CBT often involves community partnerships with exterior businesses, non-profit organizations, or non-governmental organizations. When this dual partnership exists, power and profit are often not equally shared. For example, how much say does the community have in the decision-making and administration?

To what extent does the community have curatorial power in how their culture or environment are being commodified? How is profit divided between the organization and the community?

This paper will go one step beyond CBT, by explicitly looking at community-owned tourism (COT). In community-owned tourism, the members of the community (or an association of communities) are the owners, administrators, and managers of the tourism project. While a community may partner with travel agencies and work with individuals who are not from the community, this paper is concerned with power structures where the community, as opposed to individuals, outside businesses, NGOs, etc., is fully in charge of decision-making, management, and profit distribution.

Degrowth and tourism

The foundations of a degrowth society cannot be based only on a reduction in economic activity. This is made visible by periods of economic downturns, where unemployment skyrockets and social spending is cut, often leading to reductions in social welfare (Latouche, 2009, p. 8). Instead, degrowth must be treated as social shift, which focuses not only on restructuring the economy away from a capitalist focus on profitability and economic growth, but also a fundamental reorientation of values, relationships, and livelihood practices. In the words of Paulson, what we need for degrowth to work, "is not just a quantitative decrease in production and consumption, but something much more radical: a cultural transformation that re-establishes livelihoods, relationships and politics around a new suite of values and goals" (Paulson, 2017, p. 430).

A part of this "cultural transformation" should include livelihood opportunities which provide not only fair wages to laborers, but also serve to achieve stronger social relations, communally established goals, such as ecological regeneration or social justice initiatives, and greater societal wellbeing. Gibson-Graham propose that for economies to contribute to these greater social goals, economic production should have the "capacity to produce social surplus in a variety of forms, and not just surplus value" (Gibson-Graham, 2006, p. 95). The intention is to move beyond an economic understanding which focuses on how wealth can continue to grow, to thinking about how profit, in the form of social surplus, can come to serve community goals and an interconnected sense of social belonging and wellbeing.

In thinking about tourism as a catalyst for what Gibson-Graham have termed "diverse economies" (Gibson-Graham, 2006, 2008), it is possible to imagine a variety of avenues by which tourism practices could contribute to the development of a degrowth society. In Hall's foundational article on tourism and degrowth, he lays out several possible means by which tourism can help create this vision of degrowth (2009). For example, he suggests that tourists could localize their travel as much as possible to reduce their overall carbon footprint, while ecotourism businesses can move beyond "green-washing," by ensuring lodges have a net positive environmental impact. He also argues that tourism firms can adopt a "concept of social responsibility that shifts from being 'beholden to shareholders' to one that is more stakeholder-based and includes the workers and communities on which their survivability is partly based" (Hall, 2009, p. 58).

In thinking about the diverse means by which tourism could contribute to degrowth, it is important to ensure that "degrowth" does not become another meaningless term to describe the ethics of "alternative tourisms." However, it is equally important to measure degrowth within the practice of tourism as a form of progress, rather than searching only for "utopian solutions wholly autonomous from the [capitalist] system" (Figueroa & Alkon, 2017, p. 209). This purest approach problematically bifurcates degrowth in tourism into two simple categories: 1) "Yes, achieving degrowth," or 2) "No, not achieving degrowth." Rather than thinking about economic practices in this polarized form, it is necessary to consider the spaces of creative possibility, where the practice of tourism can produce social surplus which helps meet a variety of communal goals. This does not mean that wages or profit disappear, but rather that they are not the only or primary goal of the tourism project. The practice of community-owned tourism, in particular, aligns with what Gibson-Graham have called the "community economy." Through communal management and decision making, a community economy has the potential for resocializing economic relations, where recognition of economic interdependence, cooperation, and social connections guide how economic decisions are made (Gibson-Graham, 2006).

Given that tourism is entangled in the capitalist economy, it will often continue to create new markets for capitalist expansion (Fletcher, 2011). However, tourism which combines communal governance, with diverse social surplus goals, can subvert the underlying logics of neoliberal capitalism, which centers individual profit and constant economic expansion. The remainder of this article will turn to the Kichwa Añangu Community, to consider how their model of community-owned tourism, guided by *Sumak Kawsay*, can make important contributions for thinking about the role tourism could play in a degrowth society.

Methods

This article draws on four months of fieldwork completed during two trips to the Kichwa Añangu Community (CKA) in 2015 and 2016. Prior to beginning this research, I signed a contract with CKA identifying my roles, obligations, and commitments to the community. Drawing on ethnographic methods, over two trips I lived in the community center where the Napo Cultural Center, one of Añangu's two lodges, is located. I was also able to visit the Napo Wildlife Center, which is located two hours from the community center, on two occasions. During this research, I completed thirty semi-structured interviews with Añangu Community members, ecolodge staff from outside the community, and other visitors, such as interns and volunteers. All interviews were conducted in Spanish and were recorded with the permission of the interviewees.

While in Añangu, I engaged in extensive participant observation by joining in nearly every aspect of the tourism experience. I frequently accompanied guides leading tourists through Añangu's various attractions. On two occasions, I served as a bilingual interpreter for guests, including a film crew who was creating a video for Añangu's tourism project. I frequently visited the Kuri Muyu Interpretation Center, where Mamakunas or mothers from Añangu perform traditional dances, share Kichwa history, and sell artisanal goods. I worked with employees in *varios servicios* (various services), collecting food for tourists and helping with construction projects. I also assisted in the restaurant, either working with cooks in the kitchen or helping set the dining room tables. Finally, I was able to engage in everyday activities, such as making *chicha*, a fermented cassava beverage, and playing sports, while also serving as the resident English teacher for the Napo Cultural Center's staff.

This research drew on grounded theory throughout the data collection and analysis process. At the completion of each visit, all interviews were transcribed. Transcriptions and fieldnotes were then inductively coded to identify relevant themes. The three major categories discussed in this article, "Livelihood Opportunities," "Cultural Reclamation," "Environmental Stewardship and Resource Protection," emerged from this coding process.

The Kichwa Añangu Community: An overview

The Kichwa Añangu Community (*Kichwa Añangu Llactama - Comunidad Kichwa Añangu*) (CKA) lives along the banks of the Napo River, inside of the Yasuní National Park. Añangu's founding community members, who are Kichwa Indigenous people, are originally from cities such as Tena and Archidona. In 1964 and 1977, the Ecuadorian government passed Amazonian colonization laws which encouraged migration from the Andes to the Amazon. These laws aimed to "civilize" the Amazon region, putting titles on supposedly unclaimed lands, while generating economic growth through enterprises such as cattle grazing and logging. This lead to waves of internal migration as Indigenous peoples moved further into the Amazon to maintain their traditional livelihoods (Yashar, 2006). The development of the CKA in the 1970s was a result of this internal migration and it came with many challenges. Population numbers fluctuated due to mosquito-related diseases, building on swampy land, a lack of all basic services, and a temporary military occupation which disrupted community wellbeing and resources (Amores Grandes, 2012; Torres, 2013).

Nonetheless, the community persevered. It was formally recognized by the Ecuadorian government in 1982 and gained full legal status as a *"Comunidad"* in 1994 (Amores Grandes 2012). The community chose to name itself *Añangu*, which means "ant" in Kichwa, after the leaf-cutter ants who parade throughout the Yasuní National Park, working day and night, always as a team. At the time of my fieldwork, Añangu had approximately 188 permanent community members, including nearly 70 *socios* or adult community members. Being a *socio* is a commitment. It includes participating in monthly assemblies, following community-defined rules, and attending *mingas* or communal work sessions. Not all adults are required to become *socios*, but those who do have access to land and a voice in the community governing structures. All families in Añangu have homes along the Napo River. Each family has land to build a home and plant a *chacra*, or small farm. The majority of Añangu's *socios* are employed by their tourism project, working at the Napo Cultural Center, the Napo Wildlife Center, or the main office in Quito, Ecuador.

Community-owned tourism in Añangu

To understand how tourism in Añangu serves as an example of degrowth, it is helpful to first turn to the history of tourism in Añangu. This history demonstrates the transition by which the Añangu moved from an exploitative form of community-based tourism to community-owned tourism. In the latter form, the CKA has been able to define the project's goals according to their value system and Kichwa ontologies as an act of self-determination. During the 1990s, several men from Añangu were working at ecolodges outside of the community. By 1998, it was proposed that the community should start its own tourism project. Initially, feelings were mixed. Among other concerns, it was well known that building a lodge would be expensive. Nonetheless, a small group decided to make the two-hour trek through the forest to Lake Añangucocha, where they began building cabins from local materials. Eventually, the community voted to support the project, with the initial support of NGOs, who helped fund the construction of the Napo Wildlife Center (NWC). According to a community leader, Añangu worked with three NGOs: Neblina Forest, Tropical Nature Conservation System, and the EcoEcuador Foundation.

After the Napo Wildlife Center was opened in 2000, the community signed a contract with EcoEcuador, giving them ownership of the lodge for twenty years as a community-based tourism project. According to the contract, Añangu would receive economic benefits from the NWC's profits and employment opportunities. After the twenty-year mark, the CKA would take over ownership of the lodge. The relationship with EcoEcuador fell apart when it became evident that the NGO was mismanaging funds. Añangu's former President explained that once it was clear that EcoEcuador was stealing money, workers from Añangu traveled to Quito and occupied the NGO's main office, refusing to allow the employees inside. Ultimately, the Añangu Community sued for full rights to the lodge and won the case in 2007. Today, the community maintains full control over the tourism project, which they manage through a process of communal governance.

At the time of this research, the tourism project in Añangu included the operation of the Napo Wildlife Center,[1] the Napo Cultural Center,[2] and the *Kuri Muyu* Women's Organization.[3] The Napo Wildlife Center opened in 2000 and has since become a world-renowned ecolodge. It is well known for its birding opportunities and advertises itself as offering a pristine Amazon experience. The CKA's second ecolodge, the Napo Cultural Center, opened in 2012. It is located in the community center and focuses on creating a cultural experience for guests, who are able to interact with community members by participating in a *guayusada* (early morning tea drinking with an elder), playing sports, or having lunch at a local home. This ecolodge is locally called the Mamakuna's Lodge, or Mother's Lodge. This is because it was the Mamakuna's who advocated to open the lodge, given that the community center is closer to their homes. The Mamakuna's make-up the majority of the lodge's staff, an uncommon gender dynamic in the tourism industry (Lew, Hall, & Williams, (Pritchard 2014). Kichwa women from the Añangu Community work not only cleaning rooms or in the kitchens, but also as guides and even in managerial positions, which are typically occupied by men across tourism projects. This is an example of the power communal governing can have, when all voices are equally valued in the community. In the case of Añangu, the boundaries of women's participation are defined by the Mamakunas themselves. The Kuri Muyu Interpretation Center is also located at the Napo Wildlife Center. At the Kuri Muyu, Añangu's Mamakunas or mothers share Kichwa history and traditions with visiting guests.

It is important to emphasize that community-ownership means that the project belongs to the whole community and is managed by Añangu's *socios*. There are salary hierarchies across employment positions, such as salary distinctions between the general manager, the lodge administrators, and guides, and so forth. Additionally, at the main office in Quito, there are only a few employees who are *socios* from Añangu. The remainder of the staff are largely from Quito and have specialized training in tourism management, such as marketing or accounting. However, all staff members who are employed by the tourism project ultimately work for the community. All major decisions regarding the tourism project are made during the monthly assembly meetings, which are only attended by *socios*. Furthermore, there are *socios* from Añangu who have chosen not to participate or be employed by the tourism project. Nonetheless, all *socios* have a voice in discussing, debating, and voting on projects and issues related to tourism, among all other community-related topics. Añangu is also well known in the region for the strict rules chosen by *socios*. This includes the decision to ban hunting, a prohibition on the consumption of alcohol in the community center, required participation in *mingas* (communal works sessions), and attending the monthly assemblies. Guides from other communities in the region frequently mention that Añangu's project is successful because the community follows these rules dutifully.

Ultimately, it is Añangu's communal governance which makes tourism in the CKA unique. Although tourism inevitably depends on tourists' demands and consumption, having the ability to shape the curation of the tourism experience arguably becomes an act of degrowth, where the community acts as a collective, rather than self-interested, profit-seeking individuals. Tómas summarized this process when he explained that "in the assemblies, we are always arguing. […] If there is a problem, we fix it, that's it. And in the assembly, everything can be resolved. For that reason, we have grown so much here." As Tómas notes, communities inevitably have frictions. They should never be understood as perfectly homogenous and harmonious entities. However, in Añangu, the assemblies become the place of negotiation. It is a dynamic governance process, where voices are heard, compromises are negotiated, and decisions are ultimately made around community-defined goals. In the CKA, profit serves as a medium sustaining community projects and goals, rather than prioritizing individual wealth as an end goal. The following sections will provide an overview of three initiatives prioritized by the Añangu through the development of their tourism project.

Why tourism? A look at the Kichwa Añangu Community's goals

This section will examine three goals the Añangu Community is attempting to achieve through their tourism project: livelihood opportunities, localized cultural reclamation, and environmental stewardship. Each of these goals highlights how the practice of tourism can have end-goals, which are not centered solely around an economic bottom-line. While having sufficient income to sustain the project cannot be removed from the equation, the relationship between community tourism and a degrowth society should ideally consider how profit can serve as a vehicle for achieving the common good. What is key to this argument is how the Kichwa Añangu are able to use ownership of their tourism project to focus on community needs and goals, which they often frame through the Kichwa notion of *Sumak Kawsay*.

The Añangu have publicly defined *Sumak Kawsay* as, "'wellbeing', a way of living in harmony within the communities and with nature," where they can "use their resources to promote regeneration […] to preserve and maintain their rich culture, traditions, their identity and their environment" (Comunidad Kichwa Añangu, 2017). While *Sumak Kawsay* is embedded in Kichwa cosmologies which have meanings beyond the politics of degrowth, the way the Añangu practice community-owned tourism explicitly challenges an economic growth mentality, which centers monetary accumulation. While tourism is intended to provide a basic economic livelihood for community members, it also employs a diverse economies approach which strives to keep young people in the community, sustain the practice of Kichwa traditions and beliefs, and to protect the Amazon Rainforest. Each of these goals is part of the ongoing process of creating *Sumak Kawsay*, which Carlos Viteri from the Kichwa community of Sarayaku describes as being in "permanent construction" (Viteri Gualinga 2002, p. 3).

Livelihood opportunities

One of the primary reasons that the Añangu Community has chosen to engage in community-owned tourism, is to create local jobs that align with community-defined goals, such as cultural reclamation and environmental protection. Prior to initiating the tourism project, the community was engaged in commodity agriculture, which was causing extensive deforestation. Additionally, many young people were leaving to work in cities, the petroleum industry, or other ecolodges in the region. The community's tourism project is now seen as the best avenue for bringing income into the community to support local projects, while minimizing damage to the immediate environment. It has also successfully created jobs for community members, who no longer have to leave Añangu to be able to support their families.

The challenges confronting livelihood in the Amazon were made visible to me when my friend Victor, a young Kichwa man, was considering leaving tourism to work for the petroleum industry. At the ecolodge where he was employed, he was making Ecuador's minimum wage, $366 a month. The petroleum company was offering him $800 a month with shorter working hours. Victor's case provides insight into the messy livelihood conflicts individuals frequently confront as they attempt to financially survive.

Today, much of the world's population is connected to modern globalization and the neoliberal wave of capitalism, oftentimes creating dependence on the capital and commodity-oriented market economy (Harvey, 2005; Robinson, 2003). While money may physically be nothing more than paper or digits in a computer system, the value we have assigned to it shapes our lives in infinite forms. Everything from our daily subsistence, employment, access to material resources, environmental management, and education are influenced by our economic systems and the global flow of capital. Some of us, including myself, have great flexibility in choosing a career that aligns with both our need for income and with our moral and ethical values. However, assemblages of factors including socioenvironmental contexts, historical inequities, and structural barriers, often merge to make more accessible certain job opportunities, while limiting access to others. In the case of Victor, petroleum seemed like the best opportunity to make enough money to pay for his university studies.

While Victor is not from Añangu, these livelihood challenges are present in the Añangu Community. As Añangu's youth prepare to enter the workforce, they may be tempted to leave

Añangu for the petroleum industry or a career in one of Ecuador's urban areas. Using tourism, *socios* in Añangu are engaging in an active attempt to keep young people in Añangu. As Hector explains:

> We have talked about this with the tourists, our project, our dream of maintaining our culture. Right? To not lose our culture, because it is so important. We are in this project, the project of the community to keep our children here, that way our children do not go to the West to pick up other customs. We teach them, now, us as parents, teach our children our customs, from the little that we know, we teach them.

When Hector says the "West," he is not referencing the United States or Europe. He is talking about Coca City, Tena, Quito, Guayaquil, and other Ecuadorian cities. The West is urban, it is disconnected from the land, from the forest, Kichwa culture, and a sense of home. Tourism is intended to create an opportunity for youth to see a future in Añangu, where they too will be able to contribute to the tourism project.

Students are intimately exposed to the tourism project, because their school is located only a few minutes' walk from the Napo Cultural Center's restaurant. Tourists frequently visit the school, often times bringing school supplies as donations. All high school or *colegio* students are required to study tourism as a part of their curriculum. Beyond interacting with tourists and visiting both the Napo Wildlife and Napo Cultural Centers, all high school students participate in an internship. After their third year of high school, students will be sent to different tourism projects throughout the Bajo Napo region. Some will stay in Añangu, working at one of the two lodges, while others will go off to hotels and other ecolodges. Upon graduating, students from Añangu often receive financial support from the community to continue their education. While it is recognized that not all students will return or be interested in tourism, the hope is that several will come back with the skills needed to carry the tourism project forward. Matías, a community socio who is only his mid-20s, told me, "we are young, over time, we could leave it, but no, not that. We have to work to continue with community tourism."

Another prominent livelihood challenge confronted by the Añangu Community is that they have significant quantities of petroleum under their land. In the community's book *Historia de la Comunidad Añangu*, or History of the Añangu Community, it is stated that their engagement with tourism is a reaction to the exploitation of the Amazon via petroleum extraction. In 2013, when the book was published, the Añangu hoped that there would be no drilling in the Yasuní National Park as a result of its mega-biodiversity (Torres 2013). Proactively, the community invited both former President Rafael Correa and his former Vice-President and current President of Ecuador, Lenin Moreno, to visit the Napo Wildlife Center. During Moreno's visit, a community leader stated to him that "our community will not allow any oil company to enter and will care for the fauna and flora in this place" (TransPort, 2013). By demonstrating the quality of their tourism project, the Añangu are attempting to bring both political and public attention to the success of their ecolodge. Like many Indigenous communities across the world, one of their most important goals is to protect land from its reduction to extractable economic value (Butler & Hinch, 2007).

In stark contrast to how Kichwa communities interpret *Sumak Kawsay,* the Ecuadorian government has appropriated the Indigenous term to justify oil expansion to fund their development goals and social welfare programs (Radcliffe, 2012; Republic of Ecuador, 2008; SENPLADES, 2013). Floresmilo Simbaña, a leader of the Confederation of Indigenous Nationalities of Ecuador (CONAIE), has critiqued the government's use of *Sumak Kawsay,* arguing that they interpret *Sumak Kawsay* as "access to services." The government's goal is to invest in "health, education, public works, and social services," in an effort to move closer towards *Sumak Kawsay* or "good living" (Llopis 2015). However, to accrue the income needed to provide these services, the government has relied on the extraction of natural resources, including petroleum, which is contradictory to the Kichwa understanding of *Sumak Kawsay,* which values the wellbeing of the environment. The contradiction between the state's envisioning of *Sumak Kawsay* and an

Indigenous perspective was made visible in the Yasuní National Park, where the government began extracting oil in 2016, despite resistance from many Indigenous communities who consider Yasuní and its surrounding territories their sacred and ancestral homelands (Brown, 2018; Coryat, 2015). To date, the Ecuadorian government has not made any specific threats against the Añangu's land and in 2018, a voter referendum prohibited the expansion of extraction in Yasuní (Tegel, 2018).

Nonetheless, the Añangu are aware that political winds can change. For that reason, they will continue to use tourism both as a tool for generating local employment which aligns with their communal values, while also bringing both national and international attention to the value of their tourism project. Añangu's focus on livelihood opportunities highlights that degrowth's future is not one that can be devoid of employment. However, degrowth should account for better labor opportunities, labor that aligns with communal good, ethical standards, and environmental care (Latouche, 2009).

Cultural reclamation

One afternoon, while drinking *chicha* in the *Kuri Muyu* with an Ecuadorian family, Tómas, a guide from Añangu, explained that the community started the Kuri Muyu to: "[...] maintain [culture], to teach how we lived before. Many people talk about rescuing [culture], right? But rescuing is like someone is drowning, dying. [...] We speak about reclaiming, reclaiming how our parents lived, how was the tradition." Tómas' words provide insight into the endlessly dynamic and shifting nature of culture. Rather than being passively received, the practice of a "Kichwa culture" is actively and agentively constructed through tourism and other projects developed by the Kichwa Añangu Community. Cultural reclamation or *reivindicación cultural* recognizes that the Añangu have undergone cultural shifts over decades and centuries. Like all Indigenous peoples across the Americas, Kichwas have been targeted by the colonial violence imposed by European invaders, powerful state actors, and extractivist corporations (Muratorio, 1991). They have also been subject to the Ecuadorian government's multiple attempts at imposing a fabricated myth of *mestizaje*, or racial and ethnic mixture, across the Ecuadorian state, which sought to create a hegemonic nation-state identity (K. L. Smith, 2015). Rather than characterizing cultural tourism in Añangu as a means for salvaging a dying culture, Tómas sees cultural tourism as a way of taking pride of their cultural ancestry, while using that history to shape how they want to define, perform, and share culture today. The *Kuri Muyu* serves as an important cultural space, where the Añangu are able to sustain a livelihood, while simultaneously working together to study and produce their own sense of identity.

How the Añangu chose to practice their culture through tourism, does not always adhere to the ancestral past. At times, ancestral practices must be kept alive through oral histories, rather than materialized practices. One important example of this dynamic cultural process constructed by the Añangu is their relationship to hunting. More than a decade ago, the Añangu Community decided to ban all hunting in the community. Three local guides explained that prior to the ban, the Añangu Community hunted for its own consumption and to sell trophy animals. Hunting was an important means of livelihood. However, it became increasingly clear to hunters that they were having to trek deeper and deeper into the forest to find animals due to the increasing pressures on Amazonian wildlife. In reflecting on this moment, they explained that this was a difficult decision, made during a monthly assembly meeting. Tómas says, "When we signed an agreement [to ban hunting] in this same community, with all of the members, we then had to enforce the rules of the community. For us instead of hunting, it is better to conserve the animals, caring for everything. It was really difficult, but in the community, we have agreed." Iker described how the first five years of the laws was a difficult period, because men who had traditionally supported their families through hunting had to give up their lifestyle. However, as animals returned, and the Añangu's tourism project began to grow, the Añangu eventually came to develop a sense of pride in their decision to ban all hunting. Today, this is part of how the Añangu are reclaiming their culture. It is not a process of reclamation which perfectly mimics ancestral practices, but is instead an act of self-determination, where they are able to define what cultural practices are shared and celebrated.

Given this dynamic cultural process, tourism is seen as an important mechanism for teaching future generations about how the Añangu defines culture. For example, Miriam, a *Mamakuna* explains:

> For this reason, the women, we have put together this organization, we have organized to reclaim our culture [...] for our children or our future, to not forget. Today, I see girls or sons from this very place, they no longer want to speak [...] Kichwa, they are embarrassed to speak. They are embarrassed to drink chicha, they are embarrassed to eat our typical food, and for this reason, we wanted to organize.

Here, it is clear that tourism is not focused only on the guests' experience. Instead, the development of the *Kuri Muyu* has provided an opportunity for the Añangu, under the guidance of the community's elders, to collectively reflect on and learn about Kichwa ancestral practices and traditions. The *Kuri Muyu* is also intended to provide a space for their youth to learn about Kichwa tradition of the past and present. As youth watch their mother's present in the *maloca*, or ancestral home visited by tourists at the *Kuri Muyu*, they are able to see the weapons Kichwas once used to hunt and procure their food.

During the period of time I spent in Añangu, I was able to observe small changes in how youth embraced their sense of being Kichwa. For example, in 2015, when I first visited Añangu, many Mamakunas such as Miriam, told me that their children no longer wanted to drink *chicha*. This sentiment was expressed in the high school English class I taught, where many students complained about drinking *chicha*. However, in 2016, the *Kuri Muyu* was moved from a remote location only reachable by boat, to the community center. Once the Mamakunas exclusively worked out of the community center, the sweet and slightly bitter smell of *chicha* filled the air. Daily, I would see Mamakunas sharing *chicha* with their eager teens as they meandered about the community center at the end of the school day.

Añangu Community members have smartphones, social media, and like to travel as tourists. They also cheer for Ecuadorian soccer, play Ecuavolley, are invested in national politics, and can sing the national anthem of Ecuador in both Spanish and Unified Kichwa. However, through tourism, they are choosing to combine their identity as Ecuadorians with their Kichwa identity. By communally controlling their livelihood, they decide what is best for their community and how tourism can be used to serve various goals, including cultural reclamation.

Some cultural tourism projects may attempt to hide aspects of cultural identity which do not fit neo-colonial tropes of the Indigenous Other (Davidov 2013). However, in Añangu, these aspects of their lifeways are largely not hidden from tourists. Regardless, what is key is that the community controls how they perform their Kichwa-ness (or perhaps better said, their Añangu-ness) for tourists. They have agency in the cultural reclamation process. In Añangu, cultural performances for tourists are deeply tied to an intentional process of prideful identity construction, where they are able to push forward and control their community-defined goal of cultural reclamation.

Here, we can see the connection between community-owned tourism as practiced in Añangu and degrowth. Tourism in Añangu is serving as a medium for promoting communal values, a sense of Kichwa identity, and a source of historically focused education. The goal of the tourism project is not simply to produce profit for material comfort, but is instead promoting a specific value system guided by *Sumak Kawsay*, meant to disrupt colonial efforts to erase their Kichwa identity.

Environmental stewardship and resource protection

The relationship between Añangu's tourism project and environmental stewardship has been woven into the discussions on livelihood opportunities and cultural reclamation, with an emphasis on petroleum extraction and ecological management. This section will only briefly reflect further on this discussion. Trosper proposes that for many Indigenous peoples, it is common to consider the wellbeing not only of today's generation, but of the seventh to come. He explains that "past human generations left us a legacy, and we have a duty to pass that legacy to our great-grandchildren and beyond, as far as the seventh generation" (Trosper 1995, 67). This is echoed by Oren Lyons, an Iroquois leader Trosper quotes, who says that "we are looking ahead [...] to make sure and to make every decision that we make relate to the welfare and well-being of the seventh to come" (Trosper 1995, 69). The Añangu, guided by *Sumak Kawsay*, are engaged in a similar practice. Their goal is not only to care for the wellbeing of their environment now, but to do it for their children, grandchildren, and the future generations who will someday inherit Añangu. As the tourism project's former manager explained to me, "We do not want to contaminate our land, our rivers, our air, our forest; we want to leave our children with a good inheritance."

Community-ownership of the tourism project is key to this process because they decide how money brought in from tourism is invested in community projects. After paying salaries to employees, all additional income generated by tourism is used to develop community projects, which are largely focused on resource conservation and environmental stewardship. Additionally, the Añangu's tourism projects and environmental goals have caught the attention of outside institutions, who have donated materials to help the Añangu move towards greater environmental conversation. For example, the community is striving to become increasingly energy independent. Currently, the community center and both ecolodges are largely dependent on diesel-run generators. With time, the community hopes to rely less on the generator. A series of solar panels, donated by both the United States and British embassies in Ecuador, who were impressed by the Añangu's organization, have already been installed. Currently, these solar panels are providing 24-hour electricity to the *casa comunal* or community house, the teacher's office, medical center, and the teacher's bedrooms. Individual households also have small solar panels. Eventually, Añangu is planning for the entire community center to be run on solar.

The Añangu are also using food as a part of their energy-based goals. As a tourist, when you are given your "community tour," you are taken towards a large, white cistern, which seems strangely out of place amid the surrounding trees. This is the community's biodigester, donated by Ecuador's Ministry of Industries and Productivity, which sees the community as a model of sustainability (Ministerio de Industrias y Productividad, 2013). The idea behind the biodigester is that the community will be able to produce biogas for cooking in both the cafeteria and restaurant. Unfortunately, they have encountered engineering difficulties in channeling the biogas. Nonetheless, the biodigester remains a work in progress, amid the Añangu's larger energy goals. For example, next to the biodigester is a large-scale composting project. The compost can be used in the community garden, which is managed by students and Mamakunas. Over the long-term, the community garden project, which involves a small nursery and a large greenhouse, is intended to provide locally grown foods to the tourist restaurant and staff cafeteria.

The Añangu Community hopes to become increasingly food sovereign. Currently, every family in Añangu has a small farm and chickens, which supply a significant amount of their daily food needs. This is a shift from their livelihood prior to tourism, where they were engaged in commodity agriculture. Families are prohibited from having game animals, such as pigs or cows, whose food and land needs are seen as detrimental to the surrounding forest. Overall, each of these goals serves to localize their household economies, reducing their need to purchase commodities from outside, while also limiting local resource extraction. This is particularly important because as a Trosper et al. note, land and environment for many Indigenous peoples are sacred, where the "source of knowledge is the land, not humans" (Trosper, Parrotta, Agnoletti, Bocharnikov, Feary, Gabay, & Gamborg, 2012). This process also creates an additional connection between tourism and degrowth. While these projects do not reduce tourism's dependence on international travel, how the Añangu are choosing to invest their profit from tourism reduces their need to purchase diesel fuel, gas, and food from outside sources.

Conclusions

In considering the relationship between tourism and degrowth, the case of community-owned tourism in the Kichwa Añangu Community has highlighted multiple avenues by which tourism can challenge a growth mentality in capitalist practices. Notably, its governance structure is guided by interdependent community values, where Añangu's *socios* collectively decide: 1) how the tourism project should benefit their community, and 2) how profit should be distributed to ensure fair wages and financial support for community projects. In describing the purpose of the tourism project, Tómas told me, "What we want the most, is to have a change for the good life" or *Sumak Kawsay*. What it means to achieve the good life can be viewed through how the Añangu operate their tourism project. In practice, this means that communal governance can focus on the good of the whole, rather than individuals. It also means using tourism to create a diverse economies approach which supports local livelihoods, promotes cultural reclamation, and invests in environmental stewardship, while subverting the pressures of extractivism, commodity agriculture, and urban opportunities.

Añangu's tourism project does not provide a cure-all answer to the challenges presented by the growth economy. Notably, many of the visiting tourists are foreigners, who must fly to Ecuador to visit their ecolodges. This reliance on the global market seemingly contradicts any argument that tourism in Añangu challenges capitalist practices or encourages environmental protections. However, this is where Gibson-Grahams concept of the diverse economies provides important insight. By reading for economic "difference rather than dominance" (Gibson-Graham, 2006), we can conceptualize how tourism practices could contribute to a broader degrowth society. In the case of Añangu, by decentering income and profit as the primary goals of the tourism project, the Añangu are demonstrating how tourism, when shaped by local self-determination, can be used to create social and environmental good locally.

The Añangu's tourism project demonstrates that degrowth is an ongoing process. Community-owned tourism will not radically restructure tourism's diverse forms on a global scale, at least in the short-term. Nonetheless, for the Añangu, tourism is a means for moving towards *Sumak Kawsay*, which has aspects which overlap with the broader degrowth movement. The Añangu are currently training other Indigenous communities across Ecuador in their style of community-owned tourism, called *turismo comunitario* in Ecuador, by focusing on self-determination and governance. This is an important step in considering how power dynamics and profit-goals within the practice of tourism may be shifted, as tourism moves into the hands of organized communities.

Notes

1. Website for the Napo Wildlife Center: www.napowildlifecenter.com/
2. Website for the Napo Cultural Center: www.napoculturalcenter.com
3. Information from this section is pulled from interviews and interactions carried out during my field research. Details can also be found in the community's self-published book, *Historia de la Comunidad Añangu* or History of the Añangu Community (Torres, 2013) and the community's personal website, www.comunidadanangu.org

Acknowledgments

I want to thank the Kichwa Añangu Community and all of the staff at the Napo Cultural Center, the Napo Wildlife Center, and the main office in Quito for welcoming me into Añangu and supporting this research throughout the length of my stay. I also want to thank Dr. Maribel Alvarez, Dr. Marcela Vásquez-León, Dr. Mamadou Baro, and Dr. Ronald Trosper for your support and feedback throughout this research process.

Disclosure statement

No potential conflict of interest was reported by the author.

Funding

This research was generously funded by the Kichwa Añangu Community, Yasuní-Amazona, the Tinker Foundation, the Willian and Nancy Sullivan Scholarship Fund, the Graduate & Professional Student Council at the University of Arizona, the Bureau of Applied Research in Anthropology, and the School of Anthropology at the University of Arizona.

References

Altmann, P. (2014). Good life as a social movement proposal for natural resource use: The indigenous movement in Ecuador. *Consilience*, (12), 82–94.

Altmann, P. (2017). Sumak Kawsay as an element of local decolonization in Ecuador. *Latin American Research Review*, *52*(5), 749–759. doi:10.25222/larr.242

Amores Grandes, F. S. (2012). *Implementación de buenas prácticas de turismo sostenible en el lodge Napo Wildlife Center, Comunidad Añangu*. Riobamba: Escuela Superior Politécnica de Chimborazo.

Blackstock, K. (2005). A critical look at community based tourism. *Community Development Journal*, *40*(1), 39–49. doi:10.1093/cdj/bsi005

Brown, K. (2018, March 22). Indigenous Amazonian women demand end to extraction. Retrieved July 1, 2018, from Mongabay Environmental News website: https://news.mongabay.com/2018/03/indigenous-amazonian-women-demand-end-to-extraction/

Butler, R., & Hinch, T. (2007). *Tourism and indigenous peoples: Issues and implications*. Oxford: Elsevier Ltd.

Capitán, A. L. H., & Guevara, A. P. C. (2014). Seis debates abiertos sobre el sumak kawsay. *Íconos: Revista de Ciencias Sociales*, *48*, 25–40.

Chuji, M. (2009). Modernidad, desarrollo, interculturalidad y Sumak Kawsay o buen vivir. *Ponencia Presentada En El Foro Internacional Sobre Interculturalidad y Desarrollo, Uribia (Colombia)*, *23*(5), 2009.

Comunidad Kichwa Añangu. (2017). Napo Wildlife Center showcased as an example by the UNWTO to commemorate "The International Year of Sustainable Tourism for Development." Retrieved August 11, 2019, from Napo Wildlife Center website: https://www.napowildlifecenter.com/the-international-year-of-sustainable-tourism-for-development/

Coryat, D. (2015). Extractive politics, media power, and new waves of resistance against oil drilling in the Ecuadorian amazon: The case of Yasunidos. *International Journal of Communication*, *9*(1), 3741–3760.

Dávalos, P. (2008). Reflexiones sobre el Sumak Kawsay (el Buen Vivir) y las teorías del desarrollo. *Boletín Icci*, *103*. Retrieved August 28, 2019, from America Latina en movimiento: https://www.alainet.org/es/active/25617

Davidov, V. M. (2013). *Ecotourism and cultural production: An anthropology of indigenous spaces in Ecuador*. New York: Palgrave Macmillan.

Figueroa, M., & Alkon, A. H. (2017). Cooperative social practices, self-determination, and the struggle for food justice in Oakland and Chicago. In A. Alkon & J. Guthman (Eds.), *The new food activism: Opposition, cooperation, and collective action* (pp. 206–231). Oakland: University of California Press.

Fletcher, R. (2011). Sustaining tourism, sustaining capitalism? The tourism industry's role in global capitalist expansion. *Tourism Geographies*, *13*(3), 443–461. doi:10.1080/14616688.2011.570372

Font, X., Sanabria, R., & Skinner, E. (2008). Ecotourism and certification: Confronting the principles and pragmatics of socially responsible tourism. *Journal of Sustainable Tourism*, *13*(3), 281–295.

Gibson-Graham, J. K. (2006). *A postcapitalist politics*. Minneapolis; London: University of Minnesota Press.

Gibson-Graham, J. K. (2008). Diverse economies: Performative practices for ˋother worlds. *Progress in Human Geography*, *32*(5), 613–632. doi:10.1177/0309132508090821

Greenwood, D. (1989). Culture by the pound: An anthropological perspective on tourism as cultural commoditization. In V. Smith (Ed.), *Host and guests: The anthropology of tourism* (2nd, pp. 171–185). Philadelphia: University of Pennsylvania Press.

Hall, C. M. (2009). Degrowing tourism: Décroissance, sustainable consumption and steady-state tourism. *Anatolia*, *20*(1), 46–61. doi:10.1080/13032917.2009.10518894

Harvey, D. (2005). *A brief history of neoliberalism*. Oxford: Oxford University Press.

Higgins-Desbiolles, F. (2006). More than an "industry": The forgotten power of tourism as a social force. *Tourism Management*, *27*(6), 1192–1208. doi:10.1016/j.tourman.2005.05.020

Higgins-Desbiolles, F. (2008). Justice tourism and alternative globalisation. *Journal of Sustainable Tourism*, *16*(3), 345–364. doi:10.1080/09669580802154132

Honey, M. (2008). *Ecotourism and sustainable development: Who owns paradise?* (2nd ed.). Washington: Island Press.

Honey, M. (2016). Treading Lightly? Ecotourism's impact on the environment. In N. Haenn & R. R. W. and A. Harnish (Eds.), *Treading lightly? Ecotourism's impact on the environment* (pp. 380–389). New York: New York University Press.

IPCC. (1999). *Aviation and the Global Atmosphere*. Retrieved from http://www.ipcc.ch/ipccreports/sres/aviation/014.htm.

Kallis, G. (2011). In defense of degrowth. *Ecological Economics*, *70*(5), 873–880. doi:10.1016/j.ecolecon.2010.12.007

Latouche, S. (2009). Farewell to *growth*. Cambridge: Polity.

Ministerio de Industrias y Productividad. (2013). Ministro Ramiro González inaugura proyecto productivo de uso de energía limpia en la comunidad Kichwa Añangu, en el Yasuní. Retrieved March 19, 2017, from http://www.industrias.gob.ec/bp-139-ministro-ramiro-gonzalez-inaugura-proyecto-productivo-de-uso-de-energia-limpia-en-la-comunidad-kichwa-anangu-en-el-Yasuní/

Muratorio, B. (1991). *The life and times of grandfather Alonso*. New Brunswick, NJ: Rutgers University Press.

Okazaki, E. (2008). A community-based tourism model: Its conception and use. *Journal of Sustainable Tourism*, *16*(5), 511–529. doi:10.1080/09669580802159594

O'Neill, A. C. (2002). What globalization means for ecotourism: Managing globalization's impacts on ecotourism in developing countries. *Indiana Journal of Global Legal Studies (Indiana University Press)*, *9*(2), 501–528.

Paulson, S. (2017). Degrowth: Culture, power and change. *Journal of Political Ecology*, *24*(1), 425. doi:10.2458/v24i1.20882

Pritchard, A. (2014). Gender and feminist perspectives in tourism research. In A. A. Lew, C. M. Hall, & A. M. Williams (Eds.), *The Wiley Blackwell companion to tourism* (Vols. 1–Book, Section, pp. 314–324). Oxford, UK: John Wiley & Sons, Ltd. doi:10.1002/9781118474648.ch25

Radcliffe, S. A. (2012). Development for a postneoliberal era? Sumak kawsay, living well and the limits to decolonisation in Ecuador. *Geoforum*, *43*(2), 240–249. doi:10.1016/j.geoforum.2011.09.003

Recasens, A. V. (2014). Discursos" pachamamistas" versus políticas desarrollistas: El debate sobre el sumak kawsay en los Andes. *ÍCONOS: Revista de Ciencias Sociales*, *48*, 55–72.

Republic of Ecuador. (2008). *Constitution of the Republic of Ecuador*. Retrieved from http://pdba.georgetown.edu/Constitutions/Ecuador/english08.html

Robinson, W. I. (2003). *Transnational conflicts: Central America, social change, and globalization*. London: Verso.

Rozemeijer, N. (2001). *Community-based tourism in Botswana: The SNV experience in three community-tourism projects*. Gaborone: SNV Netherlands Development Organization.

Russell, A., & Wallace, G. (2004). Irresponsible ecotourism. *Anthropology Today*, *20*(3), 1–2. doi:10.1111/j.0268-540X.2004.00265.x

Salazar, N. B. (2012). Community-based cultural tourism: Issues threats and opportunities. *Journal of Sustainable Tourism*, *20*(1), 9–22. doi:10.1080/09669582.2011.596279

SENPLADES. (2013). *Plan Nacional para el Buen Vlivr*. Retrieved from www.buenvivir.gob.ec

Sirima, A., & Backman, K. F. (2013). Communities' displacement from national park and tourism development in the Usangu Plains, Tanzania. *Current Issues in Tourism*, *16*(7–8), 719–735. doi:10.1080/13683500.2013.785484

Smith, K. L. (2015). *Practically invisible: Coastal Ecuador, tourism, and the politics of authenticity*. Nashville: Vanderbilt University Press.

Stonich, S. C. (1998). Political ecology of tourism. *Annals of Tourism Research (Elsevier Science Ltd.)*, *25*(1), 25–54. doi:10.1016/S0160-7383(97)00037-6

Stronza, A. (2001). Anthropology of tourism: Forging new ground for ecotourism and other alternatives. *Annual Review of Anthropology*, *30*(1), 261–283. doi:10.1146/annurev.anthro.30.1.261

Tegel, S. (2018, February 5). A referendum in Ecuador is another defeat for South America's left-wing populists. Retrieved August 27, 2018, from Washington Post website: https://www.washingtonpost.com/news/worldviews/wp/2018/02/05/a-referendum-in-ecuador-is-another-defeat-for-south-americas-left-wing-populists/

Thomson, B. (2011). Pachakuti: Indigenous perspectives, Buen Vivir, Sumaq Kawsay and degrowth. *Development*, *54*(4), 448–454. doi:10.1057/dev.2011.85

Torres, S. (2013). *Historia de la Comunidad Kichwa Añangu: Nacionalidad Kichwas Amazónica - Parque Nacional Yasuní*. Ecuador: Proyecto Biocomercio GEF-CAF.

TransPort. (2013, May 13). Sostenibilidad. Retrieved March 19, 2018, from http://transport.ec/hechos-y-personajes/sostenibilidad/

Trosper, R. (1995). Traditional American Indian economic policy. *American Indian Culture and Research Journal, 19*(1), 65–95. doi:10.17953/aicr.19.1.1l1w15g072k576k4

Trosper, R., Parrotta, J. A., Agnoletti, M., Bocharnikov, V., Feary, S. A., Gabay, M., & Gamborg, C. (2012). The unique character of traditional forest-related knowledge: Threats and challenges ahead. In J. Parrotta & R. Trosper (Eds.), *Traditional forest-related knowledge: Sustaining communities, ecosystems and biocultural* (pp. 563–588). London, New York: Springer.

UNWTO. (2014). *World Tourism Day: About WTD 2014 "Tourism and Community Development."* Retrieved August 28, 2019, from United Nations World Tourism Organization: https://media.unwto.org/press-release/2014-06-23/world-tourism-day-2014-celebrating-tourism-and-community-development

UNWTO. (2017). *UNWTO Tourism Highlights: 2017 Edition.* Madrid, Spain: World Tourism Organization (UNWTO).

Vainikka, V. (2013). Rethinking mass tourism. *Tourist Studies, 13*(3), 268–286. doi:10.1177/1468797613498163

Vásquez-León, M. (2012). Policies or conservation and sustainable development: fishing communities in the Gulf of California, Mexico. In J. B. Greenberg, T. Weaver, & W. L. Alexander, & A. Browning-Aiken (Eds.), *Neoliberalism and commodity production in Mexico.* Boulder: University Press of Colorado.

Viteri Gualinga, C. (2002). Visión indígena del desarrollo en la Amazonía. *Polis. Revista Latinoamericana, 1*(3).

Yashar, D. J. (2006). *Ethnic politics and political instability in the Andes* (P. W. Drake & E. Hershberg, Eds.). Pittsburgh, PA: University of Pittsburgh Press.

Buen Vivir: Degrowing extractivism and growing wellbeing through tourism

Natasha Chassagne (iD) and Phoebe Everingham

ABSTRACT

Buen Vivir (BV) is a holistic vision for social and environmental wellbeing, which includes alternative economic activities to the neoliberal growth economy. This article looks at how tourism initiatives under a BV approach can lead to degrowth by drawing on a case study of how BV is put into practice through tourism in the Cotacachi County in Ecuador. We argue that by degrowing socially and environmentally damaging extractive sectors and growing alternative economic activities like community-based tourism, a BV approach could increase social and environmental wellbeing. We refer to LaTouche's notion of degrowth as a matrix of multiple alternatives that will reopen the space for human creativity. This complements the notion of BV as a plural approach, and in turn works to decolonise the parameters of how we might understand degrowth. In the case of Cotacachi, the vision for tourism is based on the needs of the community, rather than to satisfy a Eurocentric ideal of development supported by a policy of extractivism. BV is key to how this community conceptualises the potentialities of tourism because it considers the wellbeing of the people and the environment. In this case, degrowth is a consequence of BV, rather than the objective.

Introduction

Tourism is an extractive activity, according to some scholars, undermining any genuine efforts for sustainability because of the physical stress placed on the natural environment from infra-structure, consumption and pollution and strains on local water and energy supplies (Bushell and Eagles, 2006; Gössling, 2002; Hall, 2010).

Sustainable tourism, defined as "tourism which meets the needs of present tourists and host regions while protecting and enhancing opportunity for the future" (Butler, 1999, pg.10) is one way the tourism industry seeks to shift those impacts. Sustainable tourism has been a critical concern for some tourism scholars concerned with the consequences of economic growth and its limits on host communities and the environment. However, others have argued that sustain-able tourism does not go far enough in its critique of capitalist economic growth, particularly in the era of climate change, which calls for a radical need to reconsider the growth paradigm in all facets of life, not excluding tourism (Gössling, Hall, Peeters, & Scott 2010). As Hall (2010) argues, a paradigm change is needed in relation to tourism's sustainability, one that radically questions wellbeing in terms of GDP and economic growth. While proponents of alternative tourism argue for a shift towards social and environmental responsibility in tourism practices, if these tourism ventures are managed within neoliberal paradigms that promote endless growth, tourism's sustainability will inevitably be undermined (Higgins-Desbiolles, 2010).

Hall (2009) and Higgins-Desbiolles (2010, 2017) provide an opening for tourism scholars to radically question the limits of economic growth in relation to tourism by drawing on the concept of 'degrowth'. While tourism has not been a focal point of the degrowth movement, Hall (2009) points out that tourism research has engaged with aspects of this concept through making links with alternative economic activities that emphasise alternative tourism development: tourism which puts the needs of host communities and environment first. In that respect, we agree with Higgins-Desbiolles (2009, p. 126) who argues that we should embrace the possibilities that rethinking tourism through notions such as 'degrowth' provides, inviting us "to think more imaginatively about the meaning, purpose and impacts of our tourism and travel cultures". In this article we draw on the notion of degrowth as conceptualised by LaTouche, a prominent French intellect in the degrowth space. For LaTouche (2012), degrowth (décroissance in French) is about responding to an ecological and social crisis, an escape from the logic of capital accumulation and decision making as always embedded with the logic of profit. Essentially, the concept of degrowth calls for a complete paradigm shift away from top down Eurocentric models of development and measuring wellbeing in terms of GDP. Degrowth fundamentally questions the 'spirit' of capitalism supported by an extractive economy - consumption and development as 'economic progress' (LaTouche, 2012, p. 75) - in the name of human wellbeing and the environment. It recalls the logic of the 'limits to growth' argument which affirms the impacts of human development on finite natural resources.

Rather than framing degrowth in deficit language, as a backwards slide or a 'lack', the French term employed by LaTouche, décroissance, has more positive connotations than the English translation 'degrowth'. As LaTouche argues (2012, p. 77), we must instead think of degrowth as "A-growth". Using an environmental analogy, he asks "[w[hat could be more fortunate than the fact that after a disastrous flood, a river returns to its normal flow?" (LaTouche, 2012, p. 77). Such an analogy illustrates the argument for degrowth as a consequence of Buen Vivir (BV), and the reciprocity with nature that it espouses – an approach which seeks to enhance the growth of social and environmental wellbeing, but degrow any destructive forces to that wellbeing.

Hopeful possibilities arise through rethinking growth, consistent with the Latin American concept of BV, when regarding tourism as an alternative economic practice to extractive activities. BV is an ever-evolving concept with its roots in Indigenous cosmology, and approximately translates to 'Good Living', or as Vázquez (2012) defines it "living in plenitude". It is a prominent concept in constitutional debates and transformations particularly in Bolivia and Ecuador (Vázquez, 2012).

BV has recently been connected to tourism by Fischer (2018) and Karst (2017). While we acknowledge that BV has different applications throughout Latin America and that the concept is fluid in academic discourse, some common aspects of BV include "a communitarian view of wellbeing based on reciprocity and complementarity that valorises indigenous identity and culture, and involves not only human beings but also the natural environment" (Giovannini, 2014, 71). We therefore argue that focusing on BV redefines the parameters of how we understand 'limits'. Privileging social and environmental wellbeing, tourism as an alternative economic practice under a BV approach results in the degrowth of socially and environmentally damaging sectors like extractivism. Because of the way in which the economy is conceptualised under BV, it shifts priorities away from an economic growth mentality, towards greater social and environmental wellbeing, and meaningful human connection.

Gudynas (2011, p. 446) states that there are several similarities to both BV and degrowth. Just as LaTouche's degrowth is about plenitude and growth of wellbeing rather than the economy, so is BV. The key differential is that it is not only a theoretical paradigm but a worldview which highlights nature as a part of social and communitarian relations, treating it as a subject of rights (Unceta, 2013). At this juncture, we highlight Gudynas (2011, p. 446) who conceptualises degrowth neither as a comparison concept to BV, nor an objective of BV, but rather as a consequence.

In light of these arguments, we want to highlight the positive possibilities of degrowth as a consequence of a BV approach; not a limitation, lack or a backwards step, but an opening up to how tourism can be otherwise. This involves a rethinking around the ideals of tourism as means for social cohesion, inclusivity and holistic wellbeing (Higgins-Desbiolles, 2006), and the possibility to enhance positive interactions with the environment. BV as a guide for tourism helps centre deeper engagement with places and people; where tourists can have more meaningful experiences, which in turn also brings greater wellbeing to host communities and their environment.

In this article therefore, we argue that BV can offer a way forward for communities to hold onto their cultural traditions and knowledges, ensure social and environmental wellbeing, and live the 'Good Life'. Moreover, tourism that is underpinned by BV can lead to degrowth in a positive and hopeful sense for both local communities and tourism. By 'degrowing' tourism, spaces of possibilities are opened up through the growth of intercultural learning and exchange, deeper human connections, and greater sense of reciprocity with the natural environment.

In this article we use the case study of the Cotacachi County in Ecuador to demonstrate how tourism initiatives that come from the communities themselves can provide an alternative economic activity to the neoliberal development model supported by extractivism, as a means of economic growth. Drawing on BV to guide tourism operations can also challenge top-down tourism models embedded within neo-liberal growth models, where transnational tourism operators control much of the tourism industry at the detriment of the local communities (Fletcher, 2011). The Cotacachi County is examined because of the worldviews and understandings of BV by its communities. In this case, tourism as an alternative economic activity is used as an example of how BV is practiced on-the-ground.

First, we engage in a description of BV and its principles, discussing how BV can be used as a guiding tool for tourism. Next, we turn to the case study and examine examples of tourism as alternative economic activity in the context of the relevant principles of BV, before turning to a discussion of how in the case of Cotacachi County tourism is employed to lead to the degrowth of extractivism, consequently putting limits on growth, which is not supported by a sustainable tourism approach.

Degrowth or growing wellbeing? The impetus for Buen Vivir

The main argument for degrowth rests on two key principles: 1) that economic growth must not surpass the biophysical limits of the planet, and: 2) human wellbeing takes precedence over the pursuit of wealth (Whitehead, 2013, p. 142). LaTouche's (2010) premise is that *decroissance* (degrowth) does not equal negative growth, as that would only plunge societies into distress, and compromise wellbeing. However, it does criticise certain types of economic growth, such as catch-up economic growth models that promote over-consumption and extractive industries.

In helping to refine our understanding of degrowth in the context of tourism, Hall (2009, pp. 55–56) citing the 2008 conference Declaration of the First International Conference on Economic Degrowth, reasserts that the process of degrowth has certain characteristics, including:

- Quality of life rather than quantity of consumption;
- Basic human needs satisfaction;
- Societal change based individual and collective actions and policies;
- Increased self-sufficiency, free time, unremunerated activity, conviviality, sense of community, and individual and collective health;
- Self-reflection, balance, creativity, flexibility, diversity, good citizenship, generosity, and non-materialism;
- Equity, participatory democracy, respect for human rights, and respect for cultural differences.

By centring BV into debates about degrowth in understanding tourism, we also aim to bring perspectives that legitimise and empower the epistemologies of marginalised communities (Karst,

2017). Moving away from top-down sustainable tourism approaches requires bottom-up community-based tourism initiatives that can ensure that tourism ventures are not only environmentally sensitive, but that the local communities are actually benefiting economically and socially (Scheyvens, 1999). Host communities must be ensured that they are gaining the maximum amount of benefits from tourism, economically and socially, with least effects on local eco-systems. If a community is to be empowered by tourism, their voices and needs should guide tourism development (Scheyvens, 1999; Higgins-Desbiolles, Carnicelli, Krolikowski, Wijesinghe, & Boluk, 2019). We argue that empowerment for local communities requires communities themselves to define the parameters of this empowerment within their own worldviews and cosmologies, so that communities affected by tourism become the 'producers of tourism knowledge', rather than merely the 'objects of tourism research'(Chambers & Buzinde, 2015; p. 3).

BV is not only a theoretical concept, but it is based on a decolonial worldview and way of life, meaning that it is manifested in beliefs, values and practices at the community level. BV has more practical promise than degrowth thinking alone because it can be seen as having the potential to change the way of 'thinking' and 'doing' in tourism as being Euro-centric and human-centric. BV recalls the need to consider the needs of the environment - not just human needs like degrowth - and placing nature as an actor in pursuing social and environmental wellbeing. BV also aims to work cooperatively to achieve transformational change from the bottom-up. In that sense, BV is understood as a 'community tool for practice' (Chassagne, 2018), providing a concrete path for practical alternative economic activities that subsequently result in the degrowth of socially and environmentally damaging economic activities such as extractivism. Examples of how this is so are discussed below in the case study of tourism in the Cotacachi County, Ecuador. Firstly however, we explain how BV can be used as a guiding tool for tourism.

Buen Vivir as a guiding tool for tourism

BV has real-world practical applicability, informed by decolonial epistemologies which can guide tourism practices enabling empowerment of host communities and protecting their environments. We thus propose BV as a tool that can be used to guide tourism as an alternative economic practice, but in a way that respects the limits of the environment. In that respect, it is appropriate at this juncture to shift the discussion to what BV entails, before examining how tourism as an economic alternative can fit within the framework of BV.

A conceptual and critical analysis of the literature identified 14 core principles of BV (Chassagne, 2018) (Table 1).

These principles were categorised under three pillars: Social, Spiritual and Material, and the six dimensions for BV, adapted from Álvarez (2013): Equity and social cohesion (Social), sustainability and empowerment (Spiritual), livelihood and capabilities (Material). The principles were deemed necessary, interrelated and inseparable in the aim to achieve wellbeing and sustainability under BV; therefore, they are all implicated and impacted in the pursuit of sustainable tourism as an alternative under BV. However, the most relevant principles for tourism practices are: Plurality and Community; Reciprocity and Nature; Decolonisation and Culture; Food Sovereignty and Sustainable Use of Resources; and, Wellbeing and Contextuality (discussed in the case study). For these principles to be realised, the fundamental needs of a community must also be satisfied. We now turn to the case study area of Cotacachi and illustrate the specific region's practices of tourism as an economic alternative to extractivism that align with the principles mentioned above.

Case study area profile

In 2008, under pressure from *Movimiento Alianza PAIS*, the Citizen Revolution (*Revolución Ciudadana*) the Ecuadorian constitution codified the concept of BV to bring about a'"new

Table 1. Buen Vivir Principles, adapted from Chassagne (2018).

Principles of Buen Vivir		
Core Principles		
Social		
Equity	*Social Cohesion*	
• Plurality[4]	• Community	
• Non-linear progress	• Harmony	
• Complementarity		
Spiritual		
Sustainability	*Empowerment*	
• Reciprocity	• Decolonisation[5]	
• Nature	• Culture	
Material		
Livelihood		
• Food sovereignty[6]		
• Sustainable use of resources[7]		
Capabilities		
• Wellbeing		
• Quality of life		
• Contextuality[8]		

intercultural and plurinational model of society", extending rights to nature (*Pachamama*) (Fisher, 2018). However as Fisher (2018) points out, under former President Rafael Correa, the 'conventional developmentalist strategy' still presided, privileging "expert knowledge, information technology and extractive industry" (Fisher, 2018, p. 456). Yet as Fisher (2018, pg. 456) points out, in many cases the tensions between neoliberalism and BV have given rise to new forms of tourism development that are "more ecologically responsible alternatives to mainstream development". In the case of Cotacachi Ecuador, tourism as an alternative to extractivism is a proposal put forth by various individuals, community groups and local organisations and supported by the local Cotacachi Government. Cotacachi's demographic, cultural and geological heritage demonstrate the importance of an approach to tourism which values and protects its local communities and their environment.

The Cotacachi County in the highlands of Ecuador contains some of the most ecologically significant environments on earth. The Intag region in particular contains an internationally protected area, Cotacachi-Cayapas Reserve, and is also home to two of the world's 35 internationally recognised biodiversity hotspots: The Tropical Andes and Tumbes-Choco-Magdalena. They are two of the most important ecological zones on the planet, with a high degree of endemism of plant and animal species: 49 percent of all bird species in Ecuador, seven vegetation ecosystems with 13 percent of total species of Ecuador, and 28 endangered species including the mountain tapir, spectacled bear and brown spider monkey and mantled howler monkey (Waldmüller, 2015).

The County has a population of approximately 40,036 habitants, 78 percent of whom live in a rural area (Municipio de Cotacachi, 2016); fifty-five percent are Indigenous (Saltos, 2008), mainly Kichwa, which is one of the largest concentrations of Indigenous people in Ecuador. Possibly, for this reason, the County has a strong affiliation with the ethos of BV and over the past two decades this worldview has grown stronger through communal practices as well as community and local government campaigns. The County also has a unique model of democratic participation through a participatory budget, first introduced by Indigenous Former Mayor Auki Tituaña. Through these processes, the people of Cotacachi voted for the County to be declared an 'Ecological County' in order to protect the area's biodiversity - the first in Latin America.

The field site was chosen for several reasons including the value placed on BV as an alternative by the communities there, the geographical and cultural context, and, the impetus to find alternative economic strategies to the extractive policies for economic growth pursued throughout Latin America. The communities in Cotacachi are fervently opposed to large-scale extractive activities for the social and environmental impacts they cause, and have been fighting this for decades. In response to these threats, local processes have seen communities develop community tourism initiatives, as one alternative economic approach, in line with their culture and values. In the following sections we examine their approach to tourism as alternative practice to extractive industries to achieve BV.

Methodology

The empirical data for this article was collected by the first author as part of the fieldwork for an ethnographic study on BV in the Cotacachi County. The study was part of her doctoral research on whether BV could become a viable alternative to sustainable development. The study was not specifically directed at tourism, however tourism emerged as key theme because of the possibilities it provided for locals to resist large-scale extractive industries such as mining, identified by many in the local community as being damaging to overall wellbeing of the community and the environment.

The methodology used for this study was short-term ethnography. The key task of ethnography is to "provide rich, holistic insights into people's views and actions". Pink and Morgan (2013, p.351) characterize short-term ethnographies "by forms of intensity that lead to deep and valid ways of knowing". This methodology was chosen as a way to examine understandings and practices of BV on-the-ground because, "[T]he nature of alternatives as a research question and a social practice can be most fruitfully gleaned from the specific manifestations of such alternatives in concrete local settings" (Escobar, 1995, p. 223).

A review of the existing literature on BV found that while it is an endogenous-led approach, there was a gap in understanding of what it means for communities on-the-ground, therefore a lack of coherency about what it entails in practice. The empirical study thus examined how BV is defined at the grassroots level, and what it looks like in practice.

Three main categories of stakeholders were included in the study, as identified in a previous review of the literature on BV, using a key informant approach: community, government and local civil society organisations. The methods used were in-depth semi-structured interviews, participant and non-participant observations and document analysis. An 'interpretive approach' to ethnography was taken, which means that long-term immersion in the setting was not required, rather using interview methods is an effective way to examine people's collective and individual understandings and practices of BV (Mason, 2002). Under interpretivist assumptions, people are the primary data sources to gather meaning and social norms (Mason, 2002). Therefore, semi-structured interviews was the primary method taken, which included 20 key informants: eight from community; seven from government and five from local organisations. Seven identified as Indigenous, 11 as Mestizo and two 'Other'; among which five were women. Unlike in traditional ethnography where participant observation is generally the primary method, in short-term ethnographies it is limited to a secondary data collection method, albeit an important one.

Interviews were conducted and transcribed in Spanish, with the aid of a local research assistant. All data was analysed using thematic coding techniques, in its original language (Spanish or English) through the use of data management software NVivo. A mixture of data analysis techniques was used, including Creswell's 'three-step qualitative data analysis' (2013) for interview and document data; and Strauss and Cobin's 'analysis in three steps' recapitulated by Gobo (2008) to guide the analysis of observational field notes. Using these techniques, first the data was prepared and organised, then coded; followed by a representation of the data in narrative form (Creswell, 2013). To organise the data, a deductive coding framework was used based on an initial conceptual framework and themes discovered in the literature, then the coded data was inductively added to the existing coding framework.

Tourism as an alternative practice under Buen Vivir

An approach to tourism balancing the notion of degrowth, which integrates the needs of both the local community and their environment can ensure that local communities play a key role in the planning and management of tourism in their local communities. This type of tourism needs to be locally managed and well-planned so that "tourists and hosts have the opportunity for positive encounters that can facilitate better relationships between strangers in ways that also benefit local economies and uphold ecological values" (Singh, 2011, p. 215).

Consistent with the literature, key informants in this study identified the need to move away from the neoliberal growth economy supported by extractivism, which they identified as incompatible with BV. Many key informants cited tourism as one path to help communities achieve self-sufficiency (community-based activities) and demonstrate a shift away from policy that argues the need for economic growth under a development policy supported by extractivism. This is voiced in many ways that support BV, for example, at the entrance of the community of Pucará, like many others in the region, is a large sign that says, "Welcome to Pucará, a productive, ecological, touristic and solidarity community free from mining."

Key informants affirmed that needs should be determined by the people themselves based on actual needs and not identified exogenously in relation to an individualistic, consumerist vision of needs. Communities should be the ones who decide what they really need, though the reality is that one community's idea of what they really need may not conform to the idea of what is needed for human 'progress' under Western development theory, which is largely founded on modernity, technology and economic growth. A decolonial approach to tourism development that emphasises local knowledges is thus key for communities to be empowered to make decisions about the kinds of tourism that will ensure social and environmental well-being (Chambers and Buzinde, 2015).

Many community members have identified small-scale community-based tourism in particular as a possible sustainable alternative to extractive activities and this is being carried through regional development policies (Municipio de Cotacachi, 2016). To bring together local tourism operators strengthening the capacity of tourism as an alternative to extractivism in the region, a tourist centre has been set up by the Ecotourism Network of Intag, at the cultural and natural heritage site of Nangulvi in Intag, in cooperation with several local organisations for 'Sustainable tourism as a development alternative'.

One element of BV that has been identified by both the key informants, and policy for BV, is that to achieve it and meet fundamental needs, the productive matrix must change, therefore as argued by the former Correa government, a new economic model must be adopted (SENPLADES, 2013 Objective 10). Thus, the material pillar of BV moves beyond material 'progress' or economic growth and focuses on the principles which are vital to satisfying fundamental needs and achieving the communal vision of social and environmental wellbeing. In the context of tourism, this points to the livelihood and capabilities dimensions, particularly the principles of Food Sovereignty, Sustainable Use of Resources, Wellbeing, and Contextuality.

With that in mind, BV argues for a shift towards a post-extractive society, as an extractive economy is in conflict with BV's principles and the value and agency placed on nature. Consistent with the principles for degrowth which stipulate that economic growth must not surpass earth's biophysical limits, two thirds of the key informants also argued that there are biophysical limits to the earth that must be respected, but that are not being respected because of the attitude and consumeristic ways of life in modern society, and an exogenous Western conception of needs.

To reach a post-extractive economy however, society requires concrete economic alternatives. In Cotacachi, the grassroots movement to push for alternatives to extractivism manifests in several ways, one of the most significant[1] being tourism. "We are searching for alternatives", one community member divulged[2], "to demonstrate that our communities don't need extractivism." For many people in the community, the focus is on being able to meet their fundamental needs within their worldview of BV – which aligns with degrowth, rather than the neoliberal perspective of economic growth for needs satisfaction.

BV therefore allows for a decolonial repositioning of degrowth to be reframed in a manner that focuses on the growth of more sustainable alternative economic activities to enhance social and environmental wellbeing, rather than traditional economies which emphasise growth of GDP as an indicator of wellbeing. As local government employee Emmanuel argues,

> It's [BV] the perfect excuse for developmentalists that there are people who oppose development. Some people have even told me from some spaces in [national] government that we are even against people having refrigerators, kitchen, that they get around in cars and use computers… speaking of degrowth is not very politically correct here [in Latin America] and I understand that that is why Alberto Acosta, Martinez and all these people rescued this idea of Sumak Kawsay[3] to give a more proper argument to degrowth. Then speaking of degrowth in this way [under SK or BV] I understand that it is a necessity, I understand it as the logic of historical becoming because we live in a finite world in which growth is an absurdity, the concept of permanent growth (Alberto Acosta, 2012).

The pursuit of economic alternatives which could lead to a post-extractive economy, thus degrowing those socially and environmentally damaging sectors of the economy, is part of the practical implementation of BV. These alternatives are pursued in line with the principles for BV and are paramount to it becoming a concrete alternative path for change.

In Cotacachi, tourism is thus identified as an economic alternative in response to a long history of threats of extractivism in the community. Associations like AACRI (Artisans Association of Coffee Farmers of Rio Intag), for example, work cooperatively with other organisations for sustainable small-scale alternative forms of tourism. The aim is for a "different kind of tourism" that is exchange between tourists and host communities (Bold, 2007). Many key informants also believe that this kind of tourism helps sustain the environment, and their culture.

Diego, a local rights activist comments, "I believe that we should go looking for alternatives that are in harmony with what we have". Diego voices the same opinion as many key informants and indeed community members, "We have extraordinary natural [heritage], we have beautiful landscapes, a gigantesque cultural richness, and I believe it is why we are capable of exercising tourism potential instead of petrol potential ... an alternative to extractivism. If we say no to extractivism, we should say yes to tourism."

We now turn to ways in which the local tourism agenda aligns with the principles of BV, as an example of what BV looks like in practice in Cotacachi County and guided by the principles which are most prevalent for tourism, as mentioned in the section 'Buen Vivir as a Guiding Tool for Tourism'.

Plurality, wellbeing and contextuality

BV requires plural cooperation for knowledge and capabilities on all levels. Under a BV approach, local governments have a key role as facilitators in an endogenous process by providing the structures, spaces and resources for communities to identify and meet their fundamental needs in a way that is conducive to their cultural, geographic and demographic context. This is no less true for tourism as an economic alternative. In the face of local community opposition to extractivism for economic development, the Cotacachi Municipal government has promoted the development of tourism activity, as a response to community needs and as an alternative to boost and strengthen the local economy of Cotacachi through culture, nature, ecotourism, adventure tourism, rural tourism and agritourism (Bold, 2007).

The strategy supports the strengthening of alternatives economies and the degrowth of environmentally and socially damaging extractive industries, which would be a pre-condition of achieving BV. Local government facilitates local tourism initiatives by managing lines of credit for tourist microenterprises; establishing alliances with tour operators; politically supporting the struggle of the community and local authorities against extractivism; reforesting the region with native species; capacitating communities; offering environmental education; and strengthening the Intag Ecotourism Committee (Bold, 2007).

Political will for supporting community-driven processes is imperative because although BV is an endogenous approach to social and environmental wellbeing, it does not maintain that communities must apply it in isolation, but rather that the process should be derived from the ground up, not imposed from the top-down (Chassagne, 2018, p. 7). As Delgado et al. state, "if communities could create BV for themselves entirely, it would have already been done" (2010, p. 32). This is no less vital in the consideration of tourism as an alternative economic activity to extractivism.

One of the key challenges of BV is that it is community-driven based on needs and not on an exogenous development agenda. If tourism development is genuinely regarded as a practical pathway to BV and implemented endogenously with full respect for community and reciprocity of the environment, then it is a challenge that can be overcome. Local government support can thus promote social and environmental wellbeing by allowing communities to take charge of tourism processes through a participatory democratic approach, which would work towards meeting the social and environmental needs that are contextual to that community, rather than an exogenous perception of those needs and the needs of the tourist.

The Cotacachi-Cayapas Reserve is of particular importance in this respect, because as a major source of non-economic wealth (natural, cultural, aesthetic) in the region, it encapsulates a source of both social and environmental wellbeing. It has been the focus of conservation efforts due to its importance for biodiversity and local ecosystems, and the threat of impacts from extractivism in the region. The local government's plan to protect and conserve its natural heritage has a major impact on the type of tourism which is carried out in surrounding communities. It also acts to counter efforts by national government and foreign multinational mining companies for exploration in the area.

The largest locally-driven tourism initiative is undertaken within Cotacachi-Cayapas Reserve, in coordination with the local government (Municipio de Cotacachi, 2016) to limit environmental impacts. There are more than 30 families who now work together to offer eco-tourism tours in the surrounding areas (Olivera, 2010). In the Cotacachi-Cayapas Management Plan (Ministerio del Ambiente, 2007), tourism is cited as a management instrument which can contribute to the conservation of the National System of Protected Natural Areas (of which Cotacachi-Cayapas is a part), developed with participation from local populations in the operation of tourism activities and the distribution of benefits. Impact evaluations are sustained by processes of research, biological, ecological, social and economic monitoring, and regulated by the Ministry of the Environment.

While the Reserve is vital to the region's natural and cultural heritage, like all other areas in Cotacachi, there is a challenge in ensuring that it aligns with the objectives and principles of BV, therefore that the development of tourism initiatives remains at the hands of the people, with benefits remaining in the local community; and not relegating to an exogenous idea of what the community needs. The material pillar of BV moves beyond material 'progress' or accumulation and economic growth and focuses on the principles which are vital to satisfying locally-identified needs and achieving the communal vision of sustainability and wellbeing. This is where the principle of contextuality is important under a BV approach, ensuring that any tourism initiatives align with the needs of the community, rather than seeking to increase economic growth.

At present, tourist numbers are increasing, and this can have negative impacts on tourism management. In 2014 there were 153,544 tourists to the Reserve alone, which increased to 190,377 by 2017 (Municipio de Cotacachi, 2017). To align with BV objectives and for degrowth to occur tourist numbers should remain in a steady-state or with slight growth, focusing instead on length of stay, value and benefits derived, over an increase in tourist numbers. Overall growth in tourist numbers is not the objective of tourism under BV, as it will result in the need for more complex tourism infrastructure and resources, and thus greater economic growth and consequently an increase in adverse social and environmental impacts within the community. In the context of Cotacachi County, which aims to preserve its cultural, social and environmental heritage, aligning this approach with the characteristics for degrowth is appropriate.

Reciprocity, nature and community

Communities in the Cotacachi County state that they hold a deep connection to nature, demonstrating a reciprocal relationship between the communities and their environments, grounded in their philosophical leanings toward BV. Leandro tells, "The environmental issue is extremely important. That is, we want to live in harmony with nature … we are part of this whole ecosystem. That is, we do not want to exclude ourselves [from it]." Therefore, economic alternatives will have to integrate this sense of reciprocity with nature. Tourism has been supported by the County government as part of economic alternatives to extractivism. National newspaper 'El Comercio' applauded the proposals for an alternative economic model that is "not based on petroleum and the extraction of our non-renewable resources, but on agriculture, tourism and the protection of the environment" (Entre el orgullo y el olvido, 2001).

Many informants were of the view that community-based tourism, such as volunteer tourism and community stays, are one way to ensure that tourism impacts are minimal. Pedro, a former petroleum worker says, "when tourism is badly managed, there are impacts". Arguably, whichever tourism model is adopted there are both positive and negative impacts, but the adverse impacts on the communities and the environment can be mitigated by local participation and management of tourism processes and activities, espoused by an approach to tourism guided by BV. In that way, communities are key actors in tourism development, which can help instil a sense of reciprocity and a respect for local environments in tourists. For example, Pedro argues that "when a group of tourists come and say they can do as they like, they can dump their rubbish where they like, it's bad, definitively bad. So, what we are doing is [taking charge]. We are managing and adopting [these processes] in the whole community."

Tourism underpinned by BV not only becomes an issue of respect for the environment, but also necessitates and promotes respect for the communities, their culture and ways of living and support this exchange of knowledge which not only enriches the tourist experience, but the wellbeing of the community too. Community youth leader Sofia believes this knowledge and cultural exchange is fundamental to the way tourism is conducted in the communities, and when tourists stay longer term it is an opportunity to demonstrate how the community does things. She says, "we can teach them how to work with the environment, how we sow plantations, how we recycle … and equally they can help us."

Community-based tourism has the potential to fortify both the natural environment and the cultural heritage. In that respect tourism would not be mass-tourism on a large-scale for economic development, but more holistically approached and tourists thus would not be 'left to their own devices', practices, consumption and behaviours as tourists would be guided by local worldviews.

The protection of the environment and community capacity to practice tourism as an economic alternative were deemed inseparable by key informants. Especially given the importance of natural heritage in eco or nature-based tourism activities. As Pedro affirmed, "the community is very conscious of the environment, and maintaining the environment is vital for us because … it affects animals, it affects people, it affects many things [including] that we could no longer have access to one of the principle economic activities: tourism." Protecting the ecological value of the region thus becomes a focus of tourism activities, and a reason to ensure environmental impacts are kept at a minimum through the local management of resources.

Communities in Intag in particular have embraced community-based ecological tourism, handicrafts and home gardens and agricultural practices such as panela making, beekeeping, home hydro-electricity, volunteer tourism, organic farming and the sale of local produce including honey and coffee, as community-based ecological tourism ventures. These initiatives are supported by integrated tourism development which is beneficial for local communities in terms of protecting their way of life, their livelihoods and their culture.

Decolonisation and culture

AACRI (La Asociación Agroartesanal de Caficultores Río Intag) is one such example of local products integrated into the tourism market to the benefit of local economies. AACRI is a local coffee association founded in 1998 with approximately 150-member families. It incorporates agroforestry with coffee tourism to diversify community-based economic alternatives and is an example of the role local organisations can play in BV in mediating local processes and increasing community capacity.

Head of a local environmental organisation, Felipe told, AACRI was offered "as an alternative to mining, to give people an [economic] alternative to mining." This supports the shift back to local economies which are built for and by local communities, moving those communities away from the notion of 'developed places' for the purposes of the neoliberal tourist market.

In 2008, AACRI put together a tourism proposal together with local organisations in Intag. The idea was a different type of tourism, a pathway to intercultural dialogue through an agricultural exchange with similar communities in France. Every year a group of people linked to tourism travel from Intag to France, and at the same time a group visits from France. The objective of this exchange is to understand the tourism experiences of both parties (Bold, 2007). There are formal programs of cultural exchange between families in Cotacachi and tourists, organised by several other groups and local organisations. This works to promote cultural respect and an exchange of knowledge, fundamental in a plural concept like BV. Moreover, by providing local products and other services to tourists, meaningful intercultural exchanges can occur, giving tourists an opportunity to learn from the knowledge and expertise of host communities. Promoting meaningful intercultural exchange in tourism can provide opportunities for tourists to question problematic binaries that perpetuate stereotypes of non-western communities as inferior (Everingham, 2015, 2018).

Local Intag youth leader Sofia explained that a cultural exchange is as valuable to local communities as it is to tourists, because this exchange of knowledge is not just one-way, it is an interchange which benefits both the communities and tourists. In this style of interchange, communities teach tourists about the region, the culture, language, biodiversity, the land and its history, and tourists bring their own knowledge to the table for a plural exchange.

For tourism to be meaningful it cannot be understood only in terms of tourism activities, but it must also be understood as impacting on and being influenced by other sectors of the community such as environmental management, farming and the artisanal sector, for example. And for tourism to be successful as an alternative economic activity, there is a certain level of social organisation and cooperation between civil society and organisations required. This is vital for helping communities satisfy their fundamental needs, and is necessary for effective and democratic participation, as municipal government employee Joaquin explains,

> Where there is a diverse, pluralistic social fabric it is an important step in the governance of Cotacachi, the municipality of Cotacachi. If we build the concept of the organization of urban, rural women rights, of children and youth to urban and rural areas, the organization of farmers, the tourism sector, the artisanal sector, urban neighbourhoods; we contribute to that space for citizen participation that could only be much more effective in their demands and actions.

Community-based eco and cultural tourism is being promoted within the County by the local government, through the will of the communities. The main tourism activity is undertaken within the protected Cotacachi-Cayapas Reserve, in coordination with the local government (Municipio de Cotacachi, 2016) to limit environmental impacts. There are also cultural programs organised between several different organisations and local communities. Local tourism agency Runa Tupari, for example, works with Indigenous communities from the Peasant Organisations Union of Cotacachi to organise volunteer tourism stays with local families to exchange culture and to participate in domestic and agricultural work.

Consumer products targeted at tourists or produced for locals with tourists also in mind are also considered as part of BV, in the spirit of degrowing extractive industries. Consumerism of these products brings us back to Higgins Desbiolles (2010, p. 125) call for tourism to seriously engage in the idea of 'limits', and BV provides the framework to do so.

At one roadside market a local indigenous woman explained how extractive industries are negatively impacting the handicrafts market, and the result is that traditions are being lost in the process,

> We are struggling to produce traditional handicrafts because materials have become too expensive. The traditional materials we use such as wool and natural dyes are being replaced by synthetic alternatives made from by-products of oil and petrol. Companies are taking advantage of this to mass produce handicrafts for tourists and local artisans are struggling to compete. Some have abandoned traditional ways of doing things for mass-production to sell at markets like Otavalo where tourists come to buy 'locally-made' things.

Besides providing economic alternatives to traditional consumer markets, several artisan groups like *Mujer y Medioambiente* (Woman and the Environment) in Intag work to continue traditions such as handicrafts and other handmade produce with natural materials, giving full consideration to the environmental impact of their craft. Working as a cooperative, they sell their produce for a fair price within local communities, as well as to tourist markets, providing an income for its artisans. Local cooperative employee Luis says alternative to development projects like the above-mentioned are important for building community solidarity,

> What it represents in the initial stage is learning to work together. They [community members] realise that it is easier to work together to achieve quality to later have products which can compete, and which can be sold, and which also represent where they come from.

Discussion

The economic pillar of BV is of crucial importance if the concept is to move communities beyond an individualistic growth-led neoliberal Western model of development and towards a more just economy of alternatives based on a community-led, endogenous conception of needs satisfaction, underlined by social and environmental wellbeing. Practical economic alternatives such as tourism that is managed by communities with social and environmental wellbeing in mind are vital. Adopting a BV approach to guide tourism could also ensure that host communities receive equitable redistributive socio-economic effects from tourism through strategies that come from slow, informal and bartered exchanges.

When local communities plan tourism themselves, tourism as an alternative to extractivism can act as a tool for sustainable social and environmental wellbeing, leading to deeper sets of experiences that are contrasted to highly commodified tourism, which is fleeting. The higher the community involvement the greater the benefits (Wearing et al., 2012).

The principles of BV require for such an alternative to be small-scale, local and with benefits to local communities to increase the wellbeing for all. BV necessitates plural cooperation on all levels to produce knowledge and capabilities that can enact long-term change. Therefore, BV is a plural approach that moves away from 'reform' and 'status quo' and towards 'transformation' (Dryzek, 1997, p. 12). It is in this process of transformation under BV that degrowth would occur.

Table 2 below demonstrates the parallel between the tourism practices discussed above, the relevant BV principles, and the characteristics of degrowth as reiterated by Hall (2009).

In relation to Hall's argument that 'ethical consumption' is a requirement for degrowth in tourism, tourists and locals alike have a responsibility through their consumption habits and practices to respect local practices, environment, traditions and cultures. Under a BV approach this relates to the principles of decolonisation, culture and the sustainable use of resources; and all actors have a responsibility. If the ethical consumption of products for tourism is respected by both tourists and the host communities, it can help conserve the culture of that community and create a mindset of decolonisation, bringing the power back to the community, respecting traditional ways of life and traditional expertise. This can in turn lead to the sustainable use of resources whereby products are produced by communities using traditional methods and materials, which as opposed to mass-production brings consciousness to the production and consumption process. The result would be the production of arts, crafts, food products and handicrafts which help support livelihoods and therefore assist in meeting needs rather than being produced to satisfy an exploitative capitalist consumer market.

This approach prescribed by BV supports and is supported by Hall's (2009, p. 55) argument for degrowth in tourism, as degrowth particularly calls for an observation of the principles of equity, participatory democracy, respect for human rights, and respect for cultural differences.

The tourism initiatives discussed above are by no means exhaustive examples in the case of the Cotacachi County, but they are intended to highlight some of the ways in which tourism, when considered as an economic alternative under a BV approach, engages and involves communities in bottom-up driven initiatives designed to meet fundamental needs in line with BV

Table 2. Tourism, Buen Vivir and Degrowth Parallels.

Tourism Practices	Buen Vivir Principles	Degrowth Characteristics
Cultural and knowledge exchange Production and promotion of traditional handicrafts and arts Volunteer tourism	Decolonisation and culture	Quality of life, equity, respect for cultural differences, creativity, diversity, unremunerated activity
Eco and agri-tourism initiatives Community stays	Reciprocity, nature and community	Conviviality, non-materialism, sense of community
Participatory local government initiatives	Plurality, wellbeing and contextuality	Participatory democracy, good citizenship, respect for human rights.

principles. In that respect, degrowth is the consequence of such alternative economic practices, with social and environmental wellbeing being the ultimate objective, leading to a post-extractive economy that values holistic wellbeing over economic growth.

Conclusion

Sustainable tourism is concerned with the limits to growth, but it does not go far enough in reconsidering those limits. While sustainable tourism argues for a shift towards social and environmental responsibility, it is still couched within the unsustainable economic growth paradigm that inevitably has negative effects on the environment and local communities.

Communities in the Cotacachi County seek to use alternative tourism initiatives as a way to demonstrate the viability of a move away from a growth policy supported by large-scale extractivism. This type of tourism can help shift the focus of tourism as one of an economic growth activity, to one which results in the degrowth of socially and environmentally damaging activities. The demographic, cultural and geographical heritage of the County demonstrates the importance of this vision for tourism underpinned by BV and is supported through regional development policy at the municipal level through the strengthening of local community capacity in tourism, as well as environmental and cultural heritage management developed with participation from local communities.

These tourism development initiatives constructed within the context of BV promote an alternative economic activity which has the potential to decolonise the parameters of how we might understand degrowth; as a consequence of redefining the notion of limits. Like LaTouche (2012) we see degrowth as opening-up spaces of creativity and possibilities. This reframes degrowth not as a 'lack' but a growth in social and environmental wellbeing and conviviality.

Chambers and Buzinde (2015) urge tourism scholars to incorporate non-Western perspectives into tourism, which can in turn open-up possibilities for tourism practices that are beneficial for local communities. Like Karst (2017), we use the notion of wellbeing from a BV perspective to contribute the importance of centring local narratives, Global South perspectives and Indigenous worldviews into tourism research.

BV offers a vision for "thinking across the colonial difference and opening paths towards decolonial understanding" (Vázquez, 2012, p.6). Through changing the ways of 'knowing' and 'doing' development BV opens multiple possibilities for communities to achieve wellbeing for themselves and the environment. Economically, this is pursued as a strategy to transition local economies into a post-extractive society. This is key because BV and extractivism are incompatible (Chassagne, 2018), because the latter is inherently destructive to nature and destabilises communities through adverse social and environmental impacts.

Tourism as an alternative economic practice based on the principles of BV opens up opportunities for tourists to have more meaningful experiences, while contributing to the wellbeing of host communities and their natural environments. Under this approach, all actors have a role to play, and by the local government facilitating tourism as an alternative economic activity, it enables visions to become reality. Alternative tourism initiatives such as those outlined from Cotacachi align with arguments for both BV and degrowth – moving away from Eurocentric models of development and recalling the limits to growth argument. Using BV as a guiding tool for sustainable alternative forms of tourism would result in a degrowth of the more damaging sectors of the economy such as extractivism, and growth of other local and more socially and environmentally sustainable economies related to sustainable tourism (artisan and local produce, for example), supporting the social and environmental objectives of BV. Degrowth then becomes a consequence of a BV approach, not the aim, but the inherent characteristics of degrowth are also integral to the type of tourism development needed to align with the principles of BV.

Sustainable alternative tourism that is community-based and driven is one alternative economic activity under a BV approach which supports the idea of degrowth towards a post-extractive economy. To that end, it provides local communities with opportunities to increase their capacity for economic self-sufficiency, while protecting and promoting the environmental and cultural heritage of the community and breaking the dependence on large-scale extractivism. Thus by 'degrowing' or *growing* more sustainable local economic activities using BV as a guide, spaces of opportunities are opened up through the growth of intercultural exchange, deeper human connections, wellbeing, and a greater sense of reciprocity with the natural environment.

Notes

1. Significance is analysed by the number of references across all data methods (interviews, observations and documents).
2. This does not refer to a key informant, rather was part of the participant observation data.
3. Buen Vivir, from the Indigenous Kichwa.
4. As the peaceful existence of diversity
5. The process of which supports a respect for cultural systems.
6. Assumes access to food as a human right, providing dignity to all in the food system, from producers to consumers.
7. Relates to the satisfaction of needs through livelihood, rather than the perusal or wants pertaining to economic growth.
8. Supports the notion of BV as being tailorable to each community based on its particular capabilities.

Disclosure statement

No potential conflict of interest was reported by the author.

ORCID

Natasha Chassagne (iD) http://orcid.org/0000-0003-2412-7578

References

Acosta, A. (2012). *The Buen Vivir: An opportunity to imagine another world.* Berlin, Germany. Retrieved from http://www.br.boell.org/downloads/Democracy_Inside_A_Champion.pdf#page=194

Álvarez, S. (2013). *Sumak Kawsay o Buen Vivir como Alternativa al Desarrollo en Ecuador. Aplicación y Resultados en el Gobierno de Rafael Correa (2007-2011)* (Doctorat in Economic Sciences). Universidad Complutense de Madrid, Madrid.

Bold, V. (2007, October/November). Cotacachi actualiza su plan cantonal de turismo. *Periódico Intag,* pp. 40.

Bushell, R., & Eagles, P. F. (2006). *Tourism and protected areas: Benefits beyond boundaries: The Vth IUCN World Parks Congress*. Wallingford: CABI.

Butler, R. W. (1999). Sustainable tourism: A state-of-the-art review. *Tourism Geographies, 1*(1), 7–25. doi:10.1080/14616689908721291

Chassagne, N. (2018). Sustaining the 'Good Life': Buen Vivir as an alternative to sustainable development. *Community Development Journal, 54*(3), 482–500. doi:10.1093/cdj/bsx062

Chambers, D., & Buzinde, C. (2015). Tourism and decolonisation: Locating research and self. *Annals of Tourism Research, 51*, 1–16. doi:10.1016/j.annals.2014.12.002

Creswell, J. W. (2013). *Qualitative inquiry & research design: Choosing among five approaches* (3rd ed.). Los Angeles: SAGE Publications.

Dryzek, J. S. (1997). *The politics of the Earth: Environmental discourses*. Oxford; New York: Oxford University Press.

Entre el orgullo y el olvido. (2001). *Periódico Intag*: Cotacachi, Ecuador.

Escobar, A. (1995). *Encountering development: The making and unmaking of the third world (New in Paper)*. New Jersey: Princeton University Press.

Everingham, P. (2015). Intercultural exchange and mutuality in volunteer tourism: The case of Intercambio in Ecuador. *Tourist Studies, 15*(2), 175–190. doi:10.1177/1468797614563435

Everingham, P. (2018). Speaking Spanglish: Embodying linguistic (b)orderlands in volunteer tourism. *Emotion Space and Society, 27*, 68–75. doi:10.1016/j.emospa.2018.04.001

Fisher, J. (2018). Nicaragua's Buen Vivir: A strategy for tourism development? *Journal of Sustainable Tourism, 27*(4), 452–471. doi:10.1080/09669582.2018.1457035

Fletcher, R. (2011). Sustaining tourism, sustaining capitalism? The tourism industry's role in global capitalist expansion. *Tourism Geographies, 13*(3), 443–446.

Giovannini, M. (2014). *Indigenous peoples and self-determined development: The case of community enterprises in Chiapas*. Trento: University of Trento.

Gobo, G. (2008). *Doing ethnography*. Los Angeles, CA; London: Sage.

Gössling, S. (2002). Global environmental consequences of tourism. *Global Environmental Change, 12*(4), 283–302. doi:10.1016/S0959-3780(02)00044-4

Gössling, S., Hall, P., Peeters, P., & Scott, D. (2010). The future of tourism: Can tourism growth and climate policy be reconciled? A mitigation perspective. *Tourism Recreation Research, 35*(2), 119–130. doi:10.1080/02508281.2010.11081628

Gudynas, E. (2011). Buen vivir: Today's tomorrow. *Development, 54*(4), 441–447. doi:10.1057/dev.2011.86

Hall, C. M. (2009). Degrowing Tourism: Décroissance, sustainable consumption and steady-state tourism. *Anatolia, 20*(1), 46–61. doi:10.1080/13032917.2009.10518894

Hall, C. M. (2010). Changing paradigms and global change: From sustainable to steady-state tourism. *Tourism Recreation Research, 35*(2), 131–143. doi:10.1080/02508281.2010.11081629

Higgins-Desbiolles, F. (2006). More than an "industry": The forgotten power of tourism as a social force. *Tourism Management, 27*(6), 1192–1208. doi:10.1016/j.tourman.2005.05.020

Higgins-Desbiolles, F. (2010). The elusiveness of sustainability in tourism: The culture-ideology of consumerism and its implications. *Tourism and Hospitality Research, 10*(2), 116–129. doi:10.1057/thr.2009.31

Higgins-Desbiolles, F. (2017). Sustainable tourism: Sustaining tourism or something more? *Tourism Management Perspectives, 25*, 157–160 doi:10.1016/j.tmp.2017.11.017.

Higgins-Desbiolles, F., Carnicelli, S., Krolikowski, C., Wijesinghe, G., & Boluk, K. (2019). Degrowing tourism: Rethinking tourism. *Journal of Sustainable Tourism, 1* doi:10.1080/09669582.2019.1601732.

Karst, H. (2017). This is a holy place of Ama Jomo": Buen Vivir, indigenous voices and ecotourism development in a protected area of Bhutan. *Journal of Sustainable Tourism, 25*(6), 746–762. doi:10.1080/09669582.2016.1236802

Latouche, S. (2010). Degrowth. *Journal of Cleaner Production, 18*(6), 519–522. doi:10.1016/j.jclepro.2010.02.003

Latouche, S. (2012). Can the left escape economism? *Capitalism Nature Socialism, 23*(1), 74–78. doi:10.1080/10455752.2011.648841

Mason, J. (2002). *Qualitative researching* (2nd ed.). London; Thousand Oaks, CA: Sage Publications.

Ministerio del Ambiente. (2007). *Plan de Manejo Reserva Cotacachi Cayapas 2007*. Quito. Retrieved from http://suia.ambiente.gob.ec/documents/10179/242256/25+PLAN+DE+MANEJO+COTACACHI+CAYAPAS.pdf/72c5f641-6573-4f6d-94b5-fd3b6df6227c.

Municipio de Cotacachi. (2016). Actualizacion PDyOT Cotacachi 2015-2035. Retrieved from http://www.cotacachi.gob.ec/index.php/component/phocadownload/category/61 (09 May 2016).

Municipio de Cotacachi. (2017). *Ingresos de turistas y vistantes registrado en la reserva ecológica Cotacachi Cayapas*. Cotacachi, Ecuador. Retrieved from http://www.cotacachi.gob.ec/index.php/turismo

Olivera, R. (2010). Coffee in the clouds. *New Internationalist, July 2010*.

Pink, S., & Morgan, J. (2013). Short-term ethnography: Intense routes to knowing. *Symbolic Interaction, 36*(3), 351–361. Retrieved from doi:10.1002/symb.66

Saltos, T. (2008). *The participatory budgeting experience Cotacachi - Ecuador*. B. World. Retrieved from http://siteresources.worldbank.org/EXTSOCIALDEVELOPMENT/Resources/244362-1170428243464/3408356-1194298468208/4357878-1206561986056/TatyanaSaltosPaperSession3Day2.pdf

SENPLADES. (2013). *Plan nacional para el buen vivir 2013-2017*. SENPLADES, Quito, Ecuador.

Singh, S. (2011). *Slow travel and Indian culture: Philosophies and practical aspects. Slow Tourism: experiences and mobilities*. Bristol; Buffalo; Toronto: Channel View Publications: 214–227 Transforming Our World: The 2030 Agenda for Sustainable Development (2015).

Scheyvens, R. (1999). Ecotourism and the empowerment of local communities. *Tourism Management, 20*(2), 245–249. doi:10.1016/S0261-5177(98)00069-7

Unceta, K. (2013). Decrecimiento y buen vivir ¿Paradigmas convergentes? Debates sobre el postdesarrollo en Europa y América Latina. *Revista de Economía Mundial, 35, 197-216.*

Vázquez, R. (2012). *Towards a Decolonial Critique of Modernity. Buen Vivir, Relationality and the Task of Listening. Capital, Poverty, Development, Denktraditionen im Dialog:Studien zur Befreiung und interkulturalität*, Vol 33, Raúl, F.-B. (Ed.), Wissenschaftsverlag Mainz: Aachen, pp. 241–252.

Waldmüller, J. (2015, 20 August 2015). Analysing the spill-over matrix of extractivism: Para-legality, separation and violence to integral health in the Ecuadorian Íntag. Retrieved from http://www.alternautas.net/blog/2015/3/20/analyzing-the-spill-over-matrix-of-extractivism-from-para-legality-separation-and-violence-to-integral-health-in-the-ecuadorian-ntag

Wearing, S., Wearing, M., & McDonald, M. (2012). *Slow'n down the town to let nature grow: Ecotourism, social justice and sustainability. Slow Tourism: Experiences and mobilities*. Bristol; Buffalo; Toronto: Channel View Publications, pp. 36–53.

Whitehead, M. (2013). Editorial: Degrowth or regrowth? *Environmental Values, 22*(2), 141–145. doi:10.3197/096327113X13581561725077

Degrowing tourism: rethinking tourism

Freya Higgins-Desbiolles, Sandro Carnicelli, Chris Krolikowski, Gayathri Wijesinghe and Karla Boluk

ABSTRACT

Concerns with growth have steadily advanced since the *Limits to Growth* report due particularly to human impacts on the natural environment. Since that time, neoliberal capitalism has become increasingly reliant on growth exacerbating these problems. The destructive outcomes of these strategies has led to a growing interest in degrowth. Analysts are examining how we can create economies that eschew a growth imperative while still supporting human thriving. Tourism as a key facet of capitalism is implicated in these issues and recent concerns with "overtourism" are only one symptom of the problem. This article presents a conceptual consideration of issues of degrowth in tourism. It examines current tensions in international mobility and argues just and sustainable degrowth will require greater attention to equity. This analysis suggests that essential to such an agenda is redefining tourism to focus on the rights of local communities and a rebuilding of the social capacities of tourism. This article argues for the redefinition of tourism in order to place the rights of local communities above the rights of tourists for holidays and the rights of tourism corporates to make profits.

Introduction

Concerns with growth have a long history, going at least as far back as the Club of Rome's *Limits to Growth* report (Meadows et al., 1972). Since that time, neoliberal capitalism has become increasingly reliant on growth as the panacea to the crises it inevitably creates. The destructive outcomes of these strategies have led to a growing interest in degrowth. Degrowth analysis considers ways to create economies that eschew a growth imperative while still supporting human thriving (Kallis, 2011, p. 873). But recent events draw attention to a worsening of conditions and these require considered attention and analysis for the implications they may hold for achieving sustainable tourism futures.

The year of 2017 marked a watershed moment and not only because of the inauguration of Donald Trump to the United States presidency. Because of political crises caused by civil wars and conflicts, refugees amassed at the borders of Europe in large numbers and thereby threatened the globalisation project of the previous decades (Jazairy, 2017). In terms of tourism, images of refugee bodies washing up on Mediterranean holiday beaches confronted comfortable middle class holidaymakers and highlighted divergent interpretations of what global mobility may mean for different people (Spiegel, 2015). At the same time, reports of overtourism indicated that the travel freedom of the mass tourists could no longer be taken for granted (Murison, 2017). Trump's America has placed a travel ban on people from certain (largely Muslim) countries purportedly to ensure American homeland security and locked up undesirable migrants in desert camps (Liptak, 2017; McKibben, 2018). These few cases suggest that mobility will be a key issue in social sustainability in the global future.

Fairness and justice are key facets to achieving degrowth that is socially sustainable (Muraca, 2012). Climate change, resource depletion, over-population and financial crises are likely to create more catalysts to population movements as the planet experiences greater numbers of political, environmental, economic and social refugees. Yet, we find borders being resurrected or strengthened and fervent nationalism as a response to the desperation of such peoples (seen for example, in Trump's border wall, the UK's Brexit decision and Hungary's crack down on asylum seeker transits). Simultaneously, tourists are sought in the competitive tourism marketplace to drive the endless growth that is the key to contemporary politics in many countries. This illustrates the discriminating applications of mobility in this era. Refugees are not welcome while tourism (for those privileged) is developed often without the consideration of its scale and overall impact on already overdeveloped destinations.

Reading tourism as an assertion of power and privilege, this article offers a conceptual analysis of the degrowth imperatives in tourism to demonstrate an entire rethinking of the phenomenon is required. The current situation is untenable. It is not possible to allow the mobility of the privileged for their discretionary travel needs while walling up borders for those who must move in order to survive. In this global world, we are arriving at a moment where the stark injustices are being made more apparent and impossible to ignore. This is the focus of this article.

Analysts of "sustainable tourism" and co-founders of the Journal of Sustainable Tourism Bramwell and Lane (2008) claimed in an editorial "While more researchers are beginning to look at the equality of tourism outcomes, there is still relatively little research on the wider issues of equity, fairness and social justice in tourism" (p. 2). This article addresses these gaps as relevant to considerations of degrowing tourism. This article responds to the challenge set by the Special Issue of the Journal of Sustainable Tourism on degrowth in tourism: "To seriously pursue degrowth at both global and as well as most national levels, therefore, would likely require a drastic transformation of the tourism industry and its metabolism" (Fletcher et al., 2017). This article takes an unconventional narrative approach to accomplish these goals of illuminating issues of power and privilege in tourism which we argue underpin the problem that tourism presents. In the following sections, this article: reviews thinking on degrowth; demonstrates that tourism dynamics are currently based on a pro-growth ideology that results from neoliberal capitalism and this results in growing issues with overtourism; argues that applying a social justice lens to tourism reveals injustice in global mobilities which will necessitate a radical rethinking of the right to travel; reimagines tourism as defined by the rights of the local community as a part of such a radical rethinking project; and applies the eight steps proposed by Latouche for a degrowth transition to tourism to outline a reimagining of tourism. The contribution of this work is to present a radical conceptual argument: for equitable and sustainable degrowth in tourism to occur, tourism must be redefined and redesigned to acknowledge, prioritize, and place the rights of local communities above the rights of tourists for holidays and the rights of tourism corporates to make profits.

Review of degrowth and tourism

Despite arguments made by advocates that tourism is a benign industry that makes an invaluable contribution to development (e.g. UNWTO, n.d.a), recent analysis suggests its impacts are considerable and it has implications for efforts to try to secure long-term, wider sustainable development goals. Hall (2009, p. 53) made this point:

> If tourism is to make a genuine contribution to sustainability then it becomes vital that there is greater public acknowledgement by industry and government of what the positive and negative impacts of tourism are, and thereby to see tourism as part of the larger socio-economic bio-physical system.

Hall was one of the first to link tourism sustainability to the larger degrowth movement. Hall argued: "sustainable tourism development is tourism development without growth in throughput of matter and energy beyond regenerative and absorptive capacities" (2009, p. 53). Thus, degrowth thinking offers a fundamental challenge to tourism processes, as it questions the assumptions which have been behind the continual expansion of the industry since the post-war period.

D'Alisa, Demaria, and Kallis (2015) argue: "The foundational theses of degrowth are that growth is uneconomic and unjust, that it is ecologically unsustainable and that it will never be enough" (p. 6). Demaria, Schneider, Sekulova and Martinez-Alier (2013) argued that degrowth emerged in the twentieth-first century "as a project of voluntary societal shrinking of production and consumption aimed at environmental sustainability" (p. 192), but evolved into a social movement with a focus of opposing economic growth.

According to *the Ecologist*, "the first international degrowth conference in Paris – 10 years ago this year – introduced the originally French activist slogan *décroissance* into the English-speaking world and international academia as 'degrowth'" (The Ecologist, 2018). Knowledge of degrowth is derived from numerous disciplines including ecological economics, social ecology and economic anthropology, as well as social and environmental activism (Martinez-Alier, Pascual, Vivien, & Zaccai, 2010). Kallis (2011) asserts that degrowth "is a radical political project that offers a new story and a rallying slogan for a social coalition built around the aspiration to construct a society that lives better with less" (p. 873). It is open to debate about how radical a revolution degrowth will entail. There are also considerations of degrowth versus approaches such as post-growth, agrowth, steady-state economy, alternative well-being economics, and various forms of solidarity, and community economies addressing the options and practicalities (see Gerber & Raina, 2018). However, leading degrowth thinker Serge Latouche (2006) has explored the many terms and ideas related to degrowth thinking and argued that there is largely "[…] agreement on the re-evaluation our economic system needs, and on the values that we should bring to the fore" whether advanced by degrowth advocates, post-development thinkers, proponents of sustainable development, or green activitsts.

In his succinct assessment of "why growth can't be green," Hickel countered the argument that degrowth means deprivation: "But ending growth doesn't mean that living standards need to take a hit. Our planet provides more than enough for all of us; the problem is that its resources are not equally distributed" (2018). This analysis indicates that equity issues are of prime significance to degrowth considerations. Particularly, questions arise on common but differential responsibilities and approaches that might be implemented in the countries of the Global North versus the Global South (see Gerber & Raina, 2018).

Latouche outlined eight interdependent steps to a degrowth transition: re-evaluate and shift values; re-conceptualize entrenched capitalist concepts; restructure production; redistributions at the global, regional and local scale; re-localize the economy; reduce; re-use; and recycle resources (cited in March, 2018, p. 1695). But these strategies cannot be approached as a toolkit, technological and market fix, but rather require a whole re-orientation of values and paradigm (March, 2018, p. 1695). This transformation of values is essential; "the de-growth camp would, in addition to physical critical issues, argue that downsizing is not just a matter of physically reducing throughput as it also involves decolonizing minds from economism" (Martinez-Alier et al., 2010, p. 1744). In this analysis, we take up a "decolonising" approach by offering a radically different definition and focus to tourism that is conducive to overturning the growth fetish that currently features.

Because of tourism's considerable negative environmental impacts, it is an important sector for implementing degrowth strategies (Hall, 2009). Hall (2009) advocated a degrowth perspective to address transitioning tourism to a "steady-state economy" which he described as encouraging "qualitative development but not aggregate quantitative growth to the detriment of natural capital" (p. 57). Hall (2009) described degrowth as living within sustainable limits which is "... not so much connected to downsizing per se but to the notion of 'right-sizing'" (p. 55).

Yet contemporary tourism policy is predicated on growth (Higgins-Desbiolles, 2018a). Corporate tourism plans repeatedly reference the growth of tourism. For instance, Tourism Australia's *Tourism 2020 Strategy* claimed:

> Tourism 2020 focuses on improving the industry's performance and competitiveness by pursuing new opportunities for growth and addressing supply-side factors. The Tourism 2020 goal is to achieve more than $115 billion in overnight spend by 2020 (up from $70 billion in 2009 (Tourism Australia, n.d.).

Tourism authorities devise strategies to grow tourism markets, to increase tourism visitation, spur greater visitor spending and foster repeat visitation. This occurs because growth is the logic of neoliberal capitalism and it is essential for democratic governments to get re-elected. As Higgins-Desbiolles (2018a) described:

> The structural context set by powerful corporations, subservient governments and consumerised citizenry needs to be understood. Politicians now think in short term election cycles and have become fetishist to growth, seeking corporate funding for their re-election campaigns and voter support for the jobs and growth they continually promise to deliver. Corporations have demanded in repayment for their largesse a reduction of barriers to business, elimination of "red tape" and a business-friendly investment environment; this means a hollowing out of the role of governments to use policy, legislation and regulations to govern for the public good, longer-term wellbeing of society and holistic sustainability (p. 158).

It occurs in tourism because tourism authorities are seeking to justify their share of the governmental budget and ensure that tourism economic portfolios are taken seriously as a contributor to the nation's economic development. The agenda for growth is set at the highest levels. While the World Tourism Organization (UNWTO) proclaims interest in the socio-cultural contributions of tourism, all of its documents most strongly articulate the economic values. For example, the "why tourism?" webpage articulates current trends and developments as:

- International tourist arrivals grew by 7% in 2017 to 1323 million
- In 2017, international tourism generated US$1.6 trillion in export earnings
- UNWTO forecasts a growth in international tourist arrivals of between 4% and 5% in 2018
- By 2030, UNWTO forecasts international tourist arrivals to reach 1.8 billion (UNWTO, n.d.a).

The UNWTO acts to promote "mainstreaming tourism in the development agenda" on the basis of these statistics (UNWTO, n.d.b).

As more and more developing countries follow a development trajectory seeking to attain western levels of consumption, the world community confronts a challenging equity issue in terms of the phenomenal growth in tourism consumption. As Hall (2009) noted, considering the serious negative environmental impacts of tourism, if we believe that ethics of equity should apply so that everyone can enjoy travel, we would find "there is not enough world for everyone to be the average North American or European long-haul tourist" (p. 53). The growing middle classes of populous countries such as India and China represent a lucrative opportunity for tourism multinationals and destination governments, but insufficient thought is given to equity, fairness, and justice in tourism consumption and the need to impose limits in the interests of safe futures as touring populations rise rapidly in an increasingly resource constrained world.

However, it is important to understand that the growth fetish of tourism is not new. Brian Wheeller offered critical and cutting edge analysis in 1993. Wheeller (1993) argued that the tourism industry appropriated the language of sustainability in order to achieve public relations outcomes: "while dovetailing perfectly with notions of a quality caring industry that has developed a self-rectifying mechanism, globally, it is patently obvious that the 'bugger it up and pass it down' [...] philosophy has been employed" (p. 125). He predicted the future of tourism as heading to "mega-mass tourism" as tourists numbers grew exponentially and travel destinations proliferated with the promotion of global tourism through intentional efforts. He identified the reality globally as "a capitalist society with inbuilt growth dynamics and a 'get it while you can,' grab mentality," while the rhetoric of responsible tourism and sustainability was deployed to deceive with their "slow, steady, selfless, cosy, back to nature, sustainable, eco-friendly, controlled small-scale solution to tourism problems" (Wheeller, 1993, p. 126). He asserts that the proponents who advocate sustainable tourism as the answer to the problems of mass tourism are right:

> Sustainable tourism does provide the answer. Unfortunately it is the wrong question. Rather than effectively addressing the complexities of tourism impact, what it is actually achieving is the considerably easier task of answering the question – 'How best can we cope with the criticism of tourism impact?' – as opposed to the impact itself (Wheeller, 1993, p. 122).

Wheeller's analysis cautions us to be critically analytical of responsible tourism rhetoric and the campaigns the tourism industry proposes to address its sustainability challenges. Under the logic of neoliberal capitalism, the advocates of the tourism industry are unlikely to address the real issue of degrowing tourism and can be expected to deploy deceptive campaigns to divert attention from the critical challenges we confront.

A recent case of a promotional campaign by *Wonderful Copenhagen*, the official tourism organisation of the city of Copenhagen, Denmark, captured the inherent contradiction between the "veneer" of sustainability that is presented to gain support for tourism and the centrality of the growth agenda which is still at the core of tourism policy and planning. *Wonderful Copenhagen* promised the "end of the era of tourism" and launched a tourism strategy setting a course "towards a future beyond tourism" (Wonderful Copenhagen, 2017). Entitled "localhood," the vision seems to promise an exemplar of degrowth, stating:

> [...] we wish to co-create [...] a future destination where human relations are the focal point, where the differentiation between destination and home of locals is one and the same. A destination, where locals and visitors not only co-exist, but interact around shared experiences of localhood (2017, p. 10).

On closer examination when reading this strategy in full, this vision may be viewed as a case illustrative of Wheeller's (1993) point outlined above. *Wonderful Copenhagen* acted much like any other Destination Marketing Organisation (DMO) when it focused on the economic measurements typical of other DMOs. It claimed to go "[...] beyond bed-nights in measuring the industry's value creation [...]" (2017, p. 16). Yet, this strategy contained the same emphasis on destination competitiveness, targeting of the lucrative business traveller, increasing visitor length of stay, encouraging repeat visitation, but most importantly growing new markets too, including the notorious cruise ship industry tourist. With critical reading, the localhood strategy of *Wonderful Copenhagen* was arguably a response to criticisms of overtourism in European city destinations, the homogenisation of urban destinations through globalisation and a consumer market fracturing in tastes and interests.

Ultimately, the mission of the localhood strategy of *Wonderful Copenhagen* was growth, as it aimed to "enable our destination to be shared more" (2017, p. 11). This was confirmed by its "marks of success," with the first one being a revenue target of DKK 49 billion. It did couch this as "socio-economic revenue," claiming this refocused on "broader societal impact" rather than a more narrow "tourism-economic revenue." In the next paragraph it confessed "today, we have limited means and methods to measure broader value [...]" (p. 23). The second mark of success was to measure and target "citizen's support of visitor *growth*" [emphasis added] at higher than

80% through "frequent studies to measure sentiments of the locals towards visitors" (p. 23). Clearly as a DMO, *Wonderful Copenhagen* was using localhood as an astute branding strategy to distinguish Copenhagen from other popular city destinations (see p. 13). The strategy sought local buy-in to this growth strategy with a concern to inform the citizenry of the city of the "socio-economic" value of hosting tourists in their locale and a tool of engagement through social surveying.

This was an astute if superficial reaction to the fact that overtourism indicates that local communities are becoming increasingly hostile to forms of tourism that are imposed on them and diminish the quality of life. Overtourism refers to "the impact of tourism on a destination, or parts thereof, that excessively influences perceived quality of life of citizens and/or visitors in a negative way" (UNWTO, 2018, p. 4). Higgins-Desbiolles understood overtourism in a context of carrying capacity, when she claimed:

> Overtourism describes a situation in which a tourism destination exceeds its carrying capacity – in physical and/or psychological terms. It results in a deterioration of the tourism experience for either visitors or locals, or both. If allowed to continue unchecked, overtourism can lead to serious consequences for popular destinations (Higgins-Desbiolles, 2018b).

This different emphasis matters as a carrying capacity approach suggests a notion that places sold as a tourism destinations have limits to the growth in terms of both physical and psychological attributes.

Despite appearances, overtourism did not arrive in public discourse out of nowhere. Significant to the development of overtourism has been the dominance of neoliberal ideology and the impacts it has had on economy and society. Harvey (2005) argued the neoliberal state empowers the corporate sector by ensuring a good business and investment climate leaving civil society as the site of resistance to the injustices that ensue (pp. 70–79). In the case of overtourism at tourism destinations such as Barcelona and Venice, it is the impacted, local community that has been activated for resistance (Burgen, 2018; Milano, 2018).

Understandings of overtourism should be situated in the wider context of tourism development being fostered by the capitalist economy system for profit accumulation of multinational corporations and the global elite (Fletcher, 2011; Higgins-Desbiolles, 2008, 2018a). As Fletcher (2011) argued:

> A small number of increasingly interrelated transnational tourism operators control much of the goods and services that tourists consume globally. In this respect, tourism expansion can be viewed as an instance of "accumulation through dispossession" that Harvey (2005) finds characteristic of neoliberal capitalism in general. These operators also control much of the advertising by which tourists are enticed to consume the products offered, Transnational tourism operators work hand-in-hand with other important tourism promoters, including international development agencies and national governments (p. 455).

Through this political economy lens we can see how overtourism occurs through the pressures of multinational tourism corporations and affiliated others, who press for pro-growth approaches to tourism development. They lack concern for the limits of carrying capacity that a particular destination might be subject to and in current neoliberal contexts of deregulation are not compelled to respect such limits. Fletcher (2018) indicated that capitalistic forms of tourism are not deterred from the critical crises that capitalism heralds for its dependence on the natural environment, particularly ecotourism. Fletcher viewed tourism "as a key pillar of the capitalist economy" and showed how tourism promoters will utilise strategies of "Anthropocene tourism and other forms of disaster capitalism as a 'fix' to stave off economic and environmental crises for as long as they are able" (2018, p. 11).

This capitalistic system of production in tourism is enabled by a consumerist dynamic that is never satiated and in fact seeks out newer and more novel tourism destinations and experiences (Higgins-Desbiolles, 2010). Driven by restlessness, boredom and new ways to escape reality, tourists are perpetually seeking new experiences (Cohen, 1979; Graburn, 1989). The desire to seek more and more novel ways of stimulating the senses through travel (as encouraged by the experience economy for example) continues to go unchallenged, perpetuating the growth fetish of tourism and underpinning the ability of tourism corporates to sustain profit agendas from tourism growth.

Through these dynamics outlined above, we can identify why pro-growth policies of tourism are enacted and understand how these result in overtourism in particular locales around the world (Higgins-Desbiolles, 2018b). Next, we turn to the issue of tourists and the right to travel as an essential pillar to thinking through a socially sustainable approach to degrowth in tourism.

Understanding tourism today through a social justice lens

The nature and significance of tourism has long been debated in tourism circles. One key transformation in understandings of tourism is the transition from notions of "tourism as a social force" (Higgins-Desbiolles, 2006) to seeing tourism solely in terms of it as a business sector or "industry" (Smith, 1988, p. 183). As neoliberalism has gained dominance, conceptualisations of tourism as an industry has narrowed tourism education in such important ways that it constrains our thinking and action particularly in terms of understanding tourism as a moral domain (see Ayikoru, Tribe, & Airey, 2009). In effect, the phenomenon of tourism has been usurped by those seeking to direct it to profit accumulation and this has serious implications for the future of tourism under discussion here.

A newer way of defining tourism is through a mobilities approach. Hall (2008b) claims tourism can be interpreted as "an expression of lifestyle identified either through voluntary travel or a voluntary temporary short-term change of residence" (p. 7). This mobilities definition of tourism draws attention to how tourism can be understood by the dimensions of movement through space and time, as well as the number of trips a traveller undertakes (Hall, 2008a). Such an approach indicates the complexities of contemporary tourism, particularly how it now may overlap with everyday leisure, travel to second homes, diasporic travel, emigration, business travel, and medical travel. Hall (2008a) advocated the need for "[...] understanding the meaning behind the range of mobilities undertaken by individuals, not tourists [...] by extension, a new conceptualization and theoretical approach applied to tourism must consider relationships to other forms of mobility" (p. 15). Hall's purpose here is to address new developments in tourism demand and destination competitiveness but for this discussion it exposes to us the fact that tourism is clearly the domain of the privileged. In fact, Hall could add a fourth dimension to his mobilities approach to tourism, that of money as the globally mobile are welcomed according to their ability to pay or invest in the destinations they desire (see for instance Smith, 2014). Tourism addresses voluntary and commodified travel while our world increasingly witnesses involuntary travel out of desperation.

The 2015 image of the lifeless Syrian toddler, Alan Kurdi, washed up on a Turkish beach helps us demarcate the lines between privilege and peril in this globalised world (Smith, 2015). These Aegean beaches are the transit routes through which Syrians, among many others, flee civil war and danger (See Figure 1). The holiday islands and coasts of the Mediterranean have become the frontline in this rubbing up of the privileged and the imperilled. This situation is recognised by those amenable to a justice lens. For instance, "Tourists go home, refugees welcome" featured on signs of a leftist group Arran Paisos Catalans in 2017 (Giaccaria, 2018). *The Guardian* newspaper reported:

> Early last year, around 150,000 people in Barcelona marched to demand that the Spanish government allow more refugees into the country. Shortly afterwards, "Tourists go home, refugees welcome" started appearing on the city's walls; soon the city was inundated with protestors marching behind the slogans "Barcelona is not for sale" and "We will not be driven out."

Figure 1. Photo from "Tourists versus Refugees series, "Tourists taking a morning walk at the beach pass by abandoned life-jackets from refugees that arrived on the previous night," August 2015, Kos, Greece. Copyright Jörg Brüggemann/OSTKREUZ. Used with permission.

What the Spanish media dubbed *turismofobia* overtook several European cities last summer […] But in contrast to many, as fiercely as Barcelona has pushed back against tourists, it has campaigned to welcome more refugees. When news broke two weeks ago that a rescue ship carrying 629 migrants was adrift in the Mediterranean, mayor Ada Colau was among the first to offer those aboard safe haven (Burgen, 2018).

Giaccaria analysed these events:

Within the broader rise of anti-tourism feelings and practices, the Catalan protest is particularly meaningful as it establishes a connection between two forms of mobility that are at odds with each other: (Northern) tourism and (Southern) migration. Moreover, it subverts the common feeling about which kind of mobility is desirable and which one not. Anti-tourism protesters describe tourists as invaders who endanger the social and cultural (re)production of places (2018, p.1).

Justice-oriented scholarship is also beginning to address the issues of migration in relations to environmental change caused by climate change (e.g. White, 2011). We are already witnessing whole communities in the Artic prepare to leave their homes and even whole countries, such as Tuvalu and Kiribati, becoming environmental refugees. This is the newest and perhaps gravest form of environmental injustice and environmental racism; it may also compound historical and colonial abuses (see Maldonado et al., 2013).

These few incidents briefly addressed here invite us to think about the mobilities of tourists versus the mobilities of vulnerable others through a lens of social justice as we consider possibilities of degrowth. This invites a consideration of the right to travel and tourism and how these are enacted.

The rights to travel and tourism were derived in the twentieth century in developed countries from workers' rights and pressures to legislate leave entitlements (see Higgins-Desbiolles,

2006). This led to the incorporation of the right to travel being in key international documents including the Universal Declaration of Human Rights of 1948, the International Covenant on Economic, Social and Cultural Rights of 1966, the World Tourism Organization's Tourism Bill of Rights and Tourist Code of 1985, and the Global Code of Ethics for Tourism of 1999. The Universal Declaration of Human Rights has two passages that underpin the right to travel, articles 13 (2) and 24. Article 13, section 2 states "Everyone has the right to leave any country, including his own, and to return to his country" (UN, 1948), which O'Byrne describes as underpinning the human right to travel (2001, pp. 411–413). Combined with article 24 which states "everyone has the right to rest and leisure, including reasonable limitation of working hours and periodic holidays with pay" (UN, 1948), this important pillar of our human rights structure is credited with situating travel and tourism as part of our human rights regime. This was justified because of tourism's potential value: as the UNWTO asserted, tourism is vital for "[...] contributing to economic development, international understanding, peace, prosperity and universal respect for, and observance of, human rights and fundamental freedoms for all [...]" (UNWTO, 1999).

However, clearly this human right is not universally enjoyed and there is a clear divide between the developed and developing worlds in this respect. But before the neoliberal order took hold, there was some rhetoric concerning the need to promote greater equity. For instance, the Manila Declaration of the UNWTO in 1980 declared in its opening statements:

> Convinced [...] that world tourism can contribute to the establishment of a new international economic order that can help to eliminate the widening economic gap between developed and developing countries and ensure the steady acceleration of economic and social progress, in particular of the developing countries,

> Aware that world tourism can only flourish if based on equity [...] and if its ultimate aim is the improvement of the quality of life and the creation of better living conditions for all peoples [...] (UNWTO, 1980).

Once neoliberalism held sway, the UNWTO formulated the Global Code of Ethics for Tourism (UNWTO, 1999), which still continued such lofty and idealistic rhetoric but added more practical value by enunciating the roles and responsibilities of all of the various stakeholders in tourism (e.g. tourists, the industry, governments, and "host" communities). This code was forged in the new era brought with the demise of communism and the triumph of neoliberalism; and so not surprisingly, its preamble states:

> [...] the world tourism industry as a whole has much to gain by operating in an environment that favours the market economy, private enterprise and free trade and that serves to optimize its beneficial effects on the creation of wealth and employment (UNWTO, 1999).

Reflecting concerns contemporaneous with its creation, it acknowledged the need to balance economic development with environmental protection and alleviation of poverty, and thus was informed by the sustainability discourse of the 1990s. But more surprisingly, it advocated government support of initiatives such as "social tourism" and other processes to promote access to tourism for potential disadvantaged groups in their societies such as the people with disabilities, youth, seniors and families. This was surprising that such rhetoric had survived into the era of neoliberalism. However, because there is no mention of the New International Economic Order in this document (unlike the Manila Declaration), it failed to address how such inclusivity and equity might be achieved. One can only assume that each government's ability to fulfil its "social tourism" obligations to its citizenry and thus make real their citizens exercise of their "right to tour" is dependent upon them obtaining sufficient levels of development to make conditions possible to fulfil such obligations. The only statement this code made about obligations to development in the countries of the developing world was a call that:

> Multinational enterprises of the tourism industry should not exploit the dominant positions they sometimes occupy [...] they should involve themselves in local development, avoiding, by the excessive repatriation of

their profits or their induced imports, a reduction of their contribution to the economies in which they are established (UNWTO, 1999, article 9).

Considering the *raison d'etre* of these enterprises is profit and/or returns to their shareholders, this is patently insufficient to direct tourism to developmental outcomes for local communities.

Bianchi and Stephenson (2014) have comprehensively considered free movement of people and the right to travel and concluded:

> [...] while international travel is said to be uniquely able to foster peace, development and social harmony among human beings, neoliberal discourses of "tourism as freedom" and by association, free trade, simultaneously underplay and exacerbate the material inequalities and unequal power relations that determine people's ability to enjoy freedom of movement and the right to travel (p. 139).

Situating tourism in terms of considerations of justice, Higgins-Desbiolles (2018c) advocated:

> The justice of a full mobilities approach to human travel rather than facilitating privileged tourists. Global environmental change, the conflicts induced by increasing precarities and the desire to secure better livelihoods seem set to compel human movement on an unprecedented scale. In such a context, a goal of dismantling the UNWTO and replacing it with a UN agency for the right to mobility will become more imperative (p.7).

Higgins-Desbiolles (2018c) and Bianchi and Stephenson (2014) failed to address the fact that there are currently two bodies charged with international mobility, the UNWTO and the International Organization for Migration (IOM). The latter is described as "the leading inter- national agency working with governments and civil society to advance the understanding of migration issues, encourage social and economic development through migration, and uphold the human dignity and well-being of migrants" (IOM, n.d.). The UNWTO has published a report on "Tourism and Migration" (2009) that analysed the linkages between tourism and migration and the opportunities that emerge to grow and develop tourism opportunities (such as com- munities living in diaspora representing lucrative tourism niches or the remittance workers on cruise ships sending monies home to developing country communities). That is of course the remit of the UNWTO as an organisation. What this analysis illuminates though is that such a myopic focus is no longer tenable in a resource- constrained world subject to coming upheavals induced by climate change, conflict and economic crises. Mobilities can no longer be de-coupled if degrowth is to be achieved. Taking Higgins-Desbiolles' call for a "full mobilities approach" (2018c), this analysis suggests that if degrowth is to be socially sustainable in a globalised and mobile world, tourism degrowth must come to terms with issues of equity and justice in access to mobility.

Reimagining tourism and justifying it

Higgins-Desbiolles (2007) addressed issues of privilege and peril inspired by the impacts of the "9/11" attacks and the subsequent war on terror. She turned to the work of Frantz Fanon for understanding how the powerful and privileged exert themselves to ensure their ability to dom- inate and exploit and also how resistance to such domination might occur. Fanon's *The wretched of the earth* has been described as "the greatest masterpiece of the anti-colonial struggle" (Sartre, 1967). Its content "On violence" has a warning for our times as the catalysts to violence are growing.

Fanon (1967) recorded how the colonisation process features the colonisers dehumanising of the "natives." Fanon (1967) argued that because colonisation represents relentless violence, decolonisation struggles must be willing to resort to violence. As the colonisers work to displace the native in settler colonisation, the natives are sparked into violent resistance because they react to their dehumanisation. Settler colonialism ensures that the natives understand their situ- ation and deprivations: "[...] on the level of immediate experience, the native who has seen the modern world penetrate into the furthermost corners of the bush, is most acutely aware of all the things he does not possess" (Fanon, 1967, p. 58). Additionally, the colonised natives are aware that their oppression can only be overturned by a resort to violence: "we have seen that it is the intuition of the colonised masses that their liberation must, and can only, be achieved by force" (Fanon, 1967, p. 57).

The events of Barcelona recounted above resulting in the label of "tourism phobia" (Milano, 2018; Burgen, 2018) concentrate our minds on the potential for violence from these injustices that are increasingly brought into juxtaposition. Milano (2018), who also focused on the issues of "tourism phobia" in Barcelona, argued that the solutions to issues caused by tourism are not only technical but also political, and specifically, "it is necessary to propose structural changes to the economic model in which the tourist phenomenon is currently embedded" (p. 560. *Translated by the authors).* If we are to avoid violence, strategies for degrowth in tourism must be progressive, inclusive, just and equitable. This begins with the redefinition of tourism in order to place the rights of local communities above the rights of tourists for holidays and the rights of tourism corporates to make profits.

This article has featured diverse definitions of tourism. To achieve the goal of just degrowth in tourism, tourism must be redefined. Current textbook definitions often focus on the tourists and the nature of their demand and/or the industry that supplies them through products and services (e.g. Wall & Mathieson, 2006). Tourism for sustainability and degrowth must focus on the needs and interests of the local community; what tourism industry interests have usurped for themselves under the label of the "host community." A redefined tourism could be described as: the process of local communities inviting, receiving and hosting visitors in their local community, for limited time durations, with the intention of receiving benefits from such actions. Such forms of tourism may be facilitated by businesses operating to commercial imperatives or may be facilitated by non-profit organisations. But in this restructure of tourism, tourism operators would be allowed access to the local community's assets only under their authorisation and stewardship (See Figure 2).

A model of such a way of re-orienting tourism can be found in the Statute on Tourism in Kuna Yala. Kuna Yala (now Guna Yala) is an Indigenous province of Panama that has historically experienced imposition of tourism by central government authorities and the tourism industry (Bennett, 1999). The first article of the Statute declared:

> The only tourist activities and infrastructures possible in Kuna Yala will be, strictly and solely, those that respect, conserve, value, and defend the natural resources, environment and biodiversity of the comarca [reservation], as well as the sociocultural, political, and religious Kuna norms and customs (Snow, 2001, p. 2).

Snow (2001) described this as: "[...] represent[ing] a carefully planned strategy to direct the tourism industry to the needs of the entire Kuna nation" (p. 1). The thrust of this law was to prevent outside investment in Kuna lands, assert full control over tourism projects and subject all Kuna tourism projects to an approval process of the Kuna General Congress (Bennett, 1999). It is important to note here that the Kuna first reacted with violence against tourists imposed on their communities by the Panamanian central government and the tourism industry, before asserting their rights through the Statute (Bennett, 1999). More recent research has shown that the Kuna have been able to eliminate tourism intermediaries and thereby retain more of the benefits of tourism for themselves but even more importantly present a model of local empowerment and full sharing of the tourism opportunity and its benefits (Pereiro, de Leon, Martinez Mauri, Ventocilla, & del Valle, 2012, p. 33). Another example is the Yolngu Aboriginal community's Lirrwi Tourism which asserts Yolngu authority over tourism and its conduct on their country (see Lirrwi Tourism, n.d.).

Whether such an entire re-orientation of the phenomenon is possible is of course a real issue. A historical success that showed a more modest but no less important assertion of community interests was the Tourism Optimisation Management Model (TOMM) developed on the leadership of the community of Kangaroo Island who wanted to ensure that mass tourism

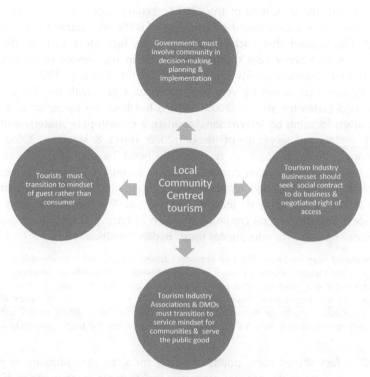

Figure 2. Community-Centred Tourism Framework as a mechanism for degrowing tourism.

developments did not diminish their quality of life (see Miller & Twining-Ward, 2005). The example set by TOMM could be taken up as a means to practically implement steady state approaches to tourism, if not degrowth approaches, as it sought community indicators of tourism impacts and ecological indicators to counter balance the more pro-growth economic indicators and tourism experiential indicators with the aim to develop responsive sustainable approaches to tourism.

There are many diverse contributions on how tourism can be made more sustainable which are more easily realised pathways to degrowing tourism. Recently, new trends including *buen vivir*, localism and slow tourism have made important contributions and potentially with real commitment could contribute to efforts towards degrowth.

Buen Vivir, or living well, is one example of a movement to abandon measures of prosperity based on gross domestic product for measures of peoples' total well-being. One example studied in tourism is that of Nicaragua. Fisher (2018) found:

> Nicaragua's Vivir Bonito, Vivir Bien is a hopeful, practical, and – yes – ideological response to a cluster of challenges that are at once endogenous, hemispheric and global. Its central concern is the many social and ecological pathways that comprise and erode collective well-being [...] In contemporary Nicaragua, as that conversation moves away from the narrow focus on markets and makes space for Buen Vivir, it will be even more important to consider how those relationships between hosts and guests, citizens and states, communities and environments, are figured and refigured, as well as how different histories, political ecologies and socio-ecological imaginaries give rise to new varieties of tourism development (p. 16).

This example of *buen vivir* reinforces that resistance to corporatised tourism and its growth agendas can also be found in articulations of tourism as a social force (Higgins-Desbiolles, 2006). Bhutan's policy and programmes based on "gross national happiness" (GNH) offer a comparable approach to *buen vivir*. As Gerber and Raina (2018, p. 357) demonstrate, Bhutan's GNH offers a practical example with the indicators of the GNH Screening Tool and the activities of the GNH Commission to build an economy based on concepts of sufficiency rather than growth.

Higgins-Desbiolles argued that social tourism and its facilitators such as the International Bureau of Social Tourism show how tourism should be in the service of human needs rather than appropriated for corporate profits and a growth agenda (2006, p. 1200). One example of a form of social tourism that would be very well suited to a degrowth tourism paradigm is that suggested by David Barkin for Mexico (2000). Mexico has been an exemplar of a country using corporatized tourism focusing on international tourists, a growth-pole strategy and mega-resorts as its approach to tourism development (Barkin, 2000; Torres & Momsen, 2005). Barkin (2000) advocated a more sustainable approach for rural livelihoods, sustainable resource management and social well-being through a mass domestic tourism approach. His work documented a number of local initiatives that featured efforts in "[…] integrating tourism into a more balanced program of productive development" (Barkin, 2000, p. 16). The form of tourism he advocated was domestic social tourism in rural communities, such as having urban school groups hosted in rural communities of Mexico for educational tours. Barkin (2000) claimed:

> The alternative model examined here offers an important counterweight with considerable benefits for rural communities and the Mexican working class. It would contribute substantially to breaking down some of the obstacles to building a more balanced national society. A program of socially oriented tourism would open a new model for decentralised development that would respond to urgent needs of present-day society. Well organized, it could be financed more readily that the international model and offers more employment and an inexpensive way to improve the quality of life for both consumers and providers (p. 19).

Barkin (2000) in fact offered some points of advice for a "tourism program as part of a strategy for autonomous sustainable resource management" that are recommended for anyone concerned with degrowth in tourism, including the "recognition of the local communities as the rightful claimants to speak for and benefit from any program that protects and exploits local resources" (pp. 17–18).

There are also opportunities offered by different models, including not for profit social enterprises (i.e. Iorgulescu & Răvar, 2015) and tourism cooperatives (i.e. Vocatch, 2010). Perhaps most radical of all, is the take-over of bankrupted hotels by workers and their operation under workers' cooperatives models such as the case of the Hotel Bauen in Buenos Aires, Argentina (Higgins-Desbiolles, 2012). Higgins-Desbiolles (2012) argued that the "Hotel Bauen provides a powerful counter pedagogy to capitalist globalization's assertion that 'there is no alternative' [… and] can reverse the logic of capitalism" (pp. 636–637).

These examples indicate that challenges to the corporate agenda of seizing tourism for profits and growth have a long and impressive pedigree. The struggle for power and control over tourism is serious and so far, the usurpers have had sound success in making us forgetful and neglectful of those thought leaders and actors that came before us. Today though the crises and the challenges that lay before us are so serious that renewed resistance is essential. Reclaiming tourism for human needs, within the wider context of autonomous sustainable resource management and allocation of wider goods and bads of development, is essential for any program planning degrowth in tourism.

As a final implement for analysis, degrowth analyses offer guidance in degrowing tourism. As previously stated, Latouche suggested eight "r's" for a degrowth transition (March, 2018, p. 1695). These provide guidance on how to transition to degrowth but as cautioned earlier must be in a context of a whole re-orientation of paradigm (March, 2018, p. 1695). These can offer an approach to considerations of degrowing tourism.

- Re-evaluate and shift values:
  Currently, tourism is defined as the business of supplying tourists with products and services or the travel motivations of tourists and the nature of their demand. This needs to be

changed. In the interest of equity and justice, tourism should be better defined as the voluntary hosting of visitors in local communities for the benefit of locals (and second, tourists). Shifting the values of tourism away from excessive commodification and exploitation is essential. Tourism must be returned to ideas of hospitality and connection. The recent work on tourism as a social force (i.e. Higgins-Desbiolles, 2006; papers of the Critical Tourism Studies 2013 conference) may provide some guidance on this. Moreover, we need to re-think how we evaluate the benefits of tourism focusing on the local community and going beyond the fragile economic benefits offered by multinational corporations with their propensity to leakages. Furthermore evaluation of tourism impacts needs to take into consideration that the tourism habits of the developed world have unjust environmental impacts on the developing world, as seen for example in climate change impacts. Finally, understandings of hospitality might benefit from a critical engagement with Derrida's challenging expositions on hosts, guests, hostility, and hospitality found within his considerations of the possibilities of (un)conditional hospitality (Derrida & Dufourmantelle, 2000).

- Re-conceptualize entrenched capitalist concepts:
  The UNWTO Global Code of Ethics for Tourism (1999) admonishes corporations to avoid extracting too much profit from their enterprises. This is idealistic rhetoric that acts as public relations spin under a system where profit extraction is the purpose of such corporations. For tourism to achieve degrowth targets, the growth agenda pursued by tourism agencies will have to be abandoned. Tourism corporations will have to accept the essential role that governmental regulation for sustainability and the public good plays and halt their advocacy for reductions in these activities as "redtape" and blocks to their development ambitions. In fact, governments could review the structures of their tourism industries encouraging, if not enforcing organisations to follow sustainable social enterprise models such those presented by Mottiar, Boluk, and Kline (2018). This would facilitate the shift from exploitative approaches performed by multinational corporations to community partnership and empowerment approaches. Furthermore, another entrenched capitalist concept to be addressed regard the excessive and compulsive consumption of tourism by some social groups which should be tackled by an educational process towards ethical consumption (Weeden & Boluk, 2014).

- Restructure production:
  Multinational corporations cannot be allowed to extract excessive profits through their ability to command terms of trade through their power in the global value chains of production in tourism, particularly when international agreements such as the General Agreement on Trade in Services cedes enormous power to them. Barkin's (2000) analysis of the role for sustainable domestic social tourism in Mexico offers one example to consider. This explored a restructure of tourism away from unsustainable forms of growth models based on international tourism to more sustainable and beneficial forms of tourism based on domestic tourism for sustainable livelihoods and community well-being. Moreover, the development of new products should be led by grassroots movements and the local community instead of being designed and imposed by external organisations and corporations such as the case of El Gouna in the Red Sea area of Egypt that has been designed and built by the multinational corporation Orascom Hotels and Development (Vignal, 2010).

- Redistributions at the global, regional and local scale:
  The right to travel will need to be rethought in the coming era of immense global upheaval caused by global climate change. The rights of tourists for holidays will have to be weighed as inferior to the rights of environmental and conflict refugees for temporary and permanent safe haven. This can be addressed through redistribution of access to mobility based on terms of justice and equity rather than wealth and ability to pay. The two bodies charged with addressing mobility at the international level, the Office for International Migration and the UNWTO, will have to be totally revamped under new charters for a new era.

Alternatively or additionally, the international community could commit to a renewed vision of the NIEO and redistribute wealth, capacity, and technology to work towards alleviating some of the conditions that cause forced migration and undermine long-term sustainability.

- Re-localize the economy:

Tourism has already embraced re-localisation as a strategy, superficially in "buy local" campaigns and more fully in neolocalism movements. The latter offers opportunities to critically analyse how the global community can negotiate pathways to post-carbon economies and transition to sufficiency economies. Neolocalism concentrates focus on the role of local production, distribution and consumption in building networks of well-being, can link people to their environment and contribute to deeper levels of understanding to support actions at personal and political levels to address climate change (Cavaliere, 2017).

The key for tourism degrowth, however, will be to embed this strategy in a more sustainable and holistic approach to sustainable development that moves beyond current approaches to "sustaining tourism" (see Higgins-Desbiolles, 2018a). Essential to this task is ensuring tourism development is only one pillar to building a diverse economy; an economy dedicated to the subsistence and well-being of its people rather than articulating to the global capitalist economy and neoliberal market system. We must abandon moves toward tourism-dependent economies as these are the antithesis of sustainable and just economies.

- Reduction, re-use and recycling of resources:

Hall (2009) addressed this in his discussion of degrowth in tourism when he noted: "sustainable tourism development is tourism development without growth in throughput of matter and energy beyond regenerative and absorptive capacities" (p. 53). This may already be addressed at a local enterprise or local site level. But this challenge should be taken up at a much broader level. One example is the "half earth" proposal (Wilson, 2016) that argues we must put whole swathes of the ecological environment under protection and conservation, with human use and access banned; even that most "benign" of industries, tourism. When tourism comes to grips with requirements that it can no longer appropriate landscapes, cultures, and peoples in a finite and stressed world, we would have stepped up to this challenge in a more meaningful manner. Concepts of reduction, re-use, and recycling in tourism are still to be more strongly embedded in carrying capacity theories. New approaches to the topic have been proposed with a new index on urban resources and environment carrying capacity by Zhang, Liu, Wu, and Wang (2018). Additionally, Muler-Gonzalez, Coromina, and Gali (2018) have proposed merging carrying capacity theory with social exchange theory where the resources identified are not only physical but also social and cultural. However, we urge academia to review the concepts of carrying and absorptive capacities in light of the current environmental and political challenges that confront us. The necessity to reduce, re-use, and recycle should also be embedded on tourism education in a push for the (trans)formation of people's consumption behaviours in tourism.

The final critical question to address is how do we turn tourism away from the power agendas that support growth dynamics? There is a full research and action agenda to pursue to accomplish this. Changing tourism education is essential so that future leaders of tourism policy and planning understand tourism in terms of a moral endeavour and in terms of its value for human well-being. Recent work on pedagogies that are critical and transformative are promising in this regard (Boyle, Wilson, & Dimmock, 2015; Boluk & Carnicelli, in press; Carnicelli & Boluk, in press; Hales & Jennings, 2017; Phi, Whitford, Dredge, & Reid, 2017). Additionally, progressive tourism developments would benefit from thinking through tourism in a context of citizenship; concerns with responsible tourism and responsibility in tourism and the influence that the NGOs that once championed these no longer have the profile they once had. Do degrowth approaches necessitate changing the industry substantially; instead of privileging unsustainable international tourism why are we not prioritising domestic tourism, social tourism and more local forms of travel? Finally, are we ready to change politics? Degrowth necessitates resisting neoliberals push to hollow out governments and their responsibilities to govern for the public good.

Conclusion

The aim of this paper was to examine the possibility of equitable and sustainable degrowth in tourism through conceptual analysis. This resulted in a redefinition of tourism, prioritising the rights of local communities above the rights of tourists for holidays and the rights of tourism corporates to make profits. Solutions offered by the corporate tourism industry are unlikely to resolve the tensions of tourism that occur as we confront the limits to growth our planet faces. Recently, Hickel (2018) reviewed the arguments for "green growth" in an analysis that followed on from the outcomes of three major empirical studies addressing the possibilities of decoupling gross domestic product from resource use. Hickel's review concluded that this is impossible on a global scale and that the promise of green growth is an illusion. Hickel stated:

> Ultimately, bringing our civilization back within planetary boundaries is going to require that we liberate ourselves from our dependence on economic growth—starting with rich nations. This might sound scarier than it really is. Ending growth doesn't mean shutting down economic activity—it simply means that next year we can't produce and consume more than we are doing this year. It might also mean shrinking certain sectors that are particularly damaging to our ecology and that are unnecessary for human flourishing, such as advertising, commuting, and single-use products (2018).

Tourism is arguably one of those "unnecessary" activities and despite claims to the contrary can be quite damaging to our ecology with its current rapacious practices fostered by a neoliberal growth paradigm. In a resource-constrained and stressed world, tourism will have to justify its existence by offering more benefits and value than it currently does. This analysis has offered some considerations of how tourism's growth agendas are symptomatic of tourism's inequity and injustice. To overturn these injustices and place tourism on a degrowth trajectory, it will be necessary to redefine tourism and to place tourism within its appropriate context of global mobilities, human well-being and sustainable futures. Tourism should be reclaimed from an industry that has defined it as a business sector for their profit accumulation, to a human endeavour based on the rights and interests of local communities in welcoming tourists. The conflicts represented by overtourism are a wake-up call; pursuing equitable and just degrowth strategies will be increasingly vital if tourism is to have a sustainable future.

Disclosure statement

No potential conflict of interest was reported by the authors.

References

Ayikoru, M., Tribe, J., & Airey, D. (2009). Reading tourism education: Neoliberalism unveiled. *Annals of Tourism Research, 36*(2), 191–221. doi:10.1016/j.annals.2008.11.001

Barkin, D. (2000). Social tourism in rural communities: An instrument for promoting sustainable resource management. Paper for the 2000 meeting of the Latin American Studies Association, Miami, USA, 16–18 March.

Bennett, J. (1999). The dream and the reality: Tourism in Kuna Yala. *Cultural Survival Quarterly*, 23.2, July. Retrieved 24 September 2018, from https://www.culturalsurvival.org/publications/cultural-survival-quarterly/dream-and-reality-tourism-kuna-yala.

Bianchi, R., & Stephenson, M. (2014). *Tourism and citizenship: Rights, freedoms and responsibilities in the global order.* Abingdon, UK: Routledge.

Boluk, K. A., & Carnicelli, S. (in press). Tourism for the emancipation of the oppressed. *Annals of Tourism Research.*

Boyle, A., Wilson, E., & Dimmock, K. (2015). Transformative education and sustainable tourism: The influence of a lecturer's worldview. *Journal of Teaching in Travel & Tourism, 15*(3), 252–263. doi:10.1080/15313220.2015.1059303

Bramwell, B., & Lane, B. (2008). Priorities in sustainable tourism research. *Journal of Sustainable Tourism, 16*(1), 1–4. doi:10.2167/09669580803489612

Burgen, S. (2018, 25 June). 'Tourists go home, refugees welcome': Why Barcelona chose migrants over visitors. The Guardian [Online]. Retrieved 3 September 2018, from https://www.theguardian.com/cities/2018/jun/25/tourists-go-home-refugees-welcome-why-barcelona-chose-migrants-over-visitors.

Carnicelli, S. & Boluk, K. (in press). Educating for critical pedagogical tourism. In S. R., Steinberg, B. Down, S. Grande, & D. Nix-Stevenson (Eds.), *The Sage handbook of critical pedagogies.* London: Sage.

Cavaliere, C. T. (2017). Foodscapes as alternate ways of knowing: Advancing sustainability and climate consciousness through tactile space. In S. L. Slocum & C. Kline (Eds.), *Linking urban and rural tourism: Strategies for sustainability* (pp. 49–64). Oxon, UK: CABI.

Cohen, E. (1979). A phenomenology of tourist experiences. *Sociology, 13*(2), 180–201.   https://doi.org/10.1177/003803857901300203

Critical Tourism Studies. (2013). Tourism and its potential as a social force. Retrieved 3 September 2018, from http://cts.som.surrey.ac.uk/sample-page/tourism-and-its-potential-as-a-social-force/.

D'Alisa, G., Demaria, F., & Kallis, G. (2015). *Degrowth: A vocabulary for a new era.* London: Routledge.

Demaria, F., Schneider, F., Sekulova, F., & Martinez-Alier, J. (2013). What is degrowth? From an activist slogan to a social movement. *Environmental Values, 22*(2), 191–215. doi:10.3197/096327113X13581561725194

Derrida, J., & Dufourmantelle, A. (2000). *Of hospitality.* Stanford: Stanford University Press.

The Ecologist. (2018). Reflections on a decade of degrowth International conferences. Retrieved 31 August 2018, from https://theecologist.org/2018/aug/29/reflections-decade-degrowth-international-conferences

Fanon, F. (1967). *The wretched of the earth.* London: Penguin.

Fisher, J. (2018). Nicaragua's Buen Vivir: A strategy for tourism development? *Journal of Sustainable Tourism*, 1. doi: 10.1080/09669582.2018.1457035

Fletcher, R. (2011). Sustaining tourism, sustaining capitalism? The tourism industry's role in global capitalist expansion. *Tourism Geographies, 13*(3), 443–461. doi:10.1080/14616688.2011.570372

Fletcher, R. (2018). Ecotourism after nature: Antropocene tourism as a new capitalist "fix". *Journal of Sustainable Tourism*, 1. https://doi-org.access.library.unisa.edu.au/10.1080/09669582.2018.1471084

Fletcher, R., Blazquez-Salom, M., Murray, I., & Blanco-Romero, A. (2017). Special Issue on Tourism and degrowth. *Journal of Sustainable Tourism Call for Papers*, Retrieved 3 January 2018, from http://explore.tandfonline.com/cfp/pgas/rsus-si-degrowth-4q2017.

Gerber, J.-F., & Raina, R. S. (2018). Post-growth in the Global South? Some reflections from India and Bhutan. *Ecological Economics, 150*, 353–358. doi:10.1016/j.ecolecon.2018.02.020

Giaccaria, P. (2018). For the sake of place authenticity: tourists versus migrants in anti-tourism discourses. Abstract for the American Association of Geographers Annual Meeting. Retrieved 3 September 2018, from https://aag.secure-abstracts.com/AAG%20Annual%20Meeting%202018/abstracts-gallery/11205.

Graburn, N. (1989). Tourism: The sacred journey. In V. Smith (Ed.), *Hosts and guests: The anthropology of tourism* (pp. 21–36). Philadelphia: University of Pennsylvania Press.

Hales, R., & Jennings, G. (2017). Transformation for sustainability: The role of complexity in tourism students' understanding of sustainable tourism. *Journal of Hospitality, Leisure, Sport, & Tourism Education, 21*(b), 185–194. doi: 10.1016/j.jhlste.2017.08.001

Hall, C. M. (2008a). Of time and space and other things: Laws of tourism and the geographies of contemporary mobilities. In P. Burns & M. Novelli (Eds.), *Tourism and mobilities: Local-*Global connections* (pp. 15–32). Oxford: Elsevier.

Hall, C. M. (2008b). *Tourism planning* (2nd ed.). Harlow, UK: Pearson.

Hall, C. M. (2009). Degrowing tourism: Décroissance, sustainable consumption and steady-state tourism. *Journal of Sustainable Tourism, 20*(1), 46–61. doi:10.1080/13032917.2009.10518894

Harvey, D. (2005). *A brief history of neoliberalism.* Oxford: Oxford University Press.

Hickel, J. (2018). Why growth can't be green. Foreign Policy (Online). Retrieved 18 September 2018, from https://for-eignpolicy.com/2018/09/12/why-growth-cant-be-green/amp/?__twitter_impression=true.

Higgins-Desbiolles, F. (2006). More than an Industry: Tourism as a social force. *Tourism Management, 27*(6), 1192–1208. doi:10.1016/j.tourman.2005.05.020

Higgins-Desbiolles, F. (2007). Hostile meeting grounds. In P. Burns & M. Novelli (Eds.), *Tourism and politics: Global frameworks and local realities* (pp. 309–332). Amsterdam: Elsevier.

Higgins-Desbiolles, F. (2008). *Capitalist globalisation, corporatized tourism and their alternatives.* New York: Nova Publishers.

Higgins-Desbiolles, F. (2010). The elusiveness of sustainability in tourism: The culture-ideology of consumerism and its implications. *Tourism and Hospitality Research, 10*(2), 116–129. doi:10.1057/thr.2009.31

Higgins-Desbiolles, F. (2012). The Hotel Bauen's challenge to cannibalizing capitalism. *Annals of Tourism Research, 39*(2), 620–640. doi:10.1016/j.annals.2011.08.001

Higgins-Desbiolles, F. (2018). Sustainable tourism: Sustaining tourism or something else? *Tourism Management Perspectives, 25*, 157–160. doi:10.1016/j.tmp.2017.11.017

Higgins-Desbiolles, F. (2018b). Why Australia might be at risk of 'overtourism'. *The Conversation*. Retrieved 3 September 2018, from https://theconversation.com/why-australia-might-be-at-risk-of-overtourism-99213.

Higgins-Desbiolles, F. (2018c). The potential for justice through tourism. *Via Tourism Review, 13*. Via [Online], retrieved 1 September 2018, from http://journals.openedition.org/viatourism/2469. doi:10.4000/viatourism.2469

International Organization for Migration (n.d.). IOM History. Retrieved 3 September 2018, from https://www.iom.int/iom-history.

Iorgulescu, M.-C., & Răvar, A. S. (2015). The contribution of social enterprises to the development of tourism: The case of Romania. *Procedia Economics and Finance, 32*, 672–679. doi:10.1016/S2212-5671(15)01448-3

Jazairy, I. (2017). *The protracted refugee and migrant crisis: A challenge to multilateralism*. Inter Press Service. Retrieved 3 August 2018, from http://www.ipsnews.net/2017/12/protracted-refugee-migrant-crisis-challenge-multilateralism/.

Kallis, G. (2011). In defence of degrowth. *Ecological Economics, 70*(5), 873–880. doi:10.1016/j.ecolecon.2010.12.007

Latouche, S. (2006). The globe downshifted? *Le Monde Diplomatique*, January. Retrieved 3 February 2019, from https://mondediplo.com/2006/01/13degrowth.

Liptak, A. (2017, 4 December). Supreme Court allows travel ban to take effect. The New York Times. Online. Retrieved 3 March 2018, from https://www.nytimes.com/2017/12/04/us/politics/trump-travel-ban-supreme-court.html.

Lirrwi Tourism (n.d.). Lirrwi tourism guiding principles. Retrieved 17 December 2018, from https://www.lirrwitourism.com.au/guiding-principles/.

Maldonado, J. K., Shearer, C., Bronen, R., Peterson, K., & Lazrus, H. (2013). The impact of climate change on tribal communities in the US: Displacement, relocation, and human rights. *Climatic Change, 120*(3), 601–614. doi:10.1007/s10584-013-0746-z

March, H. (2018). The Smart City and other ICT-led techno-imaginaries: Any room for dialogue with degrowth? *Journal of Cleaner Production, 197*(2), 1694–1703. doi:10.1016/j.jclepro.2016.09.154

Martinez-Alier, J., Pascual, U., Vivien, F.-D., & Zaccai, E. (2010). Sustainable de-growth: Mapping the context, criticisms and future prospects of an emergent paradigm. *Ecological Economics, 69*, 1741–1747. doi:10.1016/j.ecolecon.2010.04.017

Meadows, D. H., Meadows, D. L., Randers, J., & Behrens, W. W. III, (1972). *The limits to growth; A report for the Club of Rome's project on the predicament of mankind*. New York: Universe Books. Retrieved 15 December 2017, from https://www.clubofrome.org/report/the-limits-to-growth/.

McKibben, B. (2018, 3 October). The Trump administration knows the planet is going to boil. It doesn't care. *The Guardian, Online*, Retrieved 3 October 2018, from https://www.theguardian.com/commentisfree/2018/oct/02/trump-administration-planet-boil-refugee-camps?CMP=fb_gu.

Milano, C. (2018). Overtourism, malestar social y turismofobia. Un debate controvertido. *Pasos. Revista de Turismo y Patrimonio Cultural, 16*(3), 551–564. doi:10.25145/j.pasos.2018.16.041

Miller, G., & Twining-Ward, L. (2005). Tourism optimization management model. In G. Miller & L. Twining-Ward (Eds.), *Monitoring for a sustainable tourism transition* (pp. 201–232). Wallingford, UK: CABI.

Mottiar, Z., Boluk, K., & Kline, C. (2018). The roles of social entrepreneurs in rural destination development. *Annals of Tourism Research, 68*, 77–88. doi:10.1016/j.annals.2017.12.001

Muler-Gonzalez, V., Coromina, L., & Galí, N. (2018). Overtourism: Residents' perceptions of tourism impact as an indicator of resident social carrying capacity – Case study of a Spanish heritage town. *Tourism Review, 73*(3), 277–296. doi:10.1108/TR-08-2017-0138

Muraca, B. (2012). Towards a fair degrowth-society: Justice and the right to a 'good life' beyond growth. *Futures, 44*(6), 535–545. doi:10.1016/j.futures.2012.03.014

Murison, M. (2017). The challenges of mass tourism in the 21st century. Travelshift. Retrieved 3 March 2018, from https://travelshift.com/challenges-mass-tourism-21st-century/.

O'Byrne, D. (2001). On passports and border controls. *Annals of Tourism Research, 28*(2), 399–416. https://doi.org/10.1016/S0160-7383(00)00050-5

Pereiro, X., de Leon, C., Martinez Mauri, M., Ventocilla, J., & del Valle, Y. (2012). *Los turistores Kunas anthropologia del turismo etnico en Panama*. Palma: Universitat de les Illes Balears.

Phi, G. T., Whitford, M., Dredge, D., & Reid, S. (2017). Educating tourists for global citizenship: A microfinance tourism providers' perspective. *Tourism Recreation Research, 42*(2), 235–247. doi:10.1080/02508281.2017.1290738

Sartre, J. P. (1967). Preface. In F.Fanon (Ed.), *The wretched of the earth*. London: Penguin.

Smith, S. (1988). Defining tourism: A supply-side view. *Annals of Tourism Research, 15*(2), 179–190. doi:10.1016/0160-7383(88)90081-3

Smith, H. (2015, 3 September). Shocking images of drowned Syrian boy show tragic plight of refugees. *The Guardian Online*, Retrieved 3 May 2018, from https://www.theguardian.com/world/2015/sep/02/shocking-image-of-drowned-syrian-boy-shows-tragic-plight-of-refugees.

Smith, R. G. (2014). *Dubai in extremis*. Theory, Culture & Society, 31(7/8), 291–296. doi:10.1177/0263276414547775

Snow, S. G. (2001). The Kuna General Congress and the Statute on Tourism. *Cultural Survival Quarterly*, *24*(4). Retrieved 24 September 2018, from https://www.culturalsurvival.org/publications/cultural-survival-quarterly/kuna-general-congress-and-statute-tourism.

Spiegel (2015 7 August). Tourists and refugees cross paths in the Mediterranean. Spiegel Online. Retrieved 12 August 2018, from http://www.spiegel.de/international/europe/tourists-and-refugess-cross-paths-in-the-mediterranean-a-1046969.html.

Torres, R., & Momsen, J. (2005). Planned tourism development in Quintana Roo, Mexico: Engine for regional development or prescription for inequitable growth? *Current Issues in Tourism*, *8*(4), 259–285. doi:10.1080/13683500508668218

Tourism Australia (n.d.). Tourism 2020. Retrieved 2 September 2018, from http://www.tourism.australia.com/en/about/our-organisation/our-performance-and-reporting/tourism-2020.html.

United Nations. (1948). Universal declaration of human rights. Retrieved 17 January 2003, from http://www.fourmilab.ch/etexts/www/un/udhr.html.

UNWTO (n.d.a). Why tourism? Retrieved 3 September 2018, from http://www2.unwto.org/content/why-tourism.

UNWTO (n.d.b) What we do. Retrieved 3 September 2018, from http://www2.unwto.org/.

UNWTO. (1980). Manila declaration on world tourism. Retrieved 13 September 2018, from https://www.e-unwto.org/doi/abs/10.18111/unwtodeclarations.1980.6.4.1.

UNWTO. (1999). Global code of ethics for tourism. Retrieved 8 March 2018, from http://ethics.unwto.org/en/content/global-code-ethics-tourism.

UNWTO. (2009). *Tourism and migration: Exploring the relationship between two global phenomena*. Madrid: UNWTO.

UNWTO. (2018). *Overtourism? Understanding and managing urban tourism growth beyond perceptions: Executive Summary*. Madrid: UNWTO.

Vignal, L. (2010). The new territories of tourism in Egypt: A local-global frontier? *Cybergeo: European Journal of Geography, Espace, Société, Territoire*, 509. Retrieved 18 September 2018, from http://cybergeo.revues.org/23324.

Vocatch, I. (2010). ILO and cooperative tourism: Challenges and statistical measurement. Regional workshop for the CIS countries "developing national systems of tourism statistics: Challenges and good practices". Retrieved 17 December 2018, from unstats.un.org/unsd/tradeserv/Workshops/Chisinau/docs.

Wall, G., & Mathieson, A. (2006). *Tourism: Change, impacts and opportunities*. Harlow, UK: Pearson.

Weeden, C., & Boluk, K. (2014). *Managing ethical consumption in tourism*. New York, NY: Routledge.

Wheeller, B. (1993). Sustaining the ego. *The Journal of Sustainable Tourism*, *1*(2), 121–129. doi:10.1080/09669589309450710

White, G. (2011). *Climate change and migration: Security and borders in a warming world*. Oxford: Oxford University Press.

Wilson, E. O. (2016). *Half-earth: Our planet's fight for life*. New York: Liveright.

Wonderful Copenhagen. (2017). The end of tourism as we know it: Towards a new beginning of localhood; Strategy 2020. Retrieved 22 December 2017, from http://localhood.wonderfulcopenhagen.dk/.

Zhang, M., Liu, Y., Wu, J., & Wang, T. (2018). Index system of urban resource and environment carrying capacity based on ecological civilization. *Environmental Impact Assessment Review*, *68*, 90–97. doi:10.1016/j.eiar.2017.11.002

Postscript: tourism on the path to post-development

Alberto Acosta
Translated by Ivan Murray Mas

> "Leisure time is the best of all acquisitions"
> Socrates

The conventional idea of progress, and its main offspring, development, are increasingly questioned with the recognition of growing and serious social problems –particularly economic, cultural and environmental – in different parts of the planet. It has even been proven that several of modernity's "great achievements", such as technological advancement, are insufficient – and some even counter-productive – to solve the serious problems humanity faces. And in this scenario dominated by globalizing trends, many of the great ventures that are expanding throughout the world, such as mass tourism, cause new and massive disturbances.

The dangerous inertia of a failed crusade

What is of interest now is overcoming the very idea of "development", tied to a series of different qualifiers within which it has been cloaked in order to make its realization viable. We should remember that development has been pursued tirelessly over the last seven decades, and that when problems began to undermine our faith in "development", and when its theorization appeared to have come to an end, we instead looked for alternatives to "development". Like a son without a father who recognizes him, we gave qualifiers to "development" to differentiate it from what bothered us. But even so, we continue on the path of "development" – economic, social, local, global, rural, sustainable … but in the end still "development" after all.

"Development" – turned into a belief never questioned – is simply redefined by highlighting this or that characteristic. And the great majority of criticism was never against "development", but against the particular paths prescribed to achieve it.

Much was lost in that frenzied pursuit of "development", such as the cultures of affected communities, so that they become a workforce to ensure the accumulation of capital, while expanding the massive extraction of natural resources. Not only that, but community life, rurality and the joy of living without rush were regarded, and remain seen, as idle and hence causing poverty and "underdevelopment". Or, at best, and always with the aim to keep rolling the wheel of capital accumulation, communities, rurality and the joy of living are assumed to be programmable activities. In short, everything is commodified, including the well-being and organized happiness of people.

In the end, so much effort has turned out to be useless. Plagues persist, including poverty, misery and inequities, so typical of so-called "underdevelopment". But also – and simultaneously – countries assumed to be "developed" are caught within the "progress" trap. In this regard, it is enough to witness the serious contradictions, conflicts and difficulties that the so-called "developed" suffer to acknowledge just one pathology: the increasing dissatisfaction that persists even among the beneficiaries of greater material accumulation. Meanwhile, in that accelerated race for development, the fierce destruction of nature is accelerated.

In the midst of this maelstrom of modernity, the phenomenon of "leisure" has been transformed. "Leisure", instead of expressing freedom and autonomy, has become a degraded commercial space of life itself. "Leisure" has passed from an integral part of life in many communities, a moment of creativity and celebration of the sacred, to become a mere resting place to replenish the workforce to keep on producing. Or "leisure" has simply turned into a business opportunity. In this regard, mass tourism stands out as an option that promises moments of leisure life in "paradise".

This activity, considered "the chimneyless industry", has expanded rapidly in the course of globalization. Tourism has shifted from an elite activity to one for the masses. Many countries have adopted tourism as an imperative economic activity, such that tourism exceeds 10% of GDP – and in many cases far more than this – while the number of tourists, whatever their means of transport, grows exponentially at a speed that increases the consumptive capacity of the new middle classes. At the same time, mechanisms are implemented to maximize income by lowering costs. All of this has more pernicious social, economic and ecological effects for large segments of the population receiving this mass tourism – so much so that it provokes, in some parts, an increasing response that cries "tourist go home".

Currently, "leisure" – including expanding mass tourism – is one of the largest businesses in the world as it brings together millions of people and mobilizes vast amounts of capital. And, on top of this, "leisure" reflects its "utility" within a "pleasure metric" (borne of utilitarianism and even hedonism). This is why "leisure", as a consumer product, is also the object of state policies where it is planned, organized and instrumentalized as a tool to control and discipline society; the "bread and circus" of the Roman Empire is reproduced, on an expanded scale, with the speed and intensity of modern technological "achievements" and capital accumulation. And, in that process, tourism, in a parallelism with "development", seeks to adopt a series of qualifiers such as ecological, community, solidarity tourism. It does so without breaking free of its commercial elements, which in turn are increasingly more alienating.

Consequently, "mercantile leisure" – wherein we include mass tourism – is another reflection of a "mal-developed" world (Tortosa, 2011).

The complex charm of transitions

Overcoming this complex reality demands great effort and profound transformation, within the framework of multiple transitions that will acquire a growing urgency alongside the critical conditions unleashed, nationally and internationally, by globalizing capitalism, in the social, ecological and even economic realms. Tourism is one of the pending issues.

It is not just about rethinking tourism, let alone banning all trips, whose potential is enormous; as Mark Twain said, "travel is fatal to prejudice, bigotry and narrow-mindedness". Rather, we need to review the lifestyle, especially that of the elites, which serves as an unattainable guidance framework for the majority of the population. This is a review that will have to address, on the basis of real equity, the reduction of working time and its redistribution, as well as the collective redefinition of needs based on satisfiers adjusted to the capacity of the economy and of nature. Sooner rather than later, even in the same "underdeveloped" countries (not to mention the "developed"), sufficiency will have to be prioritized such that what is really needed is sought, instead of always greater efficiency – based in uncontrolled competitiveness and a runaway consumerism – which will end up destroying humanity altogether.

Perhaps the time has come to realize the reflections of Paul Lafargue (1848), John Maynard Keynes (1930), Bertrand Russell (1932), Karl Goerg Zinn (1998) and Niko Paech (2012), among others, who from various approaches suggest reducing the working time per day (to 3 or 4 hours, for example). This is a complex challenge, because it constitutes a heresy in societies committed to productivism.

In short, as the German economist Niko Paech (2012) argues, individuals and communities must "exercise their ability to live differently" (in dignity and in harmony with nature). This requires convivial proposals created from below (Illich, 2015) by individuals and communities that pressure governments to include them in their policies. The proposals of Pierre Rabhi (2013), a French farmer, thinker and writer of Algerian origin, fit within this line of reasoning, as he invites us to walk towards a society of "happy sobriety".

In the end, the task is to rethink the world of work by linking it with other worlds from which it should have never been isolated. And in doing so, it is also necessary to rethink leisure, not to regulate it, but to free it – not to make it a business, but to decommodify it by expanding its communitarian, creative and recreational potential, diversifying it for the enormous cultural pluriversity of the world. What space does tourism occupy in that other world? This is one of the indispensable questions to address.

It is time to conceptualize a world within which all worlds fit: a pluriverse (Kothari et al., 2019); a world wherein all human and non-human beings can live with dignity, where people can organize to recover and take control of their own lives, their work and their leisure. This vision, linked to Mother Earth, could be the space within which to pursue good living together (Acosta, 2013).

We must not forget that human beings, as part of nature, are not isolated individuals: we are a social and natural community, a community that has to be rethought and reconstructed more and more from the local. Will we be able to build "paradise" in those areas we call home and not look for this desperately and uselessly in distant regions, via commodified activities that awkwardly prefigure happiness? This question compels us to take a civilizing leap wherein mercantile and alienating leisure is replaced by "emancipatory leisure".

References

Acosta, A. (2013). *El Buen Vivir Sumak Kawsay, una oportunidad para imaginar otros mundos [The Good Living Sumak Kawsay, an opportunity to imagine other worlds]*. Icaria: Barcelona.
Illich, I. (2015). *Obras reunidas [Collected Works]*. Mexico: Fondo de Cultura Económica.
Keynes, J. M. (1930). "Economic Possibilities for our Grandchildren". In *Essays in Persuasion*. New York: W. W. Norton & Co., 1963.
Kothari, A., Salleh, A., Escobar, A., Demaria, F. & Acosta, A. (eds.) (2019); *Pluriverso – Diccionario del Postdesarrollo [Pluriverse: A Post-Development Dictionary]*. Icaria: Barcelona.
Lafargue, P. (2011 [1848]). *El derecho a la pereza [The Right to Be Lazy]*. MAIA ediciones: Madrid.
Paech, N. (2012). *Befreiung von Überfluss – Auf dem Weg in die Postwachstumsökonomie. [Relief from Abundance – Towards the Post-Growth Economy]*, Oekom Verlag: München.
Rahbi, P. (2013). *Hacia la sobriedad feliz [Towards happy sobriety]*. Errata Natrae: Madrid.
Russel, B. (1932). *Elogio de la ociosidad [In Praise of Idleness and Other Essays]*, Universidad Complutense de Madrid. Retrieved from http://webs.ucm.es/info/bas/utopia/html/russell.htm
Tortosa, J. M. (2011). *"Maldesarrollo y mal vivir – Pobreza y violencia escala mundial"* ["Maldevelopment and bad living – Poverty and violence at global scale"]. In Acosta, A. & Martínez, E. (eds.) *Serie Sobre Debate Constituyente*. Quito: Abya-Yala. Retrieved from https://web.ua.es/es/iudesp/documentos/publicaciones/maldesarrollo-libro.pdf
Zinn, K. G. (1998). "Machtfrage Vollbeschäftigung", *Zeitschrift Sozialismus* 3, 10–14.

Index